T0342448

Why Australia Prospered

THE PRINCETON ECONOMIC HISTORY
OF THE WESTERN WORLD

Joel Mokyr, Series Editor

A list of titles in this series appears at the back of the book

Why Australia Prospered

THE SHIFTING SOURCES OF ECONOMIC GROWTH

Ian W. McLean

PRINCETON UNIVERSITY PRESS
PRINCETON AND OXFORD

Copyright © 2013 by Princeton University Press

Published by Princeton University Press, 41 William Street, Princeton, New Jersey 08540

In the United Kingdom: Princeton University Press, 6 Oxford Street, Woodstock, Oxfordshire OX20 1TW

press.princeton.edu

Library of Congress Cataloging-in-Publication Data

McLean, Ian W.
   Why Australia prospered : the shifting sources of economic growth / Ian W. McLean.
      p. cm. — (The Princeton economic history of the Western world)
   Includes bibliographical references and index.
   ISBN 978-0-691-15467-1 (hardcover)
   1. Economic development—Australia. 2. Australia—Economic policy—21st century. I. Title.
HD82.M3345 2013
338.994—dc23   2012008056

British Library Cataloging-in-Publication Data is available

This book has been composed in Minion Pro

Printed on acid-free paper. ∞

Printed in the United States of America

10 9 8 7 6 5 4 3 2

Contents

Figures

Tables

Preface and Acknowledgments

THIS BOOK HAD ITS origins in the spring of 2006 in an office affording a breathtaking view across San Francisco Bay and through the Golden Gate to the Pacific beyond. This was an especially appropriate vantage point for the task. If California were a national rather than a regional economy, it would receive more frequent comparison with Australia, for it shares with its fellow settler economy on the far side of the Pacific many initial conditions relevant to its early prosperity, in addition to having a similarly enviable record of subsequent growth. More generally, observing Australian experience from outside the country heightens one's perception both of what seems noteworthy or unusual—thereby warranting greater consideration than it might otherwise attract—and of what seems unexceptional.

I wanted to reflect on what is surely one of the most striking features of Australia's history: its early attainment, then retention over a century and a half, of a very high level of economic prosperity. My aim was to view this achievement not only within the context of the ever-changing international economy, which has exerted such a pervasive influence on the country's economic history, but also in a comparative perspective, drawing especially on the experience of other settler economies—in particular Argentina, Canada, New Zealand, and the United States.

Another objective in writing this book has been to help fill a lacuna in discussions of the remarkable period of prosperity Australians have experienced since the last (technical) recession in the economy in 1991. Most attention in the media understandably focuses on short-run movements in key economic or financial indices, or on political aspects of whichever economic policy issue has fleetingly caught the attention of the public. It is less common to observe space devoted to providing context—historical and comparative—as to why Australia, virtually alone among the advanced economies, has enjoyed this extended period of uninterrupted growth. To gain more than a superficial understanding of the economy's performance during this recent period, I argue that it is necessary to adopt a perspective encompassing much of the country's history.

Many debts have been accumulated in the course of writing. Conversations at the design stage with Barry Eichengreen, Rui Esteves, and Kris Mitchener were especially helpful. Subsequent development of the ideas and material benefited from the comments of Raj Arunachalam, Brad DeLong, Bob Gregory, Tim Hatton, Douglas Irwin, Suresh Naidu, James Robinson, Gavin Wright, and conference and seminar participants at the University of Adelaide, the University of California, Berkeley, and the University of Melbourne. Kelly Wyett of the Reserve Bank of Australia assisted with data sources. Daniel Mabarrack provided superb research assistance in the final preparation of the manuscript. I am especially indebted to Jeff Borland, Robert Dare, and Richard Pomfret, who made invaluable and detailed comments on an earlier draft. Joel Mokyr's many contributions greatly improved the final product. Finally, I am grateful to Seth Ditchik at Princeton University Press for his editorial support, and to Karen Carter and Marsha Kunin for their production and copy-editing skills, respectively.

My greatest debt is to Barry Eichengreen and the Department of Economics at Berkeley, who, across the last decade and a half, have generously facilitated my recurrent membership in the group of economic historians among the faculty and graduate students there. These colleagues have helped shape much of my research during this period, some of which is reflected in the following pages.

Adelaide, December 2011

Why Australia Prospered

Darwin

Cape York

Kimberley

Cairns

NORTHERN
TERRITORY

Port Hedland

Mt Isa

Pilbara

QUEENSLAND

WESTERN
AUSTRALIA

SOUTH
AUSTRALIA

Brisbane

Olympic Dam

NEW SOUTH
WALES

Newcastle

Perth

Kalgoorlie

Whyalla

Broken Hill

Sydney

Adelaide

Canberra (ACT)

COMMONWEALTH OF
AUSTRALIA

Ballarat

VICTORIA

Melbourne

500 km

300 mi

TASMANIA

Hobart

CHAPTER 1

Introduction

Weaving Analysis and Narrative

> Australian history is almost always picturesque; indeed, it is so curious and strange, that it is itself the chiefest novelty the country has to offer, and so it pushes the other novelties into second and third place. And it does not read like history, but the most beautiful lies. And all of a fresh new sort, no mouldy old stale ones.
> —Mark Twain[1]

AUSTRALIANS ATTAINED the highest incomes in the world by the mid-nineteenth century, only a few decades after European settlement. Despite losing that remarkable position around 1900, they have retained to the present a standard of living that is not appreciably exceeded elsewhere. Few economies have been as successful over so long a period.[2] Some have achieved comparable levels of income only since the Second World War (think of Japan or Italy). Many are currently making good progress in catching up to these levels, though still have some distance to travel (think of South Korea). One has experienced long-term relative decline after having achieved membership into the rich club of nations in the early twentieth century (Argentina). Tragically, many less-developed economies have managed only low or intermittent growth such that they have not even begun to close the gap between their living standards and those of the richest countries. What explains Australia's enviable record of prosperity?

• • •

This inquiry into why Australia is rich adopts a historical approach because the roots of prosperity are embedded in the past: the levels of income observed in the currently rich economies are in every case the result of very long-run processes. Economies do not move rapidly from poverty and backwardness to advanced industrial status and concomitant prosperity despite the achievements of

---

[1] Twain (1989 [1897]), p. 169.

[2] The richest countries over the last 150 years include, in addition to Australia, the United States and Britain throughout; and the Netherlands, Canada, New Zealand, and Switzerland for much, but not all, of this period. See Prados de la Escosura (2000) for a review of alternative historical estimates of per capita income for the currently rich economies.

some being described as "economic miracles." Even with the impressive growth rates recently recorded in a number of poor countries such as India and China, attaining incomes comparable to the rich countries takes many decades. This is partly because incomes in the rich countries have also been rising: the poor countries must thus catch up with a level of prosperity that is moving ever higher. To illustrate, Japan began its modernization in the second half of the nineteenth century and is regarded as having turned in perhaps the most rapid growth performance among the currently advanced economies. But it was not until the late twentieth century that it attained approximate parity with incomes in the leading economies. And the evidence suggests that the level of economic development in nineteenth-century Japan was already beyond that of many less developed countries today. Or consider the roots of Britain's economic prosperity by 1850 at the end of the first industrial revolution. Historians long ago agreed it was a phase of growth that was evolutionary rather than revolutionary, and have traced its origins to an array of constitutional, social, demographic, scientific, technological, and cultural as well as economic developments stretching back several centuries.[3] Thus the importance given here to historical influences in an explanation of present-day prosperity is not something unique to the case of Australia. Economists increasingly draw on history in their quest to better account for why some countries are rich and others poor.[4]

There is an added reason to look to history to account for Australia's economic prosperity. Unlike Japan and much of Europe, membership in the rich club of nations is not a recent phenomenon. Hence the task set by posing the question "Why is Australia rich?" may be better posed as two questions to be addressed sequentially: Why was Australia so rich by the second half of the nineteenth century? And how has Australia managed to retain its position among the richest group of countries over the subsequent 150 years? Whether the answer to the first question differs from the answer to the second can be established only by historical inquiry.

The need for a historical perspective arises also because any persuasive explanation for Australia's current high-income status must highlight long-established features of its economy and society. In particular, prominence must be accorded certain of its economic and political institutions whose origins, in some cases, stretch back to the beginning of European settlement at the end of the eighteenth century. Since these institutions were adopted—or adapted—largely from British designs, their historical roots are even deeper.

The story of Australia's success in first achieving then maintaining its relatively high levels of economic prosperity over the past two centuries will here be told primarily in terms of the average *levels* of income per capita achieved in successive periods (usually of two or three decades) relative to that attained in

---

[3] For recent overviews and interpretations, see Allen (2009), Clark (2007), and Mokyr (2009).

[4] Surveys covering many countries and several centuries include Jones (1987), Landes (1998), and Pomeranz (2000).

previous periods, and also compared to the best achieved in other countries at the time. The prosperity attained in any period represents either some improvement over the previous period, some slippage, or stagnation, and our aim is to explain why we observe the outcome we do. Adding the cross-country dimension to our assessment is vital: Australia's economic achievements only have adequate context when compared with those of other countries.

Thus, one aim is that this study contribute to the literature on comparative growth, especially its historical dimension, a literature that has burgeoned in recent years. For their part, economic historians increasingly employ a comparative approach in their research.[5] And growth economists are finding not just that policies that successfully promote growth are proving harder to identify than believed by earlier generations of development economists, but that the reasons for growth—and particularly for its absence—in many cases appear to be related to factors specific to an economy's historical background. A historical case study, wherein the questions are framed such that the findings may readily be integrated with the results from other approaches to the analysis of growth, can thus make a contribution to this pressing policy challenge.

Adopting this approach, it follows that many themes or topics that would deserve attention in a general review of Australian economic history will be passed over lightly, or completely ignored. They will only be addressed insofar as they are relevant to an inquiry into the reasons for the levels of prosperity achieved. Thus no claim is made that this is a comprehensive or balanced account of the historical development of the Australian economy. Instead, my further aim is to provide those Australians who are curious about their own good fortune with an explanation for what surely ranks as one of their country's most remarkable achievements. And although there is a substantial body of writing on many aspects of the history of the economy, as will quickly become clear, no previous writer has adopted the present focus in an extended inquiry into the reasons for Australia's sustained prosperity.

This history is therefore part analysis, part narrative. The balance I strike between the two is intended to ensure the discussion remains accessible to a wider audience. And it is for this reason that I keep the use of technical terms and references to theory to a minimum, and for the most part confine my reporting of historical statistics to a limited number of simple charts.

•   •   •

The roots of current economic prosperity are not only located in the past, they are also complex. Given this, some explanatory framework is required to identify the key elements in any growth narrative, to determine how much prominence each is assigned, and to relate them to one another. Of course, explaining

---

[5]The approach is well illustrated by the studies in the recent collection edited by Hatton, O'Rourke, and Taylor (2007).

nearly two centuries of Australian economic prosperity would be less challenging were economists in possession of a theory of economic growth of universal validity—that is, for which there existed robust empirical support across all countries and at all times. They are not. But it is from the growth literature that I derive some of the insights into Australia's experience offered in this book.[6]

In the immediate postwar years, growth theory highlighted investment in physical capital as perhaps the single most important source of variation in *rates* of growth in an economy. Since then, differences in growth rates have also been attributed to differences in rates of human capital accumulation, especially formal education. And the rate of technological change completes this trinity of the sources of growth, which theory assigned a prominent role—the myriad ways in which a given level of output may be achieved with fewer inputs as a consequence of the diffusion of productivity-raising innovations.

There are two reasons why this trinity will not be center stage in this account. First, this is primarily an inquiry into the reasons for Australia's *level* of economic prosperity (conventionally defined as income or GDP per capita). To observe that a high-income country has more highly educated workers, and that they each use more equipment, provides no more than a superficial explanation as to why that country is rich: indeed such evidence is better interpreted as a corollary or a symptom of the level of its prosperity. Rather, it is necessary to ask why we observe so much more physical and human capital per worker in high-income than in low-income countries. That is, a set of more fundamental determinants of growth must be sought to account for the extremely wide variation in the levels of productivity and hence incomes across countries. And to do this, economists now look more deeply into the mechanism of growth— such as to aspects of the endowment (including natural resources, climate, location), institutional quality (the legal system, corruption, political arrangements, property rights), key policies (such as openness to trade, and intervention in markets), and cultural attributes (social norms, religion). I will explore these further in chapter 2 in discussing their relevance to the Australian experience.

The second reason for paying less attention to the proximate sources of growth is that we are focusing on the very long run—why prosperity has been sustained for nearly two centuries. If this inquiry were limited to a period within which the institutional framework, resource endowments, and other deeper influences could safely be assumed not to change, then it would be appropriate to confine attention to the immediate determinants of growth, in particular those that were amenable to policy. In the short run, fluctuations in the rate of growth of Australia's economy are likely to be influenced most powerfully by such factors as variations in the savings rate, business and consumer sentiment, the rate of immigration, and the expected profitability of new investment. Over the long run, however, many of the influences determining the level of income,

---

[6]I will have more to say about this literature in chapter 2.

but held constant in most theories of growth, cannot be ignored. They become the items of greatest interest.

One feature of the Australian experience that I therefore accord special significance is the natural-resource base—especially farmland and minerals. This economy is resource abundant in the sense of possessing a high ratio of natural resources relative to its population or labor force. In its early history, the resource sector provided much of the economy's output and was an important source of employment. More striking is that, for all of its history, exports have been dominated by a succession of resource-intensive products beginning with wool and gold. After more than 150 years of sustained high incomes, the comparative advantage of this economy still lies in its natural resources—around 65 percent of current exports are primary products. Australian history therefore offers compelling evidence against the widely held view that resource abundance is a curse not a blessing, and typically associated with corruption, low growth or stagnation, and even failed states.[7]

A second feature emphasized in the interpretation offered here is the quality of the institutional arrangements within which the economy operated. Economists recognize that institutions play a major role in explaining which countries are rich and which are not.[8] Australia is no exception to this generalization. Its sustained economic prosperity cannot be accounted for without giving priority to the role of certain institutions whose contribution has not always been appropriately recognized. In this growth narrative, several roles are emphasized. One is that Australian history yields some vivid illustrations of the importance of institutional flexibility. More than once, as evidence accumulated that an institution was operating in a manner harmful to prosperity, it was either abolished or modified to make it growth promoting. Nineteenth-century examples considered below include the transportation of convicts, the monopolization of grazing land by squatters, and the employment of immigrant, indentured labor on sugar plantations. A recent example is the reform of labor-market institutions that came to be seen as holding back potential productivity gains. The capacity of a society to adapt its institutional arrangements in the face of changed economic conditions, or evidence of the adverse consequences for prosperity of doing nothing, is a key factor explaining why there is such a wide range of income levels across countries.

Another role of institutions in this story is that political (including constitutional) arrangements likely played a key part in sustaining prosperity. One example has been of interest to political historians but less so to economists. The Australian economy has its origins as a component of the British Empire. Whereas the economic costs of imperialism in general have long been debated,

---

[7] I will have more to say on the resource-curse hypothesis in the next chapter.

[8] For a survey of the literature on institutions and growth, see Acemoglu, Johnson, and Robinson (2005).

there is no evidence of sustained or serious economic exploitation of Australia by the British. To the contrary, the Australian colonies benefited greatly from their participation as integral components of the world's most dynamic and advanced economy at that time. They had privileged access to the main market for foreign capital, and secured special trading privileges. At the political level, self-government came early and bloodlessly to the small European population in five of the six colonies in the 1850s. They in turn devised first their own constitutions and later a federal constitution for their unification in 1901, and these have served the economy well.

A final role of institutions that is emphasized in what follows is their *interaction* with resource abundance. In recent decades, to be resource rich appears typically to have led to slower growth in developing countries. This is puzzling. In theory, having more resources should raise the level of economic prosperity. Economies that are both resource rich and prosperous are therefore important counterexamples to the prevailing resource-curse hypothesis, and Australia throughout its modern history clearly fits this description. I explain the absence of a resource curse primarily in terms of the quality of some of the country's key institutional arrangements. How they were formed, how well they functioned, and how responsively they evolved in the light of experience or changed circumstances, largely determined whether the natural-resource base would be exploited in a manner that was growth promoting or wasteful of these natural assets. That is, the conditions of access to, the specification of property rights in, and the distribution of rents from the natural-resource endowment are what determined whether the growth effects of resource abundance were positive. Just one example from later discussion is the set of rules under which farming or mining could be conducted on Crown land.

In this account of the Australian economy's sustained prosperity, I also emphasize the manner in which its policy-makers responded to the major economic shocks—positive and negative—that have punctuated its history. Sometimes the shocks originated within the resource sector, such as with the discovery of gold. As noted, a favorable shock of this type need not necessarily underpin prosperity if appropriate institutions are lacking. On other occasions the shocks were negative and arose from elsewhere—the First World War, the interwar collapse of the world economy, or the oil price hikes of the 1970s. Then the critical issue is how well existing institutions coped with stress and adversity, and what policies were put in place in response to the deterioration in the economic environment. Chance events of short duration have on occasion shaped the trajectory of the economy over much longer periods. In general we will observe an economy resilient to shocks, together with policy choices made in their aftermath that were appropriate to sustaining prosperity.

One major shock to the economy widely believed to have had profound long-run implications was the depression of the 1890s. It appeared then that resource-based prosperity had faltered, and that the openness of the economy had heightened its vulnerability to destabilizing global forces. Some historians identify a fundamental shift in economic and social policies as the eventual response. The new strategy for economic growth was designed to reduce the dependence of the economy on its resources sector and on imports, thereby reducing the exposure of the community to economic fluctuations emanating from abroad. Implementing these policies required the creation of new economic institutions, especially in the labor market. The consequence was a strategy of industrialization behind rising levels of protection that was pursued for half a century. Though influential, this interpretation will be shown to require modification.

This book does not, however, simplify what is a complex history of growth to an explanation focusing solely on the interactions between resource abundance, the quality of institutions, and the development policies adopted in response to major economic shocks. Other hypotheses, themes, and conjectures feature in the narrative, countering any tendency to the overly reductionist approach to historical explanation that can follow uncritical adherence to the suggestions of any single and parsimonious theory. To illustrate with an example appropriate in a history of the so-called lucky country, due recognition is given to the role of chance.

Two other elements of the approach adopted in this inquiry warrant early mention. I do not believe a persuasive account of Australia's economic growth can be conducted as if this growth were sui generis. It is vital not to miss that which only comes into focus on looking in the mirror provided by experience elsewhere. Obviously, in its entirety the Australian story is unique. But examining the experience of other economies greatly assists thinking about many features of the Australian case. My choice of comparator will vary according to the issue and period. Until recent decades it will most often be made by consulting some aspects of the history of the other settler economies of Canada, Argentina, New Zealand, and the United States (especially its western regions). Australia has more in common with the geography, factor endowment, and patterns of demographic and economic development in these countries than it has with those observed in Britain, Continental Europe, or Japan. For recent decades comparisons with a wider set of countries and with OECD averages are often more appropriate.

I also make use of counterfactuals as devices to aid thinking about what actually happened. This approach to historical research has limitations, and will not be formally developed in relation to any issue. But posing a plausible counterfactual in order critically to assess the significance of an event or policy can be a useful thought experiment. And one way counterfactuals can be made especially apt is by drawing on comparative experience. If relevant conditions are roughly comparable in another economy, it is likely a counterfactual assessment of some aspect of Australian experience can be more persuasive and better illuminate what actually occurred.

•   •   •

To provide context for what follows, I first set out the evidence of economic prosperity (chapter 2). This covers the entire era of European settlement, and includes comparisons with the performance of selected other countries. Particular attention is paid to alternative measures of prosperity, their relationships to one another, and their limitations. As a first step toward the explanation of this evidence, I briefly review existing suggestions as to what are likely the most important determinants of Australia's levels of productivity and living standards. There are several literatures of relevance here, especially those on Australian history, comparative economic history, and growth economics—both theoretical and empirical.

I then take up the historical narrative, beginning with an assessment of the Aboriginal contribution to the economy constructed by the first European settlers at the end of the eighteenth century and beginning of the nineteenth. The British military, convict workforce, and British government financial outlays laid the early foundations of a tiny local economy at the outer margins of a vast imperial project (chapter 3). From the 1820s Australia's prosperity rested, initially, on the productivity of its labor force—convicts, emancipists, and free immigrants—and the occupation and exploratory utilization of a large area of natural grassland primarily for the production and export of wool (chapter 4). This geographical settlement and pastoral development occurred in a rapidly evolving institutional setting. Both in the economic and political spheres, institutional innovation and adaptation appears successfully to have underpinned the attainment of quite high incomes per capita even before the discovery of gold.

The gold rushes beginning in the 1850s brought not only a diversification of the economic basis of prosperity beyond that provided by the wool industry, but coincided with the de facto political independence of five of the Australian colonies through their attainment of responsible government from Britain. Critical to the maintenance and extension of prosperity during these turbulent years was the way in which the shock to the economy of the gold discoveries was mediated by the evolving economic and political institutions. The gold rushes were no flash in the pan. Gold continued to be important to prosperity for several decades, while a resumption of the expansion of the wool industry was matched by the development of other branches of agriculture (chapter 5). This is the period in which Australia came to record the world's highest income levels.

After 1890, however, these very high levels of relative prosperity were not sustained. Negative shocks from internal imbalance, external factors, and drought wrought havoc with the economy for more than a decade (chapter 6). Against this background of a major threat to prosperity, important changes occurred in the institutional framework with the federation of the Australian colonies in 1901. Though some recovery in economic fortunes occurred before the outbreak of war, it was short-lived. The First World War seriously disrupted the economy, and was to be but the first of a succession of adverse external influences on national prosperity lasting a quarter of a century (chapter 7). The breakdown of the international economic order beginning in the 1920s and culminating in the world depression of the 1930s posed major challenges to Australia. The principal policy response to this sequence of negative shocks was to promote industrialization behind rising levels of protection and accompanied by more centralized and regulated modes of wage determination.

The Second World War imparted a more favorable shock to the economy than the First. And the postwar international economic environment was much more conducive to raising incomes than it had been after 1919 (chapter 8). In the 1950s, prosperity was further underpinned by the Korean War wool boom, and by an intensification of the process of import substituting industrialization. But by the late 1960s and early 1970s, the higher level of prosperity attained during this second "golden age" was threatened. Pressures for a significant restructuring in the economy arose from a boom in mineral production, the onset of Asian industrialization, and a spike in world energy prices. These forces eventually led to the adoption of more outward-oriented policies with respect to trade and capital flows and a more market-oriented approach to the regulation of the domestic economy—policies more akin to those pursued in the nineteenth century (chapter 9). In pursuit of enhanced levels of prosperity, the policy reforms during the 1980s and 1990s were numerous and significant, requiring the abolition or adaptation of some key economic institutions. The improved productivity and incomes characterizing the 1990s have been attributed in part to this restructuring of the economy resulting from the shifts in domestic policies. But this most recent golden era has also resulted from a very traditional source of Australian prosperity—a boom in the natural resource sector driven by a combination of rising international demand for commodities, and the discovery of further significant mineral deposits and energy reserves.

When reflecting on why Australia was, and remains, so rich, two recurring themes are central (chapter 10). First, the *interactions* between the principal determinants of growth have been more important to the outcomes than the role of any one factor—such as investment, institutions, or resources.[9] And second, it is precisely due to the *shifting* basis of its prosperity that Australia has managed to sustain its status as a rich economy over so long a period and despite numerous negative shocks. Within the resources sector, the shifts have been

---

[9]This is not to deny the considerable value of single-themed interpretations. In advocating the significance of the chosen factor or influence, they thereby facilitate an assessment of its importance relative to other factors or influences.

between farming and mining; within each of these among a range of foodstuffs, fibers, minerals, and energy sources. And for part of the twentieth century, when commodity-based prosperity proved elusive, manufacturing played a supporting role. Therefore at the core of our story lies a policy and institutional adaptability in the face of markedly changed economic conditions that ensured enhanced living standards for a rapidly expanding population over most of the past two centuries.

CHAPTER 2

What Is to Be Explained, and How

[W]ealth is evidently not the good we are seeking; for it is merely useful and for the sake of something else.
　　—Aristotle[1]

IN THIS CHAPTER I first lay out the evidence that motivates this inquiry. That is, I review the conventional money-based measures of Australian economic prosperity and place these in a comparative context before broadening the focus to see whether other indicators of prosperity tell a similar story. Taken together they conveniently summarize the historical record the remainder of the book is devoted to explaining. Drawing on the literatures on growth economics and Australian history, I then introduce those determinants of this prosperity that, I will argue, are pertinent to any accounting for the variation across time in Australia's average level of income, and its changing relationship to the levels of income in other countries.

COMPARATIVE LEVELS OF GDP PER CAPITA

Perhaps the single economic "fact" about Australia most widely known among economists and economic historians outside the country is that for some period during the latter half of the nineteenth century it appears to have recorded the world's highest standard of living. Using GDP per capita, the United Kingdom held the top spot in the ranking earlier in that century, while the United States had overtaken it by the First World War. It is during the period in which the United States converges on and then surpasses the United Kingdom's lead that Australia records a higher level of income than both.

　　Australia thus makes a cameo appearance in the history of modern economic growth (figure 2.1). When exactly Australia first pulled ahead of the United Kingdom and the United States is somewhat difficult to identify, as the quality of the underlying GDP estimates declines the further back in time one presses the comparisons. We might take the midcentury estimates as a starting point. The most widely cited estimates of comparative GDP per capita for

---

[1] Aristotle (2009), p. 7.

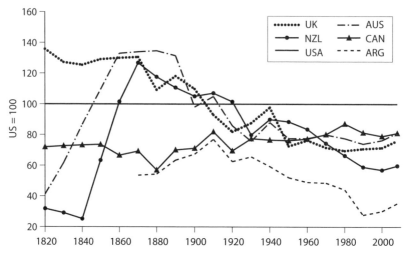

Figure 2.1. Comparative GDP per capita, selected years, 1820 to 2008 (US = 100).
Note: Based on 1990 Geary-Khamis dollars.
Source: Maddison (2010), Table 3.

1850 suggest that only the United Kingdom and the Netherlands were above the Australian level, by about 20 percent, while the United States was 9 percent below.[2] By 1860, following the gold rushes, Australia had overtaken both, but by very little in the case of the United Kingdom. The lead over the United Kingdom widens thereafter, to almost 20 percent in 1880, and was still 10 percent in 1890. The gap in Australia's favor was greater when the comparison is made with the United States, reaching 25 or 30 percent from 1860 to 1890. But following a major depression in Australia in the 1890s its clear lead was eroded, and by 1900 there was not much difference between the income levels of Australia, the United States, the United Kingdom, and New Zealand. This situation persists until the outbreak of the First World War. Canadian income levels were below all these throughout this period, with Switzerland, Belgium and the Netherlands next highest at the beginning of the twentieth century. On this evidence the clear superiority of Australian incomes over those of the United States arises with the gold rushes of the 1850s, whereas in the comparison with Britain the superiority lasts perhaps less than two decades prior to the 1890s depression.

Some cautionary remarks are in order. The economies being compared are very different in size. In 1860, for example, when Australia's population had just exceeded 1 million (and New Zealand's was only 130,000), the population of the United Kingdom was 29 million and that of the United States 32 million. Also, the quality of the national income or GDP estimates on which the

---

[2] The source for these estimates is Maddison (2010), table 3.

reported comparisons are based varies between countries and over time. The New Zealand estimates for all of this period are the least reliable because of the indirect methods by which they have been constructed, while the Australian estimates after 1860 are more solidly based than those for earlier years. In addition, there is something a little artificial about confining the comparison to national boundaries—and post-1901 boundaries at that. At this time there almost certainly existed regional economies with larger populations than Australia's that had attained higher levels of gross "regional" product (or regional income) per capita. For instance, state and regional *personal* income estimates exist for part of this period for the United States, and these, though not directly comparable with national income-based estimates, indicate that in 1880 there were regions (the Northeast and West) recording income levels above the U.S. average *by more than* the Australian lead over the U.S. average level in per capita GDP.[3] Thus California, also the location of a midcentury gold rush, almost certainly had income levels above that of Australia at this time.[4]

Concerns about the reliability of these international comparisons can be addressed in a variety of ways. First, alternative methods may be sought for converting the national GDP estimates to a common basis, such as the use of the exchange rates between currencies, or the adjustment of these rates to approximate purchasing-power parity. The most comprehensive review of alternative conversion procedures shows some variation in the duration and degree of Australia's lead during the late nineteenth century, but supports the existence of its superior income levels.[5] Second, other indicators of comparative living standards may be consulted to assess their consistency with the rank ordering between countries suggested by the GDP-based estimates. I will shortly have more to say on the question of alternative indicators, and will return to this topic in chapter 6 for a closer look at the evidence for Australia's lead in GDP per capita, the reasons for it, and why it was lost.

Although Australia surrendered its lead over the United States after 1890, the evidence in figure 2.1 indicates that during the following century it never fell far behind. There was further slippage during the period between 1914 and 1945 in the incomes of Australians relative to those of Americans, on the order of 20 percent, but no trend over the last fifty years or so either to diverge further from or to reconverge on U.S. levels. In 2000, Australian GDP per capita was 76 percent of the American figure.[6] (Canadian incomes in the same year were 79 percent of those in the United States) Since the United States is the appropriate twentieth-century benchmark for present purposes, this constitutes a

---

[3] Mitchener and McLean (1999).

[4] McLean and Taylor (2003) compare the growth histories of Australia and California.

[5] Prados de la Escosura (2000).

[6] In chapter 9 we will review studies (including a Productivity Commission report) into whether there are reasons why, irrespective of policy settings, Australia may not currently be able to achieve U.S. levels of productivity and hence living standards.

second major achievement that requires explanation. For this outcome was not guaranteed. The New Zealand experience prior to the 1960s was one of rough comparability with Australia, but since then its relative income levels have declined markedly, and by 2000 stood at only 57 percent of American levels. The Argentine experience more emphatically makes the same point. From being one of the richest countries in the world in 1913, its per capita income has fallen from 72 percent of U.S. income in that year to just 30 percent by 2000.[7] Just as there is no iron law that all developing countries will converge on the income levels of the richest, there is no certainty that having once attained rich-country status it will be maintained indefinitely.

Perhaps this is the appropriate place to note, as an aside, how "industrialization" should not be confused with growth or prosperity. Growth theorists and policy economists have emphasized the importance of industrialization as the route to successful growth, and in particular the role therein of technological change. And Britain's industrial revolution acquired canonical status in the development literature. But the tendency to conflate industrial development with modern economic growth is unfortunate. Neither the Netherlands nor Australia achieved their high income levels as a result of industrialization in the narrow sense of the term. And neither made contributions to scientific and technological progress on the order of that made not just by Britain and America but also France, Germany, and perhaps others. Thus if the criterion of "leadership" is the generation of new technology, or the size of the manufacturing sector, Australia can justifiably be relegated to minor status, and its topping of the income rankings for several decades regarded as a pesky anomaly to be consigned to a footnote.[8]

But if GDP per capita is the basis for assessing comparative economic performance, this may be raised to levels equivalent to the world's best primarily through an expansion of the manufacturing sector (as in Britain and Japan, for example), or of the natural resources sector (Australia or Norway), or of the services sector (the Netherlands or Singapore), so long as the relevant sector achieves world-leading productivity, is large enough within the domestic economy, and other sectors do not offset its contribution. This is because the principal determinant of living standards is the overall level of labor productivity in an economy. This in turn is equal to the weighted average of the productivity levels achieved in each sector, where the weights are the sectors' employment shares. To illustrate, the United States actually had higher levels of productivity in manufacturing than the United Kingdom as early as 1840, but the overall level of U.S. labor productivity was below that of the United Kingdom at that time. The United States' overtaking of the United Kingdom in income and productivity levels at the end of the century resulted from complex shifts both in their relative sectoral productivity levels and also in the relative importance of

---

[7] Maddison (2010), table 3.
[8] For examples of such consignment, see McLean (2007), p. 637.

each sector.[9] These findings have improved our understanding of the reasons for the change in leadership between these two leading "industrial" powers in their relative levels of GDP per capita. In chapter 6 we will adopt a similar comparative perspective to look more closely at the evidence of Australia's changing sectoral productivity performance during the late nineteenth century and early twentieth, and again in chapter 9 when we review the sources of recent changes in the country's rate of productivity improvement.

BOOMS, BUSTS, AND STAGNATION IN DOMESTIC PROSPERITY

The second basis on which Australian economic prosperity is assessed here is not relative to other countries' experience, but across time—that is, comparing one period with another. Since my primary interest lies in long-run trends rather than short-run fluctuations in economic activity, the relevant periods will cover several decades. Fortunately there is a substantial degree of concordance between many indicators of prosperity and measures of aggregate economic activity. The main periods of rising economic prosperity broadly coincide with the periods of most rapid population growth and of most rapid expansion in the overall size of the economy. Hence the growth in population provides a convenient initial metric for indicating these historical eras.

The European population was tiny for the three decades following 1788: around 6,000 by 1800, and 30,000 by 1820. The Aboriginal population was very much larger than this, though the number is uncertain. (I defer to the next chapter a discussion of this question, and the related issue of the extent of the Aboriginal contribution to the "European" economy—and hence prosperity.) Following these foundation years, there occurred a period of spreading settlement: in the three decades after 1820 the European population expanded rapidly, exceeding 430,000 by 1851. This period of expansion was temporarily interrupted by a depression in the economy in the early 1840s, and ended with a massive—and positive—economic shock resulting from the discovery of gold in 1851 (table 2.1). In the decade that followed, dominated by the impact of gold on the economy, the population grew by 714,000 to over 1.15 million in 1861 (figure 2.2). There followed a further three decades of economic growth marked only by regional, brief or shallow recessions, as best we can determine from available evidence. Though the *rate* of population expansion subsequently slowed, it still averaged 3.5 percent per year for three decades, a rate above that recorded during the second long population boom in the thirty years following 1945. Over these three decades another 2 million were added: by 1891 the population had reached 3.17 million.[10]

---

[9]Broadberry and Irwin (2006).

[10]Population figures are from Vamplew (1987), pp. 25–26. Of course, *rates* of population growth were highest in some of the decades prior to 1851 because the base (*level* of) population was so small. This accounts for my use here of the increase in the (absolute numbers in the) population.

TABLE 2.1. Economic and population growth rates by period, annual average percentages, 1850 to 2010

	Real aggregate GDP	Population	Real per capita GDP
1850–1860	22.3	11.0	2.9
1861–1889	4.8	3.5	1.4
1889–1905	0.8	1.7	−0.8
1905–1914	5.2	2.4	3.0
1914–1920	−1.6	1.4	−2.7
1920–1930	3.2	1.9	1.3
1930–1939	1.6	0.8	0.8
1939–1946	3.4	1.0	2.6
1946–1974	4.8	2.2	2.2
1974–1991	2.9	1.4	1.5
1991–2010	3.4	1.4	2.0

Note: Population is for year ended 31 December.

Sources: All series 1850 to 1860: Butlin (1986), Table 8, p. 113. Real GDP: 1861 to 1950: McLean and Pincus (1982), Appendix Table, pp. 29–30. 1950 to 1960: Reserve Bank of Australia, *Australian Economic Statistics 1949–50 to 1996–97*, Table 5.10. 1960 to 2010: Australian Bureau of Statistics, *National Accounts* (Cat. 5204.0), Table 1. Population: 1861 to 2005: ABS, *Australian Historical Population Statistics 2008* (Cat. 3105.0.65.001). 2005 to 2009: ABS, *Australian Demographic Statistics, March 2010* (Cat. 3101), Table 1.

The 1890s are another story altogether. A major depression ends this long nineteenth-century economic and population boom, and is followed by a severe drought at the time of federation (1901) such that for more than a decade the economy does not fully recover. Population growth slows dramatically, and in ten of the years between 1892 and 1906, there is a net outflow of migrants. From 1906 there is a return to economic growth, but the rebound is cut short by the outbreak of war in Europe in 1914, when the population had reached 4.9 million. There follows a period of a quarter century marked by two further major negative economic (and demographic) shocks and no extended period of sustained growth. The First World War seriously disrupts the economy; immigration ceases; and aggregate real GDP declines for four consecutive years. There is only a brief return to growth and immigration in the first half of the 1920s followed by deteriorating international economic conditions, and what amounts to a recession in the domestic economy. Additions to the population in the 1920s are not significantly above what occurred in the 1880s. After 1929, the world economy collapses, taking the domestic economy into its third major

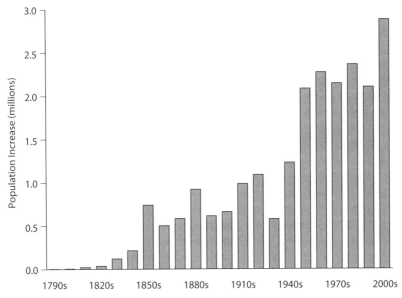

Figure 2.2. Population increase per decade, 1790 to 2009.
Notes: Population as at December 31. The indigenous population is excluded prior to 1961.
Sources: 1790 to 2000: Australian Bureau of Statistics, *Australian Historical Population Statistics, 2008* (Cat. 3105.0.65.001). 2009: ABS, *Australian Demographic Statistics, March 2010* (Cat. 3101), Table 1.

downturn in less than half a century accompanied, as in the 1890s, by net emigration. Hence the population increase in the 1930s is only about half what it was in the previous decade. The economic recovery is barely complete when war in Europe resumes in 1939. The population had by then reached 6.9 million, reflecting the much lower rate of its increase after 1914 than in the decades prior to 1890.

The economic impact of the Second World War, in contrast to that of its predecessor, was generally favorable. Indeed, by some measures the long postwar economic boom began during the war and would persist until the early 1970s. The postwar baby boom and a return to high levels of immigration lifted the rate of population increase during these years. As is clear in figure 2.2, the absolute increase in the population in the 1950s was way above what had previously been experienced, just as, at the beginning of the first long boom in the middle of the nineteenth century, there had been a marked and sustained jump in the growth of the population. But this second boom in the economy as well as in population ends in 1973 (the population was then 13.3 million), with the level of immigration 50 percent lower for the rest of that decade. Once again, negative shocks emanating from the international economy account for much of this slowdown, though without the plunge into depression that had occurred in 1890 at the end of the previous long boom. Slower economic and population growth rates characterized much of the 1970s and 1980s, with several recessions punctuating the period, such that a return to sustained high rates of growth in either the economy or in immigration does not occur until after the last of these recessions in 1990–91. The growth phase that began in 1991 when the population was 17.3 million has continued uninterrupted (that is, no "technical" recession in aggregate GDP) to the time of writing, with immigration accelerating after the mid-1990s and the population passing 22 million in 2009. Having lasted two decades, it looks increasingly like a third "long boom" in the economy, which bears comparison in respect to its duration with those running from 1851 to 1890, and from 1945 to 1973. And as is clear in figure 2.2, in the opening years of the twenty-first century, there was yet another clear step up in additions to the population.

Economic prosperity as measured by per capita GDP broadly fits the temporal pattern observed in population growth and the growth in aggregate GDP. Figure 2.3 displays this in terms of longer-period average rates of increase in order to smooth out the short-run fluctuations and more clearly identify periods of increasing, stagnant, or decreasing *levels* of prosperity.[11] One feature that stands out is the impact of the sharp declines in per capita income growth subsequent to the worst of the negative shocks and downturns in the economy: the 1890s depression, the First World War, and the depression of the 1930s. It is therefore unsurprising that each of these events was the genesis of major shifts in economic policies effecting growth that I will explore in chapters 6 and 7, especially attempts to reduce the volatility of economic activity resulting from the extent of the economy's openness to the global economy.

A second feature is the coincidence of the three long booms with periods of stability and rapid growth in the international economy. Prosperity in the Australian economy has never been sustained without that precondition. And the only period in which the domestic economy did not prosper while the world economy was expanding was between 1890 and 1904. The first period of significant integration between economies on a world rather than a regional scale began sometime around the middle of the nineteenth century and came to an abrupt end in 1914. The First World War caused a suspension of the process; attempts to restart it in the 1920s failed; and in the 1930s there was a systemic collapse of international trade and finance. Only after the Second World War did a new phase of international economic cooperation and integration begin, but it was at first gradual, restricted in geographical coverage, and limited in its reach beyond trading ties. After the 1970s, however, the pace accelerated, and more countries participated. Further, it was only at this time that international

---

[11] There is a break in the underlying estimates of real GDP between 1860 and 1861; this precludes an average for the whole of the period 1850 to 1889 being reported in table 2.1 and figure 2.3.

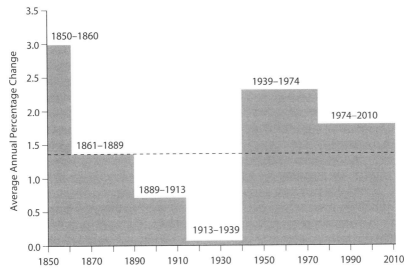

Figure 2.3. Growth rate of GDP per capita by period, 1850 to 2010.
Notes: Growth rate determined for each year and averaged over the periods shown. Average annual growth of GDP per capita from 1861 to 2010 shown as a dotted horizontal line.
Sources: 1850 to 1860: Butlin (1986), Table 8, p. 113. 1861 to 1950: McLean and Pincus (1982), Appendix Table, pp. 29-31. 1950 to 1960: Reserve Bank of Australia, *Australian Economic Statistics 1949–50 to 1996–97*, Table 5.10. 1960 to 2010: Australian Bureau of Statistics, *National Accounts* (Cat. 5204.0), Table 1.

capital markets regained the degree of integration achieved before 1914. The broad outlines of Australia's record of prosperity thus correspond as a first approximation to the periods of the first and second globalizations and the period of retreat from globalization during the decades (1914–45) between these two. This profound influence of international economic conditions on Australian prosperity will be a recurring theme in this book.

Much of "what is to be explained" has now been summarized in the evidence on Australia's *comparative levels* of GDP per capita at various times (figure 2.1), and by *changes between periods* in its GDP per capita (figure 2.3). Prior to taking up this challenge, however, it is necessary to reflect on just how satisfactory GDP per capita is as a measure of economic prosperity.

OTHER INDICATORS OF ECONOMIC PROSPERITY

Well-known limitations apply to the use of GDP per capita as a proxy measure of "living standards" or "economic well-being," though neither concept has an agreed-upon definition. GDP per capita is an *average* measure, and does not reveal the shape of the distribution from which it is drawn. Nonmarketed output such as unpaid work within the household or by charitable organizations is unrecorded. Negative externalities arising from economic activity such as pollution or traffic congestion are not directly reflected in the national accounts, though the expenditures by firms and households to offset their harmful effects may be, thus perversely increasing measured GDP. Limitations such as these may apply also in historical applications, sometimes with added force. For example, if the share of home-grown fruit and vegetables in the total consumption of these items falls as incomes rise, as it has done, the growth rate of GDP and its per capita derivative will be overstated to this extent. Or, if expenditures on commuting to work rise as a consequence of the increased distance separating the places of residence and employment, as has occurred with the growth of urban areas, this will be recorded as an increase in GDP when it is really a necessary but defensive expenditure required to produce the same level of final output.

When comparing GDP estimates across time, it is necessary to deflate the nominal values to a constant-price basis, defined in terms of a selected base year: hence the expression *real* GDP per capita indicates that this allowance for movements in the price level has been made.[12] It follows that the availability of suitable price indexes becomes critical, especially where several decades—or even a century or more—of movements in *nominal* GDP have to be deflated to a single base year. In addition, the further back in time one looks for suitable price quotations, the harder they are to find, so the reliability of the resulting price index may be less in the distant compared to the more recent past. There is also the problem of quality changes in items covered in the index: for example, the average house in 1860 was very different from that in 1960 or 2010. And new products and services continually appear while others disappear.

One response to the limitations of historical estimates of real GDP is to seek other, and preferably independent, indicators that reflect either part of what GDP covers, or what GDP omits but plausibly should be considered in any assessment of changes over time in economic well-being viewed more broadly. And economists as well as economic historians have been adept at this. For example, it can be argued that real final consumption per capita is perhaps as reflective of living standards as the broader GDP-based measure that includes investment expenditure, changes in inventories, and net exports. We do not have historical estimates of Australian consumption that are as comprehensive as those of GDP, although reasonably detailed estimates are available for the period since federation.[13] There exist some differences between the per capita trends in incomes and consumption in the alternative measures of both, but this is most noticeable only during subperiods in the early twentieth century. Hence further consideration of this topic will be deferred until chapter 7.

---

[12] Throughout this book the reported GDP-based time series are all expressed in constant prices; any exceptions will be noted.

[13] M. W. Butlin (1977), McLean and Pincus (1982), and Haig and Anderssen (2007).

In a study of prosperity that relies heavily on per capita measures, it is important to be aware of any long-run trends in economic inequality. Of particular importance are the distributions of incomes, of wealth, and of wages or earnings. Regrettably, the historical information on these for Australia is reasonably abundant only for the past few decades, and becomes increasingly patchy before then, with quantitative information for the nineteenth century especially fragmentary. What evidence we have suggests that inequality by most measures underwent a decline from sometime early in the twentieth century (but this may have begun earlier) that continued to around the 1960s. Thereafter some series show a partial reversal, with inequality rising in recent decades.[14] These trends are not smooth, with interruptions or short-term reversals during periods of war or depression, or when shocks to the economy impacted particular groups. In figure 2.4 this shallow U-shaped trend in income inequality is illustrated by the share of the very top income earners in total income. Other measures of economic inequality would depart to some degree in timing and magnitude from this particular income-based indicator. Perhaps more important is that economic inequality was never likely to have been as pronounced as in most other countries; that the relative position of the unskilled appears even in the nineteenth century to have been especially favorable; and that, as in other settler economies experiencing high immigration and population growth rates, there were more opportunities than in longer-established societies for mobility between income, wealth, or occupational groups—a feature not observable in the standard measures of economic inequality.[15]

Another indicator of economic prosperity is the trend in real wages, a measure that has the virtue of being completely independent of the national income accounts. However, it is limited by the representativeness of the particular wage rate chosen; and even maximum coverage of all "wage and salary earners" may not reflect changes in the incomes of the self-employed. Real wage trends since federation show much the same long-run pattern as per capita income, namely relatively modest increases until the Second World War with much more rapid gains thereafter.[16]

Of course, any number of social indicators might be pressed into service in order to supplement or provide an alternative to GDP per capita. However, without

---

[14] Atkinson and Leigh (2007, pp. 247–48) cite the major contributions to historical analyses of Australia's income distribution. For a study of trends in wealth inequality since 1860, based on estate data for Victoria, see Rubinstein (1979).

[15] There is limited evidence available on the historical trends in regional inequality in Australian incomes. Cashin (1995) reports incomes per capita for each colony/state from 1861 to 1991 using an indirect estimation method based on monetary data, and finds evidence of convergence between 1861 and 1901, with little change in dispersion thereafter. Sinclair (1996) directly estimates Victoria's incomes per capita. A comparison with that of the rest of Australia reveals that, with the exception of the 1850s, the difference is not marked, fluctuating generally within a range of plus or minus 20 percent.

[16] Withers (1987), p. 268. Real wage trends across recent decades will be further examined in chapter 9.

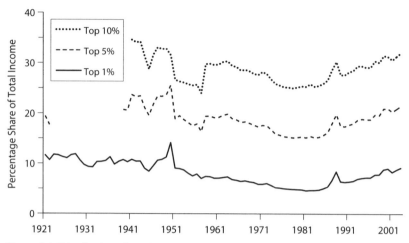

Figure 2.4. Distribution of top incomes, 1921 to 2003.
Notes: Years ended 30 June. Estimated from income taxation data.
Source: Atkinson and Leigh (2007), Table 1, pp. 251–52.

a firm theoretical basis from which to guide the selection of these partial indicators, or on which to aggregate them, they remain of limited use as *summary* measures of economic well-being. Notwithstanding this, there can be occasions when it is especially useful to highlight a particular indicator, and to contrast trends in it with trends in average incomes. To illustrate, the characteristics of housing in the decades following the gold rushes in Australia seem to me a useful complement to the high incomes at that time. The extraordinarily rapid population growth in the 1850s outpaced the construction of housing. From colonial censuses one can trace across subsequent decades the increase in the proportion of houses whose outer walls were brick, timber, or stone, and the decline in the (initially substantial) proportion that were made of canvas, wattle and daub, or corrugated iron. When the proportion of the housing stock that is constructed of inferior materials declines to a very small percentage, this particular measure no longer has much value in supplementing the GDP series. But for as long as the upgrading of the housing stock lagged the increase in incomes that made the upgrading possible, it serves as a valuable additional indicator of prosperity.[17]

A rather different dimension of prosperity is the average amount of leisure time available. This is difficult to measure directly. Often a proxy measure is obtained indirectly by subtracting from the total hours in a year those spent in employment, for which there is reasonably good information, then further subtracting an estimated number of hours spent in nonwork and nonleisure

---

[17]In a lively social history of "daily life" in Australia, Blainey (2003b) discusses many nice examples of items that might serve as partial indicators of living standards.

activities such as sleeping, household chores, commuting to work, and so on. A decrease in average annual hours worked is, other things unchanged, taken as an increase in leisure. By itself, more leisure is regarded as increasing well-being, although if income is not maintained through higher wage *rates*, the net effect on well-being is dependent on the labor-leisure preference of each individual. And doubtless, some people would prefer more hours of employment to increased unpaid leisure time. So, changes in average hours of leisure in a community over time are not without problems of interpretation as partial indicators of well-being. But they surely add to the completeness of the picture.

Little is known about trends in working hours or leisure time before the early twentieth century. Thereafter, the reduction in the former and increase in the latter is evident in historical estimates of both, with an acceleration occurring after the Second World War. If the measures of hours worked or available for leisure are converted to a lifetime basis, then note must also be made of the gradual increase in life expectancy Australians have experienced at least since 1870.[18] Putting this information together suggests that an "augmented" GDP per capita, taking into account the effects of changes in both leisure and life expectation, would show a somewhat higher rate of increased economic well-being relative to unadjusted GDP per capita between 1911 and 1947, but some reduction relative to the benchmark in the period from then until 1981.[19]

Disquiet about the adequacy of GDP-based measures of economic well-being has led not just to the search for additional indicators in the analysis of a single country's historical record, but also to intercountry comparisons. One device has been the construction of a wider composite measure, the human development index (HDI). This contains three equally weighted components: GDP per capita; a measure of educational attainment in the population; and life expectancy. The emphasis given education and life expectancy complements the economic measure with one basic measure of social progress or attainment, and another of the health status of society. The HDI has been employed primarily in the analysis of developing countries, since there the divergent trends between social and health outcomes on the one hand, and measured GDP on the other, tend to be greater than in high-income countries. However, in any historical analysis of the currently high-income countries the possibility exists that, as with less developed countries, the HDI will show differences from GDP-based indicators during earlier periods of their development.

In a recent application of the HDI methodology using historical evidence, Australia ranks first in 1870, the earliest year reported, and second after New Zealand in 1913, the only other year prior to 1950 for which estimates are given. Broadly, the results follow the GDP per capita evidence. Under either metric,

---

[18] Ruzicka (1989).

[19] Carter and Maddock (1984, 1987). See also Jackson (1992) for a discussion of these and related findings.

the same countries are bunched near the top—the United Kingdom, the United States, the Netherlands, Denmark, Switzerland, and Canada. Hence Australia's ranking at this time does not appear to be especially sensitive to the inclusion of education and longevity measures in a broader-based indicator of well-being. Similarly, comparative estimates for HDI following the Second World War show Australia holding a close relationship to the United States and ranking sixth in 1950, twelfth in 1975, and second equal in 1999.[20]

Other but partial historical indicators of well-being for the countries for which data are available also appear to confirm the relative position of Australia as reflected in GDP per capita and shifts in it over time. One such study for 1870, 1910, and 1930, and including fifteen of the then richest economies, covers measures of real wages, life expectancy, literacy, school enrolment, discretionary hours, and social spending.[21] Australia ranked highest in real wages and life expectancy in 1870, in real wages and discretionary hours in 1910, and in life expectancy and discretionary hours in 1930. In a separate investigation, it has been reported that real wage levels, especially for the unskilled, were higher in Australia than in Britain, the United States, or Canada prior to the 1890s, but that this lead was subsequently lost.[22] I will explore in chapter 6 additional evidence on real wage differences between Australia and other countries at the end of the nineteenth century and beginning of the twentieth, and consider also the possible role of increased leisure hours in accounting for Australia losing its lead in income per capita.

To conclude this evaluation, it appears that extending the search for evidence relating to "economic prosperity" beyond the conventional measure of GDP per capita to a range of alternative measures designed to capture further aspects of "living standards" or "well-being," does not significantly alter either the Australian trends in prosperity since the nineteenth century, or the position of Australia relative to other countries. This generally consistent evidence is important given the use made here of the GDP-based measures, though in using terms such as prosperity rather than welfare I am mindful to avoid unsustainable claims. Nevertheless, there are occasions when I will widen the focus beyond the conventional measures either because I worry that there are weaknesses in the Australian GDP estimates, or because there is independent evidence of trends in living standards at a particular time that do not seem adequately reflected in movements in GDP per capita. Such issues will be addressed especially in chapters 6 and 7.

One's sense of well-being or welfare typically extends far beyond the economic sphere. It is important to be clear, therefore, about what is not being claimed by the use here of the phrase "economic prosperity." For example,

---

[20]Crafts (2002).

[21]Boyer (2007).

[22]Allen (1994). Haig (1989) and Thomas (1995) also review the comparative evidence at this time, with special reference to Australian and U.K. consumption levels.

one's subjective state of well-being may not be closely related to one's material circumstances—for various reasons. People may relate satisfaction with their economic circumstances not to whether there has been an improvement in it over time, but to whether their position *relative to* some reference group has or has not improved. If the reference group is local rather than national, changes in their subjective (self-reported) well-being may not closely reflect movements in income per capita for the country as a whole. It has also been found that people in high-income countries do not always report levels of well-being higher than those in low-income countries. This is the well-known Easterlin paradox, namely that increasing a country's real GDP per capita over a wide range may not be accompanied by increases in the average reported level of overall satisfaction.[23]

The relationship between "happiness" and economic growth involves conceptual issues fundamental to economic theory, including the bases of preference formation and the malleability of preferences over time—the latter being of particular concern wherever historical comparisons of well-being are attempted. Thus the nexus between material conditions and happiness has engaged economists at least since the eighteenth century speculations of Adam Smith in his *Theory of Moral Sentiments*.[24] However the direct relevance of these issues to the present inquiry lies in the degree to which measures of prosperity such as GDP per capita, or the HDI indicator, are positively correlated with various indicators of happiness or satisfaction.

The evidence of Australia's ranking in international surveys of subjective well-being is that it is broadly similar to its ranking in GDP per capita and when using the HDI. There is some variation according to the survey data used and according to whether the questions relate to "life satisfaction" or to "happiness." Also, subsidiary questions display some variation in ranking: those relating to job satisfaction rank somewhat lower. But crude rankings of countries are less helpful in the present context than whether the Australian data are different from the conventional measures to an extent that is statistically significant. The evidence so far is that they are not. Furthermore, across the period since various international surveys of this type began in the late 1940s, Australians have consistently been among those reporting the highest levels of satisfaction.[25]

FROM EVIDENCE TO ANALYSIS

If asked why their country has enjoyed increasing prosperity for much of its history, at levels close to—and at one time even exceeding—those enjoyed anywhere else, what would most Australians offer by way of explanation? One view, which

---

[23] Easterlin (1974). For a recent critique of the Easterlin hypothesis, and survey of the literature on this topic, see Stevenson and Wolfers (2008).

[24] Smith (1979 [1759]). Fleurbaey (2009) surveys the broader literature.

[25] Blanchflower and Oswald (2005, 2006), and Leigh and Wolfers (2006).

is likely widespread, is that the country has simply been fortunate. In general usage the "lucky country" label may refer, variously, to the favorable climate, isolation from many world conflicts, political stability, or an absence of serious social divisions.[26] However the phrase also encompasses the economic sphere, a sort of "lucky economy" perspective. Taken literally, of course, attributing favorable economic outcomes simply to chance would remove the challenge, as well as any mystery, from the present inquiry. It would also greatly abbreviate its length. Treated seriously, one wants to know in what sense luck or chance have played a role, when, and with what importance relative to other sources of prosperity.

Perhaps equally widespread is a view that Australian prosperity, historically as well as currently, has derived in no small measure from its natural-resource abundance. The discovery of large areas of natural grazing land in the 1820s underpinned the wool industry's expansion, and this commodity dominated exports for most of the next century in this small open economy. Credence was thus given the popular expression that Australia "rode on the sheep's back." This became shorthand for the country's economic reliance on its rural industries more generally—a reliance that was starkly revealed during periods when the agricultural sector's fortunes turned down as well as when the good times prevailed in rural areas. But the vital contribution of the natural-resource base extended beyond pastoral and agricultural land. The discovery of gold in the 1850s gave the country its first major mineral boom. Later "rushes" and "booms" reinforced among Australians an appreciation of the importance of mining to their prosperity, particularly during recent decades as the many and diverse mineral and energy resources discovered since the 1960s have been exploited. The title of the most widely read history of Australian mining succinctly conveys something of the industry's enduring contribution to prosperity: *The Rush That Never Ended.*[27]

The twin themes of luck and natural-resource abundance are, of course, related. It was "chance" that there was plentiful land suitable for raising sheep, and large deposits of gold and other minerals, all waiting to be discovered. Not all countries are as generously endowed by nature. However, further consideration might lead one to question whether the resource discoveries can be ascribed simply to luck. In chapter 7 I will examine the degree to which the economy's resource endowment may at least partly have been determined by economic factors rather than constituting an original gift of nature acquired without significant cost or effort. Nonetheless I will be assigning a prominent role to the influence of natural resources on Australian economic prosperity, consistent with what seems to be a generally held belief.

---

[26]The epithet is associated especially with a popular book of the 1960s having this title (Horne 1964).

[27]The reference is to Blainey (2003a; first edition 1963).

Turning from popular perceptions to specialist authority, what have economists and historians believed were the principal sources of Australian prosperity? At the outset it is essential to bear in mind that any writer on historical growth is going to be influenced, whether or not the influence is made explicit, by economists' theories of growth. As these theories evolve, fresh perspectives on the past are suggested.[28] It follows that earlier writers on the history of the Australian economy worked within diverse theoretical frameworks. Since the present author is no exception to such influences, the reader deserves an indication of the theoretical and empirical literature informing the design and interpretation of Australian experience offered here, and of the relation of his perspective to those of others. Further discussion of these theses and debates in the existing literature will occur throughout the book as they become germane.

Extensive Growth and Factor Accumulation

In settler economies such as Australia the initial conditions under which growth occurred were unlike those either in early-modern Europe or nearly all currently "developing" economies. For the modern Australian economy was essentially built from scratch—the theme of the next chapter. At the time of first European contact and settlement, the continent was occupied by a relatively small indigenous population whose hunter-gatherer economy operated at very low productivity levels. The Aborigines possessed little in the way of reproducible capital stock. And, with some important exceptions, their contribution to the labor force was not significant. Only with respect to land utilization was there competition for existing productive assets; and from the perspective of the Europeans the Aboriginal use of this had not increased its productivity—it was still "unimproved." A major element in any account of the development of the economy after 1788 will, accordingly, center on the accumulation of basic productive inputs. It is not surprising, therefore, that histories of the Australian economy all give prominence to such topics as population growth through immigration, exploration and pioneer settlement, the extension of frontier agriculture, the reliance on foreign savings, the foundation of new towns and cities, and the provision of basic infrastructure where none previously existed. The early development of the United States and other settler economies may be described in similar terms.

An alternative way of putting this is to say that much of Australian economic history is about the *extensive* growth that accompanied European settlement of the continent. This refers to a situation where there occurs an expansion in

---

[28] Of course, there may be remarkable persistence in the influence on economists and historians of discredited or superseded theories, as fashion and ideology figure prominently in the sociology of both disciplines.

productive inputs and therefore in total GDP, and where this is accompanied by a rise in the population at about the same rate, with the result that GDP per capita changes little. The population and size of the economy have both increased, but living standards have not risen. This also describes periods of the more recent history of some developing economies. By contrast, *intensive* growth occurs where there is an increase in per capita GDP: the rate of (positive) GDP growth exceeds that of population.[29] This is the situation characterizing the era of modern economic growth in the now-advanced economies, frequently dated from the onset of industrialization, and also in those less-developed countries whose living standards are rising.

One reason for making the distinction between extensive and intensive growth is that it helps clarify the emphasis placed in this book on productivity, income levels, and prosperity. If this were a general history of the Australian economy, it would be appropriate to devote more space to a description of its increasing size—the expansion in the population, labor force, occupied land, capital stock, and total output—and to identify and account for the periods of faster or slower growth in each of these. To illustrate, in such a history, one central task would be to account for why the Australian population has grown from less than one million in 1788 to over twenty-two million today. But how directly relevant would this be to our central question? Total population size is not a good proxy for economic prosperity. Norway has a small population but is rich; India has a large population but is poor. The distinction I have made between extensive and intensive growth clarifies why an expansion of its total population (or labor force, capital stock, area of land in use, or output) does not of itself explain either the current or historical levels of Australian economic prosperity.

Another reason for making this distinction is that growth economics, and most theories of growth, focus only on intensive growth—the process whereby average incomes rise. One has to think that this perhaps reflects the circumstances of its origins among European economists in the eighteenth and nineteenth centuries who understandably equated economic growth with an improvement in the economic conditions of an existing population. Theirs were societies whose populations had grown slowly, had not experienced significant recent immigration, and whose territory contained no unoccupied lands or frontier regions. The conditions facing most developing countries during the twentieth century more closely approximated those in preindustrial Europe than in the settler economies, hence these same theories of intensive growth were influential also among development economists. An expansion of the population was not a primary goal of developing countries; indeed, a high policy priority was to reduce population growth as part of the effort to meet the

---

[29] Intensive growth so defined could also occur where both aggregate GDP and population were declining, but the latter more rapidly.

challenge of raising incomes per capita from initially very low levels. And both in Europe (until recent decades) and in many developing countries, emigration, not immigration, was an element in relieving population pressures. The settler economies in much of the Americas and in Australasia thus have a quite distinct demographic history arising from their strikingly different initial economic conditions.

I don't wish to exaggerate the distinction between the historical experiences of settler economies on the one hand and, on the other, those of the majority of economies be they developed or developing.[30] The distinction is clearest in the early phases of the settler economy's development. And there are features of extensive growth in a settler economy that bear directly on this inquiry because they impinge on intensive growth. For example, the growth of the total population may impact income per capita or productivity levels via scale economies. There may be a positive relation between the rate at which the total population is expanding and productivity. Frontier societies may exhibit an unusually favorable gender ratio, age distribution, and workforce-participation rate. Further, at least initially, the average age of the capital stock is likely to be lower in a settler economy than in one that is long established, with potential benefits if there have been improvements in the technology embodied in plant and equipment. It will be necessary to consider each of these. But the economic growth in focus here is primarily of the intensive kind, conventionally measured as income (or GDP) per person, and output (or GDP) per worker (that is, labor productivity). Furthermore, it is the determinants of these closely related measures of intensive growth that theory seeks to explain—not the size of economies, of populations or workforces, or of national stocks of farm land, other natural resources, or reproducible capital.

GROWTH THEORY AND AUSTRALIAN ECONOMIC HISTORIOGRAPHY

As noted in the previous chapter most models of economic growth traditionally emphasized the importance of the accumulation of more physical capital for each worker, as an increase in capital intensity was believed to be the prime determinant of the level of workers' productivity and hence of income per person. Land was assumed to be fully "occupied," hence omitted from the analysis along with the stocks of all other natural resources. This perspective on growth placed at center stage investment in machines, equipment, buildings, and infrastructure, and the mobilization of the financial resources this required (saving). The evidence from Australia's history is entirely consistent with investment playing a crucial role. A striking if extreme illustration is afforded by the low capital

---

[30]The intensive/extensive growth distinction has been made elsewhere: see Withers (1989), and Jones (1988).

intensity of production in the Aboriginal hunter-gatherer economy, which severely circumscribed any scope for productivity improvement and hence any increase in living standards before the arrival of the Europeans. One obvious source of Australia's greater prosperity since 1788 is thus its dramatically higher capital stock per worker.

During the immediate postwar decades, historians examining Australia's economic progress were influenced by these theories as well as by the supporting evidence then available from the history of some developed countries. It follows that investment activity attracted considerable attention from an earlier generation of Australia's economic historians: the levels of investment have been measured, the industries and sectors in which the investment occurred have been identified, the type of investment (such as in plant and equipment or in buildings and structures) has been determined, and this information is available annually from 1861.[31] Further, we know what proportions of Australia's investment were funded from domestic saving and from the savings of foreigners (capital inflow), and how fluctuations in foreign savings and investment imparted volatility at certain times to the Australian economy. Thus some of the most influential writings on the history of the economy bear the imprint of these earlier models of the growth process.[32]

But the capital accumulation story will take us only so far in accounting for Australian prosperity. First, as a country experiencing a rapidly rising population throughout most of its history, Australia required commensurately high rates of investment simply to prevent any fall in the capital available per worker, and hence in productivity: this is extensive growth. Second, the historical measures and descriptions of Australian saving and investment flows are at best proximate causes of growth, as previously indicated. Investment flows respond to expected profitability and, in an open economy, to rates of return elsewhere around the world. The deeper questions concerning the role of investment in contributing to intensive growth are why domestic savings were mobilized to the extent they were, why foreigners were prepared to invest as much of their savings in Australia as they did, and, critically, why investment rose at a rate that increased the capital stock *per worker*, permitting in turn increases in labor productivity.

When in the late 1950s empirical studies in a number of advanced economies revealed the limitations of models that focused exclusively on the role of investment, the growth that could not be directly explained in these models was termed the "residual"—that is, the increase in labor productivity not accounted for by increased capital intensity. Greater consideration was then given to the possible contributions arising from other sources of productivity such as new

---

[31] Butlin (1962).
[32] Ibid. (1964).

techniques of production (perhaps embodied in new capital equipment but not fully reflected in its price), increases in human capital (such as rising average levels of education), or from other changes in the organization of economic activity that raised efficiency (such as removing impediments to competition in domestic markets or exploiting the benefits arising from international trade).

These shifts in growth economics came to be reflected in the writings of Australian economic historians. For example, the introduction of new technology has always been seen by historians as a key feature of industrialization. In Australian history, the economic benefits of such innovations as stump-jump plows, stripper-harvesters, and rust- and drought-resistant varieties of wheat are well appreciated in the development of the country's agriculture. The relative contributions to increases in agricultural productivity of increased capital intensity—mainly in the form of farm mechanization—and technological change were explored, with the relative importance of the latter revealed to have risen over time.[33] But for the economy as a whole, there have been only a few attempts to assess the long-run contribution of technological change to growth.[34] With respect to the importance of trade, the "staple" export industries were seen by some scholars as critical to an understanding of nineteenth-century growth.[35] Others adopted an even wider view of the importance of Australia's international economic links, especially the macroeconomic implications of immigration and foreign capital inflow.[36]

As with capital accumulation, the growth in the size of the labor force over time, though permitting increased total output, does not of itself explain the increased output *per worker* that occurred. Indeed, the augmentation of the workforce through immigration is in part the result rather than the cause of Australia's economic prosperity—immigrants were attracted by the expected higher wages than if they remained in their homelands. However, changes in the composition and quality of the labor force may well act to raise productivity and hence living standards. Rising average levels of skill or formal education are indicators of a more productive workforce and might be regarded as proximate causes of higher living standards. And considerable attention has been paid the role of human capital in Australia's economic history, including its contribution to raising incomes through increased years of schooling or higher average skills among immigrants.[37] But these require explanation at a deeper level: Why did they occur when and to the extent they did?

---

[33] McLean (1973b).

[34] Butlin (1970) and Kaspura and Weldon (1980).

[35] Blainey (1964), McCarty (1964), and Lougheed (1968). I will have more to say on this export staple literature in chapter 5.

[36] Hall (1963b) and Boehm (1971).

[37] For example, see MacKinnon (1989a) and Withers (1989), respectively. The role of education will be examined in chapter 8.

RECENT THEMES IN GROWTH ECONOMICS

The current consensus among economists is that providing an answer to the question as to why there exists such extreme variation in levels of prosperity between countries is much more complicated than was believed in the immediate postwar decades, and that the simple if elegant neoclassical growth models of an earlier era do not provide an adequate framework for the task. The titles of two recent books by leading researchers convey the current sense of scholarly frustration (and humility?) in this branch of the profession: *The Elusive Quest for Growth* and *The Mystery of Economic Growth*.[38]

One reason for the recent shift in economists' thinking is the persisting economic stagnation in countries which have received significant amounts of foreign investment and financial assistance over many years, most conspicuously in sub-Saharan Africa. Another reason is the puzzling diversity of growth experience among developing countries even after account is taken of their investment in physical and human capital. Some of these countries are catching up to the productivity and income levels of the advanced economies, as predicted by the conventional theories of growth: East Asia is home to several prominent examples. But others—though growing—are not doing so rapidly enough, or on a sustained basis, sufficient to converge on the rich countries: some Latin American economies have had disappointing growth performances across many decades.

A further spur to economists' thinking about historical growth has been efforts since the 1980s to enrich growth models by incorporating influences previously treated as exogenous. As an illustration, one focus has been on the economic determinants of the generation of new technology such as through investment in R&D, and of its subsequent diffusion, which, in turn, raises productivity. If economic conditions determine the allocation of resources to innovation, then the rate of technological change has been made "endogenous" rather than left unexplained by the model. To date, however, endogenous growth theory has been of limited assistance to empirical or historical research.[39] Furthermore, much of growth theory still employs key simplifying assumptions at fundamental variance with the basic conditions of the Australian experience, such as the assumption that the economy being modeled is "closed"—that is, does not engage in international trade or experience immigration and foreign investment. And endowment attributes such as natural resource abundance—or recurring resource discoveries—rarely feature in these models. However, there is a two-way flow between developments in theory and their assessment in the light of evidence, including that drawn from history. And in the course of this inquiry I will have occasion to refer to insights arising from some recent developments in the growth literature.

---

[38] The references are to Easterly (2002) and Helpman (2004), respectively.

[39] Jones (1995) provided an early critical assessment; Crafts (1995) suggests a limited relevance to the analysis of the British industrial revolution.

Also contributing to the changes in economists' thinking about long-run growth has been a major increase in the amount of relevant statistical information, covering a larger number of both developing and developed countries, and extending coverage further back in time. The resulting cross-country "growth regression" literature has been criticized for the ad hoc inclusion of explanatory variables and weak specification of the implicit model. Nonetheless the empirical evidence suggests that many determinants beyond physical and human capital accumulation and the introduction of improved technology appear to be systematically and significantly related to whether a country is rich or poor. The implication is that these seemingly causal factors previously left out of consideration, or regarded as of secondary importance, need to be brought closer to the center of growth inquiries.[40] A fuller discussion of the empirical evidence and debates surrounding these so-called deeper determinants of growth will be offered later, at the point where the issues become relevant to my interpretation of the Australian story. But because of their influence on this inquiry, some further comments are warranted here in order to convey something of the diversity of the highly suggestive findings arising out of these empirical analyses of growth.[41]

In what would appear puzzling to Australians, economists found that natural-resource abundance was *negatively* associated with growth, hence giving rise to the widely held view that natural resources were a "curse" rather than a blessing.[42] This conclusion was based on particular measures of resource scarcity or abundance and was derived from a large number of country observations. As with any statistical relationship, there will be outliers. Since there is little doubt as to its status as resource rich, however this is defined, it appears Australia is just such an exception to the rule. Of course it is not alone in this respect: also qualifying as resource abundant and rich might be listed the United States and Canada since the nineteenth century, and Norway in the decades since the discovery of North Sea oil. But if Australia is an exception to the resource-curse hypothesis, the challenge is to identify why this has been—and remains—the case. A number of mechanisms have been suggested in the literature to account for the putative negative effects of resource abundance on growth, including heightened opportunities for rent-seeking behavior and corruption, neglect of investment in education, and the adverse impacts of a boom in the natural-resource sector on some other sectors of the economy.[43] Australian history, from the first pastoral boom beginning in the 1820s to the minerals and energy

---

[40]Barro and Sala-i-Martin (1995) and Acemoglu (2009) offer overviews of the literature. The most comprehensive survey of recent research in growth economics is provided by Aghion and Durlauf (2005).

[41]A more detailed survey is to be found in McLean (2004).

[42]Sachs and Warner (1995, 2001) were early proponents of the hypothesis, while Brunnschweiler and Bulte (2008) offer a critical assessment. Frankel (2010) provides a recent overview of the literature.

[43]On the political economy aspects of resource abundance, and importance of institutional quality, see Auty (2001) and Mehlum, Moene and Torvik (2006).

boom of the early twenty-first century, includes occasions where there is evidence that these mechanisms were present, but where their potentially harmful impact on prosperity was averted or contained. This theme figures prominently in what follows, beginning in chapter 4.

The growth literature also identifies the possible importance of particular characteristics of the abundant resource as a determinant of whether its presence will be favorable to prosperity or not—such as whether it is confined to a particular location such as a single mine-site (a "point" resource). In addition, it matters greatly whether the natural resource is nonrenewable, like a mineral deposit or oil or gas field, or renewable such that with careful management the potentially exhaustible resource is sustained rather than depleted, as is true in the case of the fertility of agricultural land. It will be observed that because Australia has both types of natural resource its history contains illustrations of the different challenges their exploitation poses. A further mechanism of relevance to the boon or curse outcome is how the rents from the resource are distributed. At one extreme they may be fully dissipated on current consumption such that depletion of the resource will bring a quick end to the prosperity it underpinned. At the other is some variant of a national investment (or sovereign wealth) fund into which all resource rents are channeled, and only the future income from these investments made available for consumption.[44] This topic will be raised in relation to the long boom in the economy that ended in 1890 (chapter 6) and revisited in relation to the resource boom of the early twenty-first century (chapter 9).

Some features of a country's geography also emerge in the cross-country growth literature as related to either their levels of per capita income, or rates of its increase.[45] According to these studies it is an advantage to be located in temperate latitudes rather than the tropics. It is an advantage to have coastline rather than to be landlocked. It is an advantage to be located near the centers of international trade and finance rather than at some far-flung point on the communication lines of the world economy. And it is an advantage to possess rivers and lakes such that a high proportion of your territory lies close to a navigable waterway. These econometric results also might puzzle an Australian. A significant part of the country lies in the tropics. There are no major lakes, and the few river systems are famously unreliable for purposes of transportation. Further, despite the so-called tyranny of distance, Australian prosperity was founded on an extraordinarily close trading relationship with an economy located as far away as could be found: hence the label shared with New Zealand of being "the Antipodes."[46] As in the case of the resource-curse hypothesis, Australia's prosperity appears not to be fully consistent with these broader patterns.

---

[44]For a recent discussion, see van der Ploeg and Venables (2011).

[45]There is debate as to whether geography itself, or an interaction with institutions, drives these results: see, for example, Rodrik, Subramanian and Trebbi (2004).

[46]The "tyranny of distance" is a phrase made popular through being the title of a best-selling book by Blainey (2001), first published in 1966.

One policy area important in the growth literature and also in Australia's history concerns the openness of the economy. Both economic theory and the empirical evidence from cross-country growth regressions using postwar data support the existence of a positive relationship between an economy's degree of integration with the international economy and its growth performance. Since Australia pursued outward-oriented policies in the nineteenth century and has again in recent decades, but to some degree turned inward and protectionist during the first half of the twentieth century, one major issue for the present inquiry is whether these very long-run policy shifts mattered for economic prosperity, when, and by how much. Of particular relevance to this question are two recent developments in the analysis of the relationship between openness and growth. First, debate surrounds the direction of causation in the trade-growth nexus; the positive correlation between the two is not in doubt, but it is possible that they are simultaneously determined.[47] Second, there is evidence that the nature and strength of the link between trade policy and growth have evolved over the last century: the theoretical expectation of a positive relation between free trade and higher growth, which is found to be empirically robust for recent decades in cross-country analyses, receives weak support for the interwar period and no support for the period prior to 1914.[48] These debates will inform the discussion in later chapters of the importance of trade and related policies to Australia's economic prosperity.

A further candidate for explaining why countries vary in their long-run growth performance is their response to exogenous negative shocks, which may originate in the international economy or be due to climatic forces or some other natural disaster; or they may arise from war or a major political upheaval. It has been observed that the long-run impact on growth of a comparable shock varies across countries, raising important questions not only about the policy responses adopted but also about other determinants of an economy's resilience under stress. This is well illustrated by the differing recovery experiences among the affected economies following the East Asian economic crisis in 1997. Australian economic history includes several severe negative shocks: the First World War, two major depressions (in the 1890s and 1930s), and severe droughts (especially around 1900). One objective of this book will therefore be the identification of reasons why Australia's prosperity was not permanently undermined by adverse events that, elsewhere, have been used to account for economic stagnation or even decline. In particular, this is a theme in the economic history of Argentina.

Of relevance to thinking about the Australian experience are recent findings on the long-run growth effects of imperialism. Some seventy countries are ex-colonies of European powers, and to varying degrees, they adopted, and have retained, institutional arrangements inherited from the imperial power. These

---

[47]See Frankel and Romer (1999), and Rodriguez and Rodrik (2001).
[48]O'Rourke (2000), and Clemens and Williamson (2001, 2004).

ex-colonies also vary in the levels of their current prosperity from the very rich (such as Australia, Canada, and the United States) to the very poor (such as in much of Africa). This diversity of experience has afforded an opportunity for the analysis of the relationship between institutions and growth over the two centuries or more since colonial occupation began.[49] One contentious issue is the extent to which the transference from Europe to the colonies of institutions possibly relevant to long-run growth, such as a legal system, was a function of climate. This possibility arises because the climate of a colony determined the disease environment and thus settler mortality rates that, in turn, influenced the level of European migration. A higher proportion of Europeans in the colonial population increased the likelihood that growth-promoting institutions of European origin would be introduced.[50] The causal links between institutions, geography, and colonial status on the one hand, and long-run growth on the other, are complex, but an Australian case study might usefully complement the evidence from these cross-country growth studies.

To conclude this brief discussion of some likely deeper determinants of economic prosperity, it is important to stress that the quantity and quality of both physical and human capital per worker is still a critical part of the analysis. The revision to traditional thinking is better described as accepting that its narrow focus is seriously incomplete. The economist's preference for parsimony when building theories of complex phenomena has had to be relaxed somewhat in order to increase the explanatory power of growth models. And this applies, also, to any satisfactory account of why Australia has such a long record of economic prosperity.

Also warranting emphasis is that these deeper determinants of growth, though only recently accorded serious attention in economists' models or in econometric analyses, have long been of interest to economic historians as well as to specialists in the problems of developing countries. Thus the Australian historical literature already addresses many of these topics, as economic historians never uncritically confined their inquiries to the restricting boundaries of formal growth theory. The contribution of this recent cross-country growth literature is, nonetheless, that it sharpens one's focus in the search for the key influences. This literature also provides a broader context in which to locate the experience of one country. However, in examining the Australian historical evidence, it is also necessary to be alert to the operation of special or unusual local influences that might get washed out in cross-country studies because they are rarely observed—or are less prominent—in accounting for the levels of prosperity elsewhere.

---

[49] Acemoglu, Johnson, and Robinson (2001, 2002).
[50] Albouy (2008).

CHAPTER 3

Origins

An Economy Built from Scratch?

> Were Aborigines too well furnished with food to bother about producing more? . . .
> [T]he influential concept that hunter-gatherers were "the original affluent soci-
> ety" with abundant food and leisure time is a myth, even in the richest environ-
> ments. The mistaken idea that Australian hunter-gatherers needed only about
> four hours per day to feed themselves came from a brief, flawed 1948 study of
> Arnhem Land. . . . The uncertainty of survival, the unremitting labour of the
> food quest and frequent hunger casts serious doubts on nostalgic concepts of a
> lost utopia.[1]

WHAT WERE THE "initial conditions" in the Australian economy relevant to
an inquiry into the historical foundations of its prosperity? Conventionally
the story begins in 1788 with the arrival of the first Europeans intending permanent settlement. Hence the common use of the term "European Australia"
or the phrase "since European settlement." But the Australian Aborigines had
been occupying the continent for forty thousand or more years. Thus the first
question, in a chronological as well as logical sense, is the extent to which the
pre-1788 "Aboriginal" economy formed an element in that of the later "European" economy. This can be expressed more sharply as two questions. First, to
what degree was the European economy constructed on the foundations of the
existing Aboriginal economy? And second, what was the contribution of the
Aboriginal population to the levels of prosperity achieved relatively early in the
period of European settlement?

In Europe, modern economic growth from the late eighteenth century onward
occurred in the context of societies and economies that, though undergoing
rapid changes in some regions and industries, also exhibited much continuity
with centuries past. For example, the rate of growth of the stock of productive
capital may have accelerated, but houses, public buildings, ports, roads, ditches,
fences, and so on that had been built over decades, even centuries, continued in
productive use for many years. Furthermore, institutions and production techniques of ancient lineage persisted into the period of modernization, though
undergoing varying degrees of adaptation. Similarly, when modern economic

---

[1] Flood (2006), p. 21.

growth began in Japan in the middle of the nineteenth century (and as later oc-curred in India and China), there was much to build on in terms of physical capi-tal, human capital, social organization, and political institutions in order to facili-tate the transition to industrialization and sustained higher levels of prosperity.

In contrast to the modern growth experience typical of Europe and Asia, a defining characteristic of the regions of European overseas settlement was that this economic "inheritance" was way less significant. The sharpness of the discontinuity in economic organization, output mix, and productivity levels before and after the arrival of the Europeans varied across regions within the Americas and Australasia. But the displacement of the existing with the new was generally dramatic, and the process was different from what occurred dur-ing modernization in Europe or elsewhere. Within the "new world," the most marked discontinuity occurred where the settlers encountered hunter-gatherer societies, as in Australia and some areas of Canada and the United States; rather less perhaps where settled agriculture was practiced as in New Zealand; and less again where there were significant populations of even more complex societies as in Mexico or Peru. The extent to which the European settlers had to adapt to and accommodate the existing economic system was thus a function of the size of the indigenous population and also of their mode of economic organization. In this comparative perspective, modern Australia shares with the United States and Canada the initial condition that early European settlement encountered a low-density native population who were predominantly hunter-gatherers.

The Pre-1788 Economy of the Aborigines

So, what was the "Aboriginal economy" at the time the Europeans arrived?[2] Unfortunately, it is not possible to be too confident about even some of the basic facts of relevance to this question. Take population as an illustration. The conventional estimate of about 300,000 as at 1788 has in recent decades been vigorously debated, with one source putting the figure as high as one million.[3] The reasons for this debate include the absence of any comprehensive census of the indigenous population for many decades following 1788; and the pos-sibility that European-introduced diseases that raised the mortality rate spread through the Aboriginal population prior to the first direct encounters with ex-plorers or settlers. Indeed it may be that at least some of these diseases were introduced through contacts between Aborigines in northern Australia and seafaring peoples from eastern Indonesia. For example, it has been argued that smallpox may have arrived by this means in the 1780s, then spread rapidly

---

[2]Dingle (1988) provides an introduction. Economic topics are prominent in Blainey (1983) and Flood (2006).

[3]Butlin (1983).

southward among the Aboriginal population, to be observed by Europeans in Aborigines in the Sydney area about a decade later.[4]

Since we have reasonably accurate estimates of the surviving Aboriginal population by the late nineteenth century, a principal motivation for obtaining a solid estimate for 1788 is to put some bounds on the extent of the negative demographic impact of early European settlement on the indigenous Australians—whether that resulted from disease, violence, displacement, or disruption of traditional ways of life. Unsurprisingly this is a contentious issue among historians, invested as it is with elements introduced from recent ideological and political controversies. Regarding the numbers, however, the consensus is that the Aboriginal population in 1788 was probably more than 300,000 but less than a million.[5] For our purposes, further pursuit of this debate is unnecessary. Given the size of Australia—it has an area approximately equal to that of the continental United States—this implies a very low population density. By contrast, the Maori are thought to have numbered 100,000 to 200,000 at the time the Europeans arrived, but New Zealand is less than 4 percent the size of Australia.[6] In Canada and the United States, the Native American population was at least five million at the time of first contact with Europeans.[7]

A defining feature of hunter-gatherer societies and their economies is the limited importance of structures such as permanent houses—or even their complete absence. Hence we do not observe such communities living in villages or towns or constructing durable capital works to assist food production such as by draining fields, terracing hillsides, or digging irrigation channels. By contrast, these are prominent features of those societies—both ancient and more recent—based on settled agriculture. Higher densities of population were thereby achieved in the agriculture-based societies, occupational division of labor and scale economies in production were reaped, and, to varying degrees, these societies achieved a surplus beyond immediate subsistence requirements. This was the resource "saving" that permitted not just the investment in fixed productive capital, but also the allocation of time and resources to the elaboration of crafts and culture inessential to their survival.

Why settled agriculture did not emerge in those parts of Australia that are well-watered, whether temperate or subtropical, and as occurred in both New Zealand and the highlands of Papua New Guinea, is a question with major implications for later developments. Had there been at the time of European contact a much larger indigenous population along the eastern seaboard, based

---

[4]Campbell (2002) is a recent advocate of this view, rather than the alternative hypothesis that smallpox was introduced by the Europeans following their arrival in Sydney.

[5]A figure of 314,500 for the "estimated minimum population of Aboriginal descent" in 1788 is reported in the most widely cited compilation of Australian historical statistics: Vamplew (1987, p. 4).

[6]Sinclair (1980), p. 25.

[7]Salisbury (1996, p.11) suggests a figure of five to ten million for North America in 1500.

on settled agriculture, the subsequent history of the country—including of its economy—would surely have been very different. The evidence of contacts across Torres Strait between the inhabitants of Cape York and those in Papua New Guinea suggests that the transmission of knowledge concerning agricultural practices was possible.[8] Alternatively, there is the possibility of agriculture having arisen endogenously in the hunter-gather economy of the Aborigines. This, after all, is how agriculture emerged elsewhere. The observations of surviving hunter-gatherer communities by anthropologists, together with the theoretical speculations of economists about the origins of agriculture, thus have direct relevance to the Australian case precisely because the transition did not occur. Was there no "shock" to either the economic or demographic equilibrium in Aboriginal society sufficient to induce the shift to settled agriculture? Was it because the initial stage of agriculture required an increase in risk and/or work intensity that deterred the required investment? And does the explanation for this in turn lie in preference structures (for example over family size, or leisure) that were less easily modified when opportunities arose than in some other hunter-gatherer societies?[9]

The significance of these questions is that the Aboriginal economy possessed no stock of productive capital that the Europeans could seize and immediately employ to produce output for their own needs. To be clear, the reference here is to the stock of man-made reproducible capital, not to natural resources such as land or to human capital (such as survival skills essential for living in the outback), which I consider presently. As hunter-gatherers, any equipment the Aborigines used for food production had to be easily carried, and any structures for shelter had to be built quickly, and thus would not exhibit the durability typical of the housing needs of settled populations. Hence hunting tools such as the boomerang and woomera were light and portable. Similarly, temporary shelters were made of skins, branches, and bark. There are exceptions to this generalization about the relative unimportance of fixed capital to production, and these have understandably attracted the attention of scholars. One example is the construction of nets to catch birds in flight. A second is that more substantial shelters were sometimes observed.[10] A third is the ditches or channels to divert water from the Murray River, thus trapping fish or eels apparently on a scale that required group effort to construct, and that lasted many years. But the infrequent appearance of such examples of fixed capital makes the point that there was little of relevance to the production methods introduced by the Europeans. The reproducible capital stock of the Australian economy was constructed from scratch beginning in 1788 in the Sydney area.

---

[8]Diamond (1998), chapter 15.

[9]For a recent contribution to the debate about the origins of agriculture, and references to the literature, see Weisdorf (2009).

[10]Flood (2006), pp. 198–99.

Further, a hunter-gatherer economy offers little if any scope for the appropriation of indigenous production by an invader. Under other circumstances European colonization in many places was accompanied by the taxation or diversion of existing output or trade flows by the occupying power. In principle this helped fund the costs of consolidating and maintaining the authority of the new rulers, perhaps even transferring resources to the imperial economy. Spanish rule in South America and British rule in India illustrate the possibilities. In contrast, the Aboriginal economy did not generate any "surplus" output; neither did it possess taxable reproducible wealth. Hence from their arrival the Europeans had to produce all their own output without any significant contribution from the indigenous economy. This is the economic context for the initial reliance on imported food supplies, for the urgency given to finding locations in the Sydney area suitable for growing crops, and for the establishment of a government farm.

But there was one "asset" in the possession of the Aborigines that the European occupiers came to see had considerable economic potential to them, albeit in a different use. Natural resources were fundamental to the Aboriginal economy, sustaining its production system. All food items were obtained directly by "harvesting" berries from trees or bushes, fishing in rivers and the sea, and capturing animals grazing on natural grassland or living in the bush. Mineral deposits or outcrops seem not to have been systematically exploited for productive ends beyond some stone tools; clay (ochre) and gypsum featured in ceremonial uses. Hence it was the "land" broadly defined that underpinned the hunter-gatherer society and economy. And this productive asset was progressively transferred from indigenous to non-indigenous possession with the geographical spread of European settlement—especially pastoral settlement after 1820. This transfer was rarely by mutual agreement, but through dispossession or displacement of the Aborigines. In many cases this was undoubtedly accomplished through coercion or violence, though the incidence and magnitude of this remains a subject of controversy among historians. However obtained, the exploration, settlement, and economic utilization of rural land by Europeans forms a major part of the story of Australia's economic development throughout the nineteenth century.

It is relevant to note at this point the uncertainty surrounding the extent to which Australia's land resources in 1788 were solely an inheritance of nature. Over sufficiently long periods, climate change can produce marked variation in the "natural" resources of a region such as through changes in sea levels or desertification of arable land. This aside, the impact of the Aborigines on the environment over the millennia of their occupation is imperfectly understood. For example, there is uncertainty as to whether large fauna became extinct due to climatic change or human intervention. More pertinent to our interest in the value of the resources acquired by the Europeans is the impact of the Aboriginal practice known as "firestick farming." This was the periodic deliberate burning of the native vegetation to encourage fresh growth of plants that, in turn, increased the density of the grazing native animals, thus raising the food supply or influencing its location and reliability. Perhaps this improved the productivity of the land and thus the sustainable level of population. But the reduced forestation may also have had other and adverse effects on the environment.[11] From the perspective of the pioneer European pastoralists, however, this partial "land clearing" by the Aborigines facilitated the very rapid spread of sheep on the natural grasslands by reducing the up-front costs of pastoral occupation, thus contributing to the profitability of the wool industry in its early years. The effects of centuries of firestick farming, expanding the area of natural grassland suitable for grazing sheep, might therefore be thought of as an Aboriginal contribution to Australia's early prosperity rather than an element in the country's truly "natural" resource endowment at the time the Europeans arrived.

Also contributing to growth and prosperity following 1788 is the knowledge the Aborigines had accumulated about the land they had occupied for so long, and which was to prove exceptionally useful to the Europeans. We might think of this as a form of human capital, even folk science, bequeathed to the nonindigenous population. One illustration is the assistance given the early explorers by their Aboriginal guides with respect to local topography. Less transitory in value to the Europeans were the skills needed to survive in the "bush"—such as the ability to locate or collect water in arid areas and to "live off the land." Even today large swathes of the country remain a challenging environment for human occupation.

THE ABORIGINAL CONTRIBUTION TO THE POST-1788 ECONOMY

As we have seen, there were no *reproducible* capital assets of the Aboriginal economy that might have been seized by the first settlers to form the basis for productive enterprise, as distinct from the transfer of access to and utilization of the stock of land. Thus there was no equivalent in Australia to the productive capital stock acquired through invasion as in, say, Mughal India when the British established control there in the eighteenth and nineteenth centuries. Further, the institutional structures (broadly defined) of the Aborigines were of no economic value to the Europeans. The Indian example illustrates a very different institutional environment facing the occupying power, including delegation and subcontracting to regional rulers. The relationship between the British and Maori tribes and their leaders affords a less extreme contrast with the situation in Australia. The Maori practiced settled agriculture and possessed social and political institutions that facilitated coordinated and effective resistance to the European occupiers and enabled them to negotiate a formal treaty (Waitangi, 1840) in defense of their property rights over a portion of

---

[11] See Barr and Cary (1992), pp. 8–9, and Bolton (1992), p. 8.

their land. This significantly influenced the subsequent history of European settlement in New Zealand and set it on a different trajectory from that observed in Australia.

Thus the major direct contribution of the indigenous inhabitants to economic growth after 1788 was through their participation in the labor market, although the extent of this contribution is not known with any certainty. But it is clear that the Aboriginal population was too small and scattered to permit or encourage the formation of labor-intensive methods of farming (such as plantation style) or mining (such as in Spanish America). As the Aborigines were not enumerated in the early colonial censuses or "musters" of population, these sources do not provide the historian with a basis for estimating the employment status of the indigenous inhabitants, or of identifying the industry, sector, or occupation in the "European" economy in which they were working. So we may never know what proportion of the indigenous population participated in the "formal" workforce in the decades following 1788, and how this varied over time, between regions, by gender, or by occupation. This constrains our ability to measure GDP per capita or labor productivity for Australia for the early nineteenth century. Insofar as there is an unrecorded contribution to the GDP of the "European" economy by Aboriginal labor, the estimates of per capita income or labor productivity will be overstated to the extent that the population and workforce estimates excluded Aborigines. In later discussion I will consider this further.

However, there exists a body of qualitative evidence describing the contribution of Aborigines to the labor force within the new economy, though it is fragmentary and typically specific to a particular region or industry or occupation.[12] Though often anecdotal, many contemporary observations have the value of being eyewitness accounts. What can we learn from this of relevance to our broader question? One firm impression is that Aborigines were employed by Europeans in a wide range of tasks and occupations. These included working as trackers to the police and guides to early explorers; as domestic help of various forms in the houses of settlers in both rural and urban locations; as shepherds in the wool industry and as stockmen in the cattle industry; and as whalers and sealers.

We can also see in this evidence a match of Aboriginal skills and European needs in the pioneer stage of European settlement. The labor requirement in the foundation years of the colonial economy was for brawn rather than brain—for relatively low-skilled workers to engage in physically demanding labor. This is true of urban construction work as well as land-clearing and much farming activity. As the pastoral frontier spread, the demand for skills in horsemanship and managing livestock rose, and there is evidence that Aborigines possessed an aptitude for quickly acquiring these. Though the advancing pastoral frontier led to displacement of the indigenous users of the land, and to conflict, it also afforded

---

[12] For a recent reference, see Flood (2006), who discusses this topic at several points.

opportunities for their employment in the economy of the Europeans previously only available to Aborigines located near the first coastal settlements.

The historical record of Aboriginal participation in the formal labor force becomes clearer by the late nineteenth century. Most attention in the literature focuses on the contribution they made as stockmen, especially in northern Australia, and in cattle raising. In this period and industry it has been claimed that this contribution was vital to the profitability and economic development of an area extending from central Queensland to the Kimberley region in the north of Western Australia.[13] Studies of southeastern Australia suggest a significant contribution from Aboriginal workers was also made there, in the agricultural sector.[14] But by the second half of the century the Aboriginal population had declined dramatically from its pre-European level, while the non-indigenous population had risen from zero to several million. It follows that the percentage contribution of the former to the Australian labor force had almost certainly declined markedly from whatever it had been early in the century, despite the continuing importance of Aboriginal workers in some areas and industries. In fairness to the historians who have written on these issues, their primary concern has not been with estimating the share of the total workforce that was made up of Aboriginals, or the workforce participation rates of the Aboriginal population. Their evidence and assessments are typically ancillary to inquiries focusing on other aspects of the impact of European settlement on the indigenous population, especially the extent of violence, and the cultural differences that influenced black-white relationships, including those arising in the labor market.

THE CONVICT ECONOMY AND ITS PECULIAR LABOR MARKET

Europeans were not initially drawn to Australia by the allure of riches. There were no early reports of gold or silver (as in South America), of a thriving and opulent civilization (as in India), of an existing trade to corner (as with spices in what became Indonesia), or of a product in rising demand in Europe (such as silk, tobacco, tea, or coffee). There was some possibility of supplies of timber being suitable for ships' masts, and whalers and sealers were already at work on the coasts. But this information did not figure prominently in the plans for initial settlement.

What counted more in the calculations of the decision-makers was the suitability of this remote location for a convict settlement, one that would thereby give credibility to British designs on the continent against those of possible competitor claimants, in particular the French. So Australia began the European phase of its history in rather unusual circumstances. European settlement

---

[13]Reynolds (1995) and May (1994).
[14]Pope (1988) and Broome (1994).

took the initial form of a type of prison. British convicts were sent as the workers who would establish the colony under the supervision of the military. Some 160,000 convicts were "transported" between 1788 and 1868, with free immigrants becoming significant only in the 1820s.

That Australia's European origin was as a penal settlement has never been a matter of national pride. Certainly it is not comparable to the position in American history occupied by the legacy of the Puritan origins of New England. Further, some of Australia's most influential historians have encouraged the view that the convicts were a thoroughly disreputable and criminal lot, thereby unsuited for the task of constructing a new settlement. Manning Clark wrote: "So to produce food and provide shelter the settlement had to rely on the labour of men and women who had taken up a life of crime because of their aversion to labour. Neither the fear of the lash, nor the promise of emancipation, nor special indulgences overcame this innate aversion to labour."[15] In the general population, however, any shame or embarrassment once felt at the "convict stain" appears to have faded to a more relaxed acceptance of the decidedly unusual composition of early colonial society.

It is possible to advance a more positive appreciation of the role of the convicts—at least with respect to the early attainment of colonial prosperity. From an economist's perspective a convict-worker colony has some advantages if the aim is to lay the economic basis for a well-functioning pioneer settlement. Fundamentally this is because, whatever their colorful individual histories, the great majority of the convicts sent to New South Wales were selected to maximize the workforce participation rate among the early colonial population. That is, they were selected by gender, age, and physical condition. Males far outnumbered females; the age distribution was highly concentrated in the prime working-age range; and only the healthy were transported. Fit and able people were needed quickly to clear land, construct key pieces of infrastructure such as roads and houses, and to produce food. This pioneer community could not support many who were aged, weak, or children—at least initially. Put differently, its survival required as low a dependency rate as possible. The precariousness of this extremely isolated settlement is illustrated by the food crisis following the failure of the first crops, when supplies had to be sought from the Cape of Good Hope (South Africa).

As a military-style operation under the command of a governor with wide powers, and with only remote supervision from London, it might be thought that the scene was set for serious allocative inefficiencies. But there are situations in which a "command" economy works reasonably well, as in a time of total war. However, this requires that the output objectives are clearly defined, that the incentives for effort reasonably match production priorities, and that there is no serious problem of workers shirking. In early colonial New South Wales,

---

[15]Clark (1987), p. 28.

though with hiccups along the way, the command economy performed reasonably well. It was thus not imposed on an existing society on the basis of the ideology of a ruling elite as in the Soviet Union, but adopted in response to a temporary necessity. Most important, market forces were allowed to emerge from the beginning. The "private" sector appears first in the entrepreneurial activities of the military officers, then through the commercial pursuits of the emancipists—convicts whose sentences had been completed but who chose to remain in New South Wales.

It is helpful to think of the use of convict labor in Australia as a variant in a spectrum of "coercive" labor-market systems. The limiting case is slavery, which for example existed in the southern states of the United States until emancipation in 1863. A less extreme example is serfdom, a set of feudal labor relations that also persisted into the mid-nineteenth century in Russia. There is also indentured servitude: indenture was one form of immigration into the American colonies in the eighteenth century. Closely related to this is apprenticeship, a fixed-term legal contract (the indenture) between master and apprentice, variants of which survive in the labor market to the present.

Unlike a slave the typical convict laborer had numerous legal rights. This contrasts with the impression conveyed by accounts that emphasize the experience of the minority of hardened criminals held in confinement at such places as Norfolk Island, or at Port Arthur in Van Diemen's Land.[16] The length of their sentence was fixed, as with the term of an indenture. Prior to the construction of the barracks in 1819, convicts in Sydney were not even locked up at night. It is true there was a "gang" labor component to the convict workforce. But more typically the convicts were given daily tasks that left them free once these were completed. In this free time they could work for a private employer. Thus the convict laborer was working both for the state and in the private sector, both under coercion as a "prisoner" required to provide certain labor services, and residually as a "free" laborer. Or they could be "assigned" to work exclusively for an employer other than the government—a small farmer, a businessman, later as a stockman to a pastoralist. Hence New South Wales had a dual labor market, with one part comprised of government-directed labor, the other of a free labor market. In the latter, labor was supplied from convicts with free time, "assigned" convicts, emancipists, and later, free immigrants.

Thus the portrayals of the convict experience in the best-selling account by Robert Hughes, *The Fatal Shore*,[17] or in Marcus Clarke's classic 1874 novel *For the Term of His Natural Life*, are not representative of the great majority of those transported. The careful and scholarly assessments of the evidence by historians such as John Hirst and economists such as Stephen Nicholas provide more

---

[16]Norfolk Island lies 1,600 kilometers northeast of Sydney in the South Pacific Ocean. Until 1852 Van Diemen's Land was the name for the colony of Tasmania.

[17]Hughes (1987).

balanced and nuanced bases for understanding this complex allocation of labor at a critical time in the establishment of the colonial economy.[18] The historians' emphasis on the rich detail of the convict workers' experiences, illustrated by examples of selected individuals about whom substantial information has survived, nicely complements the economists' approach. The latter seek to determine the range of convict experience by a statistical analysis of information taken primarily from the individual "indents" or files of each convict, and typically ask specific questions or pose hypotheses that are in part informed by economic theory and in part by the historical accounts of the period. Then it is possible to say how representative—or perhaps atypical—are the individuals featured in the case studies in the historians' accounts. Each approach has its limitations. But taken together, our understanding of the convict system, and of the early colonial economy in which convicts formed the principal source of labor, has been significantly advanced by the economists' recent contributions.[19]

From an economic perspective, the human capital of the convict population was appropriate to the tasks at hand. The quantitative analysis of large numbers of the indents has revealed that the convicts had attributes in addition to their age, gender, and physical health that enhanced their usefulness as the "construction workers" engaged in the establishment of the settlement. Although some controversy surrounds the veracity of the recorded information, the analysis has led to two important conclusions. The first is that basic education (literacy) rates among the convicts were comparable with those in Britain. Perhaps this is less surprising when it is recalled that the crimes for which the punishment could be transportation to New South Wales included not just rather petty acts by today's standards, but what now would be regarded as acts of political or social protest and not crimes at all. Thus the convicts included a small number of professionals and even university graduates. The second conclusion is that the range of (self-reported) occupations prior to conviction in Britain roughly matched the range of skills the colony needed during its foundation years. In particular, any view that the convicts overwhelmingly had been members of a criminal class lacking any skills or prior work experience is not supported.

It is one thing to note that the selection of convicts to be transported from among those available appears to have been made according to criteria designed to enhance the likelihood of the colony's successful foundation. A separate question is whether, within the colony, the allocation of convicts to tasks made best use of the available pool of their skills. The evidence suggests that, indeed, the convicts were allocated work assignments broadly in line with their

---

[18] Hirst (1983); Nicholas (1988). A recent contribution to this topic is Meredith and Oxley (2005).

[19] Nicholas (1988, 1990) reports the most comprehensive statistical analysis of a sample of the convict indents (over 19,000). For debate, see Shlomowitz (1990) and Nicholas (1991). The following paragraphs draw especially on the research reported by Nicholas and his coauthors.

occupational or skill categories recorded in Britain. In principle this may be taken as indicating a considerable measure of efficiency in the way the convict labor market functioned, with positive implications for colonial labor productivity. In practice, the apparent matching of prior skills and assigned tasks may reflect overstatement of the former, since no independent check can be made of the truth of what was self-reported at the time of conviction in Britain.[20] For present purposes, the matching exercise need not be given too much weight, since the nature of most skills in demand in the colony at this time were such as to be easily acquired through working with someone who already possessed them (informal on-the-job training), plus a little experience.

One further relevant feature of the convict economy is the variation in the supply of convict labor to the public sector, which would rise with the arrival of a convict ship from Britain and fall when a convict's term expired. But it also could be varied by adjusting the numbers of convicts holding "tickets-of-leave," a system enabling those still serving their sentence to be assigned to work for a private employer. This was a policy instrument useful for meeting fluctuations in the government's demand for labor services, as well as an incentive that assisted in the control of the convicts' behavior, including their work effort.

There were additional rewards and punishments in the incentive system convicts faced in the dual labor market. Convicts received a wage, though one below the rate for free labor. They might also receive nonmonetary remuneration for their labor—rations and keep. As incentives to diligence, those who were well regarded as workers could be given a ticket of leave, essentially suspending their sentence subject to continued satisfactory behavior or performance of duties. Failure to do so could result in its revocation, and a return to convict status. As a deterrent to overly harsh treatment by the employer to whom the convict was assigned, the law permitted convicts to bring legal action against their employers. (Such rights in a court of law did not exist for American slaves.) Hence, despite evidence of some physical punishment by employers, this was subject to redress. Here, especially, the circumstances of most of the convicts—who were in the workforce in one way or another—must be sharply distinguished from the conditions faced by the minority of convicts who were incarcerated in extremely harsh conditions such as at Port Arthur, though it is the latter who have come to characterize the typical convict experience in literature, film, and the popular perception.

Viewing together these elements of the convict economy and its labor market, it is less surprising to see evidence of convict labor reported as reasonably productive. There is abundant evidence about work habits, especially of those "assigned" to small farmers or, in later years, to pastoralists. This indicates that although there may have been problems of shirking and higher costs of super-

---

[20] There are obvious bounds on misreporting your skills: inflating them would not work for someone claiming to be a lawyer or clerk and found to be illiterate.

vision, and although there were instances where assigned convicts proved ill suited to regular or unsupervised employment, the majority were "profitably" employed. That is, the value of their output exceeded their wage and other indirect costs to their employer. Most contemporary assessments compare their work habits and efficiency with free labor, and not always favorably. But this is not the relevant criterion for either private profitability or the net social return of their assignment (compared, say, to their continued incarceration). The critical point is that, though the assigned convict may have enjoyed more legal rights than a slave, and faced a series of incentives as well as punishments relating to his or her work effort, this was still a partly coercive labor system. To this extent, more effort was obtained for a given outlay—the mix of wage, rations, supervision costs, and so forth—than would have been forthcoming had the worker not been an assigned convict. This additional effort was a benefit to the community—products, services, or construction activities were obtained at a "cost" below that which would have applied with free labor.[21]

The survival of the initial settlement in New South Wales, and its subsequent expansion and viability, in part reflect the command-economy characteristics of its early years, and in part the special features of its demography and workforce. A very high workforce participation rate was a corollary of the selection criteria employed to determine who would be sent to establish the colony. And the flexibility of the dual labor market that quickly emerged, with its mix of positive and negative incentives, ensured a satisfactory level of productivity from the convict element that initially dominated the labor force. Further, this flexibility included encouragement for the emergence of a private sector in parallel with the initially dominant economic role of the government. Hence there was no lock-in of potentially growth-retarding economic institutions.

All things considered, perhaps this military-directed and convict-intensive operation was well suited to the daunting task of laying the economic foundations of a viable and thriving settlement in an extremely isolated location, where the rapid attainment of self-sufficiency in basic necessities and provision of basic infrastructure were paramount. A more balanced group of initial settlers (no convicts, more women and children) may have removed much of the color and drama from the colony's early social history, but also slowed its progress toward sustainability, even threatened its existence. The earlier experience of some colonies in North America illustrates the possible outcomes, and this must have informed the thinking of the British planners of the first fleet to Sydney. Nowadays one might envisage such a project being contracted out to a large corporation rather than the military, who would perhaps employ either foreign guest-workers, or a "fly in/fly out" labor force, such that the pioneer "community" would not look so different in age and gender mix from that arriving

---

[21] This social benefit may have been offset to the extent of any direct or indirect subsidy by the government to the private employer of convict labor.

in 1788: think of the isolated communities near the natural gas fields of the North-West Shelf in Western Australia or near the Olympic Dam copper, gold, and uranium mine in South Australia's outback. And the decision-making and management structures within the company overseeing the construction project would likely bear more than a passing resemblance to those of the governor and officers in the first years of New South Wales.

Further Features of the Economy Relevant to Later Prosperity

The convict-based foundation of the early colonial economy of New South Wales (and Van Dieman's Land) may have been its most distinctive element. It may also have been a key reason both for the pioneer settlement's survival, and for the comparative prosperity enjoyed by the settlers within a few decades of their arrival. But there were additional features of the early colonial economy that deserve mention as also contributing to its fairly rapid development.

Once the small community had secured its basic food requirements from local production, it faced a new challenge. Without imports of those commodities that could not feasibly be produced locally, but were necessary, it would be condemned to a standard of living not far above subsistence. An expansion in the population at this low level of income, and hence in the size of the economy, might eventually create opportunities for local production of import substitutes, once sufficient economies of scale had been attained, thus raising per capita incomes without the benefits of international trade. In the short run, of course, the requisite imports were financed directly and indirectly by British subsidies, as I explore shortly. In the longer term, this was an unsustainable basis for economic development. The "capacity to import" thus constituted a binding constraint on growth—a theme that was to recur through the next two centuries of Australian history. It was in this context that there occurred what historians have referred to as the "search for a staple"—the need for the colony to find one or more items that could be produced locally in volume and at such a level of efficiency that they could profitably be sold in foreign markets, thus financing the importation of goods vital to development and that could not be produced domestically, or could be produced only by means of an inefficient use of local resources. And foreign demand for the staple export had to be such as to permit a rapid expansion in the size of the export sector within the domestic economy, underpinning rising levels of productivity and incomes.

Even before the arrival of the first fleet in Botany Bay, there had been speculation about the possible strategic value to Britain of naval supplies of timber such as Norfolk Island pine for masts and New Zealand flax for rope and sails. Indeed access to these has been listed as one possible motivation for the British decision to establish a colony. Whalers and sealers were active around southern coasts during the first decades of European settlement. And there were also speculative ventures into the exploitation of dugong or trepang from Australia's northern waters for export to Asia. It is possible that, were we in possession of detailed and accurate trade data for the colony in its first few decades, such commodities would feature prominently in at least some years. But for the first quarter century or so no single product was found with the potential for providing the settlers with a major export-oriented growth industry, and hence a basis for funding their own import bill. There would be extensive growth as the population increased from more convict arrivals and from natural increase. But prospects for intensive growth would be limited.

This was to change, of course, with the discovery that merino sheep could be farmed profitably for their wool in New South Wales. This commodity was in high demand by the English woolen textile industry, itself a booming sector in the industrial revolution under way at the time. The entrepreneurial activity of John Macarthur established that distance from the market was no barrier to the colonial producer successfully competing with existing English and German suppliers. In part this was due to special properties of wool: its high value to bulk and weight ratios, and the fact that it was nonperishable. More generally, the higher transport costs of shipping from Sydney were offset by some combination of lower production costs and the quality of the product. Remarkably, the first export boom Australia experienced was thus not with a relatively nearby market such as India or China, but with one that happened to be about as far away as possible on the globe. Consistent with gravity models of international trade, in recent decades the volume of bilateral trade is significantly—and inversely—influenced by the distance between trading partners. Wool was to be just the first of Australia's key exports that were exceptions to this generalization: from around 1820 Australia found a succession of products it could sell worldwide. At least in this important example there is no hint that the "tyranny" of distance shaped the country's economic development through imposing insuperable barriers on participation in long-distance international trade. Wool was to remain a leading export commodity, and Britain was to retain its ranking as the principal destination for Australian exports, until after the Second World War.

In addition to some improved "capacity to import," economic growth in the colony required appropriate institutional settings. And the institutional framework of this embryo economy has long fascinated historians. The military officers quickly assumed new roles as traders, entrepreneurs, landowners, and speculators. That is, the military nature of the colony's administration lent a particular character to the origins of business activity—public and private. The aspect that has received most attention in historical accounts is the corruption attendant on such a blurring of roles, with evidence of abuse of power and conflict of interest. (One thinks here of the role of the military in the "private" sector during China's recent economic liberalization.) And this all led to a colorful social scene and much political drama. However, with no free settlers in the initial years, this outcome was unsurprising and probably unavoidable. Indeed, the ex-convicts and ex-officers did a fairly good job of establishing a functioning market economy out of inauspicious beginnings.

The economic institution perhaps most important to this transition in these early years was the government store or commissariat. A military institution for supplying stores and equipment as needed by an army was adapted to the needs of the settlement. It issued government rations and equipment; it bought grain and other produce from local producers for storage and retail sale; it accepted a variety of forms of payment; and it extended credit. Several key economic functions were thus combined in the one institution. In particular it mediated economic activity levels in the goods market between the public and private "sectors." And it provided at least some of the functions of a commercial bank.

The supply and regulation of money was another vital need in the fledgling economy that seems to have further illustrated human ingenuity at work in the pioneer outpost.[22] The use of one particular commodity as currency, namely rum, may have been exaggerated. But there were several expedients to overcome the periodic shortage of money or liquidity in the economy, including Spanish dollars, restamped coin of various origins, and other foreign currency in domestic circulation. There was the additional and persisting complication that access to sterling (or bills drawn on the British treasury) were necessary to pay for imports, and these were vital to the functioning of the economy for many years. That is, the colony had a foreign-exchange constraint because much of the currency in domestic circulation was inconvertible. As with the commissariat's role in the market for goods, institutional improvisation with respect to money and finance appears to have worked. There is no evidence that the truly weird devices employed did other than adequately finance the growth of economic activity. But the ramshackle solutions were unsustainable as the economy grew in size and complexity. The founding of the Bank of New South Wales (now Westpac) in 1817 was one institutional landmark in the development of a more mature financial sector. Another was the imperial currency reform of 1825 in which the colonies were to adopt a sterling exchange standard and British monetary units, thus leading to the creation of an Australian pound together with the domestic acceptance of British currency as legal tender.

In addition to certain key economic institutions, the colony required for its prosperity a set of political, legal, and administrative arrangements that were growth promoting. As mentioned, the military rule initially applying in New South Wales may be seen as appropriate to the short-run requirements of the settlement, not just in light of its convict character, but also from the perspective of a major logistical exercise in constructing a remote "greenfields" project for a population expected quickly to reach several thousand. But as the population of nonconvicts—at first primarily emancipists, later free immigrants—grew, the military model of colonial administration became less acceptable to the emerging "civil" society in the colony. And as the relative size of the private

---

[22]Butlin (1953).

sector within the mixed economy increased, the "central planning" inherent in the initial military operation became increasingly inappropriate. The evolution of political, legal, and constitutional arrangements away from their initial settings was to begin before 1820. But its most important stages—at least from the perspective of their impact on growth and prosperity—were to occur from the 1820s to the 1850s. It is in these decades that the transitions occur from military rule to a type of autocracy, through a measure of representative democracy, and finally to responsible government and substantial self-rule. Consequently this topic will be given prominence in the next chapter.

BRITISH SUBSIDIES AND AUSTRALIAN LIVING STANDARDS

Of the foundations of early colonial prosperity that were laid during the first thirty years or so after 1788, there is an additional element that receives little mention in most treatments, yet is obvious to anyone who thinks about the colony's finances. This was the continuing subsidy from the British government, which permitted the settlement not just to survive its uncertain first years, but financed the investment in infrastructure and pioneer agriculture that would permit growth in the population and the attainment of a degree of economic self-sufficiency. The main questions of interest here are the extent of the subsidization by the British government of the new settlement, and the time at which this subsidy faded to insignificance such that we can think of the colonial economy as having become essentially self-financing— at least on a current basis. For the evidence of early prosperity among the European settlers and their descendants must be evaluated against the possibility that it may have been partly the product of imperial subsidy rather than of the productivity of colonial labor.

Estimating with any precision the extent of this subsidization of the early colonial economy is difficult. Much of the British contribution was made "in kind" rather than as monetary grants, loans, or "aid." The boundaries between the private and public sector are blurred—members of the military engaged in private commercial activities, and holders of many public offices were not salaried officials but had their private income augmented in various ways for their services. Convict labor was assigned to free or emancipist employers under conditions that did not fully reflect current market rates of remuneration, so essentially there was a subsidy involved. Land was owned by the Crown, but access to it took a range of forms, with the occupier not always required to pay market prices or rents—the extreme example being the extralegal practice of "squatting" on Crown land for the purposes of raising wool.

Further complicating any effort to assess precisely the extent of the imperial subsidization of early New South Wales is the fragmentary and inadequate state of record keeping. And this applies not just to the small group of officials administering the struggling colony, but also to the bureaucracy in the imperial capital. The early years of settlement coincided with the French and Napoleonic Wars, which placed administrative strains on the British government. Responsibility for the colony lay partly with the military, yet the financial burdens of empire were also of deep concern to the imperial treasury, while a centralized office for the administration of the colonies was only slowly evolving following the loss of the American colonies. Accordingly, the information necessary to assess with a high degree of confidence the extent of the British taxpayers' subsidy for the initial establishment and early development of the colony in New South Wales simply does not exist.

The most detailed attempt to arrive at some approximate estimate is due to Noel Butlin.[23] There is no bottomline, preferred figure, given the difficulties in accurately assigning expenditures to imperial or colonial revenues, the problems of double-counting and "in kind" transfers, and the fragmentary state of contemporary record-keeping. He suggests at one point that British budgetary expenditures represented about two-thirds of the value of the GDP of New South Wales and Van Diemen's Land between 1788 and 1822, and at another has a chart suggesting this ratio was about 50 to 60 percent around 1820 then fell continuously.[24] Note this is not an estimate of the proportion of GDP due to—or derived from—British expenditure, since the two are not directly comparable in concept, quite apart from all the measurement problems.

In an earlier discussion of the colonial economy, Butlin made the following qualitative assessment: "The early white settlements were . . . provided with, relatively speaking, an enormous subsidy by the British Government, much of it unwittingly and to British chagrin. Though this subsidy declined relative to Australian gross [domestic] product, it remained substantial until the early 1830s, and continued to be vital to Van Diemen's Land until 1850." Recognizing the impossibility of obtaining the desired measure, he here compiled an augmented subsidy estimate that includes British capital inflows into the colony, called "Capital inflow/Public subsidy," and reports annual data for 1788 to 1860. He explains that "[t]he word 'subsidy' is used here, insofar as these flows subsidized or enhanced Australian resources."[25] This series will overstate the true extent of the net contribution of the British taxpayer, especially after the inflow of private investment becomes significant with the expansion of the wool industry. But its magnitude and trend might be roughly indicative of what we are trying to assess. Not surprisingly this annual "subsidy" estimate is greater than colonial GDP in seven of the first ten years following 1788, declining to around 75 percent at the turn of the century. In the first decade of the nineteenth century (1801–10) it averages 49 percent of GDP, and in the second it is little changed at 47 percent (1811–20). There is a gap in the data in the mid-1820s, but the ratio falls to less than 35 percent at the end of that decade, then

---

[23] Ibid. (1994). The relevant section of this book is part III, "Public Funding of Colonial Development: 1788–1850" (chapters 5 to 10, pp. 53–93).

[24] Ibid., p. 69; and figure 11.3, p. 101.

[25] Ibid. (1986). The quotations are from pp. 101 and 102, respectively.

to 18 percent through the 1830s, to 12 percent in the first half of the 1840s, then further to 4 percent in the second half.[26]

We cannot put too much store in these figures given their unavoidably dubious quality. But they reinforce what the application of a little logic and economic analysis would have suggested in the circumstances and also what an assessment of the literary evidence had long indicated. The colony was not economically or fiscally "self-supporting" for many years after its foundation, and only with the rapid expansion of the pastoral industry from the 1820s did reliance on British government assistance or subsidy or aid, in whatever form, finally decline to trivial levels.

The significance of these subsidy or transfer estimates is that the evidence of early prosperity in the colony noted in chapter 2 has to be evaluated in this particular context. It was as if Britain funded "foreign aid" and "public investment" programs in New South Wales such that measured per capita incomes were way above what they would have been in its absence. Any small community can be made statistically rich if some foreign donor showers assistance and aid to a sufficient degree. Britain was the leading economic power at the time, and the European population of Australia was tiny until well into the nineteenth century: by 1820 it had reached only thirty-three thousand. With respect to the first years, Butlin concludes that "[t]hanks to local initiative and the British continuing to honour obligations of local Commissariat purchases and of imports on 'official' account, the settlement was able to achieve remarkably high living standards and a complex variety of economic activity at a remarkably early stage. Very much more than merely penal and defence costs were passed on to the British."[27] Indeed, and with respect to the following decades, his assessment is that "[t]he total 'subsidies' are far more important drivers or supporters of the Australian economy than wool up to 1831 and continue to be so for Van Diemen's Land to 1850." The result was that "with a direct exchange rate conversion, Australian GDP per head by 1821 was not far short of the British level (before adjustments for age and sex)."[28]

Although Butlin's are the only estimates available for Australian GDP per capita in the pre–gold rush decades, there have been other efforts to make international comparisons for that period. In the previous chapter I drew on the comprehensive cross-country estimates by Maddison for discussion of the years since 1850, but there eschewed referring to his earlier comparisons because of the fragility of the underlying data—and not just for Australia. According to Maddison, Australian GDP per capita in 1820, 1830, and 1840 lay well below that of the United Kingdom though was rapidly converging on it (figure 2.1). There are at least two reasons for the difference between this result and Butlin's

---

[26] The denominator is the estimate for "Australian" GDP. Butlin (1986), table 3, pp. 102–104.

[27] Ibid. (1994), p. 69.

[28] Ibid. (1986). The quotations are from pp. 102 and 104, respectively.

assessment that near parity obtained. First, Maddison's method for converting the two countries' GDP estimates to a common unit does not use exchange rates, and selects 1990 as a base year for the conversion exercise. Second, the two appear to have used different definitions of the relevant population. Butlin refers to his estimates as "white GDP," whereas Maddison includes an estimate of the Aboriginal population in the denominator of GDP per capita. This would lower his per capita estimates for Australia compared to those of Butlin even after augmenting "white" GDP with an Aboriginal contribution.

In an evaluation of Maddison's conversion methods for making cross-country comparisons of GDP per capita, Prados de la Escosura has recently provided historical estimates of his own, together with an alternative set using exchange rates.[29] For the period prior to 1860, he reports comparisons for 1820, 1830, 1840, and 1850, with the number of countries covered expanding from six to thirteen. Australia leads in each of the four benchmark years whether the comparisons are based on exchange rates or on Prados's own conversion methods. This appears to support the view of Australia's early achievement of relatively high incomes. Nonetheless, we have to recall the fragile basis on which Australia's GDP was calculated until the 1850s, if not through 1861; the problem of how appropriately to include some estimate of the Aboriginal population and its contribution to national income; and the very small size of the "Australian" community relative especially to the population of the United Kingdom. and the United States. It is because of limitations such as these that international comparisons relating to this early stage in the development of the domestic economy should be treated circumspectly.

By this conventional measure of economic prosperity, and mindful of these caveats, the very small community of Europeans in Australia appears, nonetheless, to have attained a relatively high standard of living very early in the life of their settlement, possibly even by 1820. This was based in part on the peculiarly favorable composition of the population—its high workforce participation rate attributable especially to its significant convict component. And in part the early prosperity resulted from the extent of the British subsidies, yielding the settlers a level of income and consumption that greatly exceeded their production. This subsidization of their living standards by British taxpayers was not a sustainable basis for prosperity. And the reliance on convict labor was, at least in the view of an increasing proportion of the colonial population, an undesirable basis for either economic or social development. Whether the transition to a subsidy-free and nonconvict economy could be made without impairing levels of prosperity would be revealed in the three decades following 1820—the era of the pastoral economy. In this era it would also be seen whether the institutional framework within which the economy initially operated would evolve further from its origins as being controlled by the military and dominated by the public sector.

---

[29] Prados de la Escosura (2000), table 9, p. 24.

CHAPTER 4

Squatting, Colonial Autocracy, and Imperial Policies

As well it might be attempted to confine the Arabs of the desert within a circle drawn on the sands as to confine the graziers or wool-growers of New South Wales within any bounds that can possibly be assigned them; and as certainly as the Arabs would be starved so also would the flocks and herds of New South Wales, if they were so confined, and the prosperity of the colony would be at an end.

—Governor George Gipps, 1840[1]

IN THE THREE DECADES following 1820, Australian prosperity was determined primarily by the relative strength of two sets of influences. On one side were the factors I have identified as critical to the level of income already achieved in the colony: the favorable workforce participation ratio due to the high masculinity ratio and an age distribution skewed toward those of working age, and the "subsidy" from the British government. If the proportion of convicts among total immigrants were to fall, and the proportion of families rise, both of the advantageous demographic sources of prosperity would be weakened, even though the European population would thereby become more "normal" in its gender ratio and age distribution. Such an outcome would, other things equal, depress average incomes. Any reduction in the British subsidy per capita would also lower average income. On the other side, and potentially offsetting these negative trends, was the prospect that the colony's development would be underpinned by the rapid growth of the recently established staple wool. But for this to occur, the profitability of wool production had to be such as to encourage the expansion of the pastoral industry on a scale sufficient to preserve or enhance average income even as the population expanded.

How these influences on prosperity played out would be determined in large part by the institutional context within which some key decisions were made. These decisions concerned the continuation of convict transportation and the terms and conditions of access to crown land suitable for pastoral occupation. The political institutions within which these decisions would be made were themselves in a state of flux. The military rule characterizing the initial phase of

---

[1] New South Wales Governor Sir George Gipps, writing to the colonial secretary in London in 1840: quoted in Roberts (1924), pp. 179–80

settlement was evolving before 1820, but the final form of its replacement was still unclear. Hence in 1820, say, the likely decisions on these key questions were difficult to predict. For example, it was uncertain how rapidly, and how far, the British government would consult with, and devolve powers to, the colonists. And equally uncertain was how representative those colonists participating in the new political institutions would be. This is one period in which any discussion of economic prosperity in Australia must assign considerable weight to the importance of political and institutional arrangements.

Why the Wool Industry Was So Efficient

The wool industry occupies a central place in Australia's political, social, and economic history. More than any other activity, sheep-raising underpinned the spread of European settlement in the nineteenth century. Life on the outback pastoral "property" (or sheep "station" or "run") features prominently in popular culture, representing what is quintessential about the country and even national character. Certainly wool was the principal export from the 1820s to the 1950s with the exception of the 1850s and 1860s when gold was more important. And because the expansion of exports was critical to economic growth, the industry deserves all the attention it has received from historians.

To give some perspective on the phenomenal growth of the pastoral industry at this time, the number of sheep increased from just over seventy-five thousand in 1816 to sixteen million in 1850.[2] Wool production, together with the quantity and value of wool exports, rose commensurately. Two indicators of the scale and significance of this export performance are shown in figure 4.1. The quantity (weight in pounds) of wool exported from New South Wales between 1822 and 1849 has been divided by the population in order to adjust for the extensive nature of growth during this period of high immigration and spreading pastoral settlement. The resulting per capita quantity measure of wool exports rises from 6 to 113 pounds. Another perspective on the importance of the wool trade is the rising share of Australian wool within the total quantity of wool imports into Britain. One source has this at 4 percent in 1810. By 1831 it stood at 8 percent, ranking third behind Germany (71 percent) and Spain (11 percent). But within two decades Australian wool was dominant in the British market, accounting (in 1850) for 53 percent, with Germany by then supplying just 13 percent of the market.[3]

---

[2]Published estimates of sheep numbers for the colonies are not always consistent and should be treated as approximate: see Vamplew (1987), pp. 81, 107, 115, and 124.

[3]The quantity of NSW wool exports, 1822–49, is reported in McMichael (1984), p. 262. The Australian share of British wool imports for 1810 is given by Roberts (1964 [1935]), p. 45; and for 1831 to 1850 by Burroughs (1967), p. 383.

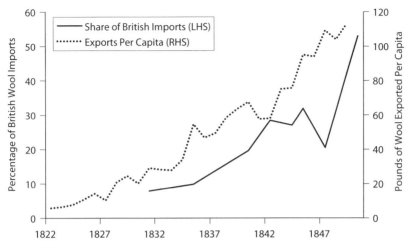

Figure 4.1. Wool trade, 1822 to 1850.
Notes: Years ended 31 December. Wool exports relate to New South Wales and the Port Phillip District only.
Sources: Wool exports per capita: Pinkstone (1992), Table 2, p. 328, and Australian Bureau of Statistics: *Australian Historical Population Statistics, 2008* (Cat. 3105.0.65.001). Australian share of British wool imports: Burroughs (1967), Appendix I, p. 383.

My interest in wool production is more focused. I wish to identify those features of the industry that not only permitted its very rapid expansion after 1820, but also account for its contribution to underpinning a high wage/high income economy even during a period of rapid immigration and population increase. An expansion of the industry and of wool exports might have occurred slowly, and been characterized by the spread of small-scale owner-occupiers living not much above subsistence—a sort of peasant agriculture much as occurred close to Sydney prior to 1820; or by using low-wage and labor-intensive farming methods such as under some form of tenancy arrangement. Under either circumstance it is likely that wages and incomes in the wool industry would have been low, reflecting low productivity levels. Instead, the pastoral expansion following 1820 had a set of attributes that permitted it to compete successfully on the world market for wool, to expand rapidly, and to remain profitable. What were they?

The Australian economy at this time may be described as labor and capital scarce, but land abundant. Actually the land abundance may not be an appropriate label until around 1820 when it was ascertained that in the central-west of New South Wales there was a large expanse of natural grassland on which livestock could be grazed. This constituted a major addition to the natural resource "endowment" of the colony, analogous to a discovery of a large deposit of gold, iron ore, or natural gas. The sudden increase in potentially productive land made labor and capital even more (relatively) scarce than hitherto. In theory, this would drive up the (relative) return to the two scarce factors of production. Hence we have an a priori explanation for the existence of a high wage economy: land abundance. But more was needed to ensure that this theoretical possibility was realized in practice.

The early pastoralists devised a quite remarkable labor- and capital-saving, but land-using, method of producing wool that reflected the factor scarcities they faced. And it would look nothing like the style of English farming, which was the template they brought with them to Australia. In the first place, the land was not only abundant but essentially priced at zero. This was due to the practice of squatting—driving sheep onto unoccupied Crown land without prior permission or property rights. Technically, the "squatters" were operating illegally. Since land was cheap and plentiful, they occupied large parcels of it. Indeed, being unconstrained, we can guess they occupied areas that maximized profits. There is no suggestion, for example, that they struggled to reach minimum efficient size. Thus two sources of their low cost and high productivity operations have been identified: free land and economies of scale.

With respect to capital inputs, the typical pastoralist at this time did very little in the way of investment in fixed assets other than sheep. The great expanse of unoccupied land available for squatting throughout southeastern Australia implied that the sheep could be left to wander, though under supervision, without the need for fencing. The mild climate made unnecessary any winter housing of livestock. No drainage or forest clearing was necessary prior to releasing the sheep to graze. And the squatters first occupied those areas that were naturally well-watered such as by containing creeks or having river frontage. Thus up-front costs of farm formation, usually a considerable barrier to entry and a significant element of pioneer farm production costs, were confined largely to the purchase of the sheep. Other relatively minor initial costs might include some rude accommodation for the shepherd, some portable wooden hurdles for folding the sheep at night, and in time some rudimentary homestead and stockyards.

It is worth noting that the one significant cost, the sheep, was a form of capital that was conveniently self-reproducing. Time, and nature taking its course, produced more sheep. Each year the capital "stock" and thus the output of wool could expand at a rate determined by biological factors without additional investment in the productive asset. Here lies a further and key element in the explanation of the rapid expansion and low cost structure of this industry.

The squatters also devised a labor-saving method of farming that accommodated the severe labor shortage in the colony. Convicts holding a ticket-of-leave were "assigned" to squatters and, together with emancipists, were a principal source of pastoral labor. The convicts were cheap (requiring less than market wages), but rarely would have had prior experience as shepherds. Given the unskilled nature of the tasks, this probably mattered less than other attributes such as reliability and the fortitude to cope with long periods living in isolation in the bush. Skills with horses and sheepdogs were vital, but easily acquired. The one labor-intensive and more specialist activity was the annual shearing, and for this, contract labor was hired from migratory "gangs" of shearers.

Finally, the wool had to be transported to a port prior to export to the British market. The absence of roads in these unsettled areas might have been an effective barrier to wool-growing. However, the high value of wool relative to its weight and bulk when baled and the fact that it is nonperishable permitted the cost of cartage by bullock-drawn wagon over primitive bush tracks to be absorbed by the squatter. At this time, little use could be made of the few inland rivers that were navigable by wool barges or steamboats, as occurred later in the century when the location of wool-growing had moved closer to the Murray-Darling river system.

From the evidence surveyed in chapter 2, the three decades of rapid pastoral expansion prior to the gold rushes were associated with high and possibly rising wages and incomes relative to those in Britain at that time. That this should occasion surprise is indicated by comparison with U.S. experience where the settlement of the Midwest agricultural regions in the early nineteenth century occurred as a result of people moving from areas of higher to lower wages and incomes. In the short run, this suggests the westward internal migration that accounted for rural expansion depressed average American wages and incomes. So, why did families uproot themselves from the Northeast and head out to the frontier to undertake the arduous task of establishing new farms and communities? The economists' explanation is that migration was driven not by short-run wage or income considerations but wealth maximization over an intergenerational time horizon. Expected future wealth, not current real wage or income differentials, was the critical economic incentive for migration. We do not possess wage or income data for Australia's regions at this time. But it is probably safe to infer that the pastoral expansion after 1820 did not operate to depress average incomes or wages, and that it instead either maintained or raised them. Such a judgment is based on the size of the pastoral settlement within total economic activity, together with the tentative evidence that no decline occurred in average Australian incomes during these decades.

There are further features of this industry that are pertinent to the explanation of its role in sustaining a high wage/high income economy during this period of rapid extensive growth and settlement. These are the indicators of efficiency and adaptability that we would expect to observe in farm firms in an internationally competitive and dynamic export-oriented industry. Typically, the wool that left the squatters' runs was not processed in any way; just crudely compressed into bales. Specifically, it was not even washed to rid the fleece of the substantial amounts of dirt or outback dust embedded there. Australians were exporting more than wool to Britain! Patently, it paid to be so slovenly. The cost of washing the wool was not recouped in the lower bulk transported or through the higher prices received in the British market for clean wool than un-washed ("greasy") wool. Washing the wool was, of course, labor intensive, even if done by means of driving the sheep into a conveniently located creek or river before shearing them. If a sheep-wash of some form had to be purpose-built, that meant more capital was required as well as labor employed. Thus adding value by washing prior to exporting the unprocessed wool did not always make economic sense—a theme that will recur in Australia's long history of exporting natural resources.[4]

Another feature of pastoral production relevant to its profitability was the exploitation of the joint-product nature of sheep: that is, they produce more than just wool. In addition to producing more sheep (lambs), they produce meat. Actually, the merinos were less suitable for this purpose than other English breeds, with a lower quality of mutton. But they were still a source of meat for those living in the interior and drier regions. More important is to note what happened when the price of wool fell. In extreme climatic or economic conditions the sheep were "boiled down" for their fat or tallow, which was then exported. This is first observed on a significant scale during the lean years of the 1840s depression in the British and colonial economies, helping counter-cyclically to maintain the profitability of pastoral operations until the price of wool recovered.

As the extensive frontier of pastoral settlement moved farther inland, an ad-ditional use of their sheep arose for longer-established squatters. They could sell some of their flock to those establishing new properties farther out and at the stage of building up their sheep numbers. Within the industry there thus developed a measure of product specialization between enterprises, depend-ing on their location and stage of development, and influenced by the relative prices of wool and sheep. The latter was determined, of course, as a derived demand based on the expected future price of wool.

In this overview of the simple analytics of squatting-based wool production in the pre–gold rush era, there is one further feature that is probably crucial to the explanation for its efficiency and rapid expansion. This is the early emer-gence of the so-called stock and station agency system, and the pastoral finance companies. Clearly the squatters were not able, individually, to arrange the trans-port, shipping, marketing, and financing of their annual wool clip, all the way to the point of final delivery at a textile mill in Britain. Specialist entities emerged to deal with these ancillary functions in the wool trade, essentially relieving the woolgrower of direct involvement once the wool passed the farm gate. And these entities formed an important part of the (backward or demand) linkages between the activities of the squatters and other sectors of the colo-nial economy. The finance requirements of the squatters were unlike the usual urban-based business or trade financing. For example, the annual wool clip

---

[4]Raby (1996), chapter 5, "Adding Value on the Station."

would be the sole or principal source of earnings for the pastoralist for the year, so provision of credit for the remainder of the year was often needed. Further complicating the credit requirements was the long delay between sending off the annual wool clip from the outback station and receiving the check from the bank in London following its sale there. The scope for intermediaries in this situation is obvious. It is testament to the innovative skills and entrepreneurial talent of the colonists that institutions and organizations emerged to fill these needs. The full development of these institutions occurs later in the century. But their origins are to be found in this period, especially in the provision of finance and the marketing of the wool.[5]

EVOLUTION OF POLITICAL INSTITUTIONS: FROM AUTOCRACY TO RESPONSIBLE GOVERNMENT

Three interrelated issues dominated political and economic debates in New South Wales after 1820.[6] One was the transition in the source of political power to the colonists from the governor, his advisers, and the British government who appointed him. The second issue concerned the continuation of convict transportation from Britain. The third related to the lack of well-specified and secure property rights in the land on which the squatters' sheep were grazing and, more generally, to the squatters' dominant and seemingly entrenched position in the political, economic, and social spheres. Although there is a close relationship between these three topics, I will discuss the evolution of institutions and policies connected with each in turn, starting with the political arrangements. This ordering is chosen because the key decisions on the two economic issues were hammered out within the framework of the evolving political institutions of the time.

The basic theme running through the political history of New South Wales is the rising demand from colonials of all classes and origins for more say in the management of their affairs. The story is complex, but the unmistakable direction of events was that the less the colonial population comprised convicts or ex-convicts, the less justification there was for the British to treat Australia as a quasi-military operation and to deny basic civil and political rights to the citizenry.[7] In 1823 the governor's autocratic position was modified by the creation of a Legislative Council of five to seven members, all appointed, though only the governor could initiate legislation. The act gave formal status to the

---

[5] Important studies included Barnard (1958) and Ville (2000).

[6] New South Wales was initially the sole jurisdiction in eastern Australia. Van Diemen's Land (Tasmania) separated in 1825, Victoria in 1851, and Queensland in 1859.

[7] Accounts of the main constitutional developments may be found in McMinn (1979, chapters 1–4), and Melbourne (1988a [1933]; 1988b [1933]).

governor's power to tax, created a supreme court, and introduced trial by jury in civil cases. In 1828 the Legislative Council was increased in size to seven official and seven non-official members, all still nominated. These arrangements continued until the Act of 1842, under which the Legislative Council was expanded to thirty-six members, twelve nominated and twenty-four elected. The elected members would be chosen by voters meeting certain property qualifications. Ex-convicts could vote and become members of the Council. But the elected members were scarcely representative, as the electoral law gave towns only one-quarter of the members while giving the country three-quarters, even though the bulk of the population was in the former. Sydney, in particular, was underrepresented. The governor and Council had wide legislative powers, but control of Crown lands and the revenue from them was retained by London.

In 1850 the British Parliament passed an act allowing all the Australian colonies to have legislative councils that were one-third nominated and two-thirds elected. A crucial provision was that the legislative councils would have considerable power to amend their constitutional arrangements. In 1851 in New South Wales, the squatter-dominated Legislative Council responded to the British act by making electoral changes that perpetuated their disproportionate representation. Of the fifty-four members, eighteen were nominated, eleven would be elected by towns and boroughs, seventeen by the settled counties, and eight by the pastoral districts. And in 1853 it drafted a constitution for the colony and forwarded it to London. This contained provisions for a nominated upper house, together with the perpetuation of unequal electorates and a restricted franchise favoring property owners. The new constitution passed the British Parliament, and came into operation in the colony in 1856.[8]

Executive authority would be located in the lower house of a bicameral parliament, ministerial responsibility would apply, and hence the governor's powers would be greatly reduced. Self-government had been achieved, though Britain retained substantial influence, such as in foreign policy. But a fully representative government had not been attained. The upper house was nominated not elected; there was a property qualification for enfranchisement, hence not even universal male suffrage; voting occurred in an open not secret ballot; and the electorates had unequal population and were heavily skewed against urban areas.

In 1856, at the first election in New South Wales under the new Constitution, the conservative interests—unsurprisingly—predominated and formed a government. But within a year, their liberal opponents gained office (for reasons discussed shortly), subsequently introducing reforms regarding the franchise, ballot, and electorates, and consolidating the supremacy of the elected lower house. A substantial measure of representative democracy had been achieved.

---

[8]Constitutions for Victoria, South Australia, and Tasmania were also drawn up. Although there were significant differences in detail, the constitution-making process in all colonies occurred in the context of the Act of 1850. I will continue to focus here on the New South Wales experience.

Symbolic of this peaceful displacement from power of the conservative landed interest was the passage, in 1861, of a radical land act to redistribute to small farmers the leased land occupied by the squatters (discussed in the next chapter). The evolution of political institutions from those of military rule in a penal colony to those of a democratic government was largely complete.

This emergence of democratic political institutions in the colony may be considered the outcome of a process in which there were three main groups of players.[9] The first was the British government and its local representative, the governor, and included the Colonial Office bureaucrats in London and the governor's appointed officials in Sydney. Initially all political power was concentrated in this group. If self-government and representative democracy were to occur in New South Wales, they would have to concur and enact legislation in the British Parliament, and, if they did not, there would have to be rebellion, following the example of the North American colonists.

In the colony itself, there was one fairly coherent group, the landed class, primarily but not totally comprising squatters. They had well-defined economic interests, in particular to secure tenure over the Crown land they occupied, and to ensure an adequate supply of low-cost pastoral labor. Their principal political interest was to attain sufficient influence over whatever local political institutions emerged to protect their privileged access to use of the public lands. John Hirst thus calls them the "conservatives."[10] They could be termed an "elite" in an economic and social sense, but in the political sphere the term is not quite apt. They dominated membership of the Legislative Council over several decades and appeared to fellow colonists to unduly influence its decisions. But, in the imperial context, the real source of power over major issues resided in London.

The remainder of the colony's population made up a third and looser group participating in the political transition. Before 1830 it comprised mainly emancipists. But after 1840 the rapidly expanding numbers of free immigrants, and the end of transportation of convicts, shifted the composition of New South Wales society toward the native born and immigrants, which included most townsfolk, wage earners, small businessmen, and small farmers. Their economic interests were diverse, but generally they were united in opposing the squatter monopoly of Crown-land occupation and the continuation of the transportation of convicts. They had no single umbrella organization through which to operate in a united fashion. Many were influenced by the debates and events in Britain concerning the extension of representative government (Chartism and the 1832 Reform Act), seeking similar rights for themselves. Hence Hirst terms them "liberals" or "democrats."

---

[9] The accounts of political and constitutional history during this period provided by Hirst (1988) and Cochrane (2006) have been helpful in developing the interpretation that follows.
[10] Hirst (1988).

It is worth stressing the limits on the governor's autocratic rule. His initiatives in the Legislative Council could face sustained opposition leading to their being withdrawn, modified, or referred to London. Sometimes the governor was supported by his immediate superior, the colonial secretary, but sometimes he was overruled. The influence of the bureaucrats in the Colonial Office over policy in the colony could also be considerable. Further, "public opinion" in the colony could not be ignored. Despite the absence of representative government, the colony had acquired a remarkably free press from the 1820s. The Sydney papers seemed fearless, lobbying for the creation of representative institutions, the expansion of the Legislative Council to reduce the influence of the landed class, and trial by jury.

What was the objective of the British in identifying with the demands of the colonists for a greater say in the management of their own affairs? In the 1820s the population was very small, and there were few free settlers, thus it would have been a bold move to make the Legislative Council more representative or to include an elected element. By the 1840s the Colonial Office appears to have taken a consistent position on the demands for self-government. Influencing their response to specific issues was the experience of the loss of the American colonies and, more immediately, problems in Upper and Lower Canada. Against this background Colonial Office policies ceded to colonial responsibility functions that did not endanger vital imperial interests. Two areas in contention were the control of Crown lands, since the British saw these as integral to their long-run imperial emigration plans, and control of colonial finances to ensure the colony not become a financial burden on Britain. The rapid growth in the population, and its changing composition with the waning of the convict and ex-convict share, were two factors making London more amenable to delegation of political functions. The economic prosperity attendant on the wool trade was surely another.

It therefore seems that, to some degree, Australians did not have to persuade the British government that it was in Britain's interest to consider favorably the demands for increased political autonomy. Both sides were aware of precedent. Threats to cause Britain trouble, threats short of open rebellion, were more credible in light of recent imperial history. So the issue was more about timing and, especially, about what form the new colonial political institutions would assume. Hence any explanation of colonial political institution building must accommodate the key role of the imperial power, and its preparedness to relinquish control. Imperial economic interests in the future of the colony were important, but these did not require that self-government or more representative democracy in the colony be withheld.[11]

---

[11]This cursory outline fails to capture the complexity of views on particular issues, the importance of some dominant personalities, the role of ideas (especially those at the center of British political debates at the time), and the demographic shifts occurring in colonial society.

For those who might be tempted to reduce colonial democratization to a deterministic process, historians of this period appropriately emphasize that chance factors may play a critical role. For example, the widening of the franchise proposed for the constitutional act of 1850 succeeded only because the high rents on Sydney housing mistakenly were thought by members of the House of Lords to be such that only wealthy people would be enfranchised.[12] The inflation following the gold rush pushed more of the population over the minimum property values required for enfranchisement. The discovery of gold in 1851 also changed the population mix in ways that could not have been foreseen by the drafters of the constitutions, strengthening the position of the liberals, and reducing the squatters' ability to maintain their hold over political affairs. And, as noted earlier, the small farmers and tenant farmers deserted the conservatives in the key New South Wales elections in the mid- and late 1850s in the face of their rising prosperity stemming from the gold boom, and of their improved prospects for farm acquisition, the liberals having promised to subdivide the squatters' large properties till then held under pastoral lease. This offset the advantage the conservatives had expected from their electoral laws giving greater representation to farming areas.[13]

The principal economic motivations for the squatters' tenacious efforts during these decades first to secure, and then to preserve, a dominant position in the emerging colonial political institutions, were the two vexed issues of convict transportation and their pastoral leases. Had they succeeded in their aims with respect to both, the direction of Australia's economic development would have been markedly at variance from what occurred, and its future growth and prosperity thereby significantly impaired.

The Labor Market: Ending Transportation, Preventing Coolie Immigration

It is likely that the majority of the European population was either convict or emancipist until about 1840, but by 1850 this ratio was less than 30 percent.[14] The transportation of convicts to New South Wales ended in 1840, but attempts to revive it continued for more than a decade. Convicts were sent to Van Diemen's Land until the early 1850s, while at the request of the settlers in the small and struggling colony of Western Australia, convicts were sent there between 1850 and 1868.

---

[12]See Hirst (1988), pp. 17–18. He concludes: "The British ignorance of colonial affairs, which could always be relied on . . . had led to the establishment of virtual household suffrage in Sydney. The House of Lords, the enemy of British reform, had picked colonial democracy out of the gutter" (p. 26).

[13]Described in Hirst (1988), pp. 83–89 and 95.

[14]This is according to the estimates of Butlin (1994), table 3.3, p. 37.

The groups aligned with the two sides of the debate on whether transportation should be ended or continued are only partly based on economic interest. The squatters wanted a supply of labor adequate for the needs of the rapidly expanding pastoral sector, so they saw the antitransportation movement as a threat to the viability of wool production and, as a result, to the economic future of the colony. The groups opposed to the continuation of convict arrivals were variously motivated. One unifying purpose among opponents of transportation seems to have been moral or ideological—that is, the desire to rid colonial society of the convict stain. There was also opposition in Britain to the transportation of convicts, evident in parliamentary enquiries in the late 1830s, and from within the Colonial Office. The free immigrants had a more direct private concern: "The newcomers, who were wage-earners and small farmers . . . were interested in high wages and regular employment, and were consequently opposed to transportation and assigned labour."[15] This, in turn, is related to the broader political struggle to restrain the power of the squatters. The balance of forces within the colony was already moving against the wishes of the employers of convict labor when a British parliamentary inquiry into transportation produced an unfavorable report, and the Colonial Office responded by declaring an end to the practice of assigning convicts to private employers in 1838 and the end of transportation to New South Wales from 1840.

Significantly, the debate in New South Wales revived at the end of the 1840s. The British government, especially the colonial secretary, Lord Grey, wanted to reintroduce transportation of convicts to New South Wales and obtained the support of the squatter-dominated Legislative Council by proposing to send equal numbers of free immigrants. The arrival of the first ship carrying convicts provoked a large public demonstration, and the Legislative Council reversed its policy in September 1850, with the British government accepting the change. In discussing opposition to this revival attempt, Hirst says that despite the popular protests, "the leadership of the movement was in other hands. The squatters' insistence that they must have convict labour outraged Sydney's merchants and professional men who were now committed to a colony of free people only. They were already disturbed by the privileged position which squatters had acquired on the land as a result of the British government's decision in 1847 [discussed below] to issue them long leases."[16] This exemplifies the nexus between land policy, transportation, and the political influence of the landed interests.

Grey's determination to reintroduce convicts to New South Wales extended to the insertion in the Act of 1850 of "clauses by which he hoped to effect the separation of the Moreton Bay District [Queensland] on terms which would permit the use of exile labour in a northern colony." However, this proposal was scrapped because his successor at the Colonial Office, John Pakington, "had little sympathy with Grey's ideas," resulting in the postponement of the separa-

---

[15]Melbourne (1988a [1933]), p. 165.
[16]Hirst (1988), p. 21.

tion of Queensland from New South Wales until 1859.[17] The antitransportation movement remained active, however, because convicts were still being sent to Van Diemen's Land at the insistence of Grey, provoking a coordinated campaign from all the colonies except Western Australia. The end of transportation to Van Diemen's Land appears to have resulted from the change of government in Britain that led Grey to be replaced by Pakington, who was "prepared to give the Australians what they wanted," illustrating how chance and personality influenced outcomes on critical institutional issues.[18]

Alternative sources of pastoral labor to that of convicts had been considered as early as the 1830s when the antitransportation campaign gained strength. And there is an intersection here with land policy. For some years the principal source of revenue used to subsidize free immigration was the sale of public land. Proposals to raise the sale price of land, or to set a fixed price, were opposed by the squatters on the grounds that if this resulted in lower revenue, the flow of "assisted" free immigrants would be curtailed, threatening their supply of labor should convict transportation end. It was in the context of the likely phasing-out of transportation, and uncertainty over the future flow of assisted immigrants that consideration was given to the importation of "coolie" labor from Asia to work as shepherds on the pastoral stations. In 1837 a committee of the Legislative Council recommended that three thousand to five thousand Indians be recruited, and a few were brought, before the British government quashed the proposal on the basis that it constituted the creation of a "slave caste."[19] The pastoralists were not deterred, making a further request in 1844, forming an "Indian Labour Association" in 1848, and employing some Pacific Islanders from the New Hebrides as shepherds, though none of these schemes was successful. The squatters then considered using Chinese, with one of the large pastoral companies recruiting 2,100 in 1854, only to lose them to the goldfields.[20] However, the influx of population resulting from the gold rushes boosted the potential supply of pastoral labor once the first phase of alluvial mining passed.

THWARTING THE SQUATTERS: LAND POLICIES TO 1847

At least as important to the economic development of Australia as the form of its labor-market institutions was the question of who was to exploit the resource endowment, and on what conditions—that is, the access to, and property rights

---

[17] Melbourne (1988b [1933]), p. 291. Roe (1974, p. 94) claims that at this time squatters both in the region that was to become Queensland, and in the northern New South Wales region of New England, considered separation from New South Wales in order that they could import convict labor, and that Grey was aware of this.

[18] Hirst (1988), p. 33.

[19] Correspondence from the secretary of the colonies to Governor Gipps in December 1837, quoted in Roberts (1924), p. 128.

[20] Roberts (1924), pp. 127–29.

in, its abundant natural resources. Land was the most important resource during much of the nineteenth century, and access to it was the principal route to acquiring private wealth. Therefore it is unsurprising that the disposal of the Crown lands would be a contentious policy issue. The first phase of land disposal ran from the 1820s to 1847 and focused on the initial occupation of natural grassland for pastoral purposes. The second stage, from the 1860s to the 1880s, concerned the reallocation of some of this land from the pastoralists to small-scale farmers, and will be examined in the next chapter.

As described earlier, wool growing had its origins in the occupation of Crown lands that had not been sold or leased to the owners of the sheep who grazed on the natural grasslands. The squatters had moved ahead of the system of land survey and disposal that initially had applied around Sydney. Anomalous maybe, but Australian economic growth after 1820 was driven by economic activity not entirely within the law. The question was how, ex post, the situation could best be regularized.

Settlement around Sydney was confined initially to nineteen surveyed counties. The form of land disposal was at first by sales, but moved to grants (with quit-rents) in the 1820s—and seems to have been at the governor's discretion. The squatting problem, however, related primarily to the spread of pastoral occupation beyond the nineteen counties.[21] In 1836, regulations were issued that legalized squatting, and the fee to hold a license was set at ten pounds annually, with no limit on the area held. By 1839 the courts had recognized the pastoralists' right of occupancy, though not against the rights of the Crown, and they could claim legal protection for their occupancy and in boundary disputes. Also in 1839 the annual fee was amended to include a levy on a per-animal basis. Because the fee was annual, any structures would be the property of the Crown or the person to whom the lease was awarded at the end of the year.

By this stage (c. 1840), the system was legal but not satisfactory from the point of view of any of those involved. The policy debates of the 1840s are thus all about security of tenure and related issues. The squatters wanted longer leases and preemptive rights over at least a portion of their runs—including the homestead and improvements—which would enable them to convert their occupancy to freehold. They had opened large areas of the country to settlement and provided it with its economic base. Their lack of property rights had arisen from inadequacies in the colony's earlier administrative arrangements for surveying and allocating crown lands. The annual license system failed to provide the type of security of property rights that would enable a more appropriate level of investment in fixed assets and provide the confidence needed to put the industry on a secure footing. They further claimed that, because of the position of the industry, the economic prosperity of the colony depended on the land tenure question being resolved in their favor. This seems an illustration of the holdup problem: potential investors were discouraged due to the lack of

---

[21] The following brief summary of the legislation is based on Roberts (1924, 1988 [1933]).

credibility of any commitment from the governor that the squatters' property rights in pastoral assets would be secure.

One might question the squatters' claims. Wool-growing was generally profitable, and the industry seemed viable given its expansion over several decades, so how serious were the (private or social) costs imposed by the squatters' lack of stronger property rights such as freehold? In theory, fixed investment in long-life assets such as fencing, dams, and buildings would be negatively impacted by a system of one-year pastoral leases with no guarantees for renewal. Raising productivity and the quality of the wool would be difficult without investment in fencing and other fixed assets.[22] But in the decades from the 1820s to 1840s, it appears that the industry flourished without much in the way of fixed assets. This seems, therefore, to be a case where more secure property rights were not essential to growth—at least in the early history of this major sector of the economy.

Any change to land tenure arrangements required legislation by the British government. Hence the squatters could try to persuade the governor to request the secretary of state for the colonies to take this up with the government. They could directly lobby members of the British Parliament, and bureaucrats in the Colonial Office—and they did. They also sought allies in their campaign. Groups offering support to the squatters included industrialists in cities in Britain where the woolen textile industry was important, and Sydney businessmen whose prosperity depended directly or indirectly on that of the wool trade. Ranged against the squatters' demands were the "systematic colonizers" (most prominently Edward Gibbon Wakefield) whose ideas about settlement ran directly counter to the policy of confirming secure property rights over a large proportion of the colony's farmland to a small number of pastoralists who had occupied the land illegally. They had influence in the Colonial Office, and their theories of colonization also provided a reasoned basis for opposition in Australia. Small farmers and would-be farmers, whether free immigrants or emancipists, saw the squatters' demands as locking them out of the opportunity to gain access to land. In addition, the squatters' demands were opposed by those who saw the likely entrenching of a "squattocracy"—the wealthy elite of pastoralists monopolizing land, hence dominating the economy and society. Given the few checks and balances in the then current political arrangements in New South Wales, and the pressures for granting more political autonomy to the colony, the fear among "liberals" and "democrats" was that the squatters would entrench and expand their already disproportionate influence during the creation of local political institutions (as described earlier).

One view was that the squatters should be treated as having no rights at all, and be, in effect, removed from their occupation. This had been the position adopted in 1834 by the governor, Richard Bourke: "the unauthorised occupants

---

[22]Butlin (1964, pp. 89–92) discusses the relation between leases and pastoral investment, but for the central and western districts of New South Wales in the 1870s and 1880s.

must not be permitted to continue as long as to create any title to the land in the occupier."[23] It was also the position of the followers of Wakefield including some in the British government and Colonial Office. That is, unless the squatters' monopoly in the market for land was broken, the development of the colony would be stymied, because the inability to obtain farmland would discourage free immigration, thereby making permanent a highly unequal initial distribution of wealth. However, evicting the squatters was not a feasible option even in the 1820s or 1830s, before the license system recognized their existence and before they had spread over much of the inland southeast of the continent. This is because the governor lacked the means: sufficient administrative and police resources were not at his disposal, precisely the reason squatting first emerged. By 1840 it would have been an impossible task to roll back twenty years of pastoral settlement and then reallocate and reoccupy vast areas of Crown lands de novo. So it is not difficult to explain why this extreme solution was not implemented—despite its being the objective of the influential adherents of theories of systematic colonization.

Instead, there was an accommodation to the squatters' demands that fell short of granting freehold title, but increased their security of tenure and gave them a privileged position in the market for land they occupied, namely, certain preemption rights. This compromise was achieved after several years of debate and policy shifts, in London and the colony. All the interests mentioned were involved. But it seems clear that the governor, George Gipps (1838–46), was critical to securing the compromise outcome. He issued regulations in 1844 aimed at curbing abuses by requiring separate licenses for each run, with no run to exceed twenty square miles or have more than four thousand sheep. He also sent recommendations to London about the broader problems, suggesting that the squatters be given preemptive rights but only over land around their homesteads and any permanent improvements they had made. However, the process for purchase was to be highly restrictive. After five years of occupation, a pastoralist could buy 320 acres, and after every additional eight years, another similar area. If the original occupier did not purchase at these scheduled times, however, another person could do so, and they would get occupancy of the rest of the run. The displaced occupier would get compensation for improvements that had been made.

When these proposals became known, there was a very strong reaction from the squatters. One authority claims that "many a group on the dusty plains gripped their rifles. . . . Even the hardest-headed pioneers spoke of resistance by force, and Australia seemed swirling in the vortex of rebellion. . . . Australia was very close to tragedy."[24] Unfortunately Gipps's regulations and proposals coincided with a marked economic downturn in the wool industry and hence

---

[23]Quoted in Roberts (1988 [1933]), p. 200.

[24]Roberts (1988 [1933]), pp. 202–203. Of this episode Roe (1974, p. 92) comments: "Feeling rose high enough to prompt talk of revolution, and Gipps asked that imperial troops stay at full strength."

the colony. It is not clear how serious this simmering discontent was; it seems to have subsided as seasons improved and the depression passed. But the next few years saw the height of the lobbying against the 1844 regulations and the proposals, with new associations formed in the colony, delegations sent to England, and attempts made to rally the wool manufacturers there. This intense rent-seeking behavior by the squatters reflects both the weakness of the institutional arrangements in the colony, and also how much they stood to lose by an adverse decision. This I see as the critical time when events may have swung in favor of a more generous accommodation to the squatters' demands. But Gipps did not accede to this pressure, and the colonial secretary backed him up. Indeed, one assessment is that, "The centre of opposition [to the squatters] came to be . . . the personality of the Governor, Sir George Gipps."[25]

In 1846 the British Parliament passed the Waste Lands Occupation Act, which was then implemented in the colony through Orders-in-Council in 1847. The pastoralists got increased security of tenure, but were not granted freehold. In a decision that would have important long-run consequences, they were granted leases of up to fourteen years in the "unsettled" districts where pastoral occupation was still in progress, and shorter leases in the settled areas where the land could be offered for sale at auction.[26] Variations on this were introduced in South Australia and Western Australia. Orthodox historiography regards what happened as a victory for the pastoralists: "the squatters acquired de facto their security of tenure and with it a monopoly of the grazing and agricultural land of Australia."[27] What is more important to the present analysis is that this apparent monopoly would survive only as long as the landlord (soon to be the colonial governments) continued to renew their leases and took no action to alter the contracts to the squatters' detriment. The 1847 regulations thus meant that the squatters' economic interests would now be determined not in London but in the colonial legislatures.

Other Determinants of Early Colonial Prosperity

The pre–gold rush economy was not, of course, simply a collection of sheep stations plus a few related activities in the transport and finance industries. Neither was it confined to the present-day boundaries of New South Wales. By 1850 settlement was well established in Van Diemen's Land, getting under way in South Australia and in what was to become Victoria and Queensland,

---

[25]Roberts (1988 [1933]), p. 200.

[26]In New South Wales in 1848–49 the number of squatters was 1,865. They occupied 85,125 square miles of pastoral land—an average of 45.6 square miles (or 29,211 acres) each. On their leases they had 5.5 million sheep and 880,000 cattle. Data based on ibid. (1964 [1935]), appendix V.

[27]Clark (1987), p. 106. This orthodoxy reflects the assumption that most of this land was suitable for small-scale family farming. Experience across the next several decades showed this was not the case.

but was only tentative in Western Australia. Sydney and Hobart were not the only towns of significance with the foundation during the 1830s of future major urban areas in Melbourne and Adelaide. The towns accommodated a range of industries and activities in services and simple manufacturing. Early examples include banking, transport, importing and exporting, wholesale and retail trade, construction (especially housing), brick making, brewing, bakeries, and boat building. Also, the rural sector of the economy was diversified well beyond the production of wool. Grain growing, dairy farming, meat and beef production, and horticulture, had been established in the first few years of European settlement, and were all flourishing.[28] This was because the growth of farming apart from wool-raising was at this time driven by domestic demand, that is, by the rapid expansion of the colonial population.

My interest is not in describing these important elements of the early colonial economy, but in assessing their contribution to the high levels of income that were achieved. Since free trade prevailed, at least with Britain, we can account for the mix of colonial activities pretty much in terms of what were nontradeable goods (houses, fresh foodstuffs, banking services), and what the colonists could obtain more cheaply by importation than by local production. In the absence of detailed data relating to these domestic industries, it is difficult to determine whether they recorded above- or below-average productivity. For some import-competing industries, the freight costs from the principal source of imports, Britain, may have afforded natural protection that thus permitted much higher-cost local production. The very small initial population further suggests that some activities may have been operating below efficient scale. Nevertheless, many activities at this stage would not be characterized by significant scale economies, so there may have been little loss of efficiency relative, say, to comparable activities in Britain. And whereas the rapid growth in population may have aided efficiency in some activities, this would be offset by the increasingly widely dispersed location of the population, fragmenting what might otherwise have been a larger single or integrated domestic market based, say, in the Sydney area. It is therefore hard to guess a priori at the *levels* of efficiency in the nontradeables and import-competing sectors compared to that achieved in the booming export-oriented pastoral industry.

One source of productivity *improvement* in the rural sector is likely to have arisen from the relocation of particular farming activities from less to more appropriate regions. This was a result first of ongoing exploration of inland areas, and subsequently of the increased information accumulated about the soils and

---

[28]Raby (1996). In the first half of the nineteenth century, grazing cattle for beef production was of minor importance compared to that of the wool industry. At midcentury there were less than two million beef and dairy cattle (the two are not separately enumerated) but over fifteen million sheep. The expansion of beef production occurred later, associated with the settlement of more arid and northern areas, especially in Queensland.

climate in any area following its settlement. This process of regional shifts of farm production began in the first year or two following 1788 with the relocation of early attempts at food production from Sydney to areas such as the Hawkesbury northwest of the town because of the increased yields obtained there. After 1820, the central-west of New South Wales offered lower-cost opportunities for wool production than earlier settled coastal regions. For the next century, we observe further shifts in the location of particular rural industries in pursuit of more profitable farming. Other things equal, this raises the productivity of agriculture and hence average incomes. In this period, we should note the beginnings of crop production and agricultural activities more generally outside the Sydney basin and Van Diemen's Land—especially in the Port Phillip District around Melbourne, and on the Adelaide Plains. In the case of South Australia, one clue that wheat production there was more efficient than in coastal New South Wales is the evidence of intercolonial wheat shipments. We can further note the intermittent export of wheat from Van Diemen's Land and South Australia in the 1840s. These trends indicate that, at least in some regions and for some products, early colonial agriculture was also at or approaching internationally competitive levels of efficiency. It would be the late nineteenth century, however, before other farm products consistently joined wool as major exports.

There is one other pre–gold rush industry in Australia that certainly was internationally competitive and export oriented, and that experienced very rapid expansion, thus making a contribution to prosperity. This is the copper industry that boomed in South Australia after the discovery of deposits there in 1841, marking Australia's first mineral boom. European settlement began only in 1836, and experienced uncertain economic times based on wool and grain farming. From the mid-1840s, copper both diversified the colony's economic base and secured its viability. The population of 17,000 in 1844 reached almost 64,000 by 1851, closing in on that of Victoria (at 77,000). The initial discoveries were in the mid-north of the colony, but in the 1860s, further discoveries were made on Yorke Peninsula. Production reached 4,700 tons by 1850, peaking at over 9,000 tons in the late 1860s and early 1870s.[29] It has been claimed that, "When Victoria led the world in gold South Australia in some years mined one-tenth of the world's copper," and that, "By the early 1870s, South Australia was the major producer of copper in the British Empire."[30] The copper boom is not just a reminder that the mining industry was contributing to Australian prosperity prior to the discovery of gold in 1851. Indeed, some coal was mined from early in the settlement of New South Wales, with unsuccessful attempts

---

[29] Population estimates are from Vamplew (1987), p. 26. Production figures are from Kalix, Fraser, and Rawson (1966), p. 136, and refer to the "copper content of ores, concentrates, etc."

[30] Blainey (2003a), p. 105; and Pinkstone (1992), p. 40.

to establish exports to Asia in the 1790s.[31] The copper boom is also a reminder that "national" income per capita is the population-weighted average of that attained in each colony or state. As in more recent decades, resource-based booms in regions that are "resource rich" can contribute disproportionately to growth Australia wide. This was a role Victoria was to take over from South Australia in 1851.

The Argentine Road Not Taken

The mechanisms whereby economies acquire growth-enhancing or growth-retarding institutions are imperfectly understood. And the hypotheses in growth economics that initial endowments and colonial inheritance may both play key roles in determining institutional arrangements, and hence growth, are the subject of debate.[32] In this chapter I have reviewed aspects of Australian historical experience pertinent to these closely related questions. It is time to explicitly consider the possibility that, given the initial conditions, there were occasions during the early colonial period when the institutional framework within which the economy operated might have taken a quite different and less growth-promoting form.

Of relevance to this inquiry is the recent attempt by Engerman and Sokoloff to explain the very different long-run growth performance of the settler economies of the western hemisphere.[33] They view the endowments of countries in the Americas at the time of initial European occupation as determining the types of institutions adopted there. Climate, soils, and other geographic considerations help determine the choice of products that come to dominate an economy. But a focus of Engerman and Sokoloff's analysis is how widely spread were the property rights in whatever resource formed the principal basis of wealth in the economy. If there arose a highly unequal initial distribution of access to, or property rights in the key resources (land, minerals, labor—including slaves), with ownership passing to a small minority of the population, the economic power acquired by this wealthy elite would likely be employed to shape early political and social institutions such as to ensure they protected their economic dominance. This characterized the early history of Latin America, but not of Anglo-America where, outside the U.S. South, the initial endowment differed, and wider access to resources led to a more egalitarian distribution of wealth.

Furthermore, Engerman and Sokoloff argue that these early institutional arrangements, both economic and political, not only persisted over long peri-

---

[31] Pinkstone (1992), p. 17.

[32] Acemoglu, Johnson, and Robinson (2005) and Levine (2005) provide recent overviews of the relevant literature.

[33] Their analysis is contained in a series of publications, including Engerman and Sokoloff (1997, 2002, 2003, and 2005a), and Sokoloff and Engerman (2000).

ods, but also help explain later institutional developments that have, in turn, impacted growth performance down to the present. If a wealthy elite emerges early, they will likely oppose the extension of the franchise, offer limited support for universal and publicly funded education, and secure an immigration program that suits their own labor requirements, thus reinforcing a skewed distribution of income and wealth in the community, and hence delaying the development of broad-based financial institutions such as a stock market. The unequal economic and political power of the elite is thus entrenched by these later institutional developments, stunting long-run growth. Where a more equal initial distribution of wealth occurs, the subsequent pattern of institutional development will be very different, and favorable to growth. In this provocative view, these causal sequences, with their historical roots in the initial endowments and in the institutions that arise to determine access to them, account for the current differences in income per capita between rich Anglo-America and relatively poor Latin America.[34] What assistance does this provide to the analysis of early Australian growth and prosperity?

I have described how the squatters became a wealthy and influential class after 1820 and how squatting was an "institution" central to the development and prosperity of the economy. Is it possible that Australia, at this stage, could have evolved into a squatter-dominated oligarchy, a "squattocracy"—politically, socially, and economically? The counterfactual story might have unfolded as follows.

Occupying the vast areas of Crown lands suitable for wool production, the pastoralists employ low-wage labor supplied by the flow of convicts from Britain. Because of the preeminence of the wool industry, they dominate domestic economic activity and the export trade. Due to their economic power within the colony and their importance to British industry, the squatters successfully negotiate with the government in London for increased control over the colonial governor, his advisory council, and his powers. In particular they use this influence to secure freehold title to all the Crown lands on which they have squatted and built their fortunes. They thus entrench in this society a highly unequal distribution of wealth—of which pastoral land is the main form—through their dominance of the political institutions they have created or shaped. To perpetuate their control of political institutions, the franchise is restricted to substantial property owners. Immigration (principally convict transportation) is carefully regulated to maintain the supply of low-cost unskilled labor required by the squatters. Indeed, if the flow of convicts dries up as a result of a change in British policy, a potential supply of cheap labor is available nearby from India, China, or the Pacific islands, which could be obtained on a contract or indentured basis. Finally, the squatters pursue free trade in order to support Britain's

---

[34]Nunn (2009, pp. 7–9) reviews several studies critical of the Engerman and Sokoloff findings on the Americas.

commitment to open markets, to secure their imports at world prices, and to discourage the growth of an urban-industrial working class that would result from any tariff protection of Australian manufacturing.

In this conjectural account Australia soon looks much like Argentina—economically, politically, and socially. And, as in any good horror story, there is enough historical verisimilitude to keep the reader accepting its plausibility despite its scary ending. The point of the exercise is that the actual ("initial") conditions in Australia in the 1820s and 1830s appear superficially similar to those in Argentina and perhaps elsewhere in Latin America at comparable times in the formation of their societies and economies.

Nothing in this stylized description suggests as an inevitable outcome that, within a few decades, the colony would have self-government, ministerial responsibility, and a good measure of representative democracy. To a student of interest-group politics, this result might be a surprise given that the landed class had the advantage over the liberals and democrats of smaller numbers but greater wealth, lower organizational costs, common goals, and greater political leverage through their dominance of the Legislative Council from the 1820s. Further, this outcome does not appear consistent with the emphasis Engerman and Sokoloff give to initial conditions. In their perspective the factor endowment from about 1820 would suggest that the landed interests in the colony, who had occupied much of the pastoral land and hence monopolized the principal source of colonial wealth, would have been able to determine the direction of political institution building to ensure their economic interests were well served and their political position remained dominant.

The important feature of the political landscape that any political economy "model" misses if it focuses only on groups *within* New South Wales is the pivotal role of the *outside* group—the British government and its local representative, the governor, who controlled the political system, but were not part of colonial society. It is imperative to recall that we are examining democratization in a colony, not in an independent polity.[35] Until self-government in the 1850s, the British ultimately determined the nature and timing of any fundamental institutional changes, even if there was significant input into decision-making from colonial interests. And, as we have seen, they were a counter to what appeared irresistibly powerful local interests—such as those of the squatters. This offsetting role seems crucial to the evolution of those institutions that had the greatest bearing on long-run growth and prosperity in Australia at this time. And, as we have seen, within a few decades Australia was developing more like Anglo-America than Latin America.

---

[35] This colonial status similarly limits the relevance to the Australian historical experience of the economic models of the emergence of democracy in the influential work of Acemoglu and Robinson (2006a).

Consider what might have transpired had the colony suddenly been cast adrift to fend for itself.[36] The squatters and their allies would have been in a much more powerful position during the formation of local political institutions. But the squatters lacked a credible commitment mechanism to satisfy the economic aspirations regarding land redistribution of the majority of colonists short of conceding a substantial measure of de jure political power through institutions based on a democratic constitution. Their alternative would be repression. And it is unclear whether this path would have been chosen as the context is so removed from historical circumstances. Nonetheless, without the counterweight against the de facto power of the squatters, emanating from the governor and from London, the Latin American outcome seems more probable. Thus any attempt to link the initial endowment to the nature of the political institutions bequeathed to a self-governing Australia must contend with the independent role for the imperial power, and its successful resistance to an unfettered domination by the squatters and their allies.

After 1850, in the early years of responsible government in the colonies, there are clear indicators of the consolidation of representative and democratic institutions. Several Australian colonies incorporated universal male suffrage in their constitutions from the outset—at least for the lower house of Parliament. The secret ballot was also adopted in some colonies in the 1850s, and in all by 1877. The property restrictions on voting for the lower houses were never high, and progressively lowered. And suffrage for women was introduced from 1894 in South Australia, and by 1906 was granted throughout Australia. There seems little doubt that the Australian experience more closely matches North American than Latin American experience in the timing of the extension of democracy.[37] And it seems equally safe to suggest that at no subsequent juncture in the country's history did the potential exist for Australian political and social development to take such a radically different direction as might have occurred in the decades covered in this chapter, a direction that would have embedded growth-inhibiting institutions so firmly into the foundations of the economy.

---

[36] In some measure this was the situation in Spanish America during the Napoleonic occupation of Spain, and this interregnum was a critical period for the formation and consolidation of political groups in its colonies in the lead-up to their independence (Elliott, 2006, chapter 10).

[37] In their analysis of political developments in the Americas, Engerman and Sokoloff point to the divergence in historical experience between Anglo America and Latin America in the nineteenth century in the timing of the widening of the voting franchise and in related democratic reforms. They account for the much earlier appearance of these in North America to the prior differences with Latin America in the initial distributions of wealth and political power. Their most explicit consideration of this contrast is offered in Engerman and Sokoloff (2005b).

CHAPTER 5

Becoming Very Rich

There is this peculiarity in gold, as an object of industry, that the quest of it disturbs all other adjacent industries.
　—Anthony Trollope, visiting Victoria in 1871[1]

IN 1851 THE DISCOVERY of gold delivered a major shock to the predominantly pastoral economy of Australia and ushered in a dramatic episode in the history of the country's prosperity. Considered in relation to the size of the economy it triggered the largest economic disruption ever experienced. And though an economic shock by origin, its effects quickly permeated the social, political, and even cultural spheres, some so deeply that their impression has lasted to the present. The importance of gold in domestic and international finance at the time made Australia akin to some of today's oil producers. Like a mid-nineteenth century Gulf state, a very small population found itself in possession of a significant proportion of the world's supplies of a strategic commodity. Crucially, this commodity had the advantage that it could be produced without the prior development of domestic manufacturing or financial services, and could be exported in an unprocessed state onto a world market that had a seemingly unquenchable desire for it. Further, the gold discoveries augmented and diversified Australia's already generously sized natural-resource endowment. Looking forward, the rural and mining sectors were jointly to provide the basis for much of Australia's growth and prosperity even though farming moved well beyond its initial concentration on wool production, and the output of the mining industry diversified beyond copper and gold.

　The primary mechanism linking the gold discoveries and the increase in future wealth they represented with the level of economic activity was the dramatic increase in immigration. The "rush" phenomenon knew few boundaries. There was no effective control over the movement of people across colonial borders or from abroad, and a "national" immigration-policy regime had to await federation in 1901. As a result, whereas in 1850 the non-indigenous population was about 400,000, by the end of the decade it had almost tripled and was over 1.1 million. The immigrants were disproportionately male and of

---

[1]Trollope (1987 [1873]), vol. 1, p. 22.

working age, hence the workforce expanded even faster than the population.[2] Of itself, the increased participation rate accompanying the rushes would likely have resulted in a rise in per capita income.

Major shocks to an economy, whether positive or negative in their impact, offer a sort of natural experiment. This is because periods of extreme stress most clearly reveal the key mechanisms and complex interactions in an economy, whether the shock is triggered by natural calamity (e.g., drought), war, an external event (a boom or depression originating in the world economy), or, as in this case, a large natural resource discovery. There is another reason why economists are attracted to the study of major shocks. Some have long-lasting, even permanent effects on the performance of the economy, including cases in which the initial cause of the disturbance quickly fades. This persistence may arise because path dependence and "lock-in" prevents a return to preshock economic conditions or performance. Although the shock itself may be of limited duration, the economy is pushed in a direction it would not otherwise have taken, and one that cannot be reversed. I believe this to be true of the gold rush episode.

There may also be enduring effects of a shock that arise from the nature of the responses to it. A shock may "stress-test" a country's economic institutions and the quality of its policy-making. Indeed some economists believe that a significant determinant of current differences in income levels across countries can be attributed to the appropriateness of the policy responses to major shocks.[3] The gold rushes will not be the only example in the history of the Australian economy I will look at from this perspective. A similar approach will be adopted with respect to the 1890s depression and drought, the two world wars, the depression of the 1930s, and the resources boom at the end of the twentieth century. But the mid-nineteenth-century gold rush offers an early opportunity to explore the implications for Australian prosperity of the policy responses to a major shock.

Two further features of the period following the gold discoveries are of particular relevance. Both are treated as rather obvious in most historical accounts, but warrant closer scrutiny here. One is that the rushes were no flash in the pan. That is, the economic effects of the discoveries were sustained, not transitory. Yet the latter outcome has often been characteristic of gold or other mineral discoveries in unsettled or sparsely settled territory, and did arise at a local or regional level following some of the minor Australian discoveries (such as in Queensland) later in the century. This is the phenomenon that produces ghost mining towns. But collectively, and viewed from a national perspective, the major discoveries in Australia had a sustained economic impact best illustrated

---

[2] The workforce estimates for 1851 and 1861 are from Vamplew (1987), p. 147.
[3] Rodrik (1999).

by those who rushed in choosing not to rush out soon after. Given our focus on prosperity and its determinants, a second key feature of the gold rush is that it constituted a *favorable* shock to the economy. Both extensive and intensive growth resulted from this major addition to the country's resource endowment. That is, despite the flood of immigrants, per capita income was 6 percent higher at the end than at the beginning of the 1850s.[4]

There were other developments during the 1850s that contributed to this eventful decade having particular relevance to the story of Australia's prosperity. The following are illustrative but not exhaustive. This decade witnessed the commencement of overseas borrowing by governments: in 1858 Victoria raised a loan on the London capital market.[5] It was also the decade in which for the first time significant numbers of Asian immigrants arrived (mainly Chinese drawn to the goldfields), thereby qualifying the usual shorthand description of non-indigenous Australians as of European descent.[6] And it was the decade in which the dominance of Sydney was challenged by Melbourne: for at least the next century and a half Australia was to have two major urban economies. The gold rush also coincided with significant political and constitutional changes. Victoria and Queensland were separated from New South Wales, creating the six colonies that are today's six Australian states. And during the decade, responsible government was granted to five of the colonies, the exception being Western Australia, the least populous, which followed suit in 1890. The colonies became, in large measure, independent political entities, with the notable exceptions of defense and foreign relations. They retained the British Crown as head of state, and the Privy Council in London was the highest court of appeal. Also, given the overwhelming preponderance of British among the immigrants, the Australian colonies remained culturally closely tied to the imperial power. But they were independent in most areas relating to their economies and to economic policy.

As the favorable impact of the gold rush on prosperity persisted for several decades, it is appropriate to treat the period from 1851 to 1890 as a single era of economic expansion, rapidly increasing population, and rising incomes. Therefore in this chapter we will range over this entire forty-year period. No similar "golden age" was to recur in Australia until the economic boom that began after

---

[4]This is based on a comparison of the three-year averages for 1849–51 and 1858–60 of real "white" GDP per capita reported in Butlin (1986, p. 113). The peak year during the decade was 1853, when per capita GDP was 32 percent above its pre-rush average. Real wages between 1850 and 1860 rose 17 percent in New South Wales, but were 8 percent lower in Victoria (Maddock and McLean 1984, p. 1055): a weighted average for the two yields a rise of 2 percent.

[5]The 1858 Victorian loan was for seven million pounds. New South Wales had raised small amounts beginning in 1856, but these did not exceed one million pounds until 1868 (Lamb 1964).

[6]Census-based estimates for 1861 record 38,742 giving China as their place of birth; this represents 3.4 percent of the population (Vamplew 1987, pp. 8–9).

(or, by some measures, during) the Second World War and ended in the early 1970s, hence having a duration of twenty-five to thirty years. By contrast the most recent period of uninterrupted growth and rising prosperity since 1991 has, at the time of writing, lasted "only" twenty years.

This time frame of four decades is not the one usually adopted. In the historical literature, discussion of the long boom in the nineteenth century conventionally begins with 1861. But there was no break in economic activity in 1861; and neither is there any basis in political or social history for marking that year as a turning point in the country's fortunes. Rather, the convention of dating the beginning of the boom in 1861 results primarily from the start year adopted in two influential historical studies. Comprehensive annual estimates of Australian GDP, investment, and the balance of payments begin in 1861 in the historical time series estimates of Noel Butlin.[7] When he followed up his statistical volume with a detailed account of the growth of the economy to the end of the nineteenth century, he chose, unsurprisingly, to start his discussion with the year in which his rich collection of economic statistics began—1861.[8] The artificial benchmark year has, regrettably, stuck. But we will not be bound by it even if the range and quality of statistical evidence on the economy vastly improves from the early 1860s.

In the three decades after 1860, incomes continued to rise at the healthy clip of 1.3 percent per annum (the average rate between 1861 and 1889). This was achieved despite rapid population growth driven in part by high levels of immigration. In 1861 the population was 1.15 million; by 1891 it had almost trebled to reach 3.17 million. That is, there was rapid *extensive* growth at the same time as living standards were both high and rising. Indeed, the aggregate economy sustained a growth rate averaging 4.8 percent per annum for the entire period from 1861 to 1889, a performance that compares favorably with the most successful among the rapidly developing economies in recent times.[9] The focus here, however, is an explanation of the sustained increase in per capita income across the forty-year boom. We defer to the next chapter an assessment of prosperity *relative to* that achieved during this period in those other economies with which it is appropriate to benchmark the Australian record.

---

[7] Butlin (1962). His choice of this year arose from its being the earliest in which sufficient information was available on economic activity for all the colonies to provide a solid basis for his Australia-wide estimates. More than two decades later Butlin extended his exercise in historical national accounting to cover years prior to 1861, but this encompassed a much narrower range of indicators and was based on more fragmentary and less reliable evidence than employed in his earlier work covering the years after 1860. Regrettably, there is a break in his constant-price estimates of GDP between 1860 and 1861. See Butlin (1986) and Butlin and Sinclair (1986).

[8] Butlin (1964).

[9] The population data are from Vamplew (1987), p. 26. The aggregate and per capita GDP growth rates are from Maddock and McLean (1987b), p. 14.

THE ECONOMIC EFFECTS OF GOLD: AVOIDING THE RESOURCE CURSE

To understand how the rush resulted in a sustained rise in prosperity, we need to examine some aspects of its short-run effects. In fact, it is possible that the initial impact of the discovery of gold on the economy was negative. Contemporary reports indicate that a sudden migration of predominantely young, male gold seekers from other occupations and colonies caused some degree of economic dislocation. Of course we lack the quarterly and monthly data now available on production and employment by industry and region that would enable a clearer picture to be drawn of what happened in those first months of the rushes. The pastoralists complained that they could not retain essential workers, such as shepherds. There are accounts of the marked absence of young men among the populations of towns, suggesting that urban employment and hence output might both have declined. Whether total output in the economy fell depends in part on whether the adversely affected industries were able quickly to find substitute labor.

But offsetting this negative short-run impact was the rise in economic activity in Victoria directly and indirectly associated with the diggings—and not just by the value of gold found. Further, we know this happened very quickly. One crucial factor was the low barriers to entry in the alluvial goldfields. Indeed, the initial rush of would-be miners only occurred because of this. All one needed was a shovel, a pan, some food, and a tent, and, perhaps accompanied by one or more similarly equipped colleagues, one headed to the diggings—on horseback or even on foot. The alluvial nature of the initial discoveries meant that individuals or small groups of miners could form a viable production unit. Hence tent encampments—small towns—sprang up almost overnight at the sites of promising gold finds. These miners had to be fed, clothed, and supplied with mining tools, so ancillary economic activity emerged from the beginning of mining operations. All this activity, including the gold found, boosted economic activity.

It was about a year until the arrival of the first immigrants whose decision to migrate was made in response to the news of the gold finds, hence the dislocation was confined initially to churning in the domestic labor market. And there is evidence that disappointed gold seekers returned to their homes and usual occupations quite quickly. One can guess at the reasons for the return flows beginning after only a short period. Some would have had access to limited savings to sustain themselves at the diggings, and if they did not find enough gold to meet expenses would soon be driven home by financial necessity. Some would have found themselves physically unsuited to the work of mining, or found that what they initially saw as something of an adventure quickly lost its romantic appeal. Others would have recalibrated the risks associated with their move to the diggings once they got there and acquired more information about the probability of striking it rich—or of just breaking even. We should not lose sight of the rush as a type of lottery in which there is the thrill of participation in the small probability of significant financial gain, but with the crucial difference from present-day lotteries that the probability distribution of outcomes was initially unknown. A few weeks panning on a given site would change that, with daily updates on the richness or paucity of the gold in the area. For these reasons a "rush" to any new location could also trigger as dramatic a reverse flow if glowing early reports proved spurious or exaggerated. Hence, this initial phase of disruption to the wider economy may have been relatively short-lived.

By 1852, with the arrival of immigrants attracted by news of the discoveries, and with the richness of the goldfields confirmed by rising production levels, the medium-term effects on the economy became clearer. One helpful way to view these is to treat the gold rushes as an example of a supply-side shock triggering so-called Dutch-disease effects, deploying the economists' models of such an event. These models will also prove useful during our examination of later episodes in Australian history. Perhaps their best-known implication is the so-called Gregory effect—the mechanism linking the expansion in the mining industry beginning in the 1960s with the subsequent decline in the relative size of the manufacturing sector (deindustrialization). The gold rushes provide an early illustration of the adjustments in the economy that occur in response to this type of shock, and—more important—assist our account as to why the economy emerged not just significantly changed but also more prosperous.[10]

In a pattern that was to be repeated—with some variation—over a century later, the "resource boom" triggered by the gold discoveries led to positive effects for some parts of the economy during the 1850s and beyond, but had a negative impact on others. Positively affected were activities directly associated with supplying the miners' needs, such as food and mining equipment, and the transport of people and supplies. In these activities, prices, wages, and presumably profits all rose, drawing labor and other resources from elsewhere in the domestic economy as well as from imports. Indeed, there may have been higher—and less volatile—earnings made on average in these ancillary employments than those made by a miner. Adversely affected were those sectors of the economy that lost labor to the diggings, and/or that had to pay higher wages to retain labor but could not pass on these increased costs in higher prices. A builder in Melbourne could recover the higher wages needed to secure tradesmen and building laborers because there was a boom in construction and house prices were rising. In contrast, the pastoralist was restricted in his ability to raise wages in order to retain stockmen tempted to seek their fortune on the goldfields, as the price of wool was determined at sales in London and this was little influenced by the commotion in faraway Victoria. This pattern of adjustments among sectors and occupations resulting from the shock of the gold

---

[10] A detailed treatment of the gold rushes from this perspective is provided in Maddock and McLean (1984).

discoveries closely fits the pattern economists have observed following comparable shocks or booms elsewhere.[11]

With the arrival from late 1852 of large numbers of immigrants, the economy began a process of re-equilibration. The labor influx was so large relative to the population that this occurred surprisingly quickly. The spikes in wages and prices in the occupations and sectors most directly and favorably affected were substantially reduced within a few years. Remember that this economy had no effective border or immigration controls to inhibit labor inflows. Also pertinent to this speedy rebalancing in the economy was its institutional arrangements: relative to a modern economy, that of the 1850s was almost totally unregulated. There were few barriers faced in establishing or operating a business or in hiring or firing labor. In the history of the Australian economy, this surely has to be the limiting case of great adaptability in the face of a major exogenous shock.

The initial rise in the general price level following the discoveries was quickly squeezed out of the macro-economy by highly responsive supplies of both immigrants and imported goods, and by the flexibility of the labor market. Hence there was no wage-price spiral, locking in the inflationary spike—as would occur following the oil price shocks in the 1970s, and bedeviling attempts to restore low inflationary growth and stability to the economy until the early 1990s. Other examples abound of responses to radically changed economic circumstances that assisted the postshock re-equilibration. Pastoralists exploited the joint-product (meat and wool) attribute of their sheep by driving them to the goldfields for slaughter as a result of high meat prices and in the face of a shortage of shearers. They also lobbied for the selective immigration of shepherds. Building workers in Melbourne enjoyed such high demand for their labor that they started trading that for leisure, securing an eight-hour working-day regime.[12]

The initial boom contained a major speculative component that could have led to a serious bust. But this potential was avoided by the speedy downward readjustments in product prices as imports rose and in wages as immigrants poured in. Hence there was no bust. Pertinent to our interest in prosperity, real income at the end of the decade had not fallen below its pre-gold levels; there was no mass exodus of disappointed fortune seekers; and the population continued to rise, albeit at a less hectic rate. And it should not be overlooked that this re-equilibration occurred without a national government, and with colonial governments in each of the affected colonies lacking many of the institutions and sources of advice now regarded as essential for macro-economic management—such as a central bank and a phalanx of economists.

---

[11] These relative price effects may be offset to some degree by the positive income effects of the boom.

[12] Hughes (1961).

An additional reason for the economy's successful negotiation of these first turbulent years was the absence of growth-retarding distributional conflict. Whatever the cultural significance of the miners' riot or rebellion in 1854, it had little economic importance—other than as an exception highlighting the generally peaceable fashion in which society allocated the rents from gold. The critical issues of determining access to, and the distribution of returns from, the resource discoveries were resolved in ways that provided wide opportunities to directly participate in the gold-seeking "lottery" and spread the indirect benefits widely. This reduced the scope for distributional conflict over sharing in the benefits of the boom. Note that the distributional issues include intergenerational ones. Here is the importance of diverting rents to investment in infrastructure and assisted immigration, and borrowing abroad on the security of the expected future resource riches to fund more development-oriented projects (of which more later).

The key elements in the story of how the benefits of the resource bonanza were shared are well known, although their economic significance is less obvious. The Victorian government at first prescribed a very small claim size on the diggings, eight feet by eight feet. One motive may have been to concentrate the miners in as small a region as possible to reduce the costs of administration and of maintaining law and order on the goldfields. The government's fears of disturbances in the mining encampments were based in part on its knowledge of the lawlessness associated with the California gold rush, and partly on the need to avoid spreading too thinly the limited police and military resources at its disposal.[13] The small claim size had the consequence, however, of increasing the numbers who had access to the lottery that constituted working on any field. Whether or not this was intended, the effect was to widen access to, and more widely distribute the benefits of, the discoveries.

The infamous miner's license and fee imposed by the government also probably had mixed motives. The government needed additional revenue to police and to administer the goldfields, and to cope with the increased demands on its resources resulting from the unexpected boom in the population of the colony. Some form of tax on the booming sector was an obvious response. At the same time, a fee to obtain a license to mine would in principle have had some deterrent effect on the disruption in the colonial labor market caused by the discoveries. It constituted a small barrier to entry into the industry (the price of the lottery ticket, as it were), and, since it had to be paid every month, an inducement to exit the industry if one's income from mining was modest.

---

[13] In contrast to the situation in California in 1848, when gold was discovered in Victoria in 1851, there was a functioning government, including a legal framework for mining. The very different institutional context in California is described in Clay and Wright (2005, especially pp. 159–71) and in the literature they cite.

Here is evidence of a government endeavoring to cope with increased demand for its services (and not just those related to law and order), while also trying to lessen the disruption to existing economic activities brought about by the rush.[14]

Whatever the intention, the license fee was considered unjust and constituted an important element in the story of the 1854 Eureka stockade "rebellion" at Ballarat, west of Melbourne. An economic perspective on this episode highlights other aspects. As a "tax," it was levied as an entry fee to employment in an industry—paid before any income could be earned in that industry. This sort of arrangement is not unknown elsewhere in the economy (think of taxi plates), but was unusual in that the probability of gain (profit) from gold mining was much more difficult to estimate at the time the up-front license fee had to be paid than is the case in most occupations or business ventures. Especially at the beginning of the rush, it was extremely difficult to predict, ex ante, the distribution of returns among individual miners, and what would determine that distribution. Again, contrast this with a lottery: the payout distribution is known to all ticket buyers; and the probability of success by any individual is known to be strictly random. The alternative ways to raise revenue from gold mining might have included a production tax levied per fine ounce, and at the point of first sale on the fields to the gold commissioners, banks, or storekeepers, but this would have been expensive to collect. Income taxes were even further beyond the administrative machinery of the times. So the hated miner's license fee was replaced with a tax on the export of gold. The levy fell on successful miners (and then only indirectly) rather than everyone at work on the diggings. And it was imposed at an administratively convenient point in the shipping of the product. One in-principle deficiency of an export tax is the incentive to smuggle, and gold is perfect for this because it is nonperishable and of high value relative to its bulk. But the incentive to smuggle is also a function of the size of the tax, which was not especially high in this case. And Australia had no land borders or close neighbors, which would have lowered the costs of smuggling. Nonetheless, we will never know the extent to which returning Chinese miners carried home their finds from the diggings, leading to some understatement in recorded gold production at the time.

The precise distribution of miners' returns during the initial alluvial phase is, of course, not known. Some indication of the *average* returns may be obtained by dividing the value of gold produced by the estimated number of persons employed in gold mining. Although the production estimates are likely to be fairly accurate, the workforce engaged in mining was in constant flux, so that estimates of the numbers of miners on the goldfields at the time of a census may not reflect the average over the year. Nonetheless, an "implicit" wage of the

---

[14]A detailed analysis is provided by La Croix (1992), who also offers a comparison with conditions on the California goldfields.

average miner has been computed by this method. It shows a dramatic rise in 1852, then a decline, relative to alternative occupations, across the 1850s, consistent with observed flows of labor to and from the diggings.[15] But the average return to mining tells us nothing about the distribution, knowledge of which would enhance understanding of how widespread were the first-round benefits of the discoveries. After all, the "rush" phenomenon is driven by the expectation of above-average gain.[16]

As gold production evolved from its alluvial to a more capital-intensive quartz mining phase there was a shift in the distribution of benefits.[17] The small group of diggers working together on a surface claim of small size gave way to corporate ownership of enterprises and the employment of wage labor in deep shaft mining covering a much larger claim. However, the wages paid to miners had to match those paid elsewhere in what remained a high-wage economy; and the shares in mining companies were publicly traded.

These relatively egalitarian distributional outcomes, achieved in a fairly benign fashion, might have been very different. In principle, access rights to each goldfield could have been assigned by the governor or auctioned off to an individual or company, and the mining undertaken by wage labor, as happened with some gold deposits in Latin America. The long-run consequences—political, social, and economic—would have been very different from what actually occurred. In practice, such an initial response was unlikely to have arisen in the prevailing conditions. Under British law all gold discovered belonged to the Crown. The alluvial nature of the initial discoveries made it hard to prevent access to the fields, which, in any event, were scattered across a wide area of almost unsettled territory. The law-enforcement resources of the state were extremely limited. And, perhaps most important, the rapidly evolving political situation in the colonies, and the general temper of a colonial society already clearly determined to resist the unequal distribution of farming land, would have cautioned the authorities against provoking popular discontent with policies that limited access or diverted the stream of benefits to narrow interests.

Note the contrast with access to the other abundant natural resource—rural land. There, the initial phase of occupation was highly skewed toward a relatively few squatters who thereby gained a high proportion of the rents from the resource. The process of broadening this access, and redistributing the rents, was politically and socially divisive, extending over several decades. In the case of gold, the conditions governing initial access to the resource were extremely

---

[15]Maddock and McLean (1984), pp. 1051–52.

[16]Lacking income data at the level of the individual, Serle (1963, pp. 85–86 and 391–92) used contemporary qualitative evidence to speculate about the variation in the earnings of individual miners.

[17]Surface-level alluvial mining was known as placer mining on California's fields; quartz mining was also referred to as reef mining and typically involved drilling a shaft to conduct underground operations.

open, encouraging mass entry into the industry. The later evolution of mining into its corporate form occurred alongside the persistence of small-scale enterprises and solo fossickers, the mix varying by location and depending on the nature of the ore body.

One indicator of the long-term economic impact of the discoveries is the level of gold output over the next four decades. Gold production averaged 3 million fine ounces per annum in the 1850s. In the 1860s this declined, but only to about 2.5 million fine ounces. In the following two decades it fell further, to about 2 million and 1.5 million fine ounces in the 1870s and 1880s, respectively. That is, more than thirty years after the initial gold rush, Australian production was still at 50 percent of its peak level. Since (nominal) gold prices were essentially stable, this trend in production closely corresponds to that in the (nominal) value of gold produced. There was no collapse of output following the initial spike, but rather a very gradual decline over more than thirty years, followed by a fresh round of major discoveries in Western Australia in the 1890s that boosted production levels back to their 1850s level of 3 million fine ounces annually. This contrasts with the experience of California. There, peak production in the 1850s was also about 3 million fine ounces annually. However it declined much more rapidly than in Australia to less than a third of this by the early 1860s, after which it remained fairly constant.[18] In this respect the two rushes on opposite sides of the Pacific have differing long-run trajectories. However, caution must be exercised in comparing these regions. From its initial location primarily in Victoria, the gold industry spread over the following few decades not just to New South Wales but also to Queensland, prior to the establishment of the Western Australian goldfields in the 1890s. Likewise in California, the discoveries at Sutter's Mill marked just the first of a succession of later finds throughout not just that state but in what would later become Nevada and beyond, with San Francisco the center of a mining-based boom extending east through the Sierras and north to British Columbia.

So the benefits of the gold discoveries were long term rather than a flash in the pan because of the sheer size of the gold deposits, revealed by the sequence of subsequent discoveries and the continuing high levels of gold production. The share of total employment in mining quickly fell from its gold-rush peak in the 1850s, but remained above 5 percent for the rest of the century—considerably higher than the share recorded in the mining boom of recent years (figure 5.1). The contribution of mining to GDP similarly fell away from its initial peak as the booming economy quickly diversified, but remained above 10 percent until

---

[18]Clay and Jones (2008), figure 1, p. 1000.

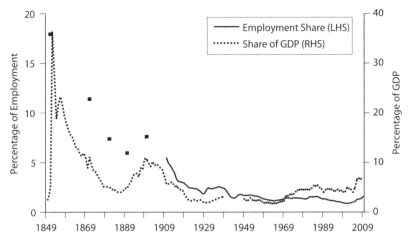

Figure 5.1. Mining shares of total employment and GDP, 1849 to 2009.
Note: Employment data before 1890 are for Victoria, New South Wales, Queensland, and South Australia.
Source: Battellino (2010), Graphs 1 and 2.

the 1870s.[19] As in the case of employment, this is a larger direct contribution to economic activity than the mining sector has made in recent years.

The sustained economic importance of gold may also be conveyed by its contribution to exports. Wool dominated export receipts to 1850, but the value of gold exports exceeded that of wool for the next twenty years. It is also important to counter the impression sometimes conveyed by historical accounts that gold was of importance in the economy only during the 1850s—often alluded to as "the gold rush decade." The rush phenomenon in its popularly conceived and demographic form was indeed confined to this decade. But the same cannot be said of activity levels in the gold industry, or of gold's continuing major contribution to the economy. In the 1870s, when wool finally regains its status as the principal export commodity, gold accounts for over 28 percent of total exports. Indeed, in the 1880s, at the height of the second pastoral boom, gold exports were still worth 16 percent of all exports.[20] By the end of the 1890s, with the collapse of the wool industry on the one hand, and on the other the Western Australian gold finds, gold exports were approximately equal in value to those of wool, each at just over 30 percent of the total.

---

[19]Detailed estimates of the value of total mineral production are available from 1861. Gold accounted for 89, 73, and 57 percent during the three decades beginning, respectively, 1861, 1871, and 1881 (Butlin 1962, table 55, p. 115). Copper was the second most important mineral by value in both the 1860s and 1870s; black coal in the 1880s.

[20]Vamplew (1987), p. 188.

A second reason a "bust" did not occur following the initial gold boom is that, as noted already, the immigrants who "rushed" in did not flow out. Some left for other occupations as the gold industry became more capital intensive with the decline of alluvial and rise of quartz mining, or left Victoria for other colonies. But the proportion that left Australia was small. Two groups who did were returning Chinese miners (though some stayed), and those attracted by the gold discoveries in New Zealand—especially to the Otago fields in the early 1860s.[21]

Why did they stay after the alluvial gold discoveries became smaller and less frequent? Perhaps the most important reason is that the colonial governments, and not just in Victoria, saw the long-run development potential from what they guessed (or feared) might be a very short-run boom-bust episode. There was no "economic planning" as we might today observe in a less-developed country, or "structural adjustment assistance" of the sort seen in a modern de-veloped economy. But, looking back, it is remarkable the extent to which the colonial governments acted *as if* they were engaged in a development strategy to garner long-term benefits from what might well be a short-lived boom if left to its own dynamic. There are numerous illustrations of policy responses consistent with this interpretation. The subsidization of young single female immigrants was not novel, having been a feature of New South Wales policies in the 1840s. But the economic benefits might include encouraging marriage and permanent settlement among the young single males who had arrived dur-ing the rush. Colonial government policies to increase the rate of agricultural development by opening additional farming areas to settlement had a similar motivation. And the advocacy by some that protective tariffs be introduced as an incentive to employment creation in colonial manufacturing was couched in the same terms—and, with some delay, implemented in Victoria. A further expression of this developmental agenda is the Victorian government's entry into the London capital market in 1858. The British funds were to be used for what we would now call public works or infrastructure spending—especially on railways and urban utilities.

A third reason for the long-term rather than transitory economic impact of the gold rushes was their demographic effect.[22] The age distribution of the population was impacted first by the preponderance of young adults in the ini-tial immigrant rush, then by the rise in the birth rate as they stayed and formed new families. The first-round economic consequences of this were to stimulate the demand for housing and, indirectly, for a range of population-sensitive con-struction. This was most evident in the expansion of urban areas—including

---

[21] Of course, the latter did not constitute a loss of population to the "Australasian" economy of the time.

[22] The long-run economic effects of the demographic shock accompanying the gold rushes of the 1850s have been well documented: see Hall (1963a) and Kelley (1965, 1968).

commercial buildings as well as transport and utilities infrastructure such as roads, tramways, railways, ports, and water and gas networks.[23] The rapid expansion of Melbourne, and especially its overtaking of Sydney as the largest city, is the clearest illustration of the impact on the urban economy of the population explosion accompanying the gold rushes.

There were also second- and later-round economic effects of the demographic shock of the 1850s. A generation later, the children of the gold-rush generation formed their own households. The initial "kink" in the age distribution had an echo around twenty-five years later. Thus the property boom of the 1880s, most pronounced in Melbourne, was in part demand driven and a lagged result of the earlier rushes. These interactions between demographic shocks and fluctuations in the demand for particular types of investment activity can be large enough to significantly determine the course of aggregate activity in the economy. And this was the case with the Victorian economy in particular in the several decades that followed the gold rush. There are multiple reasons for the prosperity associated with the 1880s, as we will later see. But the long-term impact of the gold rushes, operating over several decades through its demographic effects, made an important contribution.

These long-run economic-demographic interactions affecting investment and output levels in the economy are especially clearly illustrated in post–gold rush Australia because of the relatively large size of the initial population shock. But they are not unique to this period. Variations in the levels of immigration have frequently imparted lesser shocks to the rate of population growth and/or kinks to the age distribution. Sometimes these have economic origins. The downturn in the economy after 1890 resulted in a long period of low or negative immigration and slower population growth. And the depression of the 1930s led to postponed marriages and a decline in the birth rate as well as reduced immigration rates. War can also inflict demographic shocks with long-run economic consequences. The casualties of the two world wars were concentrated in young adult males, and on these occasions there were also declines in rates of marriage and immigration. In more recent Australian history the clearest as well as the most familiar example of the phenomenon was the post-1945 baby boom. Its origins are very different from that following the gold rushes. But demographic shocks are central elements in the two longest economic booms the country has experienced.

The long-run economic benefits obtained from the exploitation of a nonrenewable resource were also the result of the location of the midcentury gold discoveries, most of which were made either in, or not far from, settled areas, even if the settlement was new and consisted of low-density pastoral occupation. The Victorian goldfields were also relatively close (about 150 kilometers) to the

---

[23]See Butlin (1964, chapters 3 and 4) for a detailed analysis of investment in urban infrastructure during the second half of the nineteenth century.

ports and towns of Melbourne and Geelong, which, though less than twenty years had passed since their foundation, had the potential to rapidly expand in size. Further, areas of land between Melbourne and the goldfields were already being settled by farmers producing cereals and dairy and horticultural products, while the land immediately surrounding the goldfields was suitable for conversion from pastoral to more intensive agricultural pursuits in response to the rapid increase in demand for food and fuel (hay and oats for horses). These geographic considerations determined the extent to which the demand emanating from the gold rushes was lost to imports and the extent to which it became a source of growth in domestic economic activity.

At first sight this is pure luck. Had gold been found in 1851 in, say, the Pilbara region of northwest Western Australia, where a century later vast reserves of iron ore were discovered and mined, it seems highly improbable that the stimulus to the Australian economy in either the short or long run would have been anything approaching that resulting from the Victorian discoveries. There was little potential in the arid Pilbara for local production of food or other supplies, hence all inputs required by the mining camps would have been shipped long-distance. The tiny settlement on the Swan River (Perth) was the closest, at over 1,500 kilometers, and would have received some stimulus. But imports would surely have accounted for much more than they did in Victoria. That is, much of the economic activity generated by a rush to the Pilbara in 1851 would have been lost to the domestic economy. Further, there would have been no employment opportunities in the Pilbara for ex-miners as the alluvial phase of gold production declined, such as was afforded by the expansion of Victorian farming or the growth of manufacturing and service industries in Melbourne. Hence a Pilbara rush in the 1850s would likely have been a transitory affair, at best bequeathing a modest-sized and isolated settlement to the region, just as later mineral finds in the remote outback were to result in towns such as Mount Isa in Queensland, Broken Hill in New South Wales, and Kalgoorlie in Western Australia.

However, perhaps this location issue is not simply a matter of luck. Gold and other minerals were found in more remote areas of Australia—but later. So it is likely that the timing of the 1851 discoveries was in part related to the timing and pattern of exploration and initial pastoral occupation of southeastern Australia.[24] We will return to this theme in a later discussion about the mid-twentieth-century mineral and energy discoveries, and will consider there whether they can better be regarded as endogenous to economic activity, or as truly exogenous and resulting from something random and appropriately thought of as "luck" (chapter 7).

---

[24]On the determinants of mineral discovery, see Blainey (1970) and Eichengreen and McLean (1994).

Any evaluation of the contribution of gold to Australian prosperity requires an assessment of what would have happened in its absence. This is usually left implicit in historians' accounts of the period. However, constructing an explicit counterfactual is made especially difficult in this instance because the economic disturbance the discoveries unleashed was large relative to the size of the pre-gold economy and pervasive in that few regions or industries were unaffected. But it is worth sketching a thought experiment on the topic.

The massive population expansion beginning in 1852 would not have occurred without gold. Instead, there would have been more modest growth via much lower levels of immigration. Some of the positive economic effects of the discovery of gold to which we have referred constituted simply an acceleration of what would have occurred without gold, but been longer in coming; others may never have occurred. An example of the former is the timing of the Victorian government loan raisings in the London market. An example of the latter is the overtaking of Sydney by Melbourne as the largest city (until the end of the nineteenth century) and dominant financial center of Australia (until the end of the twentieth century). Rural development, the spread of settlement, and expansion of farm exports would have underpinned growth in a no-gold world, as they had prior to the gold discoveries, and to which they contributed thereafter. The growth of those rural industries not primarily oriented to export markets at that time, such as dairying and horticulture, would have been slower, and this effect may have been especially pronounced in Victoria. Perhaps the expanding wheat industry would have contributed more to exports in a no-gold Australia with its smaller population. However, since the location of rural production is largely determined by climatic and soil conditions as well as transport costs, in the long run it is likely the same mix of farming activities would have arisen, and with the same regional pattern of specialization.

With a slower expansion of population, of urbanization, and of rural development, the aggregate economy would have been smaller than it was—perhaps at any subsequent date. It is trickier to guess at the counterfactual income per capita. We have observed that the re-equilibration of the economy after the positive shock of the discoveries left GDP per person above what it had been in 1850 although below its peak. But it does not follow that per capita incomes may not also have risen in the smaller and less populous no-gold economy between, say, 1850 and 1860. This requires a more thorough modeling exercise than has been so far done, or can be done here. The safer conclusion is that, in addition to delivering a permanently larger population and economy, the discovery of gold was *associated* with a sustained rise in Australia's already relatively high incomes. Measured in terms of this key indicator of economic prosperity, the gold rush was neither a flash in the pan nor an example of the so-called resource curse.

Consolidating Democracy and Resolving the Squatter-Selector Conflict

The drafting of the colonial constitutions in the early 1850s occurred against the background of the economic bonanza and population disruption associated with the gold rushes, and historians have debated the relationship between the two. One point of agreement is that the discovery of gold accelerated the political reform already under way: "Responsible government might not have been established when it was, if it had not been for the great strengthening of the middle class brought about by the gold discoveries. Moreover, without this middle order of liberal-minded but respectable townspeople, self-governing institutions would probably not have functioned as smoothly as they did."[25] In the context of the narrative in the previous chapter, the goal of the landed interests to maintain as much of their political power as possible in the writing of the colonies' constitutions, and hence through the design of the new colonial parliaments, was made more difficult.[26]

In the battle to enshrine democratic forms in the new political institutions in the Australian colonies, one major issue was the composition and power of the upper houses of the new legislatures. And it was in the upper houses that the squatter interest retained greater influence. A key point of contention was thus whether membership in these would be by nomination or election. The former mode was adopted in New South Wales and Queensland. A second issue was the breadth of the franchise for these upper houses, especially the extent to which the property qualification would be more restrictive than for the lower houses. Other issues critical to the progress of democratic reform concerned the power of the upper houses to block appropriation bills or reject other legislation originating in the lower houses (where the government was formed), and the extent of the discretionary powers of the colonial governor in times of political deadlock between the two houses. Colonial politics for several decades was complex, messy, and fluid, with recurring serious tensions over these fundamental issues. But the squatter influence in the upper houses, though able to frustrate and delay, was never sufficient to permanently block the will of the majority in the more representative lower house. Perhaps the touchstone issue here concerned land policies that aimed to subdivide and redistribute the pastoral leases of the squatters to would-be farmers during the 1860s and 1870s.

This is important in our search for the bases of Australian prosperity because the assignment of property rights in rural land must be conducive to landown-

---

[25]Ward (1992, pp. 167–68).

[26]"Historians have warned against a temptation to find in these gold-rushes the cause of developments which would have happened, if more slowly, without them. Merchants, shop-keepers and artisans would have fought the squatters' monopoly in any case, and would in time have won their victories for 'democracy'" (Crawford, 1979, p. 104).

ers maximizing output and productivity. It is also important because the distribution of ownership of one of the major sources of wealth in the nineteenth century was at issue, and we have previously noted the relationship in the long run between wealth inequality and prosperity. It remained uncertain whether rural Australia faced a Jeffersonian or an Argentine future, despite the victories for the former outcome in the 1847 regulations and in the constitutional changes of the 1850s.

In Victoria in the late 1850s and early 1860s, there was both unemployment and out-migration to the newly discovered goldfields in New Zealand, hence the colonial government was anxious that population gains be retained, and making land available to more would-be farmers seemed the principal way to achieve this. Most likely the gold rush only brought forward a demand to "unlock" (the term used at the time) the pastoral leases that would have arisen anyway with the continued but very much slower immigration of free settlers, the rise in urban demand for agricultural products, and the growth in knowledge of the agricultural potential of land currently used solely for grazing sheep. This conjecture is supported by the fact that agitation to unlock these lands was not confined to Victoria.[27]

This second stage of the disposal of Australia's public lands looks somewhat like that which occurred in the United States under the Homestead Act of 1862, and close attention was paid to contemporary developments there. The aim was to create large numbers of medium-sized family farms for "selection" from Crown land currently on pastoral lease; hence the episode is known as the "squatter-selector" conflict. Here the economic interests are reasonably well defined, with the resolution of the conflict occurring within the institutional framework created by the granting of responsible government. However the combination of finding gold and the constitutional concessions by Britain had significantly reduced both the economic and political power of the squatters compared to their position immediately after the 1847 regulations.

Under the selection acts in the colonies, millions of acres of land were sold. Typical selection sizes were 320 or 640 acres, with survey before selection (other than in New South Wales), and a complex and changing set of auction or conditional grant mechanisms used for the allocation to would-be farmers. For contemporaries and historians alike the major issue has been the degree to which the original intention of the framers of the legislation was undermined—that is, the extent to which the squatters were able to preserve the best land for themselves and their families through corrupting the selection process. The consensus is that the squatters sabotaged the aims of the legislation and retained considerable landed wealth, an assessment that appears to support the conjectural history sketched in the previous chapter, and suggests that this

---

[27]The main pieces of legislation were Robertson's Act in New South Wales in 1861, Grant's Act in Victoria in 1865, and Strangways Act in South Australia in 1868.

squatter "victory" was a decisive outcome of critical importance to Australia's development.[28]

However, wool growing in semi-arid areas is subject to scale economies, and hence requires large land holdings. Also, both contemporary critics and most historians have judged the selection acts in terms of how much crop production expanded—in contrast to sheep numbers or wool production—employing this as an indicator of the desired "agricultural" (rather than "pastoral") development that selection was designed to promote. But the Australian climate and soils are such that even today the area cultivated remains small compared to the area of grazing land. The relevant information about soils and climate was not available at the time. Confusion about the economics of pioneer agriculture, as well as powerful ideological impulses, lay behind the campaign to break up the squatters' runs. Assessment of the agricultural as distinct from the pastoral potential of much of southeastern Australia was way too optimistic, driven by the development aims and revenue needs of the colonial governments, as well as a mistaken belief that much of the squatters' land could be turned into viable small family farms based on cropping.[29]

From a long-run development perspective, the squatters did not emerge victorious. The selection acts prevented those squatters who occupied good land from keeping all of it. In areas where small-scale agriculture was viable, they had to make way for the selectors, even if they often corruptly gained ownership of more of this land than was intended.[30] In the semi-arid zones, attempts to replace large grazing properties with small-scale crop farming failed spectacularly, and farm amalgamation or abandonment and reversion to wool production followed.[31] In the arid zone farther inland, only large-scale pastoral holdings were profitable. The chaotic selection process vastly increased knowledge about land use in Australia, however costly the acquisition of this information proved to be for the failed selectors. The squatters' economic position within the rural sector was diminished, but they survived wherever the most efficient use of land was large-scale pastoral farming.

The squatters' economic power waned for additional reasons. The emergence of the mining industry, some expansion of manufacturing, the rapid growth of the urban population, and the concomitant rise in food production (wheat,

---

[28]Historians also concur that the selection process was most corrupted by the squatters in New South Wales and least in South Australia.

[29]But this is not what is reported in much of the historical literature. An exception is the case study by Gammage (1990).

[30]"Despite the frauds and conflict which the [selection] acts produced, and their failure to promote rapid development in agriculture . . . thousands of people were able to use them to settle on the land. These success stories should not be gainsaid" (Hirst 1988, p. 152).

[31]In one of many regional studies of the implementation of the land acts, Meinig (1962) provides a clear account of the reasons for the failure of the selectors in the mid-north of South Australia.

dairy products, horticulture) all reduced the relative importance of pastoral production in the economy. A final phase of pastoral expansion into marginal inland areas in the 1880s was followed by financial collapse and drought in the 1890s. Further, the rise of mixed (wheat/sheep) farming, and the growth of the meat export trade following the introduction of refrigerated shipping in the 1880s, blurred the distinction between squatters and farmers.

Accordingly, in the analysis presented here, the squatter-selector conflict is not the potential turning point the historians make it out to be. Sequence matters. If the squatters had been granted freehold title in 1847, the outcome of the legislative fight over selection and closer settlement after 1860 would have been less certain. The squatters could, and did, fight to retain their privileged access to the land. And the historians' consensus about the squatters' ability to retain considerable chunks of good agricultural land in some areas where smaller farms might have been viable is correct. But it was a rearguard action. With the passage of the selection acts, the landed elite lost their ability to protect, by means of their dominance of the new colonial parliaments, the economic institution (large pastoral holdings on long-term leases from the Crown) on which their wealth was based. Hence they attempted to maintain their economic position by undermining the selection process in practice.

From this perspective, the squatter-selector conflict of the 1860s is better seen as a major challenge to, or test of, the political institutions created in the 1850s, but not so critical a challenge that these democratic institutions were themselves under threat. Separate and more detailed examination is required to determine whether specific aspects of the colonies' constitutions and electoral rules were influential in limiting corruption during the process of land selection, or exacerbated the problem of rent capture by the squatters and hence slowed economic growth. Nonetheless, the partial and messy re-allocation of considerable areas of Australian farmland occurred without bloodshed or revolution. The new political institutions provided the context for peacefully resolving what under other conditions might have provoked serious conflict, hence turning the country along an altogether different path of development.

The critical importance of the 1847 regulations governing the use of pastoral land, and their facilitation of the subsequent widening of land ownership in Australia, is now clear. It also was clear to a leading scholar of Argentine economic growth writing in the 1980s:

> Australian land policies are in substantial contrast to those of Argentina. For many years the British government did not surrender ownership of Australian land and, before independence, the Iberian monarchies followed a similar policy in their American domains. Sheep ranchers [i.e., the squatters] failed to get clear titles to their enormous enterprises during the crucial, formative years of Australia; opposition to their claims [came] from miners, land-hungry ex-miners, and urban groups. Ranchers remained an important

political force in Australia, but one which did not control government machinery as did landowners in Argentina. When cereals became an important Australian export, family-operated, medium-size farms were relatively more important than in Argentina, where tenant farming under contracts of about five years were more common than in Australia. A system of rural production, where tenant farmers moved frequently from one region to another, did not seem to damage Argentina's rural productivity and output growth before 1929, but it had deleterious effects on income distribution as well as on social and political life.[32]

And the marked divergence in economic performance in these two otherwise comparable settler economies after 1929 has been attributed to precisely these distributional, institutional, and political differences.[33]

OPENNESS AND GROWTH

As the contribution of the gold-mining sector to the domestic economy gradually declined, the rural sector resumed its leading role as an engine of growth, contributing both to the expansion of the economy and to increased prosperity. Before I assess the contribution of the rural industries, however, it is important to recognize how critical the favorable conditions prevailing in the international economy were to Australia's natural resource-based expansion and prosperity at this time.

International trade expanded rapidly during these decades, was centered in northwestern Europe (especially Britain), and reflected a simple geographic pattern of specialization. The industrializing "core" exploited its comparative advantage in the production of manufactured goods, which it exported to the non-industrialized "periphery" whose comparative advantage lay in natural-resource-intensive foodstuffs and raw materials. These were, in turn, exported back to the core economies. The Britain-Australia trading relationship closely fits this wider pattern. Australia exported gold, wool, and a few other rural products to Britain in exchange for a wide range of industrial goods. The Australian exports were largely unprocessed, with little value-adding occurring prior to shipment. The imported British manufactures were both investment and consumer goods, typically intensive in capital and skilled labor, and they embodied best-practice technology due to Britain's technological leadership at the time. The political links between Britain and its Australian colonies facilitated this trade, though were probably not essential to it, as attested by the similar British trading relationship with Argentina.

The importance of foreign trade to the economy may be measured by the ratio of exports to GDP, or by the ratio of trade (the sum of exports plus im-

---

[32]Diaz Alejandro (1985), pp. 101–102.
[33]See, for example, Duncan and Fogarty (1984), and Duncan (1985).

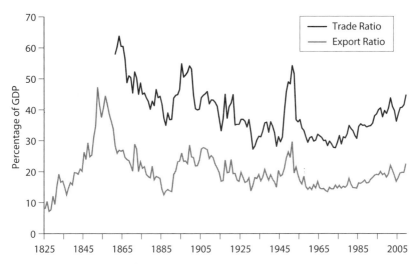

Figure 5.2. Export and trade ratios, 1825 to 2009.
Note: The export ratio is the ratio of exports to GDP, and the trade ratio is the ratio of exports plus imports to GDP, both measured in current prices.
Sources: 1825 to 1860: Pinkstone (1992), Table 63, p. 363. 1861 to 1900: Butlin (1962), Table 247, pp. 410–11. 1901 to 1949: Butlin (1977), Table IV-1. 1950 to 1997: Reserve Bank of Australia, *Australian Economic Statistics 1949–50 to 1996–97*, Table 1.10. 1998 to 2009: Reserve Bank of Australia, *Statistics*, Tables G1 and H03.

ports) to GDP, the latter being the conventional measure of an economy's openness. Figure 5.2 displays the historical trends in both. During the pre-gold pastoral boom the export ratio rises from 9 percent in the late 1820s to 26 percent in the second half of the 1840s; then, under the impact of the gold discoveries, to an average of 39 percent during the 1850s. Put differently, exports were expanding faster than domestic economic activity across more than three decades. After 1861 both the export ratio and the trade ratio trend down for the next three decades. A prima facie case might be made on the basis of this evidence that Australian growth was export-led between the 1820s and 1850s, but not during the rest of the pre-1890s boom. However, a more sophisticated analysis is required to determine the direction of causality, a topic to which we will return. What is unmistakable is that the economy was more "open" in these decades than it would be for much of the twentieth century—that is, the export and trade ratios were at a higher level.

Much of Australia's economic development during these decades has been attributed to its ability to efficiently produce and competitively sell the products of its rural sector on world markets. As we have seen, the export of wool began in the 1820s, and by the 1850s, Australia was supplying over half the market for this key input into the British manufacturing sector. And wool dominates rural exports during these decades through 1890, though agricultural products begin to make a significant contribution especially toward the end of the century: first wheat, then following the introduction of refrigerated shipping in the 1880s, also dairy products and frozen meat. This literature views the expansion and diversification of rural production for export as the principal driver of extensive growth; and also views the efficiency levels reached by Australian farmers as a principal source not only of their export competitiveness but also the prosperity of the wider community. This "export-led" growth perspective is similar to that adopted in studies of the role of international trade in accounting for the rapid growth of some East Asian economies in the second half of the twentieth century.

The nineteenth-century variant of this explanation for growth has focused primarily on the linkages that connected the export product (sometimes called the "staple") to the economy of the region in which it was produced, and thus to the wider economy. This approach is helpful in highlighting the varying impacts on the domestic economy that resulted from different staple products such as gold, wool, or wheat. We have touched on this in earlier discussion. Wool was profitably exported halfway round the world from the 1820s because sheep were self-reproducing, were grazed on (almost free) natural grassland, and required few purchased inputs beyond some labor for shepherding and shearing. A consequence is that there was no need for input supply firms to locate near to the production point: pastoralists could spread far from cities or towns. This was feasible also because wool is nonperishable and had a high value-to-bulk ratio. Wool was brilliantly suitable as a staple product with which to open up large swathes of the outback. Similarly, we have previously described how special features of gold enabled its profitable production under frontier conditions. Again, properties of the product surmounted the transport costs of getting gold from the mines, given the poor state of colonial roads, and of shipping it to London. Wool and gold thus share attributes that account for their ability to underpin Australia's early growth at a time when its frontier economy was very small and possessed little infrastructure.

In the staple view of Australian growth, wheat production is contrasted with wool for its different linkage effects. The production technology was more capital intensive, especially in the widespread use of labor-saving machinery. In this particular rural industry, labor productivity was high because of mechanization rather than land intensity. Indeed, given appropriate soil and climatic conditions, the farm-firm could be much smaller than a pastoral station. But mechanized wheat growing required local supply and repair services, so was associated with a denser pattern of rural towns. Also, wheat had a lower value-to-bulk ratio than either gold or wool, so could not be transported far without railways to reduce transport costs. Hence the wheat frontier never extended more than a short distance beyond a coastal port or the rail network. Wheat growing thus stimulated the extension of rural railways.

This focus in the staple interpretation of growth on specific characteristics of the product extends to the stimulus afforded the rest of the domestic economy as a result of off-farm processing. Gold was exported essentially unprocessed. Wool was also subject to little downstream processing. We have noted in our discussion of the 1840s how wool washing raised its value, a simple illustration of adding value prior to export. The gradual emergence of textile and clothing manufacturing in Australia absorbed some of the wool-grower's output. But most wool was processed in textile mills in Britain before being transformed there into clothing, blankets, and other woolen products.

The wheat industry was a little different from wool in terms of its downstream processing within Australia.[34] For one thing, a higher proportion was consumed domestically: Australia only became a consistent net wheat exporter at the end of the nineteenth century. In addition, the transport of wheat required not just railway infrastructure but also storage facilities (grain silos or elevators) along the rail network. The flour mills that processed the wheat may not have been especially high tech, even for the nineteenth century, but they provide an illustration of the expansion of the rural sector stimulating domestic processing of farm products. From the 1880s the dairy export industry and the frozen meat industry provide additional examples. It is appropriate to regard both dairy factories and meat-freezing works as "manufacturing" establishments, and the refrigerated butter, cheese, lamb, and mutton produced in and exported from them as "simply transformed" manufactured goods.

The expansion of the wheat industry also stimulated domestic production of manufactured inputs to an extent not seen with either wool or gold production. Perhaps the most visible, as well as the most sophisticated, was the local agricultural machinery industry. Growing out of local blacksmith repair shops, and the activities of individual inventors, agricultural implement firms flourished in the second half of the nineteenth century. Australian manufacturers successfully competed against imported British and American farm equipment, and prior to the First World War had even established export outlets for harvesting machinery.[35] These products of the agricultural engineering industry surely qualify as "elaborately transformed" manufactures for that era. Indeed, the selection of the McKay Harvester factory in Melbourne as the basis for the famous "Harvester" judgment on wages and margins in 1907 by Justice Higgins was due to its having one of the largest and most diverse skilled labor forces in a single industrial establishment at that time.

Thus export products differed in the nature and strength of their linkages to other parts of the domestic economy with implications for the pattern of settlement, the size distribution of towns and cities, the role of the public and

---

[34]Dunsdorfs (1956) provides a comprehensive economic history of this industry.
[35]McLean (1973a, 1976).

private sectors, and the growth of nonrural industries such as transport, manufacturing, and services. Some historians have gone so far as to elevate the staple model to the status of a general explanation for the growth of the Australian economy at this time.[36] This emulated research by Canadian historians who had earlier developed the staple perspective to explain the growth of their economy. Indeed, Boris Schedvin has argued that the different mix of staple products in nineteenth-century Australia (wool and gold) compared to Canada (timber products and wheat) accounts for the earlier and more rapid development of manufacturing in the latter, and that this in turn explains what he alleges to be Australia's poorer growth performance during the twentieth century than Canada's.[37]

The staple approach thus captures important elements of the relationship between international trade and growth in an economy endowed with abundant natural resources. But it does not constitute a "theory" of growth in any formal sense, for it does not endogenously explain how one dominant staple follows another, thus sustaining growth, or how economies founded on staple exports experience a transition to growth based on other sources. More rigorous analysis of the trade-growth nexus across countries, and for recent decades, has met with mixed results. Even the direction of causation is not as clear-cut as implied by export-led growth models, whether of the staple or some other variety. Further discussion of this is deferred to a later chapter. However, in explaining Australian growth in the late nineteenth century, the historians' focus on the importance of the expansion of the rural sector, and on the vital, related role of export demand, seems fully justified.

Of course international trade does not occur in isolation. A richer approach is to begin with an appreciation of the depth and breadth of Australia's integration into the international economy. The trade flows highlighted so far were accompanied by factor flows. Financial capital and immigrants moved from labor- and capital-abundant Britain to labor- and capital-scarce Australia in response to the higher returns to both factors in the latter. It is crucial to any understanding of Australia's economy at this time to recognize that these trade and factor flows were interdependent. Furthermore, it cannot be overlooked that this high degree of economic integration between Britain and Australia occurred within the political and constitutional context of their imperial relationship. This gave the Australian colonies a special position in the rapidly expanding international economy at that time. They received preferential access for their exports to the British domestic market. Colonial governments received favorable terms in the London capital market when raising loans for

---

[36] Early examples include McCarty (1964) and Blainey (1964), while Lougheed (1968) offered a critique.

[37] Schedvin (1990). Pomfret (1981) also compares the Australian and Canadian historical experience with respect to their staple commodities.

infrastructure development such as railway construction. The economic benefits extended also to their membership in a type of currency union, since sterling was the international reserve currency of the era. And their defense and security arrangements were funded primarily by the imperial government—that is, by the British taxpayer. I will defer a fuller accounting of the costs and benefits to the Australian economy of the imperial connection to chapter 7. The aim here is to broaden consideration of the role of international economic links beyond trade to factor movements.

The inflows of foreign (mainly British) investment in this period were prodigious. One measure is the proportion of domestic investment funded not by domestic savings but by those of foreigners. This averaged 35 percent between 1861 and 1889 and was higher than this during the 1880s.[38] Thus extensive growth during this long boom was critically dependent (in a proximate sense) on the importation of British capital. Since most was borrowed by the colonial governments, this added to their debt, which during these decades was growing faster than GDP (figure 5.3). The prosperity of the period covered by this chapter is thus supported in part by a fairly steady run-up in the level of public indebtedness from an initial position of no debt at the granting of responsible government. By the mid-1880s, government debt exceeded 60 percent of GDP, a level that, then as now, might be regarded as increasingly exposing public finances—and hence prosperity—to a crisis triggered by, for example, a downturn in economic activity, higher costs of rolling over existing loans, or a closing up of capital markets.

It is pertinent to observe this relationship from the other side: Australia was a major destination for British overseas investment during these decades. Since Britain accounted for a large share of all international capital flows before 1914, it follows that Australia figured prominently on a world scale as a recipient of the surplus savings of others, especially prior to 1890. Here is one indicator of Australia's importance within the world economy during this first era of globalization. Nothing comparable was to be attained during the second period of globalization in the late twentieth century with respect to Australia's significance as a destination for international capital flows.

The contribution of immigration to the expansion of the population between 1861 and 1889 was about 34 percent, and higher than it was to be again on a sustained basis until after 1945.[39] Again, we can look at this from an international perspective. Within the wider context of the mass migrations of the times, the Australian share of the (approximately) fifty million European emigrants before the First World War was much lower than that of the United States, but

---

[38]McLean (1989b), p. 16. Another measure is the ratio of net capital inflow to GNP, which also peaked in the 1880s at 9 percent (Edelstein, 1982, p. 251).

[39]It was 35 percent between 1947 and 1974 (McLean 1989b, p. 16).

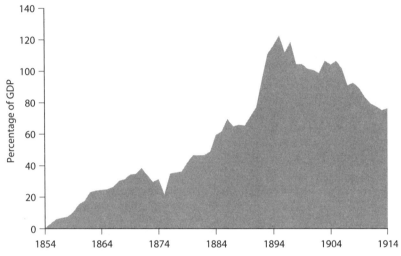

Figure 5.3. Government debt as a percentage of GDP, 1854 to 1914.
Source: Vamplew (1987), Series GF7, p. 256.

still ranked third behind Argentina and just ahead of Canada at more than 7 percent of the total.[40] In the case of Australia, its peak share of immigrants occurred prior to 1890.

These numbers suggest that extensive growth was significantly boosted during the long boom by these sizable factor inflows. However they do not indicate whether the effect on per capita income of this augmentation of domestic with foreign supplies of labor and capital was favorable or unfavorable. In the absence of evidence one can only cautiously speculate. To illustrate, it is possible that the immigrant workers on average possessed about the same level of human capital (formal education, skills, experience) as existing members of the Australian labor force. It could also be the case that the foreign-financed additions to the capital stock were such as to leave the capital *per worker* approximately the same as before. The population, workforce, capital stock, and total economy would all be larger as a result of the factor inflows, but labor productivity (and, other things equal, per capita income) would be unchanged. It follows that if the high levels of immigration and foreign investment into Australia during this long boom are to have played a role in its high and rising levels of prosperity, we have to search for evidence other than the mere size of the inflows.

One possibility is that the human capital of immigrants was above that of the native born. Britain was the dominant source of immigrants, and one study of their occupation mix indicates that the associated skill levels were on average below those of British migrants arriving after the Second World War. How-

[40]The figures refer to the period 1851 to 1915 (Kenwood and Lougheed 1999, p. 49).

ever, what is required is a comparison of the skills of immigrants with those of the existing workforce, but matching occupational data are not available for this period.[41] Another contribution of immigration to productivity and hence income at this time may also have been the immigrants' higher workforce participation rate than the resident population's; though speculative, this would result from the immigrants' higher masculinity ratio and higher working-age proportion, a topic we return to in the next chapter. A related benefit of high levels of immigration is a more flexible domestic labor market—immigrants are likely to settle where labor is in greatest demand.

A second possibility is that foreign capital financed imports of machinery and equipment that embodied technology closer to global best practice than what was (or could have been) produced from domestic sources. Britain was the technological leader at the time, and this is where most of Australia's imported capital equipment was obtained. This transmission mechanism enhanced Australian access to products and production methods that would have a favorable impact on productivity as well as on the level of output.

Another source of productivity gain from these factor inflows arose insofar as there were scale economies that would not have been realized had Australia relied just on natural increase in the population for additions to its workforce, and on domestic saving alone to finance investment. More precisely, any such gains, assessed in a given year, would simply have been delayed until the autarkic (counterfactual) economy eventually reached the same size. These economies of scale might have arisen at the level of the firm or industry, or have been economy-wide. Given the initially very small size of the Australian population and economy, it is hard to think that there were not some unexploited economies of this type. A closely related but distinct source of potential productivity improvement arises from agglomeration economies—and these are most prevalent in large urban areas. The fact that a relatively high proportion of the Australian population lived in a small number of cities possibly helped capture any agglomeration effects, offsetting to some extent the disadvantages of its small and widely scattered total population.

So far I have emphasized the favorable international economic conditions during this period and the openness of the Australian economy. But this takes us only so far in the search for an explanation of Australia's especially high incomes at this time. The expansion of the economy and population between 1851 and 1890 could have occurred with no rise in per capita income, and thus with some deterioration in Australian income levels relative to benchmark economies such as Britain, Canada, or the United States. So, why was this period of sustained and rapid extensive growth also one that delivered such world-leading levels of income? To address this question, it is first necessary to drill down further into the sources of efficiency in the farm sector during this

---

[41]Withers (1989).

golden age, and then turn in the next chapter to the comparative evidence of economy-wide productivity and income levels.

RURAL PRODUCTIVITY AND ITS SOURCES

I have previously argued (in chapter 4) that Australian woolgrowers must have achieved production efficiency levels the equal of or superior to those achieved anywhere else. When discussing the period 1820–50, several likely sources of this productivity superiority were identified, such as that land costs were low (almost free to "squatters"); that sheep grazed on natural grassland rather than sown grasses, stubble, hay, or root crops requiring repeated cultivation; that pastoral properties were largely unfenced, with boundary riders and shepherds serving as cheaper substitutes; that there was limited investment undertaken in fixed capital (dams, windmills, stockyards, but few farm buildings); that mild winters meant there was no need to keep stock indoors; and that, outside the annual mustering and shearing season, labor requirements were much lower than in European farming. These sources of efficiency are, conceptually, distinct from the scale economies that were reaped especially in the semi-arid outback regions where very large flocks were grazed at very low stocking rates per hectare. In addition, the Australian woolgrowers early developed an extremely efficient system of financing and marketing the wool clip through "stock and station" firms and their agent system. All this underpinned pastoral productivity levels during the first pastoral age, prior to the discovery of gold.

The further productivity-enhancing changes occurring within the pastoral zone between 1850 and 1890 were not especially dramatic. On inland pastoral stations where wool was the dominant if not sole product, there was further investment in stockyards, shearing sheds, and especially in securing reliable sources of water for the sheep—often the key determinant of the ability to grow wool in the semi-arid regions. There were some mechanical innovations of importance—notably the replacement of hand shears with shearing machines, and improvements in the wool press. There was an ongoing search for superior breeds of sheep aimed at raising fleece weight or quality. And perhaps most important, there were improvements in station management. These pastoral properties were sometimes quite large enterprises in terms of the value of the flock and the annual wool clip, but not in terms of their permanent workforce, which was typically small. Shearing had the seasonal peak labor requirement, but was undertaken primarily by itinerant contractors.

Although there was a further phase of spreading pastoral occupation into inland areas between 1850 and 1890, this period also saw the conversion of earlier-occupied areas closer to the coasts from wool-growing to grain farming or to mixed wheat growing/sheep raising. The rise in mixed farming in some regions reflected its increased profitability; consequently, it likely increased farm productivity. The relative importance of nonwool rural activities began to increase also in response to the rapid increase in population and its food requirements, stimulating especially dairying and horticulture. Furthermore we have to recall the importance of grains and straw as the energy source for the predominantly horse-based transport systems of that era. Again, the domestic demand for this nineteenth-century equivalent to oil grew with the population. Thus there was some change in the product mix of the rural sector.[42]

Beyond the wool industry, the period after 1850 saw many changes in rural technology and management, some quite dramatic. One source of enhanced efficiency was the introduction of wire fencing, facilitating the selective breeding of sheep for particular wool or meat characteristics relative to what is possible in open-range farming. Fencing also permitted "mixed" farming by keeping sheep separate from crops, and a property subdivided into fenced paddocks is a prerequisite for rotation cropping alongside livestock production. These may be thought of as yielding scope economies in the farm-firm.

Another source of productivity growth in nonpastoral farming across these decades was the diffusion of mechanized production methods and constant improvements to the implements and machines already in use. These include cultivation, planting, harvesting and post-harvesting equipment, and the cream separator. The "stump-jump" plow and the "stripper" harvesting machine have legendary status as local inventions assisting the spread of agriculture into areas where imported implements and machines were less suited. The imports came primarily from Britain and the United States, with the latter's agricultural machinery industry witnessing rapid innovation in the late nineteenth century. Thus not only did the amount of machinery per worker in agriculture rise, but the technology embodied in the equipment was at the world frontier. Both contributed to increasing labor productivity.[43]

Agricultural mechanization was not just a response to labor scarcity and its relatively high price, but had other productivity-enhancing or cost-reducing benefits. It raised yields by better spacing seeds during planting, compared with traditional methods of broadcast hand sowing. Cultivation implements assisted weed control. The speed of some farm operations was increased, hence more work could be undertaken under optimal conditions for planting and harvesting. And the quality of the product was better controlled with mechanized production methods.

The adoption of new machines and implements was a highly visible source of increased rural productivity at this time. But there were other important sources. This was the era of the development and adoption of new varieties of wheat—most famously those associated with the work of William Farrer. The location-specific features of soils and climate meant that imported European crop varieties did not always flourish, or were not suitable in all regions. Patient experimentation over many years by innovative farmers and colonial government

---

[42] Agricultural developments in this period are covered by Davidson (1981) and Dunsdorfs (1956).
[43] McLean (1973a, 1976).

agencies was required to identify or develop the best varieties to deal with crop disease (such as rust in wheat), poor quality soils, drought, and high summer temperatures. In part the new varieties simply permitted crops to be grown in areas where they otherwise would not have been planted at all; and in part they increased yields on land already cropped.[44]

Closely related to the mechanical and biological innovations in agriculture at this time were changes in farm management and organization. First, note should be made of the effect on average farm size of the selection acts. In many instances they prescribed maximum farm sizes that were either too small to be efficient from the outset, or, especially with the increased fixed costs associated with mechanization, were soon found to be below the acreage needed for profitable production. So, despite the wishes of the legislators, powerful market forces led farmers to seek scale economies through farm amalgamation. From about 1890 the long decline in the average size of rural holdings ended, and average farm sizes began to increase. It may be conjectured that the selection acts at first lowered rural productivity; that their circumvention had the benefit of minimizing this politically imposed inefficiency and drag on growth; and that the subsequent rise in farm size was a source of productivity gain.

Other on-farm changes also had productivity-enhancing effects, even if introduced to reduce risk and lessen the volatility in farm income, such as that resulting from drought. The rise of mixed farming diversified the farmers' sources of income and increased the viability of the enterprise in an environment where both climate and commodity prices fluctuated markedly across the seasons. Rotation cropping, fallowing, and the use of artificial fertilizers were designed to raise yields, but in most cases would also have raised labor productivity.

These mechanical, biological, and managerial innovations in farming had diverse origins. Much consisted of "folk science," or the contributions of talented pioneer farmers who over time accumulated knowledge about how to improve profitability or output. This knowledge then spread through local information networks, such as rural newspapers and annual "shows." But where the new scientific knowledge or technology originated overseas, or required professional skills, more formal mechanisms predominated. With respect to mechanical innovations, the private sector could profitably supply the new technology to the farmer as it was "embodied" in the new machine or implement, and the property rights of the inventor (typically, an agricultural machinery firm) were protected by patent. Australian farm-implement- and machinery-makers competed vigorously with the imported products of British and American firms. With respect to biological and especially managerial innovations, the private sector was much less able to meet the farmers' requirements. There are strong

---

[44] A similar pattern of biological innovation occurred in U.S. agriculture at this time: see Olmstead and Rhode (2008). And through reports in the rural press, Australian farmers were well informed of this.

public goods characteristics to the production of this type of knowledge. Thus it is no surprise that, whereas there was no demand from farmers that the colonial governments establish state plow or harvester factories, there was a demand that they establish experimental farms, botanical gardens, agricultural high schools and colleges, and departments of agriculture.[45]

There has been limited assessment of the contribution of productivity improvement to the expansion of rural output at this time, and of the possible sources of the productivity gains whether these are measured as labor productivity or multifactor productivity. The most detailed analysis relates to Victoria, which has the most comprehensive statistics on the rural sector during the period. There the mix of farming differed markedly from that of Australia as a whole, with pastoral production constituting a smaller (and declining) share of rural output, and crop production and dairying correspondingly larger (and increasing) shares. Hence the Victorian evidence on rural productivity may not be representative of the whole country. Quite low *rates of growth* in labor productivity are recorded there between 1870 and the 1890s followed by a marked acceleration. The likely sources of this efficiency improvement on Victorian farms lie in the cumulative but lagged effects of the diverse changes noted above in farm management, product mix, scale economies, and mechanization, which all began prior to 1890, but were accelerated from the mid-1890s.[46]

More important to our search for the sources of Australian prosperity is the evidence from a recent attempt to compare the *levels* of labor productivity in the agricultural sectors of Australia and the United Kingdom from 1861.[47] It appears that, in striking contrast to the contemporary assessments of "slovenly farming" practices frequently expressed in reference to Australia's farmers, where English practice appears to have been the benchmark, colonial farmers were the more efficient producers—and by a considerable margin. In 1861, labor productivity in Australian agriculture was 76 percent above that in the United Kingdom, and this sizable superiority increased markedly over the subsequent three decades to reach 252 percent in 1891. Looking beyond the period covered in this chapter, the 1901 estimate of 71 percent reflects the negative impact of the serious drought that affected rural Australia at the time, but by 1911, the large lead had been restored with a 189 percent higher productivity level than in U.K. agriculture. It is possible to extend this comparison to include Canada and the United States, albeit indirectly. The level of labor productivity in U.S. agriculture was close to that for the United Kingdom during these decades, moving within a narrow range from 92 to 112 percent between 1851 and 1911.[48] A separate study reports that labor productivity in Canadian agriculture

[45]McLean (1982).
[46]Ibid. (1973b).
[47]Broadberry and Irwin (2007).
[48]Ibid. (2006), p. 261.

was below that in the United States between 1871 and 1921, ranging from 65 to 87 percent of the American levels.[49] It follows that Australian farmers' efficiency levels were significantly higher than all three: indeed, "this suggests that Australia was the world's agricultural productivity leader at this time."[50] Comparative analysis thus powerfully reinforces the importance of the skills and enterprise of their farmers to the prosperity that all Australians enjoyed.

• • •

How do we sum up the story of post–gold rush economic prosperity? One history of the economy covering this period has the catchy title *No Paradise for Workers*.[51] Undoubtedly the average standard of living of Australians in the years prior to 1890 was below what is enjoyed today when, perhaps, we are at least closer to whatever constitutes the economic paradise the authors had in mind. But since long-run trend growth has been positive, comparisons of current with earlier prosperity will always indicate the past falls short. So this is a benchmark with limited relevance. The more conventional benchmark of prosperity in a given period is whether changes in an indicator such as income per capita are positive, and if so how rapidly it rises. Certainly the period from 1850 to 1890 saw an increase in this key measure. Though there seems no simple explanation, let alone a single cause, neither is there any deep mystery concerning the likely factors at work. Part of the story is the state of the international economy, which was particularly conducive to the rapid growth of the settler societies located in temperate zones, especially their export-oriented producers of foodstuffs and other raw materials. And the Australian producers were highly efficient, employed best-practice technology, and were innovative and adaptable in a high-risk frontier environment. A further aspect of the story lies in the sheer abundance of the natural-resource base of land and minerals that was being discovered and exploited at this stage. Finally, something did not happen that might have changed the outcome of this story. Australians did not seriously squander the growth potential inherent in the resource endowment— though, as further discussed in the next chapter, neither were their conservation and environmental-management practices especially laudatory, at least by the standards of the early twenty-first century. In short, Australians were prime beneficiaries of this first era of globalization, becoming very rich on the basis of the interactions existing between their natural-resource endowment, the efficiency with which this was utilized, the quality of their institutional arrangements, and their choice of an outward-oriented growth strategy.

---

[49] McInnis (1986), table 14.6, p. 757.

[50] Irwin (2007), p. 228. Again, this refers to labor productivity: there are no estimates available for total factor productivity for the Australian agricultural sector at this time.

[51] Buckley and Wheelwright (1988).

CHAPTER 6

Depression, Drought, and Federation

A wilful, lavish land.
—Dorothea Mackellar[1]

THE LONG BOOM that began in the 1850s came to an end in the early 1890s. And the slump that followed was both deep and protracted. Indeed, per capita real GDP fell by 22 percent by 1895 and did not regain its 1889 peak for a full two decades—until 1909 (figure 6.1). To give this context, both the extent of the fall in incomes, and the number of years that elapsed before the previous peak was regained, were greater than that which occurred during the depression of the interwar period (when they were 18 percent and thirteen years, respectively). Explaining why this stunning reversal of fortune occurred after 1890 is the central task in this chapter.[2]

The approach adopted here includes a comparative perspective on Australians' reduced levels of prosperity between 1890 and 1914. As we saw in chapter 2, Australia recorded the highest per capita income in the world for some period prior to the 1890s. This achievement has never been repeated. In this inquiry into Australian prosperity and its determinants, it therefore is crucial to explain how this ranking in per capita income was lost after 1890. Unsurprisingly, it turns out that the reasons overlap with those accounting for why the high incomes, relative to other countries, were attained in the first place, a topic not directly addressed in the previous chapter.

EXPLAINING RELATIVE INCOMES

Recent analyses of the Australian lead in incomes prior to 1890 have focused on several possible contributing factors.[3] One is that there was something unusual about the composition of the Australian population at the time that

---

[1] From the final stanza of "My Country" (1911): Kinsella (2009), pp. 127–28.

[2] There is debate concerning a possible overstatement of the extent of the boom—and hence also of the ensuing slump—in the estimates of GDP compiled by Butlin (1962). Alternative estimates have been proposed by Haig (2001), but to date these have not been assessed as clearly superior: see Maddison (2003, pp. 72–73), Broadberry and Irwin (2007, pp. 263–64; 2008), and Haig (2008).

[3] The following discussion draws on Broadberry and Irwin (2007), Irwin (2007), and McLean (2007).

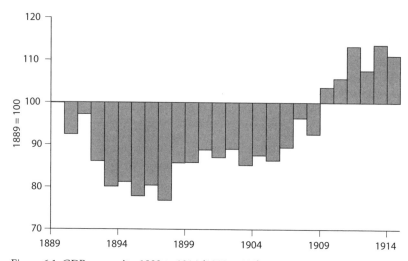

Figure 6.1. GDP per capita, 1889 to 1914 (1889 = 100).
Source: McLean and Pincus (1982), Appendix Table, pp. 29–30.

boosted measured GDP relative to that of the two benchmark economies, the United Kingdom and the United States. We have noted the role of economic-demographic interactions within the Australian economy following the population shock accompanying the gold rushes. And it appears that the higher masculinity rates resulting from the same event may have led to a higher proportion of the population participating in the workforce (since males participate more than females), and hence producing more output than would have been the case had the gender balance been closer to the norm. However, the overall (male plus female) workforce participation rate, though higher in Australia than in the United States, was below that in the United Kingdom. Thus in a comparison with the United States, about half the income superiority of Australia over the United States in 1890 can be attributed to these demographic and labor-market characteristics. In a formal sense, the remaining and unexplained half must be due to higher labor productivity—GDP per person employed. In the case of the comparison with the United Kingdom, all the income superiority must come from this latter source.

Any comparison of labor productivity between the three countries has to take into account both the differences between them in productivity levels across particular industries or sectors, and the differences in the relative importance of these sectors within each country, economy-wide productivity being the average of that in each industry weighted by its share of total employment. The evidence suggests that the source of Australia's productivity superiority over both the United Kingdom and the United States prior to the 1890s arises in the two natural-resource-intensive sectors of agriculture and mining. With respect to agriculture, the level of labor productivity in Australia in the 1880s was over twice that in the United Kingdom, which was in turn about comparable with that in the United States. Similarly in mining, Australia had almost a threefold lead over the United Kingdom in labor productivity. Of course, the importance of these sectors in the three economies differed, and thus their contribution to economy-wide productivity levels did too. The United States had a much higher proportion of its labor force in its less efficient agriculture than did Australia, whereas the share of employment in U.K. agriculture was somewhat less than the Australian share. Differences between the three countries in their productivity levels and shares of employment in other industries or sectors do not appear to contribute significantly to the explanation of the Australian lead in overall levels of labor productivity.

It can be concluded that, relative to the United States, the higher prosperity Australians enjoyed at this time had its proximate origins in part in its higher masculinity rate and workforce participation rate, and in part in the higher level of labor productivity in the farming and mining sectors. When the comparison is made with the United Kingdom, the much higher labor productivity in the same two natural-resource-intensive sectors in Australia accounts for its superior levels of income, though in this case the higher U.K. workforce participation rate partly offsets the Australian advantage in productivity.[4]

The attention devoted in the previous chapter to the long-run demographic implications of the gold rushes, and in the previous two chapters to the sources of efficiency in the pastoral and agricultural sectors, was motivated in substantial part because of this comparative analysis: they were key determinants of Australia's relatively high level of economic prosperity in the nineteenth century. This has been an important finding derived from the effort to benchmark Australian income per capita against that of the United Kingdom and the United States, and the attempt to account for the Australian superiority over both. Looking ahead, I will return in chapter 9 to review attempts to benchmark Australia's productivity performance since the 1960s against the United States in particular, but with the advantage of more comprehensive data of higher quality.

In this and the previous chapter, I have examined several sources of the economic prosperity recorded in Australia in the decades between 1850 and 1890. But this has not been an exhaustive inquiry given the many possible contributing sources canvassed in chapter 2. It should also be noted that highlighting the especially favorable international economic conditions Australia faced during these decades, and the impressive productivity performance achieved in the resource-based export industries, is not novel. So, what other sources of prosperity at this time might have had a major role to play? Two that figure prominently in growth theory probably were not so unusual as to account for

---

[4]These results are recently reported, involve many assumptions, and have yet to be subjected to intensive critical evaluation. However, see Haig (2008) and Broadberry and Irwin (2008).

the Australian lead in living standards at this time. There is no evidence to support the view that labor productivity in Australia was higher than that in the United Kingdom or the United States because there was a greater stock of capital available to each worker. Capital stock estimates that would make possible a direct estimate are not available, but evidence of investment rates do not suggest Australians were accumulating capital at unusually high rates. If physical capital per worker seems not to be a source of Australia's relatively high productivity, might it be that the accumulation of human capital was greater— that is, per worker? A discussion of human capital—especially education—in Australian growth will be deferred until we assess the economy's performance in the twentieth century. For now it is sufficient to note that there appears little difference between Australian and U.S. rates of elementary schooling in the late nineteenth century, at a time when this level of education was probably more important to growth than the higher levels (high school, university) that later assumed much greater significance. However, there is one source of measured growth that warrants consideration. Very little attention is accorded in the Australian literature to the possibility that the prosperity Australians enjoyed before 1890 may to some extent have been inherently transitory because the conventional methods of measuring GDP do not adjust for any of the resource depletion that was occurring at this time in farming or mining.

Eating the Seed Corn?

It is possible for an economy temporarily to attain higher levels of income and consumption than is sustainable in the long run by running down its stock of natural resources. That is, the *levels* of productivity and hence income attained in the late nineteenth century may have been based to some extent on an unsustainable rate of depletion of nonrenewable resources such as mineral deposits, and/or an unsustainable rate of exhaustion of renewable resources such as pastoral and agricultural land. Gold provides a clear case of the former. The discoveries of the 1850s and later were extracted at a rate that maximized current profitability in the gold-mining industry. When the deposits were mined out, or yields declined below economic levels, the mine closed and production ceased. In the case of rural land, if pioneer farming practices were lowering yields through overcropping ("soil-mining" is the appropriate term in this context), then output was higher than could be sustained without some change in farming practices, changes that likely lowered output and/or productivity in the short- to medium term. This is an intuitive exposition of what might be meant by an unsustainable level of output or income pre-1890.

Economists have tried to sharpen the discussion of what is a sustainable use of natural resources. One approach is to focus on what is done with the income (rent) generated from exploiting a nonrenewable resource. If it is all spent on current consumption, this will be boosted in the short run, but will decline if the rate of resource extraction falters, and return to its initial level if the resource is fully depleted. The higher consumption level was inherently temporary. However, if a portion of the additional income obtained by exploiting the resource is saved rather than consumed, and invested in an asset that is expected to yield income in perpetuity (government bonds, for example), a higher level of consumption can be maintained beyond the point at which the resource is depleted.[5] This, after all, is the idea behind the sovereign wealth funds of resource-rich nations such as Norway or the Gulf states today: how to maintain incomes and consumption after the oil and gas reserves have run out.

Turning from theory to history, the question is whether, around 1890, Australians were consuming too much of the rent from the resource extraction, and investing too little in alternative productive assets, in order to maintain incomes in the long run. Put differently, in 1890 how much of Australia's GDP per capita, and consumption per capita, might have been "unsustainable" in this sense? If this was significant, Australians had been bringing forward their consumption of the bounty of the natural resources they had discovered without making full provision for the maintenance of their standards of living. They had perhaps been, to some degree, "future eaters," in the colorful phrase of a recent writer on environmental sustainability.[6]

Gold is a nonrenewable resource, hence each ounce mined, minted and exported in exchange for imports was one less ounce available in the future. In this "quarry" economy perspective, the gold rush represented a rapid exploitation of the community's stock of gold and its conversion into current income and expenditure—including primarily on current consumption. The choice of present versus future income becomes more complex where the resource in question is of an unknown size, or where future resource discoveries are uncertain with respect to both their timing and value. For example, in any year following 1851, it was not known how much gold remained to be discovered and mined. The gold discoveries in Western Australia in the 1890s illustrate the difficulty in drawing strong conclusions about whether gold production in earlier decades had temporarily supported "unsustainable" levels of income and consumption.[7]

In contrast to mineral deposits, rural land is a renewable natural resource. It may be depleted, such as through overcropping, leading to a decline in its fertility

---

[5] Indeed, there will be some rate of deferred consumption (saving) from the additional income that will provide a future income stream from the alternative investments such as to maintain consumption levels beyond the depletion of the resource, and do so indefinitely.

[6] The reference is to Flannery (1994).

[7] I ignore here the role of technological change in determining the extent to which the stock of a particular resource is (economically) recoverable; and the related possibility that the natural-resource endowment is to some degree endogenous to the level of development of an economy, a topic I turn to in the next chapter.

or livestock-carrying capacity. Thus in the short run, farm output may be increased above the level that can be sustained in the long run. Given the importance of the rural sector in the economy at the time, this in turn would lead to a temporary higher level of income. But in contrast to mining activity, the productivity of rural land can be replenished, albeit at some cost.

The evidence typically used to support the view that rural production methods during these decades were depleting soil fertility is the decline in *average* crop yields during the decades in which (especially wheat) acreage greatly increased. This may have been pronounced in the early years of rural occupation of a region, when little was known about the management practices necessary in each locality to avoid declining yields. It is also possible that the financial and "improvement" conditions imposed on selectors under the land acts of the 1860s and 1870s encouraged soil-mining practices. In this case public policy operated at cross purposes, supporting maximum access to land by small farmers, but providing incentives for them to adopt a short-term revenue maximization goal instead of a long-term viability objective—financially and ecologically.

However, this evidence has to be treated cautiously, as average yields of a given crop in a colony can be shown to have declined in part because the location of crop production was shifting to regions with lower rainfall or poorer quality soils, and hence lower yields were recorded for these reasons. Even within a given region or county, yields may fall for reasons other than over-cropping.[8] We noted in the previous chapter that even before 1890, established farmers were observing adverse consequences to their own behaviors. Realizing they were depleting their resource base, they adjusted their product mix, adopted new technology and farm management practices, and turned to governments for assistance where collective action was necessary. For example, the Australia-wide average yields of wheat began to rise after reaching a nadir during the 1890s.

To have avoided soil degradation would have required a slower growth in rural settlement and output and/or a higher cost structure to farming from the outset. The result would have been lower farm incomes and productivity during this pioneering phase. How much lower is not clear. But it seems safe to suggest that the levels of farm output and labor productivity achieved in Australia before the 1890s were to some degree based on the depletion of rural land fertility. This in turn suggests that some component of Australian average incomes was likewise based.

It should not be overlooked that in each of the other high-income settler economies in the latter half of the nineteenth century—Canada, New Zealand, the United States and Argentina—natural resources played an important role

---

[8]For example, if the best land was brought into production first. Frost (1995) argues against the uncritical acceptance of declining yields as a measure of soil-mining practices by Victoria's farmers.

in their development and prosperity. Hence, before it can be suggested that Australia's *relative* income ranking might be sensitive to its unsustainable resource depletion, a similar exercise on any comparator country would have to be undertaken.

Nor should it be assumed that the evidence of declining soil fertility at this time of itself implies socially suboptimal decision-making by farmers; that is, decisions not in society's long-term interest. Some commentators on resource and environmental history overlook the extent to which Australia's pioneer farmers could only learn the characteristics of their land by using it. Further, even from hindsight it is not clear that a slower expansion of rural occupation and development, with a greater investment in higher-cost sustainable farming practices from the outset, would have produced a higher level of social welfare, though this is implied by some writers. Tricky assumptions about the welfare of different generations—some of whom would lose, some gain—are implicit in any such counterfactual.

BOOM, BUBBLE, AND BUST: A CLASSIC DEBT CRISIS

With hindsight, it is easy to be wise in observing that the long nineteenth-century economic boom eventually acquired characteristics that imperiled its continuation. If contemporaries could confidently have foreseen this, one imagines that whether pastoralist, house buyer, banker, or politician, they would have acted differently. For their part, historians have, if anything, overdetermined their explanations of the crash of the early 1890s.[9] The list of suspects in the crime is long, but different investigators have lists that only partially overlap. Identifying the key elements among the many plausible contributing factors requires the assistance of a particular model, approach, or perspective. That adopted here is the one most commonly employed to analyze debt crises in small, open, developing economies, since the boom and bust in late-nineteenth-century Australia has much in common with these all-too frequent events.

The pastoral occupation of inland Australia would eventually encounter its geographical limits, and in southeastern Australia, this appears to have occurred by 1890, at least temporarily. But of itself, this need not have precipitated an economic crisis. As we have seen in the previous chapter, the application of new technology and improved management methods permitted increases in output on inframarginal farms. Encountering the geographic limits of rural occupation may, however, have increased the *cost* of additional production relative to when this additional production was achieved by moving out the frontier of rural settlement. But this may not have been apparent to contemporaries, at least immediately. That is, there may have been an element in the *expected*

---

[9] Important treatments are by Boehm (1971) and Hall (1968).

profitability of the pastoral industry in the 1880s that relied on its continued low-cost geographical expansion. As already noted, the frontier occupation of farmlands was also a process of acquiring relevant information about the suitability of the area in question for rural development, as it was difficult, if not impossible, to acquire this information prior to making the initial investments in land and livestock.

Rapid expansion was also elevating risk in the urban sector. High levels of immigration, combined with the "echo effect" of the gold-rush-induced kink to the age distribution, created strong demand for residential construction as well as ancillary urban infrastructure such as tramways, suburban rail lines, and water and sewerage systems. The urban construction boom is most famously associated with Melbourne in the 1880s. Supplying much of this infrastructure fell to the government sector, which financed its spending in large part with foreign borrowing. Although there was nothing inherently unsound in such a debt-financed urban expansion, the dangers lay in the levels and forms of the borrowing. The social overhead capital that was created would not immediately generate sufficient revenue to fully service the loans, and the fact that it was not private sector but colonial government borrowing (and investment) meant that any failed project would directly and negatively impact public finances. Private developers could go bankrupt, but the colonial governments could not so easily default on their debts. Hence any misdirected public investment would be a burden on future taxpayers.

There are many ways to illustrate the run-up in debt that accompanied the boom. One is to cumulate the current account deficits that were a persistent feature of the decades before 1890, thereby obtaining a rough indicator of total foreign debt exposure: according to one recent estimate, this rose from a trivial proportion of GDP before 1861 to over 100 percent by the end of the boom, then, as GDP fell with the ensuing slump, the ratio climbed above 150 percent.[10] A more conventional indicator is the level of government debt (figure 5.3). This, too, was very low at the beginning of the boom, at a mere 3 percent of GDP in 1855, but rose rapidly thereafter to reach 71 percent by 1890, peaking during the depressed decade that followed at 123 percent in 1895.

The financial sector also grew rapidly, providing the conduit linking savers with borrowers. Critical to the sound allocation of these funds among competing projects by the bankers and other intermediaries was their knowledge of the risks and returns to which lenders were to be exposed. Also critical for financial stability were the institutional checks and balances both within financial institutions and across the financial sector. However the rapid growth in the sector led to a scarcity of bankers with relevant experience, especially of rural Australia. It led also to a proliferation of numerous small banks with limited

---

[10] The methodology and estimates are by the Reserve Bank of Australia: see Belkar, Cockerell, and Kent (2007), figure 3.

diversification in their investment portfolios, whether across asset types or by colony. And this rapid growth occurred in a regulatory regime that was very laissez-faire. This was a finance sector with the potential for a serious decline in prudential standards.[11]

The high level of investment that characterized the long boom was the result of decisions taken both in the public and private sectors, and financed both from domestic and British sources. An important issue is thus whether there was serious misallocation of this investment. Related questions include whether any such misallocation was primarily due to government decisions or those made by market agents, and whether any such tendencies were clearest in the 1880s when the boom in asset prices peaked.[12] With respect to the run-up in public-sector debt, some attempts have been made to evaluate the investment decisions of the colonial governments. Of particular interest has been the case of railway construction, often subject to the assessment (both at the time and by historians) that lines were built with political rather than economic considerations uppermost, or that there was wasteful construction due to intercolonial rivalry—especially between New South Wales and Victoria to service the transport needs of the Riverina region on their common border. The evidence does not support an unqualified judgment of sustained or substantial misallocation of investment in railways, though debate continues.[13] And any assessment has to ask whether a better allocation could have been made with the information available to the decision-makers, or only with the advantage of hindsight.

At the level of the macro-economy, the potential for crisis lay in any sudden and significant change in the key elements supporting growth previously enumerated: the inflow of foreign capital that augmented domestic savings and financed about 40 percent of domestic investment; the ability of colonial governments to service their rapidly growing foreign debt; and the rate of immigration, which was underpinning the urban construction boom. To illustrate this vulnerability, figure 6.2 shows the proportion of export earnings required in each year to service the existing debts held abroad. The run-up in this debt-servicing burden prior to 1890, and most rapidly during the 1880s, is striking. Only in the depth of the depression of the 1930s was this level of debt burden briefly exceeded.

In the early 1890s all these props were fractured. The London capital market became increasingly concerned about the expected returns on further lending to Australia, at least partly in reaction to events in Argentina (the Barings crisis of 1890). This is the contagion effect, familiar from recent financial crises such as those among Asian economies in 1997. And the popping of a speculative

<hr />

[11] A summary analysis of developments in the financial sector at this time is provided by Merrett (1989).

[12] The weakening of investment criteria is a theme central to the analysis of Butlin (1964).

[13] See, for example, Davidson (1982) and Frost (2000).

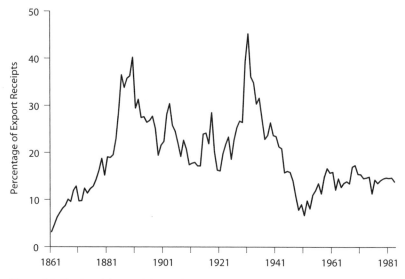

Figure 6.2. Foreign debt-servicing ratio, 1861 to 1983.
Notes: Foreign debt-servicing ratio is defined as property income debits as a percentage of total credits on the current account of the balance of payments. The Australian dollar was floated in 1983.
Sources: 1861 to 1900: Butlin (1962), Tables 247 and 248, pp .410–14. 1901 to 1949: McLean (1968), pp. 83–88. 1950 to 1983, Reserve Bank of Australia, *Australian Economic Statistics 1949–50 to 1996–97*, Table 1.10.

bubble in land and housing in Victoria led to a crisis in the financial sector in 1893 with the collapse or temporary closure of many banks leading, in turn, to the loss or freezing of deposits and a decline in lending. Growth there slowed, reducing colonial government revenues, thereby restricting Victoria's capacity to continue funding high levels of public investment in infrastructure and further slowing domestic economic activity. The downturn in economic prospects in the colonies more generally (with the exception of Western Australia) at first slowed the rate of immigration, thus compounding the negative demand forces in their economies, then led to a complete drying-up of immigration as the depression deepened.

The complex interaction between these internal and foreign sources of the boom bedevils any neat attribution of the causes of the bust that followed. As with most complex macroeconomic events, simple explanations are rarely persuasive. The weakening of investment criteria by pastoralists, governments, and others is part of the story, but begs the question what changed investors' attitudes toward risk in the 1880s. We now have a better appreciation of the dynamic role of expectations during asset price bubbles, yet they recur because each generation seems to think this time it is a sustainable run-up in the value of land, houses, and shares.[14] The event that changed the psychological underpinnings of the 1880s bubble may have been the reconsideration by British investors following the Barings crisis of the risk of further lending to colonial governments. This led to a reduction in colonial loans raised on the London capital market. But the vulnerability of the Victorian economy in particular to any slowdown in foreign investment was entirely the result of prior borrowing decisions made in the colony. The drastic reduction in government spending that occurred in Victoria in the 1890s (described below) illustrates this vulnerability—albeit after the event.

There are at least two interesting questions about this particular boom and bust that seem central to the analysis of long-run growth and prosperity in Australia. First, was the bust avoidable, or could it have been greatly attenuated? Second, were the gains or benefits of the boom sufficient to outweigh the losses or costs of the ensuing bust? With respect to the first question, the issue is under what conditions sustainable growth could have continued through the 1890s. Had growth in the 1880s proceeded at a lower *rate*, with smaller inflows of immigrants and foreign capital, and a slower extension of the area under pastoral occupation, there would have occurred a correspondingly slower run-up in public debt and in the value of assets such as land and housing. And perhaps a slower rate of pastoral expansion would have resulted in a more sustainable occupation of marginal lands. But some major adjustments in the colonial economy toward the end of the century would still have occurred. International commodity prices would still have declined until the mid-1890s. The demographic echo effect from the gold rushes would still have run its course. The Barings crisis would still have triggered a reassessment of the growth prospects of the Australian colonies resulting in a lowering of the expected risk-adjusted returns on further investment there by British lenders. And the droughts that set in during the 1890s would still have delivered a serious blow to rural prosperity. Furthermore, with no national government, there was no institutional framework within which a coordinated tweaking of the growth strategies of the individual colonies could occur. Indeed, a central element in the pre-1890s boom was their competitive pursuit of rapid growth in their populations and economies. Perhaps intercolonial rivalry became a negative-sum game to the extent that it encouraged high-risk behavior in the private sector and unproductive public-sector investment.

Backing off from such counterfactual speculation, we may still ask whether the boom was, in some sense, worth it. The assessment of historians is that the 1890s depression was a social and economic disaster. But disaster avoidance

---

[14] For a nice historical account of the role of expectations in asset price bubbles in the United States, see Shiller (2000), chapter 5, "New Era Economic Thinking."

comes at a cost. Put differently, who gained and who lost from what happened? In one perspective, the costs and benefits were borne by different generations of Australians. Those whose adult lives spanned the 1850s to the 1880s gained most from four decades of prosperity. Someone who arrived at working age (say, age fifteen) in 1889 enjoyed the fruits of prosperity only as a child. Thereafter, unemployment increased and, as is clear from figure 6.1, per capita incomes were little higher in 1914 (by which time this individual would be age forty) than in 1890, and for most of the intervening years were below it, with both the higher unemployment and reduced living standards due in some measure to the negative consequences of the boom—or at least its final stages.

Shifting our attention from the experience of different age cohorts to that of the macro-economy, many historians have implicitly assumed that there were "excesses" of the pre-1890 boom that are identifiable simply because of the crash that followed. But this is post hoc reasoning. First, as just suggested, there are beneficiaries of a boom despite its having acquired speculative attributes. Also, in the wake of recent experience, we are now more circumspect in assuming either that the speculative element in asset prices could have been identified ex ante, or that feasible policies could have been adopted that would have avoided both the excesses of the boom and the resulting crash. If there exists a strategy for ensuring sustained rapid growth without risk of major crises and hence interruptions to prosperity, then we have yet to discover it. Even the most successful developing countries over the last half century or so have witnessed periodic booms, crises, or busts. It may be that rapidly developing *settler* economies were even more likely to experience periodic major interruptions to their growth. The high but variable rate of immigration added to this inherent instability—because of the economic-demographic interactions previously described. And the lack of information about the economy's resource base was a further destabilizing feature, as its characteristics were established primarily through the inherently speculative investment necessary to occupy the frontier and tap its resources, whether via pioneer farming or mining.

The economic crisis of the 1890s thus has many of the traits of the economic and financial crises that pepper the history of the international economy. But there is one further feature of the Australian crisis that warrants mention: It was not uniformly felt across the colonies. The epicenter was Victoria. In contrast, the very small colony of Western Australia was to enjoy a boom in the 1890s—courtesy of the gold discoveries there. And it should also be noted that the seventh Australasian colony had experienced its debt crisis in the 1880s following a borrowing boom in the 1870s. Hence New Zealand was in recovery mode, strongly so after 1895 when international commodity prices rose. This is critical context to any understanding of the decision by New Zealand not to join the federation at the end of the decade.

WHY WAS RECOVERY SO SLOW? COMPARISON WITH
OTHER SETTLER ECONOMIES

There were economic downturns, recessions, and/or financial crises in a number of economies in the early 1890s, hence the Australian experience invites comparison with them. I have already noted, and shortly will return to, the case of Argentina. In the United States a major financial panic occurred in 1893, and the associated downturn there is sometimes referred to as a depression. More generally, the first half of the 1890s saw a continuation of a downward trend in international commodity prices that had set in around 1873 and was to continue until they turned up following 1895. In British agricultural history, this was long known as the "great depression." Indeed, throughout much of Europe this period was associated with falling rural incomes, the importation of new-world grains, and mass rural migration to the cities and also overseas to the settler economies, especially the United States. The first globalization, from which Australia, and especially its farmers, was a major beneficiary, was wreaking economic and social dislocation on the European countryside. And the mass international migrations that occurred at this time reflected the changing comparative advantage in (and hence location of) agricultural production as international trade in food and fiber boomed.[15]

From the mid-1890s the long downward trend in commodity prices and associated gentle deflation went into reverse. More broadly, the period from 1895 to 1914 was one of rapid growth and prosperity in the other settler economies—Argentina, Canada, and New Zealand—each of which was highly integrated into the international economy. Australian experience, however, was an exception. There was no quick bounce-back from the crisis of the early 1890s. The economic indicators do not show a sustained upward trend until about 1904. Australia "lost" a decade of growth when viewed in comparative perspective. And when growth did return, it was not sufficiently robust during the decade prior to the First World War to make up for its delayed onset. This is the only extended period of its history when Australia's domestic economy did not enjoy prosperity during a boom in the international economy.

The explanation for this anomaly in Australian experience can be approached from a national or a comparative perspective, and I will do both. With respect to the former, there is one major fact concerning the delayed recovery from the 1890s depression, and one major interpretation of it, and they both warrant emphasis. The fact is the onset and persistence of what has become known as the federation drought, which extended over much of the settled area of the country for several years, reaching its peak early in the new century. This, I like to imagine, is what the poet had in mind when choosing the adjective "wilful"

---

[15]Hatton and Williamson (1998) and O'Rourke and Williamson (1999).

to qualify her description of Australia as "a lavish land": she would have had direct experience of both depression and drought having been born in Sydney in 1885.

Because prosperity at that time relied much more than it does now on the fortunes of the rural sector, the prolonged run of poor seasons, coming on the heels of the economic depression, had a major negative impact on the economy. One dramatic statistic is that the number of sheep, which had peaked at 106 million in 1892, fell by half to 54 million in 1903: this suggests an economic catastrophe. But, as always, statistics need careful handling. Not all of the re-duction in the national flock was the result of low rainfall. Some of the decline represented a rational disinvestment in pastoral assets (destocking) following the speculative excesses of the 1880s. This was especially the case on the fron-tier where the marginal climatic conditions for profitable wool-growing were most savagely exposed. Since sheep in the arid zone had lower fleece weights of poorer quality, the *average* fleece weight rose as the number of sheep de-clined. Hence wool production—a more pertinent economic indicator than sheep numbers—fell by only 36 per cent between its peak in 1892 and through in 1902.[16]

The diversification of agricultural production that occurred during the pe-riod covered by this chapter illustrates farmers' adaptability in responding to a sequence of shocks, financial and climatic, that cushioned their economic fortunes and thereby those of the country. The rise of "mixed" farming where farmers combined sheep-raising with crop production had been occurring for some time: the advantages of producing wool and wheat rather than one ex-clusively were obvious to farmers as they adapted to fluctuations in commod-ity prices and climatic conditions. In the 1890s the diversification of both ag-ricultural output and exports accelerated. Critical to this diversification was the introduction of refrigerated shipping in the 1880s, permitting the export of frozen meat (lamb and mutton) and of dairy products to the British market. The frozen meat trade allowed the farmer to exploit the joint-product nature of some breeds of sheep beyond the supply of fresh meat to the domestic market. Also, for the first time, Australia became a consistent net exporter of wheat.

In order to assess more rigorously the contribution of the drought to the delayed recovery requires an economic model that would chart the fortunes of both the rural sector and the wider economy through the 1890s and beyond under "normal" or average climatic conditions. The gap between the counter-factual (that is, drought-adjusted) and actual GDP would then represent the economic impact of the drought. This exercise has yet to be attempted. How-ever a partial analysis of the topic has been undertaken, assessing the likely path of rural sector output had there been average rainfall during the period. Drought-adjusted rural production still falls, though only until 1896, indicat-

---

[16]Vamplew (1987): sheep numbers on p. 81; greasy wool production on p. 82.

ing that factors other than the climate negatively impinged on the farm sector during these years.[17] The general equilibrium effects on the aggregate economy are far more difficult to measure. Because the drought persisted for several years, economic agents adjusted in myriad ways to offset its negative impact, so the net (but still negative) effect on the whole economy is likely to have been less than that on those most directly affected—the farmers. Nonetheless, there is no question that the federation drought placed a constraint on the recovery.

Also warranting emphasis is an interpretation of the delayed recovery from the 1890s depression, sometimes explicit, but mostly implicit in the literature, according to which it was the result of the severity of the imbalances in the economy that had accumulated prior to 1890 and that had to be corrected before sustainable growth and prosperity could return. I call this the "symmetry" hypothesis, as it suggests that both the depth and the duration of the slump were inversely related to the scale and seriousness of the preceding boom and bubble. Since the boom was sustained and the bubble substantial, there should be little surprise, from this perspective, that the subsequent slump was severe and recovery slow. But this scarcely constitutes a persuasive analysis of the causal economic mechanisms in play. Negative shocks can be followed by an "asymmetric" bounce-back: consider, for example, the rapid recoveries in some of the devastated economies following 1945, especially West Germany and Japan. More generally, comparisons of recoveries from economic crises covering long spans of history have revealed complex forces at work.[18] For example, the presence of a financial or banking collapse tends to attenuate recovery, and just such a collapse occurred in Australia in the 1890s.

Contributing to the slow recovery was the adjustment required in the balance sheets of households, firms (including banks), and colonial governments. The end of the debt-fueled boom required what is now loosely described as "deleveraging." Households' balance sheets were negatively impacted by the decline in asset (house, land, and share) prices, and by bank collapses that resulted in frozen deposits or their complete loss. At the same time, unemployment rose and job security declined. The result was a desire by the household sector to increase its savings rate so as to rebuild its capital losses, and also for precautionary reasons given the deterioration in the labor market. It follows that the desired savings rate would be above the actual rate applying prior to the slump. But to raise their savings rate, households would have to cut consumption, and this would negatively impact private demand. In the short run, with unemployment

---

[17] The modeling of rural sector output under conditions of normal rainfall is reported in *The Impact of the 1895–1903 Drought on Australian Rural Production*, an unpublished honors thesis in economics at the University of Adelaide in 1997 by Patrick James McDonald. The main findings are summarized in McLean (2006).

[18] A recent survey and analysis is reported by Rogoff and Reinhart (2009); however they give limited attention to the Australian episode in the 1890s.

rising, there would be little scope to make this desired adjustment to household finances. Rather, the deleveraging would mostly occur only when the slump phase ended and gave way to the first signs of recovery, but it would thereby weaken that recovery.[19]

A closely related influence was the virtual cessation of foreign investment. In the 1880s boom, the savings of foreigners had financed about 40 percent of domestic investment. The drying up of capital inflow in the following decade could, in principle, have been offset by an increase in domestic saving, sustaining domestic investment and thereby countering in some measure the other negative pressures on economic activity. Indeed there is evidence that foreign and domestic sources of finance for investment in Australia at this time moved inversely—that is, capital inflow was in part a substitute for domestic saving, permitting higher levels of consumption to be sustained at any given level of investment.[20] But following the economic and financial crises in the early 1890s, Australian households were in no position to offset the sharp fall in capital inflow by raising their savings rate.

Neither were the colonial governments in a position to contribute to domestic savings by moving into budget surpluses. They experienced declining revenues as economic activity slowed, but faced fixed debt repayments, so deficits increased. Victoria was the most severely affected (figure 6.3). Modern macroeconomic theory and practice would prescribe that some increase in deficit-financed public-sector stimulus to the economy might be warranted to offset the collapse in private-sector investment and employment. Given its existing debt levels and rising debt-servicing ratio, however, the Victorian government also needed to deleverage, and in any event faced a less receptive London capital market for further colonial issues. Hence there was some substitution of colonial issues. But short of negotiating a rescheduling of its existing debt obligations—a policy option apparently not contemplated but adopted elsewhere at this time, as will shortly be described—there was no alternative but to cut recurrent government spending. This, of course, worsened the slump and delayed the recovery.[21]

Adopting a comparative perspective assists the explanation of the slow recovery, and raises further doubts about the thesis that it may be regarded simply as a consequence of the size of the problem to be corrected. In particular, the Argentine experience is in many ways apposite. These two settler economies were at comparable stages in their development. Argentina had experienced a resource-based boom prior to 1890 based on close trading and investment

---

[19]I further explore this mechanism in a comparative analysis of Australia, Canada, and the United States: McLean (1994).

[20]Bentick (1969) analyzed the Victorian experience at this time in terms of the macroeconomic relationships linking asset prices, private wealth, foreign borrowing, and the fiscal position of the government.

[21]This, and the following comparative analysis, draws on the discussion in McLean (2006).

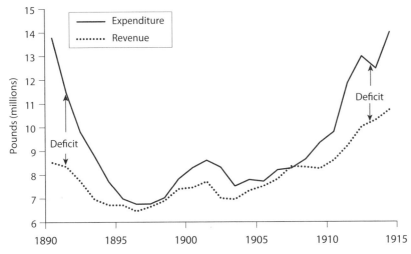

Figure 6.3. Victoria: government revenue, expenditure, and deficit, 1890 to 1914.
Note: Years ended 31 December.
Source: Vamplew (1987), Series GF67 and GF75, p. 262.

links with Britain, the expansion of rural settlement on the pampas and beyond, and an urban construction boom based on high levels of immigration and centered in Buenos Aires. Broadly speaking the character and dimensions of the booms in the two countries were similar, and the initial financial crises also appear to have had much in common. Indeed the comparability of the situation in the two explains why the contagion effect seems to have played a part in the Australian story. The reaction of London-based lenders to the Barings crisis in Argentina in 1890 was to re-rate the risk of investing further in the Australian colonies.

What the Argentine story suggests, however, is that it is possible to achieve a rapid recovery from a severe crisis at the end of a long boom: the recovery need neither be delayed nor slow. So, how did Argentina manage to recover so rapidly, and from 1895 fully participate in the two decades of prosperity in the international economy that ensued? One simple indicator of the divergence between these two settler economies that occurred at this time—uncharacteristically in Argentina's favor—lies in their population growth (figure 6.4). In 1890 the populations were similar: 3.2 million and 3.4 million for Australia and Argentina, respectively. By 1913 the Australian population had reached 4.9 million, while that in Argentina was 7.7 million, a figure Australia was not to attain until 1949.

There were two significant policy responses to the crisis in Argentina not undertaken (or feasible) in Australia, and one difference in their stage of rural settlement, that may go far to account for the quick and vigorous bounce-back in the former. The Argentine government secured a rescheduling of its debt

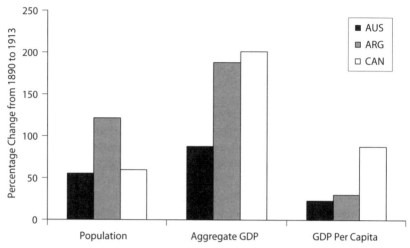

Figure 6.4. Growth indicators: Argentina, Australia, and Canada, 1890 to 1913.
Note: Percentage changes are based on end years.
Source: McLean (2006), p. 217, Table 1.

obligations with its British creditors that both lowered the rates of interest charged and lengthened the period of repayment. This is a standard maneuver for a country hit by a severe debt crisis. The downside is the reputational effect: given the history of debt default, the heightened sovereign risk may cause international capital markets either to close against future borrowing for some period, or to add a risk premium to the rates charged.[22] The advantage to the economy in crisis and seeking debt relief is that it frees up resources from servicing the foreign debt for reallocation toward stimulatory government expenditure that will boost domestic demand, hastening the recovery.

The second important policy response to the crisis observed in Argentina but not in Australia is that the former effectively devalued its currency. In fact it introduced a dual currency system, a gold and paper peso, holding the value of the former but allowing the inconvertible paper peso to depreciate relative to the gold peso. The devaluation was substantial—more than 50 percent between the late 1880s and the mid-1890s. Again, there is nothing surprising about this response to an external crisis in a small, open, developing country operating under a fixed exchange-rate regime, of which the gold standard is the archetype. The prices of imported goods rise when measured in domestic currency, so expenditure switches to domestically produced substitutes, stimulating local production.

---

[22]Historical studies of the extent to which defaulters are subsequently penalized do not show a uniformly negative outcome; other factors seem also to matter. But, ex ante, the *future* attitude of the international capital markets to a defaulter seeking fresh raisings is unknown.

And the incomes of Argentine exporters increased because their products were more competitive in foreign markets, and they received higher prices (measured in paper pesos), with both effects increasing domestic demand and employment. Argentine economic historians attribute the fiddling of the exchange rate, together with the debt relief, as major factors accounting for the brevity of the Argentine crisis and the rapid turnaround in its economic fortunes in the 1890s. I think that, had an IMF existed at the time, its advice would have been to do pretty much as the Argentine government did, so close were its policies to modern orthodoxy.

Why did Australia not follow suit, as Australians were not unaware of events in Argentina and could see the similarities in the antecedent conditions to the crises in both? First, there was no national government in Australia—until 1901. Indeed, during the debt rescheduling, the national government in Argentina had to assume responsibility for the reckless borrowing of some of its provincial governments. In Australia the colonies were on their own in their dealings with the London capital market. Even had federation occurred prior to the crisis, one may venture to suggest that the national government would not have followed the Argentine example in responding to the crisis. This stems from an assumption underpinning the responses of Australian political leaders to the situation they found themselves in by the early 1890s that, whatever the cost, it was unthinkable to default on, or seek a rescheduling of, foreign debts. Perhaps this was culturally determined: a matter of trust or reputation with "kith and kin" in Britain—both the imperial government and the London banks. The belief that future dealings with the London capital market would be seriously impaired for a prolonged period appears to have been implicit in the near-complete absence of discussion of seeking a rescheduling of the debt as an option. Similarly, the prospect of currency devaluation in some guise, with the aim of raising the incomes of Australian exporters and also stimulating activity in the import-competing sectors, was never seriously canvased. Indeed there was more discussion of the possible advantages of moving to a bi-metallic standard—no doubt of advantage to domestic silver producers. So, partly for institutional reasons, and partly for reasons of imperial affinity, the fairly obvious policy recommendations that would now be high on any list, and were adopted in Argentina, were not implemented by any of the Australian colonies.

Of course a comparison with Argentina has its limitations: there are many other differences between it and Australia that might also account for their very different postcrisis economic growth performances. Relevant to longer-run influences on growth is the issue of the extensive margin of rural settlement or "frontier" and its role in boom and bust, as previously considered. Australian land settlement and initial rural occupation occurred ahead of that on the pampas or the Canadian prairies and, with some regional exceptions, especially in Western Australia, had been completed by 1890. In the other two settler economies, the period 1895 to 1914 was a boom time, and in each case a boom closely associated with the geographical expansion of agriculture, especially wheat production.[23]

TROPICS, CROPS, AND MELANESIANS: ANOTHER ROAD NOT TAKEN

Australia is unusual among advanced economies in that a significant part of the continent lies in the tropics. In some current debates among economists, latitude matters: the tropics seem not to have been as conducive to economic growth as more temperate-zone regions.[24] And the settlement of tropical Australia has indeed lagged that of the rest of the country: the population there remains small, and there are no large urban areas. One early attempt to expand the regional economy illustrates some of the obstacles to development in the tropics, but also draws our attention once again to the critical role of institutions in the course of economic growth in Australia. Accordingly it is important to review the circumstances surrounding the importation of Melanesian indentured labor into Queensland, an arrangement devised primarily to assist in the cultivation of sugar there.

The combination of sugar production and imported (coerced) labor is a central element in the pattern of development that arose out of the initial endowments characteristic of regions in the Caribbean: labor-intensive crop production subject to scale economies at the level of the firm but a shortage of local labor leading, in turn, to the importation of slave or indentured workers for the plantations. The resulting unequal distribution of wealth and political power persisted, and the path of development led in the long run to relatively low incomes despite reporting some of the highest incomes in the Western Hemisphere in the eighteenth century.[25] Was north Queensland in danger of adopting similar growth-retarding economic institutions?

Early economic development in coastal north Queensland has some similarities with that of the Caribbean sugar economies. The newly established Queensland government had received permission from the secretary of state for the colonies to import "coolie" labor from India, and in 1861 passed an act for its regulation. However attempts to secure Indian or Chinese labor for the pastoral industry failed in the face of British and Indian objections. The Pacific islands were an alternative source. In 1863 sixty Melanesians were brought to the Brisbane area to work on a private venture to grow cotton, which was experiencing high prices as a result of the American Civil War. But it was primar-

---

[23]Comparative studies of Argentine and Canadian agricultural development at this time are to be found in Solberg (1987) and Adelman (1994).

[24]See Hall and Jones (1999), and Easterly and Levine (2003).

[25]See, for example, Engerman and Sokoloff (1997), especially pp. 270–72.

ily the sugar industry that took off in the 1860s. Initially production was on "plantations" that grew, milled, and refined their own sugar, using Melanesian labor. Between 1863 and 1904 more than 62,000 indenture contracts were written, though because of the practice of re-indenture, this overstates the number of Melanesians brought to Queensland. The average annual number recruited was 1,699 in the 1870s; 2,536 in the 1880s; and 1,307 between 1893 and 1900.[26]

The labor came on "contracts" for fixed periods, so appears to have been voluntary. However there is uncertainty over the degree of coercion used in recruitment in the islands, and over the extent of the Melanesians' understanding of the terms and conditions they were agreeing to. It was certainly indentured labor, regulated by the colonial government, but at the time, and since, it has often been regarded as semicoercive. From the beginning there was widespread opposition to the system in the rest of Queensland, in the other Australian colonies, and in London. Partly this was on moral grounds, as with the earlier antitransportation—and the British antislavery—movements.[27] Partly it was on economic grounds, the fear that cheaper labor would lower agricultural and pastoral wages. And partly it was on social cohesion—or outright racist— grounds. So who was in favor?

The sugar industry was locating in coastal areas in tropical Queensland, and the pastoral industry was also extending inland in the north of the colony. They both sought cheap labor. It is unclear how much the demand for imported labor reflected cost pressures—that white labor could only have been obtained at wages and conditions that would have rendered sugar or pastoral production unprofitable. The other factor discussed at the time was climate. The planters appeared to believe they needed non-European labor; and one governor of Queensland was "dubious of the possibility of cultivating sugar-cane in the tropics with white labour," but the colony's premier disagreed—"The same thing used to be said about Moreton Bay [Brisbane]."[28]

The extent to which the colonial government supported the planters varied. When opposition in the colony to the Melanesian labor arrangements mounted, the response in the north was to threaten separation—the formation of a new colony that, presumably, would be unfettered in devising its own labor recruitment policies and labor-market institutions. This intensified following an election fought on the issue of imported Indian and Melanesian labor, and the passage of legislation in the Queensland Parliament in 1884 to limit the employment of the Melanesians to unskilled occupations in tropical and semitropical agriculture, and to make it illegal to import Melanesians after 1890

---

[26] Cited in Shlomowitz (1982, pp. 345 and 349). This source provides an excellent overview of the key institutional and economic features of the market for Melanesian labor in Queensland.
    [27] There was related concern at evidence of high death rates among new arrivals: see ibid., pp. 346–48.
    [28] Samuel Griffith, quoted in Shann (1988 [1933], p. 312).

(a decision that was reversed in 1892). The pressure for separation reached a turning point in 1887. The British government alone had the power to change boundaries, but decided it would consider the request it had received from the northern separatists only after a majority vote in favor of separation in the Queensland Parliament—which, of course, would not be attainable.[29]

Part of the story of the gradual demise of the use of Melanesian labor in sugar production was the rise of the "central mill" system for crushing the cane and refining the sugar.[30] It was found that by shifting these two stages of production from the plantation to a local sugar mill and refinery, scale economies were realized, lowering costs, and making smaller cane growers competitive in the cane-growing stage. Hence by the mid-1880s, sugar plantations were being subdivided, and the colonial government provided financial support for the construction of the central mills on condition they buy cane from farms employing only white labor. However, white labor was generally confined to the mills, with the small cane-growers each employing a few Melanesians—who were not permitted to own land.

Following the federation of the six colonies into the Commonwealth of Australia in 1901, one of the first pieces of legislation in the federal Parliament was the Pacific Island Labourers Act, ending indentured labor in (the now state of) Queensland through the deportation of the Melanesians beginning in 1906, with compensation paid to the employers—bounties and subsidies/ protection for the sugar industry. In some small part, the Commonwealth was brought into existence to remedy a perceived failure in the existing institutional arrangements.[31]

Perhaps the most interesting aspect of the story of indentured Melanesian labor in Australia is thus not why it emerged—the preconditions seem to have been similar to those found elsewhere in terms of climate, crop, and factor endowment—but how it ended. Contrary to the impression of institutional lock-in and persistence central to the perspective that initial endowments determine fundamental institutional arrangements, and hence long-run growth, the practice of using indentured labor was abolished. This was partly as a

---

[29]Shann (1988 [1933], p. 311) suggests that the reasons the British might have taken this position include a fear that a precedent might otherwise be set for secession elsewhere in the empire (including home rule for Ireland); and a fear in the City that Queensland bonds might be less secure from repudiation after the loss of the north, as had happened in the United States during the formation of new states.

[30]These organizational changes in the industry are described in Shlomowitz (1982), pp. 339–44.

[31]There was a fear in the other colonies that the Melanesians brought to Queensland might subsequently move, unrestricted, elsewhere on the continent. Since federation would lead to the transfer of immigration powers to the federal government, this fear would be assuaged. It is important to note that the discussion of the Melanesian problem in the debates leading to federation were often linked to the wider debate on immigration policy, and that the act relating to the Melanesians in the federal Parliament was followed by the Immigration Restriction Act of 1901— the origin of the notorious "White Australia" policy.

consequence of the changes in production methods that made alternatives to plantation-based sugar-growing more efficient (although colonial government regulations and subsidies encouraged these market forces), partly through popular opposition from within Queensland expressed within the framework of existing political institutions, and partly through a newly created institution— the Australian Parliament. The interaction of economic and political institutions here seems central to this outcome.[32]

Might it have ended differently? The critical point seems to have occurred in 1887 when the north Queensland separatists failed in their bid to gain support from the British government for the creation of a new colony. Had the British agreed—they only had to follow the same procedure that had led to the separation of Queensland from New South Wales in 1859—would a society and economy have emerged that looked similar to those in the antebellum South of the United States or in the Caribbean? Writing in 1933, a leading economic historian considered that "[p]olitical separation for north and central Queensland, had it come in the [eighteen] 'eighties, would have set up a type of colony which Australia had escaped, an aristocracy of white planters seeking the wealth needed for their ascendancy by the obsolete and stagnant method of semi-servile labour."[33] Blainey has also ventured an explicit counterfactual: "In North Queensland in the 1880s arose the kind of separation movement which, had it existed thirty years earlier, would have had quick success"; and "The refusal of the British government to create a separate colony in the late 1880s was probably a turning point in our history. At the time it seemed a decision of no great importance but it probably prevented the emergence of a seventh colony which could have become a stronghold of coloured labour."[34] The poor long-run growth outcomes recorded by similar economies suggest that the failure of the north Queensland separation movement was indeed an important episode in the history of Australia's economic prosperity.

ECONOMIC EFFECTS OF FEDERATION

The federation of the six colonies into the Commonwealth of Australia in 1901 ranks with the granting of responsible self-government in the 1850s as a major turning point in the constitutional and political history of the continent. Since growth economists increasingly identify the set of constitutional and political arrangements and institutions as one of the "fundamental" determinants of why some countries are rich and others poor, this inquiry must include a brief

---

[32] This is consistent with the analysis of institutional persistence and change in Acemoglu and Robinson (2006b).

[33] Shann (1988 [1933], p. 313).

[34] Blainey (1982), pp. 198 and 201.

assessment of the impact of federation on the prosperity of Australians.[35] Identifying this impact is relatively straightforward in the short run—say up to the First World War, the period that is the main focus of this chapter. Thereafter disentangling the influence of constitutional and political arrangements from all other influences on growth and prosperity proves increasingly difficult.

Initially the new federal government comprised little more than the postal service—the Postmaster General's Department. It would take some years to organize a separate federal bureaucracy for such purposes as the collection of customs revenue or the compilation of statistics. Indeed, the new Commonwealth Bureau of Census and Statistics (CBCS), forerunner to the Australian Bureau of Statistics (ABS), issued its first annual *Year Book* only in 1908. In addition, there was no central or reserve bank to assist the monetary and financial management of the new nation. The Commonwealth Bank, established in 1911, was primarily designed to offer depositors a publicly owned alternative to the private institutions that had proved so prone to collapse in the 1890s, and from 1913 it assumed the role of banker to the federal government. It acquired note-issuing powers in 1924, but it was to be much later before wider central-bank functions were added, and not until 1960 that a stand-alone Reserve Bank of Australia was created.

Any short-run impact of federation on the course of economic affairs, and on national prosperity, would thus arise only through the economic policy decisions of the new federal government. Some are well known. An early act of the federal Parliament related to the accession by the Commonwealth of powers over immigration. As just indicated, the context was the issue of Melanesian contract labor in Queensland. But the wider issue of the racial or ethnic composition of Australia's immigrants was also in play: this was the origin of the so-called white Australia policy, though restrictions and exclusions had earlier applied within the colonies. The short-run economic implications of this policy, beyond its effects on the sugar industry in Queensland, were small. However the story was different in the longer run. An immigration policy that de facto excluded classes of immigrants who would possibly have been prepared to work for lower wages and less favorable conditions than those currently enjoyed by many workers would be a key element in the effort to maintain a high wage economy in Australia.

Under the Constitution the power to set a common external tariff was given to the federal government, while all intercolonial tariffs (indeed, all barriers to interstate trade) would be abolished. The level of the new national tariff, implemented in 1902, was a compromise arrived at in the context of the colonies having had different levels of protection: New South Wales had been the least protectionist, Victoria the most. Nonetheless, there seems little doubt that the

---

[35] A major contribution to the growth literature on this topic is that of Persson and Tabellini (2003).

average *level* of protection increased for the country as a whole since bargaining between the states resulted in the uniform national tariff rates being set mainly in reference to those prevailing in Victoria. In theory this would have a negative effect on national economic welfare. A related question is whether the subsequent adjustments to the tariff down to the First World War, notably the Lyne tariff of 1908, had any significant economic impact.

Any immediate effects of the transition to the new tariff structure are difficult to discern because of the concurrent economic dislocation and downturn resulting from the severe drought. Thus accounts of particular firms or industries facing trading difficulties in the first years after federation may reflect the impact of the new tariff regime, or may be due to the unrelated deterioration in market conditions. Because the economy was operating at less than full employment due to the drought, the lift in protection may even have had a positive net effect on employment and thus domestic economic activity in the very short run. Thereafter the *average* level of tariff protection changed little in the prewar period. Thus it is unsurprising that there is no clear evidence suggesting a significant effect, either positive or negative, of the federal tariff on growth or prosperity before 1914.[36]

In the labor market, important institutional innovations were made in the area of industrial-disputes resolution, and key decisions regarding minimum wages were announced within this new regulatory regime. These decisions flowed directly from the constitutional provisions regarding federal powers over aspects of labor relations, and gave disputes settlement and wage determination a quasi-judicial and increasingly centralized character that, broadly speaking, was to persist until the reforms of the 1990s. The Commonwealth Conciliation and Arbitration Court was established in 1904 with the power to determine wages and conditions in cases where industrial disputes crossed state boundaries, and to impose compulsory mediation. Most intensively examined in the history of wage determination in Australia has been the Harvester judgment of 1907, which established a "living wage" for a worker (and his family) that became the benchmark for subsequent determinations of the "basic" wage. Yet despite these innovative institutional and policy changes, there is scant evidence they had any discernible effect on the operation of the wider economy prior to the war.[37]

Closely related to these federation-era institutional and policy changes may have been changes in social norms (including of fairness) or expectations (including of government in providing welfare and economic "security" or stabilization). Perhaps it is through these mechanisms that the experience of the

---

[36]The most recent estimates of the average level of tariff protection at this time are by Lloyd (2008). Forster (1977) and Irwin (2006) analyze the short-run economic impact of the federation tariff.

[37]Evaluations are provided by Forster (1985, 1989) and Issac (2008).

1890s depression bequeathed its greatest imprint on society, though it is difficult to directly identify any causal links. It is clear, though, that the strikes and unemployment associated with the depression greatly influenced the agenda and world view of the labor movement in its search for improved working conditions and economic security, a search pursued through enhanced political representation and the creation of new labor-market institutions, especially at the federal level. The key question here, however, is whether New South Wales, Victoria, or any other colony would have experienced a significantly different growth path between 1901 and 1914 had federation not occurred. Constitutional, political, and related legal arrangements would all have been different in such a counterfactual. But within this time frame, neither the level nor the distribution of incomes is likely to have been greatly affected.

When we look instead to the consequences of federation for growth and prosperity after 1914, the conclusion is likely to be very different. During the twentieth century the size and scope of federal government involvement in the economy greatly expanded, its policies with respect to the tariff and regulation of the labor market evolved markedly, and the ascendance of macroeconomic policy priorities gave it increased influence relative to that of the states. On closer inspection, however, it is evident we must look beyond the constitutional and political arrangements surrounding federation if we are to account for these later changes in the role and impact of the federal government. Other developments, not foreseen by the founding fathers, interacted with the foundational arrangements they constructed. That is, the federal Constitution began to influence economic performance only in the context of subsequent events. Most significant among these were a succession of major negative shocks, beginning with the First World War. This war, the difficult international economic environment of the 1920s, the depression of the 1930s, and the Second World War, were the immediate causes of the most important changes in national economic institutions and policies during the first half of the twentieth century. The federal structure was the constitutional framework within which these challenges were responded to, new institutions were created and policies amended. But there was nothing inherent in federation itself—or that was an inevitable consequence of it—that determined the form or timing of these key institutional and policy outcomes over following decades. Thus it is not easy to distinguish the effects of "federation" per se from subsequent and probably more powerful institutional and policy influences on growth and prosperity. This is a theme to which I will return in later chapters.

Of course, there exists something of a natural experiment on whether the individual colonies would have been better off economically if they had not federated—ever. Seven colonies participated in the discussions leading up to federation but one stayed aloof. So the New Zealand economic experience since 1901 may help in thinking about the counterfactual of a no-federation world. Specifically, to what extent, and within which periods, was growth and prosperity in New Zealand some indication of what might have been the experience of at least some of the Australian colonies? Until 1960 there is no evidence of per capita GDP in New Zealand falling markedly behind that of Australia, although this does not rule out that it may have been even higher as the seventh state. Nor does it establish that one or more Australian states may have diverged (up or down) from their historical growth experience had they, too, declined to join.[38] After 1970, New Zealand's economic performance fell behind Australia's, despite increased economic integration across the Tasman Sea (figure 2.1). Many influences bear on the recent comparative performance of the two national economies, just as there are well-known sources of the changing patterns of growth among the Australian states.[39] Identifying the contribution of federation per se to the observed outcomes may be difficult, but this is the challenge if it is to be assigned a key role as an institution underpinning long-run prosperity.

ACCOUNTING FOR THE LOSS OF THE "TOP SPOT" IN INCOME PER CAPITA

Between 1890 and 1914 Australia lost its position as having the world's highest incomes. Why? The depression of the 1890s and slow recovery from it are clearly contributing factors in the short run, since neither the United States nor Britain experienced comparable economic conditions, especially after 1895. But there must have been other and deeper factors in play, or despite some delay in bouncing back from the depression, the previous sources of relative prosperity should in the longer term have reemerged and returned Australia to its former ranking. One way to identify these is to return to the framework previously adopted to account for how Australia had secured the top spot. It turns out that the specific advantages identified as underpinning the relative prosperity of Australians before 1890 did not persist much beyond then. And the reasons for this are not directly due to the depression or the slowness of the recovery from it.[40]

By 1914 Australia's per capita income was only 3 percent above that in the United States: given the quality of the historical data we can say that there was

---

[38] Western Australia has occasionally exhibited secessionist tendencies—though mainly rhetorical in nature. In 1901 its population was only 184,000, less than 5 percent of the Australian total. Its impressive growth and prosperity date from its postwar mineral discoveries: prior to this it may have struggled as an independent entity—in comparison, say, to the much larger New Zealand economy.

[39] In this context, the relative contribution of natural-resource-based activity in Australasia's regional economies may be an important source of the differences in their long-run performance. I will have more to say in chapter 9 concerning the possible sources of the different performances of the two national economies during recent decades.

[40] The following discussion draws on Broadberry and Irwin (2007), Irwin (2007), and McLean (2007).

rough parity in incomes in the two countries. The Australian advantage of 40 percent or more prior to 1890 had been all but eliminated. Since we are looking at the *ratio* between incomes in the two countries, and how it changed over time, we have to be alert to the possibility that American demographic, labor force, or productivity trends changed in a favorable direction *by more than* occurred in Australia. And this seems to have happened with respect to workforce participation rates: by 1914 they were similar in the two economies. Because the participation rate (or employment to population ratio) is the outcome of many diverse influences operating by region or by gender—to give just two examples—it is not yet clear precisely why this occurred. With respect to the gender ratio, the unusually high masculinity rate observed in the Australian data prior to 1890 gradually fades. With its origins in immigration accompanying the gold rushes, if not earlier, this is a clear case of one favorable influence on Australian incomes that was independent of the 1890s depression experience and that gradually weakened over several decades.

But there is more to the decline in Australia's relative position than can be attributed to demography and workforce participation. This can be illustrated by assuming that the relative advantage in labor productivity Australia enjoyed in 1891 was preserved until 1911, then re-estimating the ratio of incomes relative to the United States in that year. Australian incomes would have been 20 percent above American incomes, but the gap would still have fallen by about half from what it had been in 1891. That is, the loss of a clear superiority over U.S. incomes after 1890 must substantially be due to a decline in Australia's relative productivity performance. And the explanations for this are more speculative.

One possible drag on Australia's productivity performance would have arisen had there occurred a significant re-allocation of labor from higher to lower productivity sectors in the economy. A theme of much discussion in the twentieth century was that just this was happening with respect to the declining share of agricultural employment and rise in that of manufacturing, a point made especially in relation to the potentially adverse consequences of encouraging industrial development behind high levels of tariff protection. Whereas farming was export oriented, hence had to be internationally competitive, the same could not be said of manufacturing. Whatever the magnitude of this drag on national efficiency in later decades (a topic we revisit in the next two chapters), it was unlikely to have played a major role before 1914. For one thing, the significant lift in tariff protection for manufacturing came in the interwar period, not prior to 1914. Also, there was no substantial reallocation of the labor force at this time: between 1891 and 1911, the share of manufacturing employment rose only by between 3 and 4 percentage points.[41]

The other resource-based industry, mining, which like agriculture was characterized by high levels of productivity and export competitiveness, experi-

---

[41] Based on alternative estimates provided by Butlin and Dowie (1969), pp. 144 and 153.

enced a major boom in the 1890s in the shape of the Western Australian gold discoveries. This would in principle help sustain overall productivity during a period of depression and drought adversely effecting output in the rest of the economy. But by 1914 the peak of the gold boom had already passed. Unlike the gold rushes of the 1850s—following which gold production declined gradually over several decades, and gold retained its position as the most important export for two decades—the decline in production from the Western Australian goldfields was more rapid. Australia-wide gold production peaked at 3.8 million fine ounces in 1903, but fell to 2.1 million by 1914, though this was above what it had been in the late 1880s. The share of GDP from the production of all minerals was almost the same in 1911 as in 1891.[42] Hence the mining industry is unlikely to have played a significant role in the decline of Australian comparative productivity performance at this time.

As labor productivity and incomes rise during the course of economic development, one result may be a change in workers' demand for leisure. That is, an increase in labor productivity may support an increased wage, reduced hours of work (increased leisure) at the same total wage, or a mix of the two. There is evidence that both American and Australian workers in the late nineteenth century and early twentieth were increasing their average hours of leisure. However the Australian workers were showing a much stronger preference for substituting leisure for labor. From a welfare perspective, there is no difference in the two situations insofar as they were freely chosen, and hence simply reflect differing preferences, as mentioned in chapter 2. But output would be lower in the society that chose more leisure. Could this have contributed to Australia's decline in measured incomes relative to the United States? With the data presently available, we can only guess that it may have. One study has estimated that if average incomes are augmented by the higher leisure in Australia, then the "augmented-income" per capita there in 1913 would be 13 percent above that in the United States rather than 4 percent by conventional estimation.[43] The methodology is different from the productivity analysis such that a direct comparison is not possible; but this exercise suggests that the differing labor-leisure choices made in the United States and Australia might be a contributing factor to the closing of the income gap between them.

Our analysis of Australian prosperity in relative terms is helpful in highlighting what might otherwise go unremarked, but such an analysis requires care. One should hesitate before attributing a fall in relative performance wholly to the Australian economy when closer inspection may reveal that it is the performance of the benchmark economy that needs explanation—as we have seen with respect to workforce participation rates. Similarly, in the case of the

---

[42]Gold production is from Kalix, Fraser, and Rawson (1966), p. 177; the share of mining in GDP from Butlin (1962), pp. 10–11.

[43]The analysis is to be found in Huberman (2004).

slowdown in the rate of increase of GDP per capita after 1890, we should ask whether the U.S. performance is, rather, the more unusual and requires explanation. Referring back to the comparisons across a number of economies previously made indicates that this is not the case. Canada, Argentina, and New Zealand also did much better than Australia in growth performance from 1890 to 1914. Thus, the emphasis on the seeming underperformance of Australia during this time appears warranted.

Anticipating later discussion, from 1914 to 1939 there was continued very low growth in per capita GDP in Australia, such that the half century from 1890 to 1940 is considered a period of near stagnation according to some measures of prosperity. But Australia was not alone in this inability to resume more rapid growth after 1914, suggesting common forces were in play throughout the world economy up to the Second World War. Only in the period between 1890 and 1914 is Australia out of step, underperforming compared to its peers, and recording a much lower rate of growth in incomes than had been experienced over previous decades. In the Australian story the end of the long nineteenth-century boom occurs in 1890, whereas for the international economy, and for other rich economies in both the Old and New Worlds, the boom continues another quarter of a century until the outbreak of the First World War.

• • •

I have argued in this chapter that the crisis of the early 1890s was neither the fundamental cause of the stagnation in incomes in the quarter century following 1890, nor a sufficient explanation for the loss of Australia's position as having the highest incomes. The depression was clearly a searing experience, influencing individual expectations and social beliefs alike. But its impact on so many levels was profound only because of the four decades of prosperity preceding it and the failure to resume similar growth rates after the recovery from it. If, as has been suggested, the boom was in part inherently transitory or unsustainable, then the boom, slump, and subsequent poor economic performance have to be viewed jointly, as must their wider social and political consequences. Would the individual and collective responses to the experience of the 1890s have been different had there been a clear appreciation at the time of the basis of the country's prosperity between the gold rushes and the 1880s? Perhaps such an appreciation would have led to the adoption of different policies in the colonies during the boom years, policies that would have lessened the severity of the slump itself, and hence mitigated the painful adjustments that followed. Indeed, one might speculate that federation might have appeared less attractive (as illustrated by the case of New Zealand), the labor movement given less momentum at the industrial or political level, and hence the ideological and institutional legacies of the 1890s been less significant.

Finally, one must consider whether the depression and slow recovery in the 1890s might be interpreted as, at least in part, some variant of a resource curse. In the *very* long run Australia has clearly avoided an Argentine fate of dropping out of the rich club of countries. And as seen in chapter 2, it has generally managed to hold a position within that club alongside the best performers in terms of living standards, despite never having regained equal ranking with the United States. But over shorter time periods, such as the quarter century discussed here, might the abundance of natural resources in farmland and minerals discovered and exploited before 1890, in myriad ways and often indirectly, have contributed to a set of expectations and behavior that contributed to the severity of the required adjustment after 1890? Clearly the answer to this question is yes. But I have also stressed that in several respects the boom and depression look similar to many others, then and since, in small open economies. So it is not necessary to be resource rich in order to experience a foreign debt crisis or currency crisis or terms of trade collapse sufficiently serious to usher in a period of lower growth and reduced prosperity. And as emphasized in this chapter, the principal institutional weakness in the "Australian" economy exposed by the crises—the lack of a national government—was addressed with some alacrity in the movement toward federation.

CHAPTER 7

A Succession of Negative Shocks

The clash of progress and security . . . [1]

DURING THE QUARTER CENTURY following 1914, the Australian economy was battered by a sequence of external, negative shocks. So severe were they, and so limited were the recoveries from each, that incomes show very little improvement between 1914 and the postdepression peak in 1938. If real per capita GDP is set to 100 in 1914, it is below that level in every subsequent year until a postwar peak in 1925 when it stands at 103 and (with the exception of 1927) does not regain 100 until 1938 when it stands at 105. The alternative GDP estimates recently provided by Bryan Haig tell a similar story of very low per capita growth across the period as a whole: the 1914 level of GDP per capita is not exceeded until 1924, and by 1939 has risen by only 13 percent (figure 7.1).[2] An increase of either 5 or 13 percent over twenty-five years is not very different from no change at all. By this measure there occurred only a very small rise in the level of prosperity experienced by the average Australian across the period as a whole, and in many years, their incomes were below what they had enjoyed prior to the war. The purpose of this chapter is to account for this quarter century of near stagnation.

There were two really bad shocks, with one smaller one in the middle that merged into the second serious episode. The First World War hit the Australian economy hard—a very different impact from that delivered by the Second World War, as we will see in the next chapter. There followed a brief and anemic recovery in the early 1920s before problems in the postwar international economic environment took their toll on the health of the domestic economy—from 1925 by some measures or from 1927 in others. The domestic economy had thus turned down decisively before the stock market crash on Wall Street in October 1929 and the global economic collapse that ensued. For Australia the slump persisted through 1931 in the annual GDP figures (aggregate or per capita), though labor market conditions continued to deteriorate until 1933.

---

[1]Title of a depression-era book on the Australian economy: (Fisher 1935).

[2]Criticism of the Haig's GDP series has related mainly to his estimates for the years prior to the First World War: see Maddison (2003), pp. 72–73, and Broadberry and Irwin (2008).

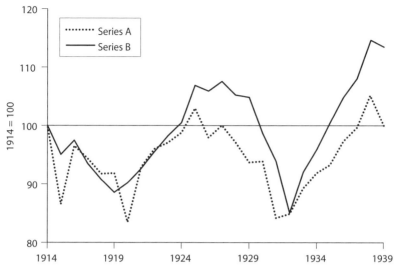

Figure 7.1. Alternative estimates of GDP per capita, 1914 to 1939 (1914 = 100).
Note: Years ended 30 June.
Sources: Series A: McLean and Pincus (1982), Appendix Table, pp. 30–31. Series B: Haig (2001), Table A2, p. 30; and Australian Bureau of Statistics, *Australian Historical Population Statistics, 2008* (Cat. 3105.0.65.001).

Recovery from the depression was sprightly but, as indicated, did little more than return per capita incomes to 1914 levels.

These external shocks emanated from the drastically changed international economic environment Australia faced in the three decades after 1914. And Australians' prewar living standards were extremely vulnerable to a serious or protracted deterioration in external economic conditions. As a small and open economy, highly integrated into world labor, capital and commodity markets, the country's prosperity depended critically on the health of the international economic system, based as it was on a high degree of production specialization in a narrow range of primary commodities exported to a limited spread of foreign markets.[3] Prosperity was also dependent on continued foreign investment to augment domestic savings and hence growth. And economic activity depended partly on immigration boosting the labor supply. Britain dominated these trade, labor, and capital links, and was, in addition, the hub of the prewar classical gold standard.

The First World War destroyed the international economic system that had functioned so well for the best part of a century. Obviously there was considerable

[3] Blattman, Hwang, and Williamson (2007) explore the impact of terms of trade volatility on incomes in commodity exporters including Australia between 1870 and 1939.

short-term disruption during the war, but a well-functioning world economy did not quickly reemerge. Indeed further dislocation was experienced in the 1920s followed by collapse in the 1930s. Thus 1914 marked the end of what now is seen as the first period of globalization. Only after the Second World War did the international economy again flourish as well as it had before 1914. It therefore is no surprise that we now speak of the first and second eras of globalization, attribute the end of the first to the shock delivered by the war of 1914 to 1918, and view the period between 1914 and 1945 as an interregnum between these two eras. Further, we now see the interwar collapse of the global economic system as comprehensive, beginning in 1914, worsening in the 1920s, and reaching its nadir in the depression of the 1930s. Even after 1945 it would take several decades to restore the international economic order to where it had been in 1913. From hindsight, all this is clear.

This nexus between war and systemic change in international economic conditions is not without precedent. Throughout modern history it appears that major wars have frequently marked the transition between eras in the history of the world economy.[4] For Australia, in so many respects itself a creation of the nineteenth-century international economy, and whose growth was so dependent on it, the war-induced collapse brought serious and persisting challenges to efforts to regain and surpass prewar levels of prosperity.

It might appear paradoxical, but this period of repeated negative shocks to the Australian economy affords an opportunity to assess the significance of what economists have identified as a potentially important determinant of long-run growth. In this view, such shocks constitute something of a natural experiment in which the economy and society are put under intense stress. The *responses* to exogenous shocks of this magnitude provide important evidence concerning the capacity of a polity to enact growth-restoring policies and also reveal the resilience and flexibility of a society's norms and institutions in the face of adversity. For responses to such a shock may either mitigate its initial negative impact or, by contrast, amplify its unfavorable consequences.[5] So what can we learn about the bases of Australian prosperity in the long run by examining the performance of the economy in the face of repeated adverse shocks between 1914 and 1939? My assessment is that there was limited scope for Australians to protect their prosperity from the severity or duration of the negative impact of these international forces. This will become clearest in discussing policy responses to the slump of the early 1930s. But it applies also to the war years of 1914 to 1918 and to the 1920s. Of course there were important domestic policy decisions taken throughout this quarter century whose

---

[4]See Findlay and O'Rourke (2007).

[5]See, for example, Rodrik (1999). This theme is especially prominent in the literature on Latin America's disappointing growth performance over many decades.

consequences would impinge either positively or negatively on the stagnant or declining levels of prosperity experienced. But the possibility for avoiding completely these adverse external influences by deft adoption of feasible alternative policies was zero. Ameliorating their domestic impact may have been all that was attainable.

This period also provides clear evidence of the capacity of Australian institutions and social norms to absorb these negative shocks without serious political or social consequences. Had they been less resilient, the deterioration in economic conditions could well have been magnified. During the war the most divisive political issue related to conscription, but it did not derail wartime economic policies or outcomes. The more stringent test came with the depression. Remarkably, the prolonged experience of unemployment and markedly reduced living standards experienced by a significant proportion of the population did not lead to serious social unrest or undermine trust in key social and political institutions. The harsh economic conditions were endured with great forbearance—an outcome beneficial to economic recovery, but not one observed in all countries during the slump of the 1930s.

Why Was the Economic Impact of World War I So Severe?

From an Australian perspective, the First World War was clearly an exogenous event in that its origins lay in the unstable competition between the major European powers, competition that extended across the economic, diplomatic, colonial, and military spheres. Australia, like Canada and New Zealand but unlike the United States, entered the war in support of Britain at the outset in August 1914. The war's duration was a little over four years, until the armistice of November 1918, but the economic consequences were more long-lasting. It was also Australia's first experience of "total" war, its earlier and limited military participation in imperial missions in the Sudan and the Boer War in South Africa having had little impact on the domestic economy.

That the First World War delivered a sizable economic shock to the economy is not always appreciated.[6] Yet the magnitude of its negative impact is readily conveyed. Real aggregate GDP declined across the six years 1914 to 1920 by 9.5 percent, while the mobilization of troops contributed to a fall in civilian employment of more than 6 percent through 1918. Population growth remained positive across the war period, albeit at about half the prewar rate. Hence per

---

[6]Puzzlingly, economic historians have written little about this war. Specialist economic analysis is very thin: Forster (1953) on manufacturing and the war is a bit of a rarity. The only recent overview is by Haig-Muir (1995), who makes a good start on key questions. Otherwise it is back to Copland's chapter (1988 [1933]) and Scott's book (1989 [1936]) for extended discussions.

capita incomes declined more sharply than aggregate GDP—by over 16 percent.[7] Had this occurred in peacetime it would be classified as a depression.

There are perhaps two levels on which to respond to the question of why the short-run impact of the war was so severe. The immediate causes are fairly clear. There was a return to serious drought conditions in the rural sector; a closing of the London capital market for development loans; an extreme scarcity of shipping combined with a high dependence on imports for essential products; the loss of manpower from the civilian labor force into the military; and a slump in the housing industry. Wartime economic-policy options were also constrained because the federal bureaucracy was new and small, there was no central bank, and unlike the situation in 1939, there was no recent experience of running a war economy.

There are deeper reasons, too, and these tie in to themes pursued throughout this book. As had occurred with the downturn in the early 1890s, the war-induced disruption after 1914 revealed the downside of the seemingly successful growth strategy of the decades preceding 1890 and also during the decade before 1914. Since analogous considerations have been addressed in the evaluation of the causes of the 1890s depression, I need not elaborate this point. However, it is important to note that this vulnerability was recognized by contemporaries as having been exposed by the war. To illustrate, the states' development programs were jeopardized by any wartime restriction on their continued borrowing in the London capital market, while British government officials were highly critical of how these funds were invested: "Australia outdoes South American republics in its desire to live on loans" wrote one official in 1917.[8] In the 1920 debates on the tariff, the minister for trade justified the need for an expanded manufacturing sector by referring to "one or two outstanding lessons of the war. I do not know anything which has emphasized the isolation of Australia and its dependence upon outside sources of supply more than the violent struggle, through which we have passed, has done."[9]

WHY NO RETURN TO NORMALCY?

In the 1920s the principal social objective and policy goal in Australia as in many countries was the restoration of prewar prosperity, universally thought to entail reestablishing the full panoply of prewar international trade patterns and

---

[7]Maddock and McLean (1987a), pp. 353 and 362; McLean and Pincus (1982), p. 30. In the alternative estimates of Haig (2001), real aggregate GDP declines between 1914 and 1918, and by 7.2 percent. A recent attempt to estimate the "cost" of the war in terms of human capital lost through death and injury is reported by Glick and Taylor (2010).

[8]Quoted in Attard (1989), p. 156.

[9]Greene, quoted in Forster (1953), p. 227.

financial arrangements. It was going to take more than a decade of failure, followed by a worldwide slump, for politicians, economists, and other observers fully to comprehend that a return to "normalcy" was unattainable. But much of what was written about the condition of the Australian economy at the time, and of the policies thought appropriate to the challenges it faced during the 1920s, was based on the premise that the world had not changed fundamentally.

One clear link between the war and its adverse impact on postwar prosperity can be seen in the methods adopted to pay for war-related expenditure.[10] Two related questions are how to pay for a war, and how to estimate the effect of the choice of war financing on postwar growth or welfare. With respect to the first, one option would in principle place the entire burden on the generation experiencing the war, such as by financing the war effort entirely through increased taxes targeting current consumption. Resources would thus be diverted from consumption to fund the war effort without negatively impacting investment and hence postwar growth. Alternatively, the burden of paying for the war could be passed entirely on to future generations by financing it solely through government borrowing, whether this was achieved by raising loans abroad or domestically. A further option would be to finance wartime deficits by printing money. In practice, national income taxes were introduced alongside state income taxes; but the war was financed primarily by loans—domestic raisings and loans in London.[11] By the end of the war, war-related expenditure accounted for just over half all Commonwealth government expenditure from consolidated revenue, and it stayed at this level at least until 1922. This includes war pensions, interest on war loans (domestic and imperial), and repatriation expenditure—appropriately treated as the economic burden of the war carried into the 1920s. Note that following the Second World War, Australia did not carry such a large debt burden into the postwar era, for reasons canvased in the next chapter.

Thus a significant damper on prosperity, and constraint on postwar economic policy, was the war debt burden that resulted from earlier decisions about how to distribute the costs of the war between reductions in present and future consumption. Had a higher proportion of the costs been borne by reduced wartime consumption, the debt burden in the twenties would have been lower, but so too would have been the initial postwar *level* of consumption. The situation in 1919 was that there existed a war debt that required servicing, but the resources devoted to this added nothing to current output. The federal government had few

---

[10]This does not appear to have been addressed in any thorough way in the historical literature, though a few comments may be found in the secondary literature (for example, Meredith and Dyster 1999, p. 97). Data relating to the wartime loans, and the "costs" of the war, are summarized in the *Year Books* published during the 1920s by the Commonwealth Bureau of Census and Statistics (later, Australian Bureau of Statistics).

[11]Note that the domestic loan raisings had a major long-run impact on the evolution of the domestic capital market: Merrett (1997), pp. 192–93.

options in theory (service, reschedule, or default), none in practice. Some part of the drag on prosperity in the 1920s is therefore this direct legacy of the war. But the debt was augmented by the postwar resumption of state-government borrowing to expand spending on public works, infrastructure, and especially rural development schemes (figure 7.2). An associated institutional innovation was the creation of the Loan Council. This effort to better coordinate the overseas borrowing efforts of the state and Commonwealth governments reflected a recognition that they faced a straitened international capital market compared to its condition prewar. Australia was highly exposed to any deterioration in the borrowing conditions facing debtor nations.

Another consequence of the war was oversupply in the international markets for agricultural commodities. The disruption to trade during the war had directly encouraged increased farm production, especially in the United States, and this additional capacity was a factor depressing prices in the 1920s. An indirect result of the war was that the newly created states in Europe adopted a policy of stimulating agricultural output as a means to absorb postwar unemployment and as one of the few avenues available to earn the scarce foreign exchange needed to finance the capital goods imports required for their planned industrializations. The war had thus bequeathed to the 1920s serious imbalances in agricultural markets, and Australian farmers' prosperity was vulnerable to these. Under such conditions it is not surprising that the 1920s witnessed a proliferation in various forms of agricultural assistance, subsidy, and support schemes in Australia. Some involved the creation of new institutions—such as state marketing boards. The collapse in demand as a result of the worldwide slump of the early 1930s saw commodity prices fall further. Although there was some relief in the late thirties, full recovery did not occur until after 1945 with the return of buoyant trading conditions in the international markets for many rural commodities.

A further link between the war and postwar growth is the contribution of the war economy to Australian industrialization. There was no dramatic overall expansion in the share of manufacturing in GDP or of total employment: in marked contrast to what would occur during World War II, there was no war-induced "spurt" in Australian industrialization. One oft-cited example of industrial advance during the war was the opening in 1915 of the BHP steel mill at Newcastle in New South Wales, and there is no question that this marked a significant step toward a more mature and diversified domestic manufacturing capacity. Though timely in permitting a reduced dependence on vital imports, its construction was planned before the war and thus cannot be attributed to the changed market conditions that followed the outbreak of hostilities. Beyond the expansion in steel production, there were other compositional changes in the manufacturing sector that gave this brief period special significance in the long-run industrialization of the economy. Key growth areas of manufacturing included iron and steel products, chemicals, electrical equipment, and textiles,

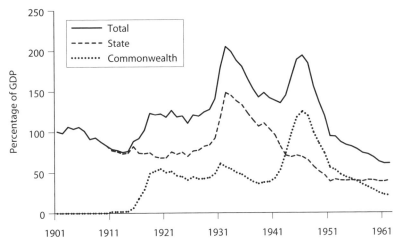

Figure 7.2. Government debt as a percentage of GDP, 1901 to 1962.
Notes: Years ended 30 June. Treatment of local government is not consistent between states or over time.
Source: Derived from Vamplew (1987), Series GF6 and GF8, pp. 256–57.

clothing and footwear. In some cases war-related demands stimulated domestic production, such as with army uniforms and boots. In many others, however, wartime disruption of traditional sources of imported supplies encouraged a rapid expansion of domestic production of import substitutes.

In the short run, and other things equal, incomes probably were lowered by these changes in the composition of manufacturing. The war disruptions to shipping availability had created a period of "natural" protection for import-competing producers. In most cases these producers were less efficient than the foreign firms previously exporting into the Australian market. Wartime exigencies thus led to a switch from lower- to higher-cost sources of supply, pushing up prices for consumers and reducing economic prosperity. Of course, not too much importance would be assigned these events if the cessation of hostilities in 1918 had brought a swift return to the status quo ante. The production of import substitutes during this period of protection afforded by the war was, however, to have longer-run consequences.

These war-induced firms and product lines faced a short life expectancy unless they received some measure of protection from imports following the return of peacetime trading conditions. The political economy of the Greene tariff (1921) is thus fairly clear, with its passage to a degree "locking in" the wartime changes in the composition of industrial activity.[12] In one view, the resulting hike in some tariffs marks the origins of a significant degree of protection

---

[12]See Forster (1953, pp. 226–28).

for Australian manufacturing. And the particular adjustments made may have been effective in sustaining activity in respect to the targeted goods and their producers such that the war led directly to the change in the *incidence* of tariff protection. But the *average* level of the tariff does not appear to have risen at this time (figure 7.3). And the overall level of protection to manufacturers may have been little changed, as any tariff rises were offset by changes in transport and other costs.[13]

These effects were addressed explicitly in the Brigden inquiry of 1929, which also considered the relationship between the tariff and wage regulation, and the spread of assistance schemes to the export (rural) industries.[14] The counterfactual to the policies actually pursued was fairly clearly laid out in the inquiry. What would have been the effect of the adoption of a free-trade regime on economic prosperity during the decade? It would depend a bit on whether prosperity was measured by real wages or income per capita. The redistributive effects of the tariff favored manufacturing workers, the burden falling on the rural sector. The Brigden report concluded controversially that although the actual level of the tariff as at 1926 had possibly raised the real wages of workers in general relative to a hypothetical free trade regime, it may not have had much impact on levels of income per capita. More recent attempts to empirically estimate the effect of the tariff on income levels have not yielded any clearer consequence.[15] Perhaps this is not so surprising an outcome. The tariff on manufacturing was not raised as dramatically in 1921 as it would be in the early 1930s, which is clear in figure 7.3, and thus any adverse impact on living standards would be more evident later in the interwar period. Also the manufacturing sector as a whole was still not that significant within the economy— about 15 percent of GDP during most of the twenties: it was to become almost twice this in the 1960s.

There were also important war-related changes to the labor-market regime in the early 1920s. The wartime inflation, and declines in real wages as money wages failed to keep pace, are part of the background to important decisions on the basic wage, such as an increase in its level and the introduction of automatic cost of living adjustments in 1922. It is agreed that the economic consequences of these changes to the labor-market regime, unlike those made prewar, were nontrivial. One further issue both at the time and for historians is whether the increasing regulation of the labor market, and especially the level of award minimum wages imposed after the war, lowered the demand for labor, reduced export competitiveness, and hence slowed growth. Most assessments focus on distributional issues arising from the changes, and regard them as benign or desirable. Their implications for growth, however, were likely deleterious. Given

---

[13]Lloyd (2008) reports estimates of the tariff; Pope (1986) discusses the offsets to its impact.

[14]Brigden (1929).

[15]See Tyers and Coleman (2008).

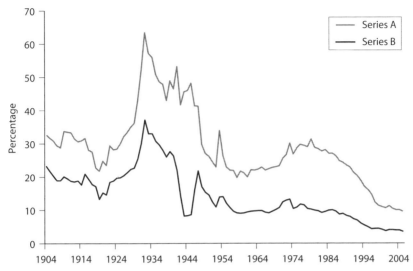

Figure 7.3. Tariff protection, 1904 to 2005.
Notes: Series A: Average duty (customs plus primage, net)—dutiable clearances only, adjusted for revenue duties plus method of valuation. Series B: Average duty (customs plus primage, net)—all clearances adjusted for method of valuation. Years ending June 30.
Source: Lloyd (2008), Table 5, pp. 123–25.

the deteriorating international trading environment Australia faced in the early 1920s, a mandated increase in real wages (or real unit labor costs) was not conducive to securing productivity gains, encouraging employment, or improving international competitiveness.[16]

So, how great would have been the impact of a more flexible labor market on prosperity in the 1920s? This is a question about the short- and long-term growth consequences of alternative institutional arrangements. Australia since the 1980s has not just debated these questions but has also implemented reforms to increase efficiency in the labor market and raise productivity and hence living standards. Bearing in mind both later theory and experience, what are the chances that a deregulation of the labor market in the 1920s would have stimulated higher living standards than those achieved at that time? A priori, it is likely that the effects of even quite radical labor-market reform would have had a number of hard-to-predict distributional consequences (maybe lower unemployment, maybe more working poor), but would not have kick-started the Australian economy into a phase of more rapid growth and hence significantly higher incomes through the decade. The sustained downward trend in international commodity prices from mid-decade was of a magnitude that

---

[16]For assessments, see Pope (1982), Forster (1989), and Issac (2008).

could not be offset to any significant extent by reductions in the cost of domestic labor.

Pursuing Rural Development—A Field of Dreams?

It is against this background that we should note the priority given further rural development in the 1920s, as it constitutes crucial evidence that the pre-1890 outward-oriented growth strategy had not by then been entirely superseded with some inward-oriented alternative. The clutch of policies promoting assisted empire migration, subdividing farms for closer settlement, extending rural branch-line railways, encouraging soldier-settler farming schemes, cross-subsidizing rural telephone services, and more, all point to the continued primacy of the view that the critical bottlenecks facing Australia's development were its need for more people and for a greater capacity to import. Rural development and the expansion of agricultural exports remained the principal means to attain these objectives, albeit amid rising concern that the rural sector would be unable to create significant additional employment opportunities. The Empire Settlement Scheme (1922) is an institutional embodiment of this strategy: the British and Australian governments jointly funded British migrants to Australia, and subsidized their settlement in rural areas, with the intention of boosting food production in the latter for export to the former. These policies have been excoriated in later evaluations by economists and economic historians as resulting in misallocated public investment and regulatory inefficiencies.[17] It appears that much of this money was wasted on largely unproductive projects, that the return on additional investment in rural production was low and falling, that many of the closer settlement and soldier settlement schemes were in the longer run economically unviable and socially a tragedy, and that the empire migration program was similarly of dubious benefit to prosperity.

So, did the war or the 1920s mark any shift in the dynamics of Australian growth? Of course there is value in asking of any period whether it qualifies as having special significance, and in what ways. It is the view of Gus Sinclair that the 1920s indeed marked a turning point in the "process of economic development in Australia," the title of his 1976 book.[18] One element in this thesis asserts that in this decade, the extensive margin was reached—though he doesn't use this term. A second is that during the 1920s a "fundamental disequilibrium" in world markets came to an end. This seems to be his main point, namely that there was more or less continuous excess demand from the 1820s to the 1920s for certain primary products in which Australia had a comparative advantage,

---

[17] For example, see Sinclair (1970) on public investment.
[18] Ibid. (1976).

and that this underpinned Australian growth. When these favorable external trading conditions ended in the late 1920s and early 1930s, there was limited potential for further rural-based development. But Sinclair ties himself in knots trying to run this single-period analysis across a century.[19]

Nonetheless, the idea that the time at which the extensive margin for rural occupation was reached might have significance for the underlying mechanism of Australian economic growth is one worth considering. Certainly the cultural or social significance of reaching the spatial limits of European settlement (which might be another description) was vast. The "outback" has a hold on the Australian imagination in part because it has defied all but very low population densities.[20] However the geographical limit to rural occupation was reached at different times in different colonies or states. For New South Wales it was around 1890, because in the 1890s depression and drought, there was a retreat of the pastoral frontier. For much of South Australia and Victoria, it was earlier, though clearing land in Gippsland in eastern Victoria came later, and the spread of cropping in the mallee lands in both states came later still—beginning in the late 1930s. In Tasmania it may have come much earlier—before 1850. In Western Australia the spread of rural settlement persisted until after 1914. In Queensland, farmers are still engaging in land clearing. So the extensive margin has been encountered over many decades in different parts of the country. No decisive turning point can thus be associated with the decade of the 1920s.

To the economist, the geographical area utilized for farming is of less importance than the production generated from that area. And as described in previous chapters, land use patterns and rural output are constantly fluctuating in response to changes in the weather, in relative prices, and in agricultural technology. When one or more of these influences turns negative over several years (as in the 1890s, and again in the late 1920s and early 1930s), there is a decline in most indicators of rural production. When market and other conditions improve, rural production revives—even if significant shifts in its composition, location, or production methods have occurred. Looked at in this way, there is nothing special about the 1920s. Indeed, however grim economic conditions were for farmers during the interwar period, there was an extraordinary expansion of activity in the sector after 1945. The area under cultivation, the production of grain and wool, and the numbers of sheep or cattle—these all doubled or more than doubled, relative to their interwar peaks, by 1960 or 1970. Thus Australia in the 1920s had not reached some barrier to increasing

---

[19]Reviewers of the book recognized the problems with Sinclair's attempt to develop an analytic structure in his interpretation of Australian growth in the long run: see Gould (1977) and Schedvin (1979).

[20]Note the parallel with the role of the "frontier" (and its "closing" c.1890) in the United States.

rural production in the long run so significant that it marks the end of an epoch in the "process of economic development."

Behind the economic debates during the 1920s over the country's growth prospects was the idée fixe that the prime goal of policy was to expand the Australian population. Of course this was to be pursued conditional not just on the composition of the population remaining overwhelmingly European (actually, Anglo), but also on the condition that there be no reduction in real wages resulting from an immigration program intended to achieve the desired population expansion. The population objective was thus a further key constraint within which policies to sustain and raise levels of prosperity in the 1920s had to be designed, again making relevant the distinction between extensive and intensive growth. It was a deeply embedded social goal not seriously questioned until the debates of the 1970s regarding the possible trade-off between population growth, living standards, and environmental quality.

At the time, economists (and not just the Brigden team) worried about these questions and canvased options. They knew that further increases in rural output and exports could not be attained by bringing fertile new land into production at low cost as had happened during the pre-1890 spread of settlement. They knew that increased output could be obtained by changes in existing land use and the application of new technology such as mechanization, but this would not be possible without considerable investment, and might not be profitable unless world commodity prices recovered markedly. They also knew that providing additional jobs in a more highly protected manufacturing sector would lower productivity and hence incomes at some point, even if they were unsure whether that point had already been reached. They canvased possible offsets, such as scale economies, infant industry arguments, learning by doing, and some types of external economies that might arise. It is also intriguing to see the one event mentioned that would bring salvation from increasingly dismal economic prospects: a major mineral discovery. Alas, the existence of vast deposits of bauxite, iron ore, oil, natural gas, copper, uranium, and other mineral and energy resources were not known at this time. Implicit in this wishful thinking is their appreciation of the importance of the mining industry to Australian prosperity in earlier decades: its relative insignificance in the interwar period is a topic to which I will return shortly.

Thus it is difficult to see how a significantly higher level of prosperity could have been attained in Australia in the 1920s under an alternative growth strategy. Policy options were heavily constrained by the burden of war debt, by the unfavorable international economic climate, and by the narrow basis on which domestic prosperity rested. After 1945 much improved trading conditions returned, the terms of trade rose, there was some diversification in the range of agricultural products exported, an expansion occurred in the importance of manufacturing, and there were major mineral discoveries. Postwar living standards rose on the back of a combination of these influences. The possibility of transposing these to the 1920s by implementing alternative domestic policies seems remote—especially since several were beyond the remit of Australian policy-makers.

Growth in Other Settler Economies

Looking at Australian experience over the period between 1913 and 1929 from the perspective of other settler economies can be helpful, first, in drawing attention to features in Australia's story that stand out only when viewed from outside, and second, in prompting one's imagination about what might have been and why it did not occur. Both Argentina and Canada experienced a more rapid rise in per capita incomes across this period (15.0 and 13.9 percent respectively) than did Australia (2.1 percent).[21] By this measure, their levels of economic prosperity were catching up to the higher levels Australia still enjoyed. For Argentina, 1929 was to be as close as they got, a relative decline setting in during the 1930s and persisting many decades. For Canada, approximate parity with Australia was temporarily attained at the end of the 1920s, lost during the 1930s, regained by the end of the Second World War, and sustained ever since. Why did these two economies, similar to Australia's in many respects, perform better between 1913 and 1929?

One possibility is the continued—or faster—expansion of "frontier" agricultural development in Argentina and Canada than in Australia. This is tricky, partly because of statistical issues, primarily the lack of comparability in definitions of land use. Partly, also, because an addition to cultivation of a hectare of land on the extensive frontier with the geographic spread of rural settlement across the prairies or pampas may be no different from an economic viewpoint to a hectare of natural grassland in an area long occupied for pastoral grazing being brought under the plow for the first time—the more typical Australian experience in the 1920s. The distinction only matters if there are systematic differences between the two situations in cost or productivity that would account for the slower expansion of land under cultivation in Australia than in the other two at this time.[22]

In the case of Canada, this is perhaps the appropriate place to indicate a difference with Australian experience that has not been investigated closely in the comparative literature. Manufacturing appears to have accounted for a much larger proportion of GDP in Canada by 1914 than it did in Australia at that time. Indeed, from the 1870s, over 20 percent of Canadian GDP is derived

---

[21] Maddison (2010).
[22] This issue is discussed in McLean (2006), pp. 234–38.

from manufacturing, a figure not reached in Australia until the 1940s, though there may be significant differences between the two countries in definitions of what constituted a manufacturing establishment that account for at least some of this striking gap.[23] Recall the discussion in chapter 5 that the nature of the export "staple" may determine the extent to which a stimulus is imparted to domestic industry, and the suggestion raised that in the late nineteenth century, Canadian timber products and wheat may have provided a greater boost to manufacturing than did Australian wool or gold. In this context it is perhaps noteworthy that confederation in Canada preceded the construction of the transcontinental railways, and that this "national" project in turn stimulated the domestic manufacture of steel as well as rolling stock. Notoriously, the Australian colonies constructed independent railway networks of different gauges with rolling stock imported from Britain. Domestic steel production, as previously noted, began in Australia only in 1915.

Another feature of Canadian economic history before 1929 is the rapid rate of industrialization based on abundant natural resources other than farmland. The key natural-resource-intensive industries by the 1920s were pulp and paper (especially newsprint) and the smelting and refining of minerals (e.g. nickel). These are described in the Canadian literature as nontraditional exports or as second-generation staple exports. And the emergence of these export-oriented manufacturing industries is explained in terms of the proximity of a booming U.S. market; the lower cost of Canadian than American forest products (inputs into paper); government policies regarding the taxation of Crown lands containing timber; the availability of cheap electricity; and tariff and related agreements with the United States.[24]

One issue for Australian observers is whether, against this background, Australia missed any opportunities to base an enhanced industrial development on its natural resources, or whether Canadian downstream processing of, or adding value to, commodity exports was the outcome of local factors. For its part Australia did expand its refining and smelting capacities and exports of some minerals at this time, especially under wartime demand conditions. Had a major expansion occurred in, for example, woolen textiles and clothing production, transforming a high proportion of the wool clip into manufactured products for export, Australia would have had something comparable to the Canadian timber products story. But I know of no serious suggestion that Australia "failed" to take advantage of any such potential export opportunity in manufacturing. The textile and clothing industry is generally described as

---

[23]The Canadian data on manufacturing as a share of GDP at factor cost are in Urquhart (1986, table 2.1, pp. 11–15), while Green (2000) discusses the links between successive staples and the manufacturing sector.

[24]An attempt to untangle the relative importance of these factors in the case of Canadian newsprint has been made by Dick (1982).

arising only because of tariff protection, and hence would have been uncompetitive internationally. With respect to other rural industries, there is a limit to the value-adding possible with grains, meat, dairy products, or fruit prior to their export. And this limit had probably been reached by 1914.[25] So perhaps Australia was "unlucky" in its resource endowment relative to Canada in that there were in the early twentieth century no comparable opportunities for underpinning export-oriented industrial development. This recalls the "staple trap" hypothesis, which was raised in chapter 5, where it was noted that an exception in the Australian case was the emergence of an agricultural engineering industry—an industry that also flourished in Canada. These observations also suggest the possible relevance of the "commodity lottery" interpretation of growth. The potential for raising incomes by specializing in producing a commodity for export depends in some measure on the particular characteristics of the commodity itself. However, whether or not a commodity is exported is a function of comparative advantage and thus determined by the initial endowment, which is a matter of "luck."[26]

This speculation about the weak dynamic links between the natural-resource base and later industrialization in Australia is warranted not simply because of what happened in Canada. The limited industrialization experienced in Argentina has also been contrasted with what occurred in Canada.[27] More striking is the evidence that links industrialization in the United States to its natural-resource abundance. Far from any Dutch-disease effect resulting in a contraction of manufacturing, American industrial development in the late nineteenth and early twentieth centuries was based directly on its abundance of land and minerals. As late as 1940, U.S. trade in manufactures still reflected this natural-resource intensity.[28] The very much larger domestic market in the United States undoubtedly helps explain the positive role resource abundance played in its industrialization. Also of possible relevance was tariff protection, low-cost water-transport links between key mineral locations, the rise of the modern corporation that brought scale economies in production, marketing and distribution, and a favorable climate for risk-taking by entrepreneurs.

Thus the United States was able to industrialize directly on the basis of its natural-resource abundance. And Canadian industrialization also appears, at least into the interwar period, to have been dynamic and bound up with its resource base, though in a setting where its propinquity to the American market for some products may have been critical. In contrast Australia, like

---

[25] This is also the view of Greasley and Oxley (2009) in their evaluation of the role of refrigerated food products in the expansion of New Zealand's manufactured exports.

[26] See Blattman, Hwang, and Williamson (2007) and Hausmann, Hwang, and Rodrik (2007) for two discussions relevant to this theme.

[27] See Cortes Conde (1985).

[28] See Wright (1990).

Argentina and New Zealand, did not at this time develop export markets for its manufactured products, with the partial exception of the simple processing of meat, sugar, fruit, and dairy products. Australia's exports were still dominated by commodities that had seen little or no domestic processing or value-adding—wool, gold, and grains. Comparative analysis suggests this partly reflects endowments, partly the scope for further processing of the particular export commodities in which Australia had a comparative advantage, partly the small and fragmented domestic market, and partly geography—isolation from potential markets.

Debt Crisis, Then Depression—Policy Responses and Constraints

To depression-era observers, the 1920s seemed—and not unreasonably—a time of relative prosperity. For it was a decade of welcome change in most people's experience, with the arrival of cars, a range of consumer durables, electricity, movies, jazz, and rising hemlines. But by the second half of the 1920s, and several years prior to the crash on Wall Street, Australia faced a severe economic crisis. Aggregate real GDP peaked in 1927 and declined 3 percent over the next two years by one set of estimates, and was essentially flat across the three years according to a second set: by either measure per capita GDP was falling prior to 1929. This crisis therefore constituted the "initial conditions" in the domestic economy prior to the arrival of the international depression. Of course, our perspective on the 1920s is colored by our knowledge of what ensued. And the economic and social calamity of the depression of the 1930s tends to cast the preexisting problems in the economy as minor by comparison. They were not. As we have seen in figure 7.1, Australian prosperity in the 1920s barely exceeded the level attained before 1914. As the incipient debt crisis foreshadowed, even that modest achievement was unsustainable.

The debt crisis has its origins in the war-related borrowing of the federal government, some of which was foreign debt. But the borrowing programs of the state governments during the 1920s considerably augmented the total debt outstanding, as was shown in figure 7.2. As mentioned, there is doubt as to the wisdom of some of the public expenditure and investment decisions financed by these borrowings, especially in rural development. With foreign-domiciled debt, there was the additional requirement that the investments it financed would generate, directly or indirectly, the foreign exchange needed to service the loans. This was especially important since the foreign component of the war debt had contributed nothing to net foreign-exchange earnings through either export growth or import replacement. Short of sovereign default there is no escaping the debt burden. And, as discussed in the previous chapter in relation to the 1890s, governments did not default—though New

South Wales premier Jack Lang was dismissed in 1932 by the state governor for threatening just such a move.

An additional source of risk associated with the high levels of foreign public debt was a decline in debt-servicing capacity. This could arise because of a decline in export earnings due to a downturn in the international prices for Australia's exports of farm products, a decline in export volumes, or both. And the reasons for the deterioration in world agricultural commodity markets during the 1920s have already been noted. One measure of this vulnerability is the proportion of export earnings needed in any year to pay interest on the debt outstanding and repay any principal due. And in the 1920s this foreign-debt-servicing ratio rose sharply—from 16 percent in 1920 to 27 percent in 1928 (figure 6.2). The economy's capacity to import was eroded by the diversion of foreign-exchange earnings to service past debt rather than to purchase investment or consumer goods needed to enhance domestic growth and prosperity. And at some point foreign lenders would reassess the risks of additional loans to Australian governments, raise their interest rates, withdraw from supplying new funds, or refuse to roll over existing loans at maturity. These were the murky and treacherous waters into which Australia had sailed in the second half of the 1920s.

This crisis of the late 1920s has some of the characteristics of the one in the early 1890s. And it is of a type with recurring crises in the history of many developing economies down to the present, variously described as a balance-of-payments crisis, a foreign-debt crisis, or a currency crisis, depending on the precise causes and symptoms. Even during the post-1945 era, there were occasions in which Australia faced less pressing variants of the same problem. But it is in the interwar period that the balance-of-payments constraint on growth was most binding since the debt crisis of the late 1920s morphed into an acute phase with the collapse of the international economy following 1929.

The magnitude of the downturn in the domestic economy is readily conveyed. According to the alternative available estimates, aggregate GDP declined between the pre-depression peak and the trough by 11 percent or 19 percent, per capita GDP by 18 percent or 21 percent.[29] The conventional indicator of the economic and social impact of the slump is the unemployment rate. This had been below 5 percent in some years during the 1920s, had risen to 8 percent by 1929, and peaked at 20 percent of the workforce in 1932. There is debate about the extent of possible understatement in these figures due, for example, to underreporting, the discouraged-worker effect, and informal work-sharing schemes. Unemployment rates among trade-union members peaked at 29 percent (figure 7.4).

---

[29] These are based on the estimates, respectively, reported by McLean and Pincus (1982) and Haig (2001).

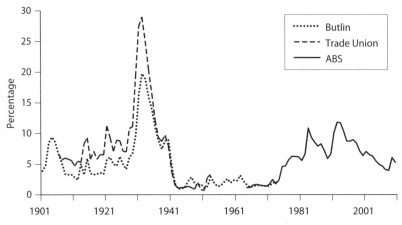

Figure 7.4. Unemployment rate, 1901 to 2010.
Note: The trade union estimates relate to years ended 31 December; the other series relate to years ended 30 June.
Sources: Butlin (1977), Table IV.5, pp. 90–92. For trade union estimates, Vamplew (1987), Series LAB88, p. 152. For ABS estimates 1964 to 1976, Reserve Bank of Australia, *Australian Economic Statistics 1949-50 to 1996-97*, Table 4.15; from 1977, Australian Bureau of Statistics, *Labour Force* (Cat. 6202.0.01).

The slump in the world economy during the early 1930s, which dragged down an already weakened Australian economy, has probably attracted more analysis by economists and historians than any other event in the economic history of the twentieth century. Significantly, debates about its causes are still not settled, which says something about the complexity of the event itself, but also reflects the inability of economic theories to provide an explanation commanding universal support. The origins of the slump are not solely, or even primarily, to be found in events in the United States in 1929. The primary product-exporting countries, such as Australia, and regions such as the American Midwest, were suffering lowered incomes and high levels of indebtedness from the midtwenties. And the reasons for agricultural distress lay deeper, in events during and after the war, and even in the vast increases in agricultural output that accompanied the extension of farmlands in the settler economies in the nineteenth and early twentieth centuries, and the remarkable productivity and output enhancing changes in agricultural technologies that accompanied that expansion.

There were additional problems in the international economy following the war.[30] International trade was permanently altered by the wartime disruption, Australia not being alone in engaging in domestic production of previously

---

[30]Major studies include Kindleberger (1986) and Eichengreen (1992).

imported goods during the conflict, then protecting the infant manufacturers after the war with higher tariffs. So world trade conditions were less open than before 1914. Further, the international monetary system, which had been based on the classical gold standard, was not quickly restored, and capital flows did not return to prewar levels. Partly this was due to the permanent shift in Britain's position within the international economy. It emerged from the war in a much weakened position, hoping to provide the lynchpin to the system as before 1914 but unable to do so. It had significantly reduced its overseas assets as part of financing the war effort while, in contrast, the United States emerged as a net creditor nation. Furthermore, British industry suffered a loss of international competitiveness, especially relative to American industry, due to wartime inflation and the deferral of investment during the war.

In Continental Europe, too, recovery following the war was inhibited by a number of factors, many war related. One was the creation of a number of new countries in Central and Eastern Europe. These struggled to maintain price stability and maintain full employment, hence resorted to protectionism. More famous are the reparations imposed on the defeated Germans. Their defiant response contributed to the hyperinflation of 1923, further weakening the key industrial economy in Europe. The rise of political extremism in Italy and Germany increased uncertainty. No wonder, perhaps, that the first attempt to provide an institutional framework for international cooperation, including in the economic sphere, should prove ineffective: the League of Nations was never able to exert the beneficial impact on the world economy achieved by its successor organizations after 1944.

It is against this international background that the question of whether Australian responses to the depression could have sustained a higher level of prosperity must be addressed. For there was no escaping the impact of the depression. The most that could be achieved would be to ameliorate its effects, and the policies designed to do this have been vigorously debated ever since.[31] These debates extend into the social and political realms, appropriately reflecting the pervasiveness and severity of the episode. Hindsight has revealed the perverse or inconsistent nature of some policies when viewed through the lens of modern macroeconomics. In the immediate post-1945 decades, when there was a belief that Keynesian theories and policies provided policy-makers with the analysis and tools to prevent the recurrence of a depression, many assessments of depression-era policies were confidently made and rather damning. But they now look somewhat partial, a reflection of the period in which they were made. Macroeconomics is now less influenced by Keynes or his followers. And history has delivered further evidence of the difficulty of combating major financial and economic downturns in advanced economies—such as experienced by Japan in the 1990s and by many countries after 2007.

---

[31] Major surveys include Schedvin (1970) and Gregory and Butlin (1988).

Because this book is concerned with explaining Australia's prosperity in the long run, it is not necessary to treat the depression experience in detail, as would be appropriate in a more general survey of economic history. Indeed, if the passing of the crisis had quickly restored prosperity to its pre-1929 peak there might be a case for arguing that the depression had no permanent impact. But this is too strong. Most accounts explicitly reference the unemployment rate as a key indicator of the timing and magnitude of both the slump and recovery phases, such that the year in which unemployment returned to its pre-slump level—1941—might be said to mark the end of the depression. If we use either aggregate GDP or per capita GDP, we see different dates for the duration of the depression, namely 1935 and 1938, respectively.

The policy decisions that have received most attention by historians and economists are those relating to the exchange rate, the level of wages, the extent of deficit-financed government stimulus, and monetary (interest rate) policy. If an appraisal of these responses indicated that they deepened the slump or delayed the recovery relative to alternative policies that would not have had such an effect, then these policy decisions aimed at short-run goals would be pertinent to our inquiry because they would have pushed the economy further into depression than the external negative influences were already doing.

Despite being the subject of considerable political controversy at the time, the key policy responses of the federal government to the slump probably had only minor impacts on the broad course of economic events. The decision to devalue the Australian pound relative to the pound sterling in 1931 is viewed as appropriate. Indeed, there exists evidence that the earlier in the depression a country abandoned the gold standard, and the greater the extent of the subsequent depreciation, the earlier and faster was that country's economic recovery. Australian experience fits this pattern.[32] With respect to policies on wages, interest rates, and government spending, the evidence suggests that there were limits to what could be achieved. Considered in isolation, policies of cutting interest rates and boosting government expenditure might have muted the impact of external forces on the domestic economy. One difficulty (as seen in the Premiers' Plan of 1931) was that elements of government policies worked against one another.[33] But such inconsistencies were not so evident at that time, prior to the emergence of modern macroeconomics.

Perhaps the more important finding of later research into the depression is that, as an economy already experiencing a crisis in servicing its foreign debt and financing crucial imports, attempts to boost domestic demand and hence

---

[32] See Eichengreen and Sachs (1985) and Eichengreen (1988).

[33] The 1931 agreement between the state premiers and federal government to stave off external default and hasten recovery in the economy included reductions in interest rates but at the same time increased taxes and cut government expenditures: Schedvin (1970, chapters 10 and 11) offers a detailed analysis of the Plan.

employment by either expansionary fiscal policy or looser monetary policy would quickly have hit external constraints. That is, the domestic stimulus would have increased the demand for imports, thus worsening the balance of payments crisis that predated the depression. The foreign holders of Australian debt would be even less inclined to extend loans; foreign exchange reserves would be further depleted; and speculation of a further devaluation would increase. In this view, policy-makers were limited in their ability to offset the negative impact of the depression by virtue of the structure of the economy and its poor state of health prior to the world economic downturn.[34] This sobering assessment of the limited scope for ameliorative action would still apply if the decision-makers at the time had access to present-day economic policy tools, including especially the full range of economic statistics. Recovery in Australia thus had to await recovery elsewhere as only then would the external constraints on more rapid domestic growth be relaxed.

IMPERIAL ECONOMIC LINKS—DECLINING NET BENEFITS

It has been a refrain in this story that for much of its history the Australian economy was highly integrated with that of Britain. Though located in the antipodes it was essentially a region within the economy of a "Greater Britain." This integration is most evident in the closeness of trade, investment, and migration links, but is evident also in technology transfers, in the existence of a currency union, and in shared banking institutions. Beyond these were further links operating in the political, constitutional, legal, and cultural spheres. Initially the integration with Britain was pervasive, but even as the political and constitutional links attenuated with the granting of responsible government in the 1850s and with federation in 1901, the economic links proved amazingly durable. Until the Second World War, Britain remained the dominant trading partner and the principal source of both immigrants and foreign investment. What were the consequences for Australia's growth and prosperity through to 1940 of this 150-year experience of first formal, then later informal, economic integration?

There is a literature that poses this question differently since it rests on the assumption that the industrialized metropolitan power dictated colonial development such as to maximize its own interests, not those of the colonists, whenever the two diverged. There is an implicit counterfactual here: by exercising its imperial power, Britain diverted the development of its distant colonies from a path they would have taken if independent, an alternative path that would have led to greater prosperity for Australians. The historians writing in this tradition

---

[34]For macroeconometric analyses of alternative policies during the 1930s, see Valentine (1987, 1988) and Siriwardna (1995).

included those who were radical nationalists, anti-imperialists, and Marxists. The intellectual roots of this perspective go back at least to Hobson and Lenin on the economic aspects of imperialism. The most comprehensive interpretation of Australian economic history in this vein was that of Brian Fitzpatrick.[35] This approach was not represented in the postwar flourishing of research into the history of the Australian economy, though elements of it survived in the writing of the heterodox "political economy" school of economists. And it is from this background that David Clark provided an important overview of the question posed here.[36] The title of his essay, "Australia: Victim or Partner of British Imperialism?," indicates that he does not assume a particular result at the outset. He identifies many of the key historical events and issues on which such an assessment would be based, concluding that there were both benefits and costs to Australia of the imperial economic relationship.

Before looking further into that, it is important to note the reverse side of this question, namely, what was the net economic benefit to Britain of its imperial possessions? Of course a finding that Britain received benefit from the empire does not rule out benefit accruing also to the empire. The economics of imperial relationships can be a positive sum game, as with other forms of international economic relationships. And any generalization regarding the benefits or costs to the British colonies in aggregate need not apply in the specific case of Australia. However, the consensus among scholars is that the *net* benefit to Britain was small when expressed as a percentage of GDP. These modest net benefits varied over time, and were rising in the period immediately prior to World War I.[37]

With respect to the economic effects of empire on Australia, it is important to recognize that they were, to a substantial degree, the effects of what is now described as globalization. In the pre-1914 period there emerged for the first time a global economic system, a significant portion of which comprised the empires of the European nations, and of these the British Empire was by far the most important. London became the world's financial center, the pound sterling the key reserve currency of the era, and Britain the industrial and technological core of the world trading system until challenged by the United States and Germany toward the end of the nineteenth century. As an integral component of the British imperial system, Australia was, ipso facto, an integral component

---

[35]His two volumes (Fitzpatrick 1971 and 1969) were first published in 1939 and 1941, respectively, and retain their value as a significant contribution to economic historiography, but on the topic of the net benefits to Australia of its close economic relations with Britain, they are no longer a reliable guide.

[36]See Clark (1975).

[37]Edelstein (1994) provides estimates of British GDP in 1914 without the empire, based on alternative assumptions, which range from 1 to 5 percent below the actual GDP in that year. If the assessment date is moved later than 1914, however, it has been argued that the net benefits to Britain were enhanced by the contribution of the empire to its defense in the First World War: "If there was ever any subsidy to the dominions, it was amply repaid" (Offer 1993, p. 235).

of the vigorously expanding global economy. Thus the economic advantages and disadvantages of Australia's colonial status in large measure were those associated with its being deeply embedded in the international economy at the time. The question then is whether the benefits to Australians of participation in the international economy in the nineteenth century were augmented or diminished by its status as a member of the British Empire.

Recent research suggests that during the pre-1914 era countries who were part of an imperial system recorded higher levels of trade than those who were not, after accounting for the other likely determinants of their levels of exports and imports. These other influences included whether or not the country was on the gold standard, a measure of the size of the economy, distance from trading partners, whether the country was landlocked and the extent of its railway network, whether it had a common border with countries with whom it traded, whether the trading partners shared a common language, and whether there was some form of imperial preference granted or a currency union. One study using this approach concluded that "being in an empire roughly doubled trade relative to those countries that were not part of an empire."[38] Since the effects of a common language independently boosted trade flows, and since language is arguably a good proxy for a range of cultural links and social networks favorable to trade, it is suggested also that the British dominions such as Australia secured more benefits than other colonies lacking these same attributes.[39]

The advantages of membership in the British Empire extended to lower costs of borrowing in the London capital market before 1914—the most important at this time. The belief that this was the case is not novel, as it was held by some contemporary observers. Recent estimates of the effect suggest it was considerable: "All other things being equal, the yield on a bond would be about 100 basis points lower if the issuer came from the British Empire."[40] Among the other things included in the analysis that might also have had a bearing on the terms on which capital could be raised were the borrower's debt and fiscal positions, their trade balance, whether they had a history of loan default, and whether they were on the gold standard. Empire membership not only conferred lower costs of international borrowing but also had the related effect of increasing the amount of capital raised. Michael Edelstein attributes the higher costs of nonmembership to "the greater risks of foreign political pressures and court systems" and notes that British investment in Argentina was, on a per capita basis, only about 70 percent of that in the British settler colonies that were self-governing.[41]

---

[38] Mitchener and Weidenmeir (2008, p. 1806). Their inquiry employed a gravity model to examine bilateral trade flows between 1870 and 1913.

[39] See ibid., p. 1827.

[40] Ferguson and Schularick (2006), p. 297. See also the analysis by Obstfeld and Taylor (2003), which considers interwar as well as pre-1914 evidence, including that for Australia.

[41] Edelstein (1994), p. 209.

These exercises relate to the economic benefits of empire membership in general, and their magnitude will have varied across colonies in a manner that only case studies of each can discern. But the general point remains: in the flourishing international economy before 1914 there were significant economic advantages in being part of the British Empire rather than independent. The economic benefits and costs to Australia of its imperial connections would, however, have varied over time. As we have seen (chapter 3), for many of the earliest years of European settlement, Australia was heavily subsidized by the British government, to the undoubted benefit of the European inhabitants. And until 1890 the net benefits in the economic sphere would most likely have remained positive. In the crisis of the 1890s, however, the assessment becomes harder. On the one hand the favored access to the London capital market may have eased the financial stringency and deflation forced on the colonies.[42] On the other, evidence suggests that some policy options to mitigate the economic downturn—such as seeking a rescheduling of debt domiciled in London, or a devaluation of the currency—were not seriously considered, in part because of the ties of "kith and kin" between Australia and Britain.[43] As we saw in chapter 6, Argentina had no such inhibitions, and may have experienced a milder and shorter depression as a consequence.

Thus it is difficult to see how Australian growth and prosperity would have been enhanced in the nineteenth century by dropping out of the British Empire at, say, the time of responsible government in the 1850s: the complementary trading relationship with Britain would almost certainly have survived as the dominant one for an independent Australia. To this extent the example of Argentina seems instructive. It became closely tied to the British economy for its imports and exports, and to the London capital market, though its immigrants came mainly from Spain and Italy. For an independent Australia before 1914, there were no significant markets for its exports or its sources of immigrants or capital that were rendered unavailable as a result of its membership in the British Empire.[44]

Arriving at a judgment about the net benefit of the imperial economic connection for the years after 1914 is more hazardous. The direct economic costs to Australia of its participation in the First World War were enormous, even if we consider just the loss of human capital in those killed or disabled in battle,

---

[42]"[T]he country risk of colonies was much less sensitive to changes in the perception of the average riskiness of foreign investment. Even in times of crisis (during the Barings crisis), colonial risk premia remained low. The empire effect was therefore strongest during crisis periods" (Ferguson and Schularick 2006, p. 302).

[43]This is discussed in McLean (2006).

[44]The sources of immigration may have been influenced more by the imperial connection than the level. Offer (1999, p. 710) suggests that "Had there been no Empire, these territories [the Dominions] would not have remained undeveloped. Settlers would have come from elsewhere in Europe, North America, or even Asia."

and the financial burden, including the legacy of the war debts.[45] How does one compare this with the economic benefits reaped across the preceding century, or factor in the non-economic considerations such as empire sentiment or loyalty to the mother country in her hour of peril which, at least ex ante, motivated participation in the conflict? If Australia had been independent politically in 1914, would it have stayed neutral throughout or, like the United States, participated only toward the end of the conflict?

In the interwar period the economic relationship with Britain became more complex. The trade policies of the two countries were potentially in conflict as Australia encouraged its nascent manufacturing sector to expand at the expense of imports—mainly from Britain. This marked a historic departure from the mutually advantageous specialization that had previously characterized trading ties. In the 1920s some American corporations began direct investment, especially in the manufacturing sector, ending the near monopoly position occupied by British firms. However, cooperation is also evident in the 1920s schemes of empire settlement that encouraged immigration from Britain and augmented British investment in Australia. In the 1930s the close financial and trade relationship between the two countries was severely tested by the world depression. The devaluation of the Australian pound, the closing of the London capital markets to new issues, and the attempts to increase imperial preference in trade are all elements that must be considered in any assessment. It is possible that the diversification in export markets away from a traditional concentration on Britain, which had begun modestly prior to 1914, was stalled or even partially reversed by the imperial orientation of Australia's interwar economic policies. And the closeness of economic ties with Britain may, by the interwar period, have led Australian firms to give preference to their traditional supplier when importing capital equipment, even though it is possible Britain was no longer the sole source of best-practice embodied technology.

After the Second World War the economic ties with Britain fade rapidly. As we will see in the next chapter, a steady decline occurred in the share of Britain both as a destination for Australia's exports and as a source of immigrants. A vestige of the imperial economic connection may be observed in the arrangements in the sterling bloc in the immediate postwar years to pool scarce U.S. dollars. Symbolic of the radical shift in economic ties was the decision by the British to enter the European Common Market. Though the first attempt was unsuccessful, the union was consummated in 1973: Britain's trading priorities had moved on from its imperial past. Some Australian rural industries and regions were adversely affected by the application to Britain of Europe's agricultural protectionism (the Common Agricultural Policy), but the aggregate impact on Australian prosperity was modest and transitory. Unlike New Zealand,

---

[45] The number of war dead was 58,000 out of a population just under 5 million, and defense-related expenditure peaked in 1918–19 at close to 20 percent of GDP (Grey 2008, pp. 119 and 121).

whose long-run growth prospects were significantly impacted by the British decision, Australia had by then diversified its production base, the composition of its exports, and the markets into which it exported.

Could the Post-1960 Mineral Boom Have Occurred Earlier?

The might-have-beens of history have been considered at several points already in this story. Mostly this has involved speculation about a possible alternative to what happened where that alternative would arguably have resulted in a *less* prosperous outcome for Australia. What if the squatters had been given freehold title to the land they occupied, or if north Queensland had seceded and developed a plantation-style sugar economy based on indentured Melanesian labor? There is also scope for posing the opposite form of counterfactual—whether there occurred missed opportunities for enhanced prosperity, as we have touched on with respect to policies countering the effects of the depression. Another candidate is the hiatus in the contribution of the mining industry to economic activity following the end of the Western Australian gold rushes. Also described as a period of "doldrums" in the industry, this extends for about half a century to around 1960.[46] Vast deposits of, for example, iron ore, coal, bauxite, and natural gas were awaiting discovery and exploitation during decades in which Australian growth and prosperity languished relative to that achieved before 1890 or after the Second World War. Could these mineral and energy resources have been accessed much earlier thereby providing the powerful economic underpinning to living standards that they delivered beginning in the 1960s?

A spur to this line of thinking has been the recent suggestion by three American economic historians that there are grounds for regarding the timing of the postwar expansion in Australia's mining industry as the result of the abandonment of earlier policies that, they argue, had for some decades inhibited the exploration, discovery, and exploitation of the natural-resource base.[47] The broader context of their observations about Australian mining development is an interest in the question of the extent to which the known natural-resource endowment of an economy is endogenous—that is, determined by economic conditions rather than being a gift of nature. Their principal focus is the role of natural resources in accounting for the growth of the U.S. economy, which they argue has been large and persistent. By the end of the nineteenth century, the United States was dominant in world production of many key minerals. Further, the industrial supremacy it attained at that time was due in part to this successful exploitation of its minerals: industrialization was heavily resource

---

[46] The term is Doran's (1984), p. 69.
[47] David and Wright (1997), and Wright and Czelusta (2007).

intensive.[48] These economic historians argue that it was the high initial incomes in the United States that permitted the investment in world-class science and engineering education and research during the nineteenth century, combined with a particularly conducive regulatory environment for exploring and developing its mineral resources, which in turn accounts for the expansion of mineral production there.

They see the Australian experience in striking contrast to that of the United States. Since Australia was also a high-income country with stable political conditions and the rule of law, the environment there for mining exploration and development must, they reason, have been much less conducive since from hindsight we know that these world-ranking deposits were awaiting discovery. They dismiss as possible causes of the delay the lower population density in Australia compared to the United States and harsher climatic conditions; rather they argue that particular policies and regulations inhibited the earlier discovery and exploitation of the mineral wealth until the 1960s. They single out the regulatory environment governing mineral exploration, especially in Western Australia; the embargoes on mineral exports at particular times; and a possible underinvestment in education in areas relevant to mineral discovery and development. And they draw attention to the prevalent belief during the interwar period that Australia was not abundantly endowed with minerals, especially iron ore, which led to policies of "conservation" rather than development.

Why has this period during which mining was in the doldrums not prompted similar questions from Australian historians and economists? It is not that the fading of the mineral sector's contribution to economic prosperity has gone unnoticed, or that its relative decline has not been examined. In the classic survey of mining history by Geoffrey Blainey, there are numerous explanations proffered, usually in relation to a particular mineral, since the circumstances and timing of the stagnation or decline in production varies markedly across minerals—itself a cautionary warning to those wishing to generalize.[49] Here, and in other accounts, the principal reason offered is that the profitability of mining declined from around the time of the First World War and did not recover until the 1950s, and that this was due primarily though not solely to trends in world commodity prices.[50] Indeed, when they rose, as illustrated by gold prices during the depression of the 1930s, production expanded. But other factors are admitted as contributing, including the small scale of mining operations, the withdrawal of British capital during the 1920s, and the fractious state of labor relations in the industry. With respect to iron ore, previous writers have noted the belief that Australia was not well endowed with deposits, the embargo against some mineral exports, and the existence in Western Australia of regulations acting

---

[48] On this theme, see an earlier contribution by Wright (1990).

[49] Blainey (2003a).

[50] Doran (1984) offers an economist's perspective on many of the key issues raised here.

as a disincentive to exploration.[51] If anything, the hiatus in the fortunes of the sector is overdetermined.

The thesis that policy barriers in place during the first half of the twentieth century resulted in a long delay in mineral development in Australia warrants more careful scrutiny than it can be given here. But from the perspective of the early twenty-first century some further points might be made. A high proportion of Australian mineral production is exported rather than forming the basis for large-scale domestic industrialization as happened in the United States. Thus international demand conditions, and especially the fluctuations in world prices, are central to the story about timing. And the interwar period was one of depressed commodity prices. By contrast, booming world minerals prices are well understood to account for a large part of the terms of trade-driven prosperity in the Australian economy in the first decade of the twenty-first century. A second element on the demand side present today is the rapid industrialization of much of Asia with its concomitant demand for mineral and energy supplies. Japan led the way, in the interwar period, but its impact on the demand for Australia minerals at that time was truncated by a government ban in 1938 on iron ore exports following Japan's invasion of China.

However, even had there been no restrictions on trade with Japan, it is unclear whether high transport costs would have precluded the Australian miners from receiving the prices they needed in order to make a large-scale expansion of mining profitable. That is, in advance of the invention of the supertankers and bulk-ore carriers, which today form the obvious link between Australian mineral and natural gas deposits and Asian industry and energy utilities, what scope existed for the export of large volumes of coal, iron ore, bauxite, and the like? And land transport costs must also be considered. The rail lines constructed from inland mines to the coast in both Western Australia (iron ore) and central Queensland (coal) run in some cases for hundreds of kilometers and have been built by the mining companies. But such large up-front fixed costs are recoverable only in a world of very large and long-term export contracts, and it is difficult to see that these potentially existed but went begging before the 1950s. Again, comparison with the American experience is instructive. Not only was U.S. mineral development not primarily export driven. But also, U.S. industrialization was concentrated during the nineteenth century in the Midwest, where iron ore and coking coal deposits lay adjacent to the Great Lakes, permitting low-cost water transport of bulky raw materials over relatively short distances. Australia was "unlucky" in this regard. Though the steel mill at Whyalla in South Australia owes its location to nearby deposits of both iron ore

---

[51]"Until 1961 [the government of Western Australia] refused to grant prospectors or companies a title to explore for iron ore. They also gave no assurance to a discoverer that he could keep what he found. Deposits were to be awarded, not to the finder, but to the company which promised to bring manufacturing industries to Western Australia" (Blainey 2003a, p. 346).

(Iron Knob) and coal (Leigh Creek), the largest and cheapest sources of these key inputs into the steel industry are located on opposite sides of the continent.

I have earlier described in relation to the convict system and the disposal of Crown lands how, if policies or institutions appeared to be standing in the way of maintaining or increasing prosperity, the economic and political system eventually responded to remove or reduce the barriers. This record of adaptability suggests that had industrialization in Asia and the invention of bulk-ore carriers and supertankers occurred earlier, the pressure on Australian governments—state and federal—to modify their regulations and policies on mineral exploration and exporting would have been irresistible.

The Debate over Stagnant Living Standards

We are now better placed to reflect further on one of the most striking features of Australian economic history initially noted in chapter 2, namely, the near stagnation in real GDP per capita lasting half a century from the end of the late nineteenth-century boom in 1890 to the Second World War. Since this is the conventional summary measure of a country's standard of living, it is often interpreted as evidence that it, too, stagnated over the five decades. Yet some skepticism has surrounded this conclusion ever since the historical income estimates of Noel Butlin were published in 1962. And there are reasonable grounds for such skepticism. One is that his GDP estimates may not be reliable, and thus may understate the "true" improvement across the period. A second is that a period of such length without any trend increase in living standards in an "advanced" economy is highly unusual, especially in the absence of some massive destructive event such as descent into persistent civil war.

Despite legitimate concerns with Butlin's estimation methods, there has been no comprehensive revision to his historical GDP series.[52] The specific revision, which by itself would most change the picture of the fifty-year stagnation, relates to the possible overstatement of the boom of the 1880s. That is, if the *level* of GDP around 1890 is overstated, but any systematic upward bias in the series is absent by the First World War, a substantial part of the puzzle would be solved. There would remain slow growth in real GDP per capita from 1914 to 1939, but this would halve the duration of the stagnation. More important, it would be more readily explicable given the succession of negative shocks the economy experienced during that period, and given that anything resembling normal conditions in both the domestic and international economies was absent in all but a few years.

Aside from these justifiable statistical concerns, other approaches have been adopted to assess the hypothesis that Australian living standards stagnated between

[52]I have previously discussed the alternative and partial estimates by Haig (2001).

TABLE 7.1. Social indicators, 1891 to 1947

	1891	1911	1933	1947
Infant Mortality (per thous.)	115.3	68.5	39.5	28.5
Housing				
Rooms per dwelling	5.05	5.04	4.94	4.82
Inmates per dwelling	5.12	4.78	4.26	3.96
Rooms per inmate	1.09	1.15	1.28	1.35
Education (percentage attendance)				
Age 5–14	62.2	67.7	79.5	88.9
Age 15–19	N/A	7.6	11.4	11.3
Age 20–24	0.43	0.75	1.7	4.9

Sources: Infant mortality: Vamplew (1987), MFM 154, p. 58. Housing and Education: McLean and Pincus (1982), Tables 2 and 4, respectively.

1890 and 1939. One has been to focus on per capita consumption rather than GDP as an alternative—but still aggregate—measure of economic well-being. The most recent estimates begin in 1900 and show a modest rise of just 19 percent across the four decades to 1939 (whereas in the subsequent four decades the increase would be 110 percent).[53] Another has been to look to partial measures of well-being that are independent of the national accounting approach and see if they also show little trend increase before the Second World War. No one of these by itself carries much conviction, but if a consistent pattern were observed across many such partial measures, this would constitute valuable evidence for or against the stagnation hypothesis.[54] In general, these "social indicators" show trend rises across the period consistent with the impression that living standards broadly conceived were much improved by 1939 compared with 1890. Some indicators of health, housing, and education are shown in table 7.1 and based mainly on census data. Not only did infant mortality dramatically decrease during this period; life expectancy at age one also increased significantly from fifty-three to sixty-five years for males and fifty-six to sixty-nine for females.[55] The standard hours of work also fell—from forty-nine hours per week in 1914 to forty-four in 1939, implying an increase in leisure

---

[53] Haig and Anderssen (2007), table 2, p. 421.

[54] Relevant studies include Carter and Maddock (1984, 1987), Jackson (1992), McLean (1987), and McLean and Pincus (1983).

[55] Vamplew (1987), p. 61. The estimates quoted compare the years 1881–90 with 1932–34

time.[56] A different contribution to the debate has come from the investigation of anthropometric indicators of well-being. These focus on such measures as average height and weight in the population and, though controversial, constitute intriguing and independent evidence. For example, the heights of male recruits into the military increased between the 1890s and 1920, whereas their body mass index (BMI) showed no clear gain: "the overall BMI improvement of World War II recruits compared to their World War I counterparts was marginal at best."[57]

An alternative approach to the issue of whether living standards stagnated is to ask whether Australians adopted some of the iconic new consumer products of the era such as motor vehicles, radios, and telephones at a rate comparable to that in other high-income countries. In 1939 there were 115 motor vehicles registered per thousand people in Australia compared to 224, 123, and 54 in the United States, Canada, and Britain, respectively; there were 17 radio sets per one hundred people in Australia compared to 21, 11, and 19, respectively, in the other three countries; and there were 105 telephones per thousand people in Australia compared to 165 in the United States and 128 in Canada.[58] No consistent pattern of Australia falling behind the others emerges from these measures.

If we revert to the use of GDP per capita as the measure of prosperity and look at what happened elsewhere, then for the quarter century covered in this chapter the Australian experience of very slow improvement was not so unusual. This is especially true if we focus on the interwar years 1919 to 1939. Australia's *relative* performance appears to have deteriorated only between 1890 and 1918, rather than between the wars strictly defined. This implies that any stagnation in prosperity between 1919 and 1939 had primarily international causes. By contrast, the severity of the negative impact of the First World War on Australia's economy appears to have had local causes. These seem less to do with domestic policy decisions at the time, however, than the unhappy consequence of a growth strategy that relied crucially on the maintenance of a well-functioning international economic system, especially with respect to British demand for Australia's narrow range of export commodities and the willingness of British lenders to supply sizable flows of capital.

---

[56]Vamplew (1987), p. 158. These do not include any increases in the number of public holidays or in annual leave.

[57]Whitwell and Nicholas (2001), p. 170; see also Whitwell, de Souza, and Nicholas (1997).

[58]McLean and Pincus (1982, pp. 13–16). These data may not be strictly comparable across countries.

CHAPTER 8

The Pacific War and the Second Golden Age

The final vindication of high protection was provided by the remarkable achievements of Australia's secondary industries in the manufacture of munitions and war supplies. Without the foundation of equipment and skill that was laid in the years before the war, Australia could never have made so substantial a contribution to her own defense and to the common war effort of the Empire and the United Nations.[1]

I HAVE DESCRIBED the First World War as delivering a severe negative shock to the Australian economy. By contrast, the Second World War was a much "better" war than the First when assessed solely in terms of its economic effects on Australia. Real GDP in 1919 was 4 percent below its prewar level in 1914, whereas between 1939 and 1946, real GDP increased by 26 percent. Considering per capita rather than aggregate trends requires caution because wartime population figures were affected by departing and returning troop movements as well as war casualties. But the contrast between the two conflicts is preserved. GDP per capita fell 8 percent between 1914 and 1919, but rose more than 17 percent between 1939 and 1946. Of course, these are output-based measures of activity that include the production of military goods and services, though by selecting starting and terminal years just outside those of peak military mobilization any distortion should be lessened. If we further narrow the focus to civilian consumption, the massive diversion of resources into the defense sector predictably resulted in a decline in consumption expenditure per capita during both wars, but by less during the Second World War (−5.9 percent) than during the First (−10.4 percent).[2] With this caveat, it seems appropriate to describe the Second World War as delivering on balance a positive shock to the Australian economy. We therefore have to account for this very different economic response to the outbreak of international hostilities in 1939 compared to that in 1914.

There is a second major difference between the economic effects of the two wars pertinent to our story. Following the First World War, per capita income remained below its prewar level until the mid-1920s, as discussed in the previ-

---

[1] Walker (1947), p. 406.

[2] Maddock and McLean (1987a), pp. 362–64, and McLean and Pincus (1982), p. 30. The alternative estimates of Haig (2001) do not report GDP for any years between 1939 and 1949.

ous chapter. By contrast there was no serious interruption to growth between the end of the Second World War and the immediate postwar years: though widely anticipated, a relapse into depression did not materialize. Neither was there a rerun of the transitory prosperity that characterized the mid-1920s; after 1945 prosperity was sustained for a quarter of a century. Thus it is appropriate in this discussion of long-term trends to integrate the period of war and the postwar long boom. In this perspective 1945 is not a break point or watershed in economic history the way it is in military, diplomatic, and social history. Furthermore many of the sources of postwar prosperity can be found in wartime events and experience. Hindsight thus assists in identifying features of the war economy important in any attempt to account for the long boom, which lasted—in this view—from 1940 to the early 1970s. And this is the limited aim here, as I am not engaged in a comprehensive analysis of the war economy.

WHY THE PACIFIC WAR FOSTERED DOMESTIC GROWTH

From an Australian perspective the war passed through three phases—in terms of both the strategic situation and its economic impact. Between the outbreak of hostilities in Europe in September 1939 and the Japanese entry into the war in December 1941, Australian military contributions to the war effort were made primarily in the European and North African theaters. This was because there was no immediate threat of Australia coming under direct attack, though there was growing concern at the possibility of Japan extending its military activities beyond its engagement in China. The economic adjustments during this initial phase were thus aimed primarily at supporting Britain as part of a collective empire effort. There did occur a restructuring of the economy to meet wartime needs, but it was not pursued at the level of urgency that was to follow. For with the attack on Pearl Harbor in December 1941, the fall of Singapore, and the bombing of Darwin in February 1942, the principal theater of conflict from an Australian perspective became its immediate neighborhood. The redeployment of Australian troops from North Africa back to Australia reflected this dramatic deterioration in the country's strategic situation.

In early 1942, with Japan seemingly poised to invade Australia, a second phase of the war effort began. Now the economy was placed under intense pressure to convert to a total war footing to meet the urgent requirements of the military. Adding to this "domestic" demand was the positioning in Australia and nearby in the southwest Pacific of a very large U.S. military presence. Eventually numbering more than three-quarters of a million, this force was directed from MacArthur's headquarters first in Melbourne then in Brisbane. It made sense to supply and equip these U.S. forces as far as possible from Australian sources instead of by ship across the Pacific at a time when the Japanese navy threatened the security of their supply links.

When the Japanese advance into Papua New Guinea and adjacent islands was eventually halted, and following U.S. naval victories in the Pacific, the threat of invasion receded. At the same time it became evident that the extreme demands made on the manpower and production capacity of the economy were unsustainable. Therefore, from 1943 a third and final phase may be distinguished in which there was a reorientation in the war economy with a reduced emphasis on achieving the maximum level of military mobilization and greater priority given to the provision of materiel for the predominantly American forces fighting in the southwest Pacific. One indicator of this was the reassignment of manpower from military to strategic civilian sectors. The consequence of these events and policies was that in each of the first four years following the outbreak of the Second World War, a dramatic expansion of economic activity occurred. By the peak year of the war effort, 1943, aggregate GDP was a remarkable 41 percent above its prewar (1939) level, and this achievement was almost repeated the following year. Thereafter, as the intensity of the war effort was reduced, output fell.

Part of the explanation for why the economic impact of the Second World War was broadly positive lies in the very different capacity of the economy in 1939 compared to 1914 to meet the needs of the military and, just as important, to substitute domestic production for the imports curtailed by the interruption to international trade following the outbreak of hostilities. This is a supply-side story. By 1939 the manufacturing sector was more important in the economy than it had been in 1914, but also more diversified into branches of industry vital to supplying both civilian and military needs. Consequently when the war broke out in Europe in 1939, Australia was much better placed than it had been in 1914.

There is, of course, a path-dependent element to this improved industrial capacity to meet wartime exigencies. As discussed in the previous chapter, the First World War had exposed the vulnerability of the economy to any major disruption to international trade, and led to the establishment of manufacturing capacity in certain key areas. It was these wartime products and firms that obtained protection from resumed imports after the war in the 1921 Greene tariff. With the downturn in the economy in the late 1920s, a further and larger increase occurred in 1929 (the Scullin tariff—clearly evident in figure 7.3) as a means both to increase employment opportunities in manufacturing as the prospects of further rural expansion faded, and to respond to the deteriorating current account balance by promoting import substitution.

Several features of the expansion in war-related manufacturing activity after 1939 are relevant in accounting for the positive impact of the war on domestic activity levels and in the relationship between the war economy and postwar prosperity. One is the link between the interwar industries, often the recipients of import protection, and those that played a critical role in the production of weapons and munitions. An example is the car industry, which in the 1930s had moved beyond the making of car bodies and assembly operations to parts manufacture, a development assisted by the Scullin tariff. The contribution of firms such as General Motors–Holden to military aircraft production has been described as follows: "Without its automotive industry Australia would not have been able to build aircraft on the scale attained at the height of the war. The industry's experience in sub-contracting made it an ideal coordinating contractor, accustomed as it was to bringing parts and sub-assemblies from hundreds of different factories and assembling, testing, and delivering to a pre-arranged timetable. The automotive industry was able to inject into aircraft production the experience and training of its executives, production supervisors and foremen."[3]

A second feature is the changed scale, composition, and location of manufacturing that occurred under wartime pressures. The numbers employed in manufacturing grew from 615,400 to 834,100 between 1939 and 1944.[4] The areas of greatest importance to the war effort were iron and steel products, refining and smelting, chemicals, shipbuilding and repairing, ammunition, military vehicles, and aircraft, as well as clothing and footwear. Many of the orders for equipment and supplies for the military went to firms in or near Sydney and Melbourne. But the war saw a geographic dispersal of munitions production to other cities and even to a number of country towns with existing small factories. This was designed in part to reduce the vulnerability of the nation's industrial capacity to Japanese aerial or naval attack, as well as to tap potential workers who were regionally immobile. The wartime boost to manufacturing in South Australia, especially at Adelaide and Whyalla, is an illustration of decisions about industrial location and expansion that would leave their imprint on manufacturing for many decades after 1945.

A third feature of note is the increased technical sophistication of the military equipment manufactured, reflecting in turn an improvement in workforce skills in a short period. This qualitative advance is not easy to assess, as the usual market forces were absent. A locally built tank seems to have been less than successful: one military historian comments dryly that "fortunately it never saw action."[5] The military aircraft made domestically did, though with mixed reviews of their performance. But as a measure of industrial progress, this is perhaps a better illustration of what was achieved by Australian firms. "To have produced 3,500 aircraft of nine different types and nearly 3,000 aircraft engines of three types, must notwithstanding the mistakes and miscalculations that occurred, be ranked among the great achievements of Australian industry,

---

[3]Mellor (1958), p. 394.
[4]Vamplew (1987), p. 149.
[5]Grey (2008), p. 185.

especially when it is remembered that the fighter aircraft was one of the most highly complicated examples of precision engineering."[6]

Another feature of the economy that helps account for the difference in domestic activity levels between the two wars is the greater contribution of women to the labor force after 1939. Thus, part of the explanation both for the rapid growth of output after 1939, and for the rise in measured GDP per capita until 1943, is not simply the reentry into the labor force of those still unemployed at the end of the depression decade, but also the wartime rise in female workforce participation.[7]

To round out this discussion of the supply-side reasons the Second World War witnessed growth in aggregate economic activity, it is worth taking a longer-run perspective on the changing importance of the manufacturing sector within the economy. Simply put, if any decade in Australian history is to be singled out as one of "industrialization," it is the 1940s (figure 8.1). Between federation and the end of the First World War the share of GDP originating in manufacturing increased only slowly from 12.1 to 13.5 percent. This gradual shift toward industry reached 16.7 percent by 1929 and 18.5 percent by 1939. But in the next decade, there occurred an unprecedented spurt such that by 1949 (and therefore beyond any wartime distortion), the share of manufacturing had reached 26.2 percent.[8] Over the next two decades of the postwar boom, there was some further small rise in this share, but it never reached 30 percent of either output or employment before beginning a secular decline. What the war accelerated, postwar economic conditions and policies supportive of the manufacturing sector consolidated—a topic discussed below.

There is also a demand side to any explanation of the difference between the economic impacts of the two wars. The First World War was fought primarily in Europe and the Middle East, remote from potential domestic sources of supply. The war-related demand for Australian-sourced materiel was limited. This was due in part to the higher transport costs relative to alternative sources such as Canada, where these "costs" included the risk of nondelivery: in wartime, the greater the shipping distance, the greater the exposure to enemy interdiction. Although the Second World War had also begun in Europe, we have noted the drastically changed situation facing Australia at the beginning of 1942. Now the demand was for war-related production to be delivered at home. An additional demand-side difference was the decision to source from Australia some of the supplies and munitions for the U.S. forces in the southwest Pacific. The more diversified manufacturing sector, acquired in the previous quarter century, and the enhanced skill base of the industrial workforce, made feasible the

---

[6] Mellor (1958), p. 422.

[7] One estimate has the female workforce rising by 29 percent between 1939 and 1944 (Keating 1973, p. 344).

[8] Based on GDP at factor cost. Maddock and McLean (1987b), p. 19.

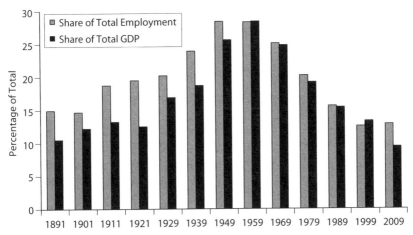

Figure 8.1. Manufacturing share of total employment and GDP, 1891 to 2009.
Note: The concepts and definitions of "manufacturing" and of "employment" may not be strictly comparable across all years.
Sources: Share of employment: 1891 to 1959, Butlin and Dowie (1969), Table 6, p. 153; 1969 to 1989, Reserve Bank of Australia, *Australian Economic Statistics 1949–50 to 1996–97*, Table 4.10c; 1999 and 2009, Australian Bureau of Statistics, *Labour Force* (Cat. 6203.0). Share of GDP: 1891 to 1939, Butlin (1962), Table 3, pp. 12–13; 1949 and 1959, Vamplew (1982), Series MANF142, p. 301 and Butlin (1977), Table IV.1, p. 79; 1969 to 1989, RBA, *Australian Economic Statistics 1949–50 to 1996–97*, Table 5.9; and 1999 and 2009, ABS, *National Accounts* (Cat. 5204.0), Table 5.

domestic production of a wide range of products to support the Australian and U.S. forces fighting in Papua New Guinea and nearby islands and waters. The list included food, clothing and boots; rifles and ammunition; field guns; transport and armored vehicles; transport and naval ships and ship repair services; fighter and bomber aircraft and aircraft engines; and ancillary equipment that was high-technology by the standards of the times.

Hence, a striking characteristic of the war economy was the division of labor that developed between the two allies in their struggle against Japanese expansion. This extended beyond the allocation of production orders for particular goods or services to include also the strategic decision in 1943 to partially reallocate Australian manpower resources from the military to the domestic production of strategic items. For their part the Americans would be able to obtain more of their supplies locally, but would thereby contribute a higher proportion of the troops fighting in the southwest Pacific. This is the context for the previously defined third phase of Australia's wartime experience.

Critical to this shared military and economic effort was the operation of Lend Lease arrangements between the two countries. In the early phase of the war, Lend Lease was designed to permit Britain and its commonwealth partners access to U.S. supplies and equipment on favorable financial terms. After the entry of Japan—and hence the United States—into the conflict, these arrangements were extended and modified to include Australia's relations with the United States more directly. One crucial element of this was its reciprocity: the program was called Mutual Aid. This wartime division of labor and the associated payments arrangements between the Australians and the Americans had the consequence that Australia emerged at the end of hostilities in an enhanced international financial position. "At the beginning of the war government policy had been to restrict dependence on external loans as far as possible and avoid the crippling accumulation of fixed-interest obligations that accompanied the war of 1914–18. . . . However, the extent of the achievement to the point of a reduction in net overseas indebtedness exceeded all expectations, and was due primarily to the rapid development of manufacturing capacity for the production of military equipment and to the inflow of Lend-Lease."[9] One indicator of this improved foreign-indebtedness position was that the debt-servicing ratio fell dramatically to levels (below 10 percent by the end of the 1940s) not seen since the 1860s, a striking contrast to the situation following the First World War (figure 6.2). Another is the rapid decline at the end of the 1940s in government debt as a proportion of GDP—again in contrast to the experience in the 1920s (figure 7.2).

The sources of domestic finance for the war effort changed in the middle of hostilities to reduce the reliance on loan finance and increase that from taxation. Within categories of tax revenue, a decline occurred from prewar proportions in the contribution of customs and excise duties and a rise in the contribution of income taxation.[10] The success of domestic loan-raising efforts suggests that the war effort had strong community support, especially once Australia seemed threatened with invasion. But it may in part also reflect the supply of savings in the community resulting from the buoyant economic conditions stemming from the war mobilization effort.

Much has been written about wartime economic policy,[11] one reason for which lies in the view that a significant contribution to the successful macroeconomic policies of the immediate postwar decades was the experience gained in the running of a substantially planned and centralized economic system between 1939 and 1945, together with the wartime planning for postwar reconstruction. The magnitude of the resource reallocation that occurred is reflected in the rise in war-related expenditure from $111 million in 1940 to a peak (in current prices) of $1,124 million in 1943 when it represented 38.5 percent of GDP.[12] In the labor market, there was conscription for military ser-

---

[9]Butlin and Schedvin (1977), pp. 598–99.
[10]See tables in Butlin (1955), p. 395, and in Butlin and Schedvin (1977), p. 571.
[11]For an early example, see Walker (1947).
[12]Butlin (1955), p. 395, and Butlin and Schedvin (1977), p. 582.

vice (although with a restriction about the theater to which conscripts could be sent)—a contrast with the bitter opposition to the introduction of such a policy during the First World War. There was also a substantial degree of planning and direction of civilian labor, especially to the manufacture of munitions and to certain rural industries. In product markets, the most visible indicator of wartime planning to contemporaries would have been the imposition of price controls and rationing of basic items, and the conversion and extension of manufacturing plants to meet orders for war supplies and equipment. Behind all this lay the extensive administrative and bureaucratic machinery extending from federal cabinet through greatly expanded and redesigned government departments to individual enterprises. Despite understandable distortion and waste, the transition to a semi–command economy was reasonably well accomplished considering the novelty and magnitude of the task undertaken under conditions of extreme stress on Australia's political, administrative, and economic systems.

The Golden Age Was Not Uniquely Australian

The period between the Second World War and the early 1970s is conventionally referred to as "the postwar boom" and as "a golden age" for the Australian economy. At several decades remove, our perspective on this era has in some respects changed. Yet there has been no fundamental challenge to the favorable assessment of economic performance and prosperity implied by these labels. That they are widely used attests to the popular impression of the period, not just the consensus among scholars. I note in passing that it was during this era that another label for the Australian experience—ranging well beyond the economic—was coined: the lucky country.

My interest in "the long boom" thus derives not from a wish to reassess the achievement of sustained growth but from a desire to explain its occurrence—in particular its origin, its duration, and why it ended when it did.[13] As with any complex event, there may never be a fully settled explanation. In this case the reason is unlikely to be because new economic data will overturn seemingly settled facts and interpretations: such an event is improbable because of the vast improvement in the quality and quantity of statistical information about the economy that dates from the end of the war.[14] Rather, shifts in interpretation of

---

[13] The reasons for the end of the "golden age" will be canvased at the beginning of the following chapter.

[14] It was in the late 1940s that Australia's first official national income accounts were compiled by what is now the Australian Bureau of Statistics. As a consequence, and compared to the estimates for earlier years compiled by economic historians, the estimates of GDP and related series used extensively throughout this book are much improved in quality.

the boom are more likely to arise because of developments in economics that enable scholars to reexamine the historical evidence equipped with new tools of analysis. In addition, each generation has a new vantage point from which to view the past. Both these influences have affected my own views on this era of economic prosperity. It is also an era of which I have firsthand—if immature—acquaintance.

Perhaps the most important fact about the long boom is that it was not unique to Australia. Precisely the same labels refer to what was almost a worldwide phenomenon in its characteristics and timing. Indeed, all the industrialized or advanced Western economies participated. In addition, the Soviet Union and its East European satellite economies, though in many respects operating in self-imposed economic isolation, also experienced respectable growth rates during these years. And in at least some parts of the so-called third world (to employ the nomenclature of the period), there were examples of poorer countries achieving respectable rates of growth, though there were important exceptions such as India, China, and much of Africa. With growth at this time so widespread, it is clear that the international economic system must figure prominently in explanations of the national experience of any economy. At one extreme a working hypothesis might take the form of the adage that a rising tide lifts all boats. That is, as a small and open economy, Australia was passively buoyed up by the same forces operating to benefit so many other economies, leaving limited scope for domestic determinants to have played a decisive part in the story.

In the literature on the Australian boom, however, most attention is given to the contribution of local decisions, policies, and events. There is a tension here that we have met previously in relation to earlier periods and topics. If the aim is to offer a detailed *description* of the Australian experience of the long boom, it is appropriate to dwell primarily on the domestic scene. However, if the intention is to provide an *explanation* of such key features as its timing, duration, and magnitude, then a comparative perspective is more appropriate. It is imperative to avoid the fallacy of constructing a tailor-made explanation of what is but one example of a general phenomenon, as if the Australian experience were unique.

As seen in table 2.1, the aggregate growth rate across the three decades following the Second World War (4.8 percent on average) was the same as that for the three decades prior to 1890. However, as population growth in the late nineteenth century was higher than in the postwar decades, per capita income growth was almost twice as high in the latter—2.5 compared to 1.3 percent. Unemployment during the immediate postwar decades averaged just 1.9 percent—a figure not equaled at any other time since federation (figure 7.4). I shall begin the discussion of this impressive record by reviewing the explanations given for the long postwar boom in the world economy. Only then is it possible to see the degree to which Australia's experience closely mirrored that elsewhere, thus delimiting the scope for any country-specific interpretation of the golden age in the domestic economy.

The initial period of rapid growth in many economies after 1945 was in part the result of deferred consumption and investment during the war years. Given the limited period of prosperity between the depression and the outbreak of war, this "backlog" in demand had probably been accumulating for a decade and a half rather than just during the war period. On the consumption side, product innovations introduced in the 1920s, such as cars and a range of electrical appliances, had by no means reached full market penetration by the time of the depression. Hence they are prominent in the list of postwar household expenditure items. Private investment had also fallen sharply in the depression, and remained at low levels during the war. The stocks of housing and of industrial plant and equipment had aged and been run down. Thus by 1945 there was a latent demand for large amounts of new investment. It would take some years to satisfy this pent-up consumption and investment demand, thereby imparting a lasting stimulus to aggregate demand once the war was over and incomes rose. There was also a technological backlog, or cluster of recent innovations, some war related, that further raised the expected profitability of postwar investment. In the immediate postwar years of low unemployment and rising incomes these conditions spurred growth of a "rubber-band" or "bounce-back" nature. How long this was a major force underpinning prosperity is debated. It has no clear definition, though seems intuitively reasonable.

A further source of prosperity in the immediate postwar years was the emergence of a stable and well-functioning international economic system. That this occurred was contrary to expectations: the end of hostilities, it was thought, would swiftly be followed by a return of the depressed and chaotic conditions associated with the 1930s, nationally and internationally. Neither was it like the experience after the First World War when attempts to resurrect the pre-1914 open international economy failed. After 1945 there occurred in a reasonably short time frame the genesis of an international monetary system (devised at Bretton Woods in New Hampshire in 1944) that was to perform reasonably successfully until serious strains began to emerge in the late 1960s. After 1945, also, there was a progressive liberalization of international commodity trade under the aegis of the General Agreement on Tariffs and Trade, though this was primarily confined to trade in manufactured products. In addition, after 1945 there was a gradual rise in levels of international capital flows compared to those of the interwar years: it would be several decades, however, before world capital markets would exhibit the degree of integration lost in 1914. Finally, there was a surge in international migration following the war to levels not seen since the early 1920s. Together these elements of the postwar international economy facilitated an enhanced degree of openness and stability that in turn underpinned domestic economic confidence. The foundations were being laid for a second period of globalization. Most important, there was no return to the isolationism, protectionism, and even autarky that had characterized much of the period between the wars.

Given this international environment, the only surprising outcome for the Australian economy after 1945 would have been slow growth, stagnation, or decline. In thinking about this bleak scenario, recall that between 1895 and 1914, when the international economy was performing extremely well, Australia failed to share in the international prosperity for most of this period, for reasons canvased in chapter 6. Historical experience thus cautions against the temptation to assert it was inevitable that favorable conditions in the world economy after 1945 would translate automatically into equally favorable domestic outcomes. Perhaps a more helpful formulation is to ask how successfully Australia exploited the opportunities opened up to it by the golden age of postwar international growth.

Export Growth, Factor Inflows, and the Korean War Wool Boom

One policy response to the opportunities offered by the end of hostilities was a substantial increase in levels of immigration (figure 8.2.). The gap in living standards between Australia and most European countries was wider in 1945 than it had been before the war, and prospects for future peace and prosperity in the devastated continent must have seemed bleak at the time. In addition there were large numbers of Europeans displaced from their homelands by war and the extension of Soviet political control into Eastern and Central Europe. From Australia's perspective these conditions represented an increase in the potential supply of immigrants. That this opportunity was taken—and vigorously so from 1947—reflects a significantly heightened Australian desire for an increased population through immigration. The Japanese entry into the war on the side of the Axis powers in 1941, and what appeared to be a serious threat of invasion in 1942, reinforced anxieties among Australians concerning their long-term security. The inability of Britain to provide effective military assistance in the crisis, and the crucial role played by the United States in first halting then rolling back the Japanese threat, underscored both the vulnerability of the country to attack from Asia and its dependence on distant allies. These wartime experiences gave a powerful boost to the long-standing national objective of an increased European population.

From Britain, from the displaced persons camps on the continent, then later from Southern Europe, a wave of immigrants were enticed, many arriving under government assistance schemes. Immigration increased aggregate demand, especially for such sectors as housing, related urban infrastructure, consumer durables, and cars. These same sectors were also experiencing high demand as a result of other demographic changes under way, notably the start of the postwar

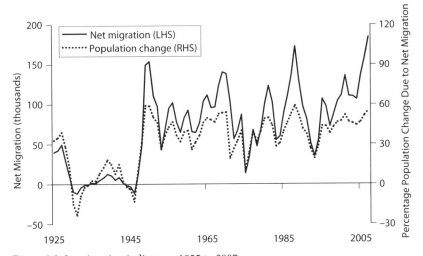

Figure 8.2. Immigration indicators, 1925 to 2007.
Note: Years ending 31 December.
Sources: Australian Bureau of Statistics, *Historical Population Statistics, 2008* (Cat. 3105.0.65.001), Table 8.1, and ABS, *Australian Demographic Statistics, March 2010* (Cat. 3101), Table 1.

baby boom. Marriages had been delayed and birth rates had fallen in the 1930s and early 1940s. Here was a clear illustration of economic activity being stimulated as a lagged response to the effects of depression and war.

Foreign investment in Australia also resumed in the postwar years following the disruptions to international capital flows that had characterized much of the interwar period and their cessation during the war. In contrast to earlier periods of inflow, the capital was predominantly privately raised, took the form of direct investment, and was sourced in the United States as well as from Britain; in addition, more was directed into the manufacturing sector. These funds permitted a higher level of domestic investment than would otherwise have been possible without reducing consumption. It is also likely that this direct foreign investment was associated with productivity-enhancing transfers of technology and managerial know-how to a degree perhaps greater than occurred in the 1920s, and certainly than in the nineteenth century.[15]

If Australia's prosperity at this time is regarded as still heavily reliant on the international market for rural commodities, then the years following the war were much more favorable for farmers than the years immediately following the First World War. Export prices had risen between 1919 and their postwar peak in 1925 by 38 percent, and the terms of trade rose by 80 percent to its

---

[15]Brash (1966), chapter 6.

peak in the same year, underpinning the brief prosperity of the early 1920s. By contrast, export prices between 1946 and 1951 rose 343 percent, and the terms of trade by 140 percent.[16] Thus Australia experienced a terms-of-trade boom in the late 1940s and early 1950s beyond anything it had seen, or was to see again until the minerals and energy-related commodities boom at the beginning of the twenty-first century.[17] Unlike the interwar experience, the terms-of-trade boost to the post–Second World War economy was sustained for over a quarter of a century despite its retreat from the peak years of the short-lived Korean War wool boom (figure 8.3). This is important to remember given the pessimism engendered by the secular trends in the terms of trade of primary producing countries during these decades.

From an Australian perspective, the Korean War (June 1950 to July 1953) was more important for its effects on the domestic economy than for the military contribution Australia made to the United Nations forces engaged there. This was because of the strategic value of wool, the price of which rose spectacularly. In particular, the demand for wool by the U.S. government in 1951 pushed the price to a peak in March of that year. A short-term supply response was not possible—it takes farmers several years to increase sheep numbers; so it is not surprising that we do not observe any rise in wool production. Hence, this brief boom was substantially the result of a demand-driven price spike, contrasting with the mid-nineteenth century gold rushes. As we saw in chapter 5, that boom was a supply-side shock resulting from discoveries in an industry that faced an (infinitely) elastic demand at the prevailing price—a price that was fixed internationally.

In the late 1940s wool remained the single most important of Australia's exports, though it was less dominant than in the late nineteenth century. Hence an increase in the wool price index of 143 percent between July 1950 and its peak in March 1951 was certain to have wide repercussions.[18] The rise in wool prices rapidly flowed through to an increase in export receipts and on into farm incomes. There was an immediate increase in foreign exchange holdings, itself of significance in a period of fixed exchange rates, capital controls, and long-standing concerns about the balance of payments. And as spending by farmers out of their increased incomes rose, the effects of the wool-price boom spread more generally into the domestic economy. In part this increased expenditure leaked into imports. Given the straitened circumstances of the immediate postwar years, it is unsurprising that there was a suppressed demand for imports, which therefore rose as rapidly as had export receipts. Indeed, when the Americans pulled out of the wool market in April 1951 and prices fell sharply, there

---

[16]Pinkstone (1992), pp. 354 and 367.
[17]This assessment is based on the available terms-of-trade indexes, which begin in 1870.
[18]Wool prices quoted in Waterman (1972), p. 78.

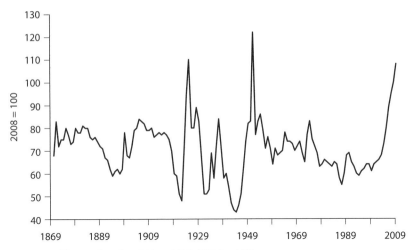

Figure 8.3. Terms of trade, 1870 to 2009 (2008 = 100).
Source: Battellino (2010), Graph 3.

were still high levels of orders for imports in the pipeline. The result was a sudden turnaround in the current account into deficit, and a crisis for domestic economic management.[19]

My interest lies less in the short-run macrostabilization story than in the longer-run effects of this episode for Australian growth and prosperity. And with the advantage of hindsight, several features are seen to have contributed to prosperity throughout the 1950s. One was the mandatory retention of some of the receipts from the sale of wool into farmers' bank accounts that then could be accessed only gradually. This lowered the short-run stimulus to aggregate demand, spreading it over the following years. There was also a voluntary aspect to farmers' spending patterns: they saved a proportion of their above-normal incomes and later invested it back into the farm. In part this may be read as an illustration of the backlog effect—for example, the replacement of aging farm equipment long deferred due to the depression and war. This higher level of farm investment thus persisted throughout the fifties, underpinning in turn a number of productivity-enhancing changes in agricultural production methods. In addition to more up-to-date machinery, farmers invested in rabbit eradication, crop diversification, the application of fertilizers and agricultural chemicals, fencing, water conservation, and irrigation. Further sustaining rural prosperity for some years was the maintenance of, or only gradual fall in, farm product prices, though a decline in farmers' terms of trade occurred through

---

[19]For a detailed account see Waterman (1972), chapter 3: "The Korean War Episode, 1949 to 1953" (pp. 64–98).

the 1960s. But there was no international collapse of agricultural prices and incomes as had occurred in the late 1920s and early 1930s. Neither were these years marred by serious or recurring droughts to match those that had afflicted farmers at the time of federation. Hence, from the late 1940s through the fifties and beyond, rural Australia shared in the golden age.

There is another element in the response to the Korean War wool boom that helps explain why its benefits were more enduring: the associated surge in the general price level was transitory. Had expectations of higher future inflation taken hold, leading to a wage-price spiral, the wool boom could have triggered problems similar to those that would characterize the stagflation experience of the 1970s. The initial inflationary shock was certainly severe. Indeed, the highest annual rate of inflation Australia has experienced since the gold rushes was 22.5 percent if measured by the CPI (in 1952) or 25.6 percent if measured by the GDP deflator (in 1951). Yet within two years consumer price inflation had plummeted to 2 percent. Part of the explanation for this beneficial outcome lies in the suspension of the system of wage indexation then operating. What could have been a mechanism for triggering a wage-price spiral was temporarily disconnected. In essence, the price rises were not fully compensated in increased nominal wages via the centralized wage-setting system, despite these institutional arrangements having been put in place to maintain workers' real incomes.

There may be a deeper component to any explanation of this outcome—one which looks remarkable by the standards of the 1970s and 1980s when the fight to reduce inflation was both protracted and very damaging to economic prosperity. The key is to identify why the anti-inflationary policy response to the wool boom of the early 1950s was accepted—by workers and by voters. The answer probably lies less in the institutional arrangements in the labor market as such than in the expectations of the working and voting populations at that time, in particular their expectations regarding economic prosperity and threats to its continuation. The great majority of adults in 1951 had lived through a decade of depression and hesitant economic recovery in the 1930s, then five years of wartime hardship. In the six years after 1945, most therefore experienced either their first spell of economic prosperity, or the first in two decades. It therefore seems plausible to conjecture a readiness to accept a temporary downturn in living standards in order to stabilize the economic system in the face of the wool price shock.[20] Making this acceptance easier would have been a widespread understanding in the community of the precise cause of the price spike, and an appreciation that it was likely to be a temporary phenomenon associated specifically with events in Korea impacting the wool industry. Key institutions and social norms appear to have worked in combination to

---

[20]Giuliano and Spilimbergo (2009) provide cohort evidence of the lasting effect of recessions on expectations.

diffuse what could have been a serious derailment to early postwar prosperity in Australia.

MACROECONOMIC THEORY AND POLICIES—WHAT ROLE?

Following the positive shock associated with the Korean War, the Australian economy continued until the late 1960s on a path of positive growth without encountering any serious or protracted recessions, and accompanied by low inflation and low unemployment. Compared with experience back to the mid-1920s, if not to 1914, this seemed to contemporaries a very welcome outcome, if not good luck. Among macroeconomists, however, there was growing confidence in their understanding of its causes and, especially—but more troublingly for their reputation in the long run—of their ability to sustain it. For this is the golden era also of the Keynesian school of macroeconomic theory and policy and of its influence over governments.

The view that gained acceptance at the time was that the application of Keynes's theories concerning the behavior of the macro-economy across the business cycle could form the basis of short-run policy adjustments, especially in fiscal policy, which would result in the avoidance of a slump like the one in the early 1930s. Macroeconomists advising postwar governments drew on not just the theoretical contributions of Keynes and his followers but also the considerable experience gained in managing the wartime command economy. When the anticipated return to depression following the end of the war did not materialize, this was interpreted as one piece of evidence supporting the efficacy of Keynesian policies.

Here was a compelling illustration of the power of ideas on economic policy and, seemingly, also on economic outcomes. A particular branch of economic theory had emerged from its Cambridge (England) origins, partly in response to the challenge of the depression in the 1930s but partly as a response to the perceived policy limitations of existing theories, the ideas of Keynes having reached Australia during the 1930s. The comparatively orderly conversion of the economy to a total war footing in the early 1940s appeared to support the view that governments could intervene in an economy to a greater degree than hitherto with desirable economic and social benefits. Further supporting the new direction in macroeconomic policy was the availability of improved statistical information about economic activity: the systems of national income accounts set up throughout the advanced economies in the 1940s, including in Australia, were based on Keynesian concepts. Later, several cohorts of postwar economics students were trained in the new macroeconomics. Alternative (pre-Keynesian) perspectives appeared discredited, so disappeared from the curriculum. It was a great era to be an economist—or, more precisely, a macroeconomic policy adviser to governments.

Ambitious macroeconomic goals were set by governments from 1946, including a commitment to the maintenance of full employment, while purposive countercyclical fiscal policies can be dated from the early 1950s.[21] At the time, the positive correlation between the new orthodoxy in macroeconomics, its application by Australian adherents in policy positions of influence, and the steady growth, low inflation and low unemployment experienced in the 1950s and 1960s seemed evidence enough to make the case. But how influential were domestic macroeconomic policies in producing the observed economic outcomes?

There are grounds for qualifying the contribution of Keynesian ideas and policies in any explanation of the golden age of prosperity, and thereby of the role of economists: correlation does not establish causation. The first of these is that the postwar prosperity ended in the 1970s without any change having occurred in the general direction of macroeconomic policies, either in Australia or elsewhere. Indeed, for mainstream (i.e., Keynesian) macroeconomists the emergence of persistently high inflation and unemployment alongside slower growth in the 1970s was an acute intellectual as well as a puzzling policy challenge. Their theoretical framework was inadequate to explain stagflation, let alone provide a basis for confidently prescribing policy solutions to it. The intellectual challengers (notably Milton Friedman and the monetary school) now attracted more adherents. There was thus an end to the consensus among macroeconomists that had marked the quarter century since 1945, replaced by a number of competing and evolving schools and approaches.

A second basis on which to question a major role for macroeconomic policy in the postwar prosperity in Australia lies in the fact that, although prosperity was evident in many countries, there was considerable variation between them in the policies they adopted. This was a period of relative prosperity even in the centrally planned economies, where Marxian economics was ascendant. In most of the West European democracies, the government sector was comparatively large, ambitious commitments to social welfare were pursued, and national governments generally made frequent use of discretionary fiscal policies in short-term macromanagement. In the United States, by contrast, the government sector was smaller, and the move toward a welfare state begun in the New Deal of the 1930s had not progressed as far as in most West European countries. Even more striking is that the shift to more activist use of fiscal policy to stabilize the economy was much less in evidence there. Indeed, the conventional dating of this is the 1964 tax cuts. In the short-run management of the U.S. economy, a greater role was accorded monetary policy, in part because of the institutional barriers to making speedy changes in policies on taxes and spending that resulted from the separation of powers between the execu-

---

[21]Waterman (1972, p. 86) writes of the 1951 budget that "The most important feature of this document was its explicit recognition, for the first time in Australian history, that the budget can and should be used for anti-cyclical purposes."

tive and legislative branches of government. In this comparative perspective, a close adherence to Keynesian policies does not appear to have been necessary to participation in the postwar boom.

Yet a third reason for being cautious about the contribution of macroeconomic policies to postwar Australian prosperity is that the economy faced no serious negative shocks over a twenty-five-year interval after 1945, that emanating from the Korean War being both relatively brief and, of course, positive. To find a period of reasonably stable growth of comparable length in Australian history one must go back over half a century to the decades before 1890. The absence of major negative economic shocks is also a feature of the international economy after 1945. When such a shock occurred in the early 1970s the standard policy prescriptions failed. This failure at their first serious test suggests that the concurrence of the heyday of Keynesian macroeconomics and the postwar era of economic prosperity in Australia may have lacked any tight causal relationship.

It is important to note that my interest is in the impact of macroeconomic policies on Australian growth and prosperity over the long run, rather than on short-run goals such as the maintenance of full employment, equilibrium in the external balance of payments, avoidance of marked fluctuations in aggregate economic activity, and stability in the general price level. Hence the debate concerning the degree to which the severity of postwar business cycles was reduced through the application of countercyclical policies, in Australia or elsewhere, has a different focus from the one adopted here. It is also important to highlight the distinction between theory and policy. However dominant the Keynesian school was at the time in academic circles and among professional economists, it does not follow that policy closely followed its prescriptions. Selwyn Cornish has persuasively argued that a more nuanced view is required of the influence of Keynes on Australian macroeconomic policy formation during this period.[22] He ascribes much of the direction taken by policy to other influences, such as the retention into the postwar years of various wartime interventions in the domestic economy, short-term political imperatives, party-political ideology, and external events such as the postwar dollar shortage and Korean War boom.

LOCATION ADVANTAGE: ASIAN INDUSTRIALIZATION AND
  CHANGING TRADE PARTNERS

Perhaps more important to the explanation of Australia's prosperity after 1945 than the contribution of macroeconomic policies was the shift under way in the country's trading relationships. A theme of this story so far has been the closeness of the economic ties between Britain and Australia, dating from Australia's

---

[22]Cornish (1993).

founding as a colony. The durability of this relationship is one of the most striking features of Australian history. During the 1930s, Britain still accounted for
just over half of Australia's exports. But this heavy reliance on a single market
changed after the Second World War (figure 8.4). In the latter half of the 1940s
Britain's share of exports fell to 36 percent; in the 1950s it averaged 34 percent;
and in the 1960s just 18 percent.[23]

The significance of this historic redirection of exports to our understanding of the sources of postwar Australian prosperity is that major new markets
opened up at this time. Some export market diversification had occurred prior
to the First World War (especially toward Continental Europe) and in the interwar period (toward the United States and Japan), but, as noted, this was limited
such as to leave Britain in a still dominant position. Britain's post-1945 decline
in relative importance was not subsequently reversed. Neither was Britain replaced by a single, dominant new export market: no country has subsequently
accounted for anything approaching half of Australian exports. Hence the postwar diversification of Australia's export destinations reduced the risk of over-
reliance on a single market, a risk inherent in the high degree of dependence on
the British market that had persisted for over a century, and first highlighted in
the economic downturn of the early 1840s.

The single most important market to emerge during these years was that of
Japan. In the late 1940s, following its defeat in the war, Japan accounted for less
than 2 percent of Australian exports. Over the next two decades, as Britain's
share fell, Japan's rose, the latter surpassing the former for the first time in 1967.
By 1970 Japan accounted for 25 percent of exports, Britain only 12 percent.
The historic trade relationship with the former imperial power had finally and
permanently been reduced to relatively minor significance.

One of the curious features of Australia's history to this point, which I
have noted in earlier chapters, was its remoteness from its principal trading
partner(s) and sources of immigrants, capital, and technology. In this sense,
distance was never a tyrant: the exceptionally long-distance economic relationship with Britain was integral to sustaining Australia's high level of prosperity
for almost one and a half centuries. Nearer Asian economies did not offer anything like comparable trading opportunities before 1914; nor at that time did
the West Coast of the United States. Only with Japan's industrialization, which
commenced in the late nineteenth century, did the prospect arise that Australia's comparative advantage in resource-intensive products might become the
basis of a significant trading partnership with an Asian country. Early evidence
for this emerged in the interwar period. Whereas in 1913, exports to Japan accounted for only 2 percent of the total, in the 1920s, this had risen to an average
of 7 percent, and in the years 1930–36 it averaged 10 percent, before falling
sharply due to international trade embargoes, then ceasing with the outbreak

---

[23]Pinkstone (1992), pp. 356–57 and 382.

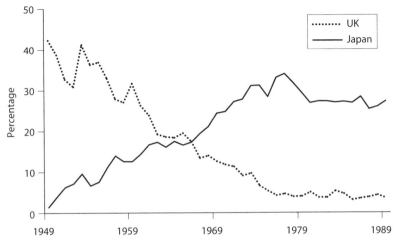

Figure 8.4. Shares of total exports to Japan and the U.K., 1949 to 1989.
Note: Years ending 30 June
Source: Pinkstone (1992), pp. 356, 382, and 389.

of the Pacific war.[24] In the (hypothetical) absence of Japan's military excursions into China in the 1930s, and its 1941 entry into the war on the side of the Axis powers, it seems safe to suggest that the trading relationship between these two western Pacific economies would have continued to grow. Instead it was interrupted for almost two decades, resuming with special vigor only after the 1957 treaty, which brought to an end restrictions dating back to the 1930s.

In a pattern that would be repeated by later East Asian industrializing economies, Japan's demands for food and raw materials were matched by its growing ability to sell an increasingly sophisticated range of manufactured products to Australia. This pattern of exchange had, of course, been precisely that which for so long characterized the trading relationship with industrialized Britain. Hence the resumption of Japanese industrialization after 1945, itself an important part of postwar growth in the international economy, was especially beneficial in underpinning Australia's prosperity. This favorable outcome for Australia of economic growth in Asia would be illustrated again in subsequent decades, with the "tigers" (such as South Korea, Taiwan, Hong Kong, and Singapore), then with China, then more generally (including especially India) in the early twenty-first century. Australians today are well aware of the link between their present high living standards and the economic modernization under way in their not-so-distant northern neighbors, a link that first became important during the golden age of postwar growth. Asian economic development

---

[24] Ibid., pp. 338 and 356.

thus reinforced Australia's comparative advantage in commodity or resource-intensive production for export. This came from the "demand" side, in a sense, and is an element of the second globalization. The discovery of minerals and energy resources from the 1960s, operating on the "supply" side, reinforced the traditional (or original) development strategy Australia had followed.

HIGH TIDE FOR AUSTRALIAN INDUSTRIALIZATION

As discussed earlier in this chapter, industrialization received a powerful impetus arising out of the particular circumstances of the Second World War. After 1945 the expansion and diversification of manufacturing continued (figure 8.1). Indeed, the historically peak shares of GDP and of employment in this sector were recorded in the late 1960s. Thus industrial growth during the long boom slightly exceeded that in the economy as a whole. Large numbers of immigrants were employed in factories and associated service industries. And foreign investment at this time went primarily into manufacturing, not farming or mining. To many contemporaries it must have seemed there was a causal connection at work, namely that the switch from farm to factory as the principal source of employment growth was contributing to the rise in postwar living standards. Economists, then and since, have had their doubts about any such influence.

The discussion of the contribution of manufacturing to Australian prosperity at various times in its history has focused on the role of the tariff and other forms of protection or assistance. In contrast to mining and farming, much of the manufacturing sector was not internationally competitive. In principle an increase in the share of a relatively inefficient sector of the economy will lower average productivity, though this conclusion rests on many assumptions and a careful definition of terms. The presumption is that living standards will be lower than under a scenario wherein the internationally competitive sector increases its share of economic activity. A fuller exploration of this complex issue, one that continues to generate debate, will be undertaken in the next chapter. This is because it was in the 1970s and 1980s that serious problems first confronted sections of manufacturing, the burden of protection to industry became a major political issue, and important decisions were made to restructure the sector. Here it is sufficient to set the scene for later discussion.

The growth in manufacturing after the war was associated especially with such industries as cars and car parts, building and construction materials, consumer durables, pharmaceuticals, footwear, textiles and clothing. This growth was driven primarily by domestic demand, not exports. The sources of domestic demand were the surge in the birth rate and in household formation, the greatly increased levels of immigration (also directly boosting demand for housing, appliances, furnishings, and cars), and rising real wages. There was also the backlog element previously mentioned as a cause of the boom in other countries: after fifteen years of depression and war there was pent-up demand by Australian households for both replacement and new products. This fortunate conjunction of factors sustained a virtuous circle of spending, production, and employment favorable to the manufacturing sector.

An additional stimulus to postwar manufacturing expansion resulted from the disposal of federal government assets built during the war for the production of defense materiel. As described earlier, these facilities were numerous, often extensive in scale, in many locations, and included sophisticated production machinery. Australia had a large stock of capital in government ownership that was potentially of considerable value if turned to civilian uses. The South Australian experience is instructive in this respect because the state premier, Thomas Playford, exploited that potential in a pioneering example of state-managed industrial expansion. This included negotiating with the federal government to release the now idle facilities, then enticing domestic or foreign manufacturing firms to locate in and convert these wartime production sites. The state government connected the sites with road, rail, water, and power services if they lacked these; offered subsidies or reduced taxes and charges; and provided low-cost state housing for (often state-assisted immigrant) workers such that their real wages would be competitive with other states'. Since the nineteenth century the South Australian economy had exhibited an emphasis on engineering and metal-using industries. But the wartime decisions to locate a number of defense-related production facilities in the state, and Playford's skill in seeing the potential boost this would provide to postwar industrialization, reinforced the reliance of South Australia on manufacturing. The deft promotion of manufacturing underpinned a period of expansion and diversification in the state's economy, though in more recent decades this has exacerbated problems of structural adjustment for this region.[25] Similar forces were at work elsewhere, particularly in Victoria, the other state economy where there was a continuing emphasis on manufacturing.

Although the domestic market was the principal source of demand for locally produced manufactures, manufacturing exports in this period rose—not just in absolute but also in relative terms. Manufactured items roughly doubled their share of exports across the 1950s and 1960s from about 11 percent (just after the Korean War wool boom) to around 25 percent. This is of special interest because it occurred at a time of high and rising protection for manufacturing.[26] The conventional wisdom is that tariffs should have encouraged the expansion of firms that were internationally uncompetitive resulting in a

---

[25] The South Australian industrialization experience is discussed in Stutchbury (1984) and McLean (1989a).

[26] A study of productivity in the Australian manufacturing sector concluded that "Whatever the 'costs of protection' in the [1950s], they may not have been as high as commonly supposed. . . . [H]igh protection in the fifties did not preclude a significant advance of manufacturing productivity then" (Haig and Cain, 1983, pp. 196–97).

decline in manufactured exports. It is surprising that the opposite is observed. This surge in manufactured exports occurred in both the "simply transformed" and "elaborately transformed" export categories, hence cannot be dismissed as arising only from the processing of primary products. Although there are difficulties with the definitions employed, and changes in them over time, this surge seems unlikely to be merely an artifact of the statistics. And for some manufactured items, the export successes of the period are well known. These included products of the chemicals, steel, automotive, and engineering industries. The main markets for these more sophisticated manufactures were New Zealand, South Africa, Papua New Guinea, and southeast Asia, whereas those for the more simple products were Europe, the United States, and Japan. One authority on trade history has written that this "rise of manufactured goods exports represented the most important diversification of the Australian export structure since the early twentieth century" when wheat, dairy products, and frozen-meat exports reduced the dominance previously enjoyed by wool and, from time to time, gold.[27] Thus, part of the industrial expansion that was a central feature of the postwar boom was export oriented. Looking ahead, by 2009, manufacturing exports as a share of total exports of goods and services again stood at just 11 percent.[28]

It is unclear whether Australia missed an opportunity at this time to consolidate a larger and more internationally competitive manufacturing sector. Several influences may have worked against such an outcome. Many exporters were foreign-owned corporations, wherein production-location decisions were made on a global basis, not necessarily coincident with Australian national interests. The mining booms and energy price shocks of the subsequent decades were to impact negatively on the nonbooming tradeables sector, most conspicuously manufacturing. Economic orthodoxy was swinging away from policies of protection and subsidization of industry in order to provide employment and economic diversification, and toward policies aimed at greater openness, allowing market forces to determine the survival of enterprises. And the continuing process of manufacturing development in the Asian economies provided relentless import competition from the products of these lower-wage countries. Whether an alternative set of policies from those adopted could have mitigated the dramatic decline in Australian manufacturing by building on the sectors that were export competitive in the 1960s is an open question.

As an aside it is worth noting one contrast in the distributional consequences for Australia of the first and second globalizations. We observed in chapter 6 that Australian farmers were major beneficiaries of the relocation of some agricultural production from Western Europe to the more efficient farms of the settler economies. European farmers, however, faced severe dislocation and

---

[27] Pinkstone (1992), p. 175.

[28] Australian Bureau of Statistics, *Australian Economic Indicators*, November 2010, tables 4 and 5.

hardship resulting from the inflow of cheap grains from the new agricultural exporters. This decline in their international competitiveness led to outmigration from rural areas to cities within Europe, as well as to large-scale emigration to the Americas and Australasia. In the second globalization it was the manufacturing sector rather than the agricultural one that relocated as a result of a shift in comparative advantage. Deindustrialization occurred in all the advanced and high-wage economies as many of these jobs moved to the lower-wage- and unskilled-labor-abundant developing economies of Asia, Eastern Europe, and Latin America. In the late twentieth century Australian manufacturing workers, like Europe's farmers a century earlier, were the losers from this second global relocation of particular industries. Unlike the economically distressed farmers of nineteenth-century Europe—whose options included starting a new life in the booming new world with reasonable prospects of thereby improving their standard of living—no such opportunity was available to Australia's displaced manufacturing workers in the 1970s and subsequent decades.

UNDERINVESTMENT IN HUMAN CAPITAL?

The fundamental importance of education to the attainment of high levels of labor productivity, and hence of living standards, is well understood. In the poorest countries priority is given to the eradication of illiteracy and the spread of elementary schooling in an effort to reduce poverty and initiate economic growth. As development proceeds and incomes rise, educational priorities shift to secondary education and technical training. In the advanced economies, educational-policy goals extend to the quality of the educational experience, to raising high school retention and completion rates, and, especially, to the expansion of higher education. The result is that rich countries have accumulated much more human capital per person than poor countries: on average, the number of years of formal schooling rises with levels of income.

Though positive, this cross-country relationship is not perfect.[29] For example, there is considerable variation even among the richest countries in the proportion of their young people in universities or other forms of posthigh-school education. There are also problems of comparability between schooling systems: the "quality" of education is not necessarily well captured by input-based measures such as completed years of schooling, accounting for the recent

---

[29]There is also some debate about the direction of causation. Particularly in empirical studies where the dependent variable is the rate of growth (in income or labor productivity), faster growth may permit more investment in education, thus lifting average levels of schooling. The possibility of reverse causation suggests we should again consider using the term "correlate" rather than determinant of growth when discussing the contribution of education. Note also that here I am concerned with levels and with the long-run, not short-run relationships between rates of change in the variables.

interest in international comparisons of test scores in key subjects. Nonetheless, one of the key determinants of the level of prosperity enjoyed by the advanced economies is their high level of human capital, especially average educational attainment.

Care must be exercised before these results can be applied in an historical inquiry. The positive relationship they suggest may not have held in an earlier era when the human capital requirements of best-practice technology were lower than today. After all, in the early nineteenth century Britain became the industrial workshop of the world, achieved the highest income per capita, and dominated the world economy with—by present-day standards—a remarkably low proportion of the population having attended high school, and with just a handful of universities. It is therefore necessary to consider both the demand for and supply of human capital at different times in Australian history, and ask whether the level of prosperity was ever constrained by underinvestment in human capital—relative at least to that which was achieved elsewhere at the time.

There is only fragmentary evidence on average levels of basic literacy (ability to read and/or write) among Australians in the first half of the nineteenth century. We have noted (chapter 3) the evidence based on the convict indents regarding the proportion of those transported to Australia who were literate, and that this suggests their average educational attainment was not markedly different from that of most people in England at the time. It was also noted that the human capital requirements for the early stages of settlement in the colonies were probably well supplied by the educational and skill backgrounds of the convicts, particularly when combined with those of the officer class and of the free immigrants who arrived in numbers from the 1820s. By the second half of the nineteenth century, the colonial censuses included questions about the ability to read and write, but from the outset report very high literacy rates. So this indicator of one of the most basic skills is not helpful in charting any rise in educational attainment in Australia at the time when the country achieved a relatively high level of income. Some international comparisons of schooling at the elementary level for the late nineteenth century exist, though these are fraught with problems such as differences across countries in the compulsory starting age or in the number of hours of schooling per year. Broadly, evidence suggests that Australian average schooling levels were comparable to those in the small number of other economies for which data are available.[30]

The increase in average years of formal education subsequent to 1900 has not occurred smoothly. Whereas elementary education was made universal in the later nineteenth century, the extension to a significant number of years of

---

[30]Lindert (2004, table 5.10) reports estimates of students enrolled in primary education per thousand children aged 5–14 for many countries including Australia from 1860, Canada and New Zealand from 1870, and the United States from 1880.

high school education was long delayed. Many public and private high schools were founded before 1900, but relatively few students continued their education beyond the compulsory leaving age. This pattern changed decisively only in the post–World War II era. If we consider high school retention rates to age seventeen, the big surge occurs only from the 1960s and 1970s. Prior to this period, Australia did not meet international best practice. Indeed, there is a lag of many decades behind the leader in high school retention rates—the United States (figure 8.5.). There the rise in high school attendance began early in the twentieth century. In 1910–11 just 6 percent of seventeen-year-olds were at school in Australia, whereas the American figures were 34 and 36 percent for boys and girls, respectively. By the early 1930s the Australian figures were little changed, at 10 and 7 percent for boys and girls, but the U.S. figures were then 47 and 49 percent. As late as 1960–61 the difference had widened further: the Australian rates were 15 and 10 percent, the American 76 and 75 percent. Only in the 1960s did the gap narrow, but by 1970–71 Australia still just matched the participation rate of seventeen-year-olds in high schools that the United States had achieved in 1910.[31] This gap is so large as to survive any problems of data comparability. The key issue here is its significance for Australian comparative productivity and prosperity. In particular were the somewhat lower levels of income per capita in Australia compared to the United States that have persisted for much of the twentieth century attributable in some measure to the delayed expansion in secondary-education participation rates in the former?

Australia's laggard status in high school attendance and retention rates was not unique. Other advanced economies during the interwar and immediate postwar decades also recorded high school retention or graduation rates well below the U.S. rates, though in the case of Canada the gap was smaller than for Australia or countries in Western Europe.[32] There is a broader issue here as to whether the significant lead in secondary education that the United States maintained for several decades contributed to its preeminence in productivity and incomes through the twentieth century. Here we confine attention to the pair-wise comparison with Australia, recalling that the United States dislodged Australia from its income per capita leadership at about the time the American expansion in secondary education began.

That there is no single path to prosperity has been repeatedly emphasized in this book. Australia's lower high school retention rates over much of the twentieth

---

[31] These figures are drawn from MacKinnon (1989a), table 1. She reports the participation rates for each age from 14 to 17, but the gap is evident across all ages. In 1910–11, for example, 42 percent of Australians age 14 were in school compared to over 80 percent of Americans of the same age.

[32] Note that it is two resource-rich economies that led the world in high school retention rates in the twentieth century. This historical evidence contrasts with the claim, based on cross-country evidence for recent years, that resource abundance is associated with lower investment in education and thus lower growth: see Gylfason (2001).

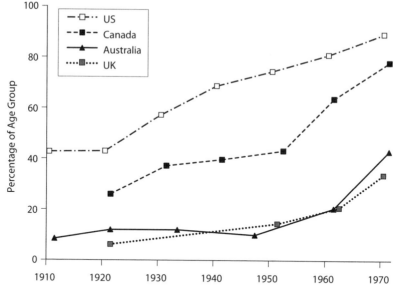

Figure 8.5. Comparative education participation rates at ages 16 and 17, 1910 to 1971.

Notes: The observations are for different years across countries. It is also likely the definition of the year varies. The observations have averaged the participation rates of boys and girls.

Source: MacKinnon (1989a), Table 1, p. 63.

century may have had little impact on average productivity if, for example, the educational requirements of its economy had been lower than those of the United States. This lower educational requirement might have arisen because of differences in their economic structures and hence demand for skilled labor. Of possible relevance here is the higher proportion of the Australian workforce in farming and mining activities compared to manufacturing than in the United States. For if the productivity benefits to the average worker of a secondary education were at that time greater in industrial employment than in agriculture or mining, the lower high school attendance rate in Australia would have less economic significance than would be the case had the two countries possessed identical mixes of sectors and occupations. Of course there is the possibility of endogeneity: higher participation rates in high school in Australia earlier in the century may have raised the share of manufacturing at that time if a lack of suitably educated workers constituted a constraint on its expansion.

It may be that the apprenticeship system, absent from U.S. workplaces but prominent in Australia's, was at least a partial substitute for the skills that might otherwise have been acquired through an earlier expansion of high school attendance.[33] It is also important to remember that education is an activity not solely undertaken to enhance worker productivity, but in part for consumption and cultural reasons that will not make any contribution to national efficiency. Hence too much can be read into the dramatic secondary schooling lag in Australia. Indeed, analysis of the interstate variation in the rise in high school participation rates *within* the United States suggests that who led and who lagged the national average was not entirely driven by expected higher private or social returns, and that cultural and economic determinants were both significant.[34]

If there existed any foregone productivity gain due to the lag in increased schooling at the secondary level it is likely to have become more significant over time as an increasingly sophisticated economy required a higher proportion of university graduates among entrants to the labor force. In the United States an expansion of college and university systems occurred in the immediate postwar years, building on the foundation provided by the interwar expansion of high school graduation rates. In a modern advanced economy the links between graduate education, university-sponsored basic research, commercial R&D, and industrial and technological progress are well known. Partly because it had largely completed the expansion of its secondary schooling by 1940, the United States was uniquely positioned to pioneer and exploit these links to enhance its industrial and scientific ascendancy during World War II and after 1945.[35] But this ascendancy is attributed also to other factors, including the unequaled size of the American domestic market. Therefore, even had the expansion of Australian secondary education occurred in parallel with that in the United States, it does not follow that this alone would have narrowed the gap between the two countries in their levels of labor productivity or income.

Turning from general education to the adequacy of more industry-specific skills, we might observe that, at least in agriculture and mining, international competitiveness has been sustained up to the present. This does not rule out the possibility that even higher levels of productivity in these sectors might, at particular times in the past, have resulted from more or different investment in education and skill acquisition. But no serious and persistent failure can have occurred. This constitutes indirect evidence of institutional and policy responsiveness when there arose in these industries a demand for more or different skills. More direct evidence is available. We have noted (in chapter 5) that an expansion of agricultural education was one of the responses to the challenges confronting late-nineteenth-century Australian farmers, with the founding at

---

[33]MacKinnon (1989a) considers this possibility, together with a number of other differences between economic conditions in Australia and other advanced economies that might have mitigated any adverse productivity effects of the Australian lag in secondary education rates. See also MacKinnon (1989b).

[34]Goldin (1998).

[35]See Nelson and Wright (1992).

that time of agricultural high schools and colleges by the governments of the colonies. Similarly, schools of mining were established in the colonies most directly impacted by the discovery of gold and other minerals.

However, it has been suggested that Australia may have underinvested in one profession of importance not just to the mining sector but also to construction and manufacturing as well, namely engineering. In a study of the supply of engineering graduates since the nineteenth century, Michael Edelstein has compared the "intensity" of engineers in the population with other countries at various dates in an effort to assess the adequacy of the supply of this particular form of human capital. His estimate for 1920 is 47 engineers per 100,000 of the population for Australia, which compares with "intensity" rates of 128, 104, 96, and 59 for the United States, France, Germany, and Sweden respectively in 1914. Another comparison is reported for 1955, in which Australia was the lowest (apart from New Zealand) among developed countries with an engineer "intensity" of 163 compared to 203 for the United States, 213 for the United Kingdom, and 273 for Canada.[36] But these comparisons are fraught with similar problems to those noted with respect to differences across countries in schooling. In particular, the differences in the composition of industrial sectors and the mix of occupations could render such comparisons nugatory: industrialization in Australia occurred much later than in most of the comparator countries. This assumes, of course, that an expanded supply of engineers would not have led to earlier or greater industrial development.

Another dimension of this topic, already touched on, is that Australia imported human capital in the form of immigrants—beginning with that brought by the convicts. Hence the local education system was not the only source of supply. The larger the contribution of adult immigrants to the workforce, the greater the potential impact from this source. And if immigrants possessed higher (lower) skills than did the native born, immigration served to raise (decrease) the average skill level of workers. To a degree, immigration was a substitute for domestic investment in education and training. There is some evidence that in the latter part of the nineteenth century and early decades of the twentieth, immigrants were on average no more skilled than the resident population, whereas in the postwar period the average skill level of immigrants was higher than that of nonimmigrants.[37] In recent decades immigration policy has given preference through the "points system" to those applicants for immigrant visas who have more years of education, fluency in English, and skills relevant to whichever occupations are currently experiencing shortages in the domestic labor market. Under these conditions it is less clear what constitutes "underinvestment" in the domestic education and training systems.

---

[36] Edelstein (1988).

[37] Withers (1989), p. 66. The evidence for the earlier period is fragmentary, and based on British data on emigrants' occupations. Withers also points out that as immigrants in both periods have been younger than residents, their human capital levels may be understated

The Debate over Postwar Growth Performance

With the slowdown in growth and slower improvement in living standards in the 1970s and 1980s, a perception emerged that Australia's economic performance was also deteriorating relative to that in comparable countries. Although inflation and unemployment were the key indicators referred to in discussions of the deterioration of domestic macroeconomic performance after 1973, in the cross-country comparisons the principal measure of Australian performance was per capita income. And, focusing on this measure, it at first appeared that there had indeed been a relative deterioration in Australia's growth performance over the entire period since the Second World War. The Brookings Institution study of the Australian economy in 1984 noted that: "During the 1950s and 1960s Australians were reasonably satisfied with their economic growth. Only in recent years have many Australians become aware that other nations have passed them by."[38] It has been suggested that this increased awareness was the result of a prior focus by Australians on a wider definition of growth (what I called extensive growth) giving way in the 1960s and thereafter to an emphasis on per capita measures.[39] Also the historic consensus among Australians concerning the social goal of expanding the population, subject to at least the maintenance of real incomes or wages, was beginning to dissolve during these postwar decades. Perhaps there simply were changes in social values; and maybe the rising concerns in all rich countries about overpopulation of the planet, and preservation of the natural environment, played a role.

There were three ways in which this relative decline in growth performance was defined and illustrated. One was to compare the *growth rates* (of GDP per capita) of Australia and other OECD countries since the war. A second was to compare Australia's *ranking* compared to other countries in the *level* of GDP per capita, and observe changes in this ranking over time. The third was to compare the level of GDP per capita in Australia with that in a *benchmark* economy such as the United States, and observe how the *difference in levels* between the two—usually the Australian level expressed as a percentage of that of the benchmark—moved over time. The focus was primarily on the first two of these. And with both measures the comparative evidence appeared unflattering to Australia.

Rates of growth in average incomes (or per capita GDP) from the war through the 1970s were higher in most other OECD countries than they were in Australia. This was especially true of Japan, West Germany, and some other West European economies. Australia came near to having the lowest growth rates using this measure, along with Canada, New Zealand, and the United States. Perhaps the more frequently cited measure of the deterioration in economic

---

[38]Caves and Krause (1984), p. 2.
[39]Gruen (1986), p. 183.

performance was Australia's rank position in terms of per capita income. In an influential study published in 1986 and entitled "How Bad Is Australia's Economic Performance and Why?," Fred Gruen reported that whereas in 1950 Australia was fifth (behind the United States, Canada, New Zealand, and Luxembourg), by 1977 its rank had fallen to thirteenth among the then twenty-four OECD economies. Consistent with the "league table" approach, Gruen comments on this change in rank as if it is a race: "Over this period we have been passed by Sweden, Denmark, Iceland, Germany, France, the Netherlands, Belgium, Norway and Japan, whilst we in turn managed to pass New Zealand." And demonstrating further agility with metaphor, he refers to this outcome as "our slide down the income-per-head totem pole."[40]

However totemic had become this measure of Australian prosperity, the distorted representation it offered was, fortunately, soon revealed. Growth economists in the 1980s observed that among the OECD countries, those that had recorded the highest growth *rate* across the postwar era had been those with the lowest *level* of GDP per capita at the start of the period, Japan providing the clearest example. Conversely, the lowest growth rates of income after 1945 were recorded in the countries with the highest level of income at the end of the war—Australia, Canada, and the United States all in this category. This pattern was attributable in part to the extent to which an economy had been devastated by war, with the bounce-back or reconstruction effect especially noticeable in West Germany with its postwar *Wirtschaftswunder*. But economists detected something more at work in these comparative growth statistics. Unrelated to the reconstruction effects following the war was a source of growth that would become known as the "convergence" or "catch-up" phenomenon. This richer view of long-run growth would resolve the puzzles concerning differential postwar growth rates—and, much more significantly, remove the inference that Australia had seriously underperformed after 1945—thereby putting to an end the muddled debate about its causes.

The convergence hypothesis identifies as one source of economic growth the advantage to a country of being relatively backward. A poor and underdeveloped economy is able to see the blueprint for its future prosperity in the advanced economies. It can buy, imitate, or steal the technology, institutions, and policies that underpin their higher productivity levels. There may be a considerable amount of adaptation required in this transfer. But the keys to prosperity are, broadly speaking, known to the poor country. The rich economy, in contrast, is already at the frontier of technology, operating at or close to best-practice levels of productivity. Improvements are possible only by the expensive and usually slow process of undertaking research and innovation. For this economy there are fewer off-the-shelf options to copy from somewhere else: it faces little potential for catching up in this sense. Hence it is unsurprising that

---

[40] Ibid., pp. 181–82 and 180.

at least some low-income economies will exhibit faster rates of growth than the most advanced economies. It follows that it is inappropriate to judge the performance of rich countries by comparing their growth rates against those recorded by lower-income economies undergoing rapid convergence.

Economic historians have described this process for earlier periods. Most famously, the faster rates of industrial growth in Germany in the late nineteenth century and in Russia in the twentieth century, compared to that accompanying the industrialization of Britain that began in the late eighteenth century, were described by Alexander Gerschenkron as attributable to their "relative backwardness."[41] And trade economists have long stressed that one benefit of participation in the world economy is that it provides opportunities to transfer best-practice technology from the advanced to developing economies through the importation of capital equipment or by facilitating foreign direct investment. A convergence or catch-up component is now standard in growth theories. And in empirical studies of comparative development it is a widely observed regularity that one significant determinant of a country's growth rate over a specified period will be its initial level of income (or productivity) at the beginning of that period, where that level is measured *relative to* the level of income (or productivity) in the leading economy. The relationship is robustly inverse. That is, the further behind the leading economy you are, the faster will be your subsequent rate of growth. But the convergence phenomenon is not a universal or iron law of growth. Other things are critically important—otherwise all poor countries would have caught up to the first industrializers.

The clarification of the debate on Australia's alleged postwar underperformance was made by Steve Dowrick and Tom Nguyen using a convergence model. They concluded that:

> in view of the fact that Australia was one of the richest nations in the world after World War II, it is perhaps not surprising that its growth rate has been below the average rate for the OECD as a group. . . . Australia's post-war growth rates have been neither exceptionally high nor abnormally low. Instead, they have been approximately equal to, or marginally higher than, the rates predicted by the models. In other words, Australia's growth performance has been about as good as one would expect from an average OECD country, were it to be endowed with Australia's characteristics in several important respects.[42]

This assessment stands. The alleged underperformance, based on superficial comparisons of postwar growth rates, can be seen to result from the application (usually implicitly) of an inappropriate economic model.

---

[41]Gerschenkron (1962).
[42]Dowrick and Nguyen (1989), pp. 34–35.

The convergence perspective also changes the interpretation to be placed on the second criterion of economic performance mentioned earlier, namely, Australia's rank among countries in terms of its level of income. If there is a tendency for countries to converge on the level of income of the leading economy, there will be a bunching among the income levels of the converging economies. Hence it is entirely possible for a country that was initially relatively rich to retain an income or productivity level that is close to that of the reference leading economy, but slip in the crude rankings as others catch up and bunch closer to the leader. And this is what happened among OECD countries between 1945 and the 1970s. If we take the United States as the benchmark, Australia's income per capita relative to this leader was stable across the immediate postwar decades.[43] A number of others—including Japan—caught up and bunched around those (such as Canada and New Zealand) in the top group. This is why the focus on rankings as a measure of performance can be seriously misleading without looking more carefully at the data and being aware of the analytical framework through which the data are being interpreted. This, too, was made clear by Dowrick and Nguyen.

Rankings (or league tables or totem poles) carry little relevant information by themselves and, as the debate in the 1980s about Australia's postwar growth performance has clearly shown, too readily become weapons in the hands of incautious participants in policy debates and those who comment thereon. Nonetheless, comparative analysis of the Australian economy with other countries, appropriately selected in light of the question, is one of the most important vantage points from which its performance can be evaluated. The debate in the 1980s served to sharpen understanding among a wider segment of the community than just economists as to the pitfalls of comparative benchmarking of Australian economic prosperity.

At the end of the postwar boom, Australia enjoyed living standards much higher than ever before. And the prosperity was widely shared—income inequality declined (further) during this period. Relative to all other countries, Australia remained among the richest. Relative to the other rich settler economies, there was little movement in income *levels*. For example, GDP per capita compared to that of the United States was 77.5, 77.6, and 80.0 percent in 1950, 1960, and 1970, respectively. The level of GDP per capita in Australia was almost identical to that of Canada in both 1950 and 1970, but it rose in relation to that of New Zealand—from 87.7 to 107.5 percent between the same two dates.[44] There is nothing in this evidence to suggest any significant "failure" by Australia to share in the global era of postwar prosperity.

---

[43] This fairly constant gap between Australian and U.S. incomes has continued to the present. We will return to this comparative analysis in discussing more recent experience in the next chapter.

[44] Maddison (2010).

The long period of prosperity Australia experienced after the Second World War is, therefore, not a mystery. The international economy was flourishing and, like many other national economies that were highly integrated into the global trading system, it shared in the general postwar boom. This was reinforced through increased openness to inflows of both labor and capital. There were no major negative shocks during the period, to either the international or domestic economies. Domestic economic management was such as to do no serious harm, no small achievement in itself, though it is doubtful it can be accorded a major role in securing the prosperity Australians enjoyed. The brief positive shock resulting from the Korean War wool-price spike did not derail prosperity. And industrialization in Japan underpinned that country's growing importance to Australian trade and prosperity.

Deeper influences that may have been essential to the maintenance of prosperity were recognized only after the event—when changed circumstances brought them to the surface. These included the set of expectations held by households and firms in 1945 that may have been more favorable to saving, to wage restraint, and to tolerance of the stabilizing policies that raised unemployment and lowered incomes in the short run, than were the set of expectations held by the next generation. Also transitory was the productivity effect of the backlog of investment opportunities and new technologies whose diffusion had been stalled by years of depression and war. Furthermore, the international financial system, initially imparting stability to the global economy, came under increasing strain during the 1960s. Thus the favorable conjunction of factors underpinning the golden age in Australia as elsewhere came to an end. And in part this was endogenous—produced by the sustained period of prosperity itself. I will take up this theme in the next chapter.

CHAPTER 9

Shocks, Policy Shifts, and Another Long Boom

This time is different.[1]

FOR MUCH OF the 1970s and 1980s, it is likely most Australians felt they were living through years of diminished prosperity relative to the immediate past. And they would certainly have been aware of an increased volatility in economic conditions. For the growth rate of the overall economy slowed markedly after 1974; unemployment and inflation both rose sharply; and a series of economic shocks buffeted the country for the next decade or more, the two oil-price spikes of 1973 and 1979 being the most prominent. The ugly term "stagflation" was coined to describe an economy simultaneously experiencing higher inflation, higher unemployment, and lower growth rates of aggregate GDP. What constitutes "high" or "low" in this context may lack a precise definition. However the contrast with the boom decade of the 1960s was striking. The annual inflation rate as measured by consumer prices averaged 2.5 percent in the 1960s but 9.8 percent in the 1970s. The abrupt rise in average unemployment rates from below 2 percent in most years over the previous quarter century to consistently above 5 percent is clearly evident from figure 7.4. The average annual growth rate of *aggregate* GDP declined from 4.7 percent in the last fourteen years of the long boom (1961 to 1974) to 2.2 percent in the nine years immediately following (1975 to 1983).[2] The growth in the population, which had been running at historically high levels after the Second World War, also slowed in the 1970s. The result was that, considering the same subperiods, the average annual increase in per capita incomes fell by almost two-thirds: from 2.5 to 0.9 percent after 1974.

Before looking at the circumstances lying behind the slowdown in rates of improvement in living standards following the early 1970s, and consistent with my emphasis on longer-run trends, it is important to put this evidence in perspective. First, the focus on prosperity and various measures thereof implies that some of the macroeconomic indicators dominating contemporary assessments of the economy's performance across these decades may not always move in the same fashion as those of greatest interest here. For example, most

---

[1] Title of a recent book investigating historical booms and crashes: Rogoff and Reinhart (2009).
[2] Australian Bureau of Statistics, *National Accounts* (Cat. 5204.0), table 1.

economists, policy-makers, and media commentators focus on aggregate (real) GDP growth as the principal measure of how well the economy is perform- ing, thereby influencing, one suspects, feelings of well-being in the community. Where population growth is significantly determined by immigration—the hallmark of a settler economy—changes in rates of immigration have to be kept in mind before inferring trends in average incomes from what is occurring in the aggregate economy. Also, inflation may be a major concern of those re- sponsible for macroeconomic management, but, short of becoming severe and entrenched, it does not directly impinge on prosperity in the sense I am using the term. The picture of the most recent decades that emerges from putting per capita real GDP center stage is not the same as that conveyed by inspection of aggregate growth, inflation, and even unemployment trends in the Australian economy.

That these general observations are warranted with respect to the period covered in this chapter may be illustrated by the evidence summarized in figure 9.1, which shows the growth rate in (real) GDP per capita each year since 1951.[3] Averaging these annual growth rates across any subperiod requires care since the marked short-run fluctuations clearly evident in the underlying series can result in considerable sensitivity of any average to the choice of start and end years. One approach is to search for years in which the economy experiences compa- rable macroeconomic conditions—perhaps with respect to unemployment—or to define a subperiod with respect to the interval between two recessions. An- other, and that adopted in the first paragraph above, is to pick end years that most clearly make a particular point. In figure 9.1 the subperiods are the six (calendar) decades since 1951, and the resulting average annual rates for each decade are shown as horizontal lines. This provides a suitable backdrop to the discussion in this chapter of both recent trends in prosperity and particular events impacting them. To illustrate, any impression that the 1950s and 1960s can be treated as a single period of growth and prosperity is belied by the con- siderable difference in the average rate of improvement in incomes between the two. A second example is the clear impact of the global financial crisis of 2008 on the average rate of improvement in prosperity across the first decade of the twenty-first century. A third is that even during the long period of recession- free growth in the economy after 1991 the average increase in per capita GDP fell short of that recorded in the 1960s. But I am getting ahead, and need to pick up the story of the difficult economic conditions that arose in the early 1970s.

Although the "golden age" was over, there was no plunge into depression after 1974 like that following the earlier long boom before 1890, or that fol- lowing the much shorter period of prosperity in the 1920s. But there was a clear step down in rates of improvement in economic prosperity in the early

---

[3]The start year was chosen, since the official "historical" estimates of real GDP commence with the year ending 30 June 1950, hence the first annual change relates to the following (financial) year.

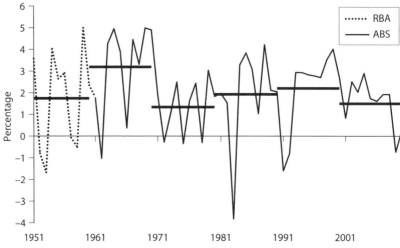

Figure 9.1. Annual growth rate of GDP per capita, 1951 to 2010.
Note: The average annual growth rate for each decade is shown as a horizontal line, where the decades are defined as running from 1951–1960, 1961–1970, etc.
Sources: 1951 to 1960: Reserve Bank of Australia, *Australian Economic Statistics 1949–50 to 1996–97*, Table 5.10; Australian Bureau of Statistics, *Australian Historical Population Statistics, 2008* (Cat. 3105.0.65.001). 1961 to 2010: ABS, *National Accounts* (Cat. 5204.0), Table 1.

1970s, and it was not until after the 1990–91 recession that there occurred a sustained return to both low inflation and lower unemployment in a period without major economic shocks.

WHY DID THE POSTWAR ECONOMIC BOOM END?

The postwar global boom ended in most other advanced economies at approximately the same time and with many of the symptoms and consequences as did the boom in Australia. Any explanation of the end of the postwar era of Australian prosperity therefore must encompass factors that were common to many economies and stress events in the international economic system imparting negative and coincident worldwide shocks. Some aspects of the Australian experience at this time did, however, reflect local conditions.

The deterioration in the world economy in the early 1970s was in part the result of forces having deep historical roots. One of these was the end of the growth spurt traceable to the reconstruction and bounce-back phases of those economies that were badly affected by the Second World War—especially in Western Europe and Japan. As noted previously this positive influence on growth may have lasted longer than many commentators have recognized.[4] Also contributing to the end of the global postwar boom were the institutional and even psychological influences mentioned earlier in our discussion of the reasons for the boom itself. In this perspective the war and the preceding depression created conditions in which the major interest groups of labor, business, and government implicitly or explicitly agreed on certain "rules of the game" regarding wage claims, profits, and the growth strategies of firms. The resulting social consensus supported noninflationary growth in the years immediately after 1945. Furthermore, this consensus persisted, and encouraged a virtuous economic circle in the 1950s and early 1960s in many countries. Perhaps the benefits of these arrangements were inherently transitory. After a generation or so their very success might well engender a quite different set of expectations. By the late 1960s the bulk of the workforce had known only prosperity and full employment. Workers might then have seen less justification for accepting pay restraint to ensure future employment than in the vastly different economic circumstances of the late 1940s and early 1950s. This postwar accommodation over factor shares and growth strategies therefore weakened. The rise in the inflation rate and the productivity slowdown in many countries in the late 1960s are seen as consistent with this interpretation—both of the boom and of its demise.[5]

A major contributing factor to the deterioration in the performance of the global economy in the early 1970s was that the international financial system came under increasing strain. By the 1960s it was clear that Japan and West Germany in particular had undervalued exchange rates relative to the U.S. dollar, evidence for this being the gradual deterioration in the American balance of payments and the persistence of current account surpluses by the other two. The asymmetric pressure to adjust arises because running current account surpluses is sustainable under a fixed exchange-rate regime, but running deficits is not. The changing competitive positions of these economies required cooperative changes in policies. But Japan and West Germany were reluctant to do this—their rapid postwar growth was in significant measure based on manufactured exports whose competitiveness abroad was enhanced by their undervalued currencies. (There is a parallel here with recent tensions between China and the United States over their bilateral exchange rate.) In addition, the fixed exchange-rate regime in place under the Bretton Woods arrangements came

---

[4]For a recent survey of the literature and contribution to the debate, see Vonyo (2008). Australian "reconstruction" was very modest compared to the situation in Japan and much of Western Europe; but there were still some bounce-back elements in its postwar experience as detailed in the previous chapter.

[5]Eichengreen (1994, 1996) develops this thesis in the context of the postwar experience of Western Europe. The prolonged effect of periods of economic hardship on expectations is explored by Giuliano and Spilimbergo (2009).

under increasing strain as the liberalization of international capital markets occurred in the 1960s. Any IMF-approved adjustment to a country's pegged exchange rate required evidence of a "fundamental," not just temporary, disequilibrium in a country's current account. But well before the IMF approval was granted, this same evidence would be available to speculators, giving them a one-way bet. Hence the system was increasingly prone to destabilizing flows of speculative capital.

Finally, among the major contributors to stresses in the international economy was the acceleration in world inflation in the late 1960s. The standard explanation begins with the policies pursued by the United States to finance the War in Vietnam and its "Great Society" program of expanded social welfare. The large expenditures incurred were not fully financed out of higher tax revenues, and this led to increased federal deficits. The resulting boost to aggregate demand pushed up prices, and this inflation was transmitted to the rest of the world, in part, through the higher prices of American exports. Then in 1971 the first serious cracks in the Bretton Woods system appeared. In August the United States withdrew the commitment to exchange U.S. dollars for gold at $35, a decision that would eventually lead to the abandonment of a regime of fixed exchange rates and the adoption of floating rates in most countries. This was followed in 1973 by the first oil-price shock, which, at the time, seemed the compelling explanation for the end of the postwar boom. The increase in oil prices was large, and it was readily understood how the higher price for this vital input spread cost increases through the economy—pervasively and rapidly—resulting in confidence-sapping economic dislocation (the relative price effect) as well as triggering a rise in the general price level. However, with the advantage of hindsight, it appears that deeper forces were already at work: a slowdown in productivity growth had begun in the late 1960s, and at the same time, inflation was accelerating.

Given this deteriorating global environment, it would have been remarkable if the Australian economy had continued to sustain its impressive achievements of the 1960s throughout the following decade. No advanced economy managed such a feat. This observation explains the attention I have assigned to these international forces and the timing of their impact. However two features of the domestic economy at this time operated to mute the negative influence of external events. First, as seen in the previous chapter, the mix of Australia's trading partners underwent a historic shift in the postwar decades, with a much reduced reliance on Britain and greater reliance on other markets, especially that of Japan (figure 8.4). In a process that has been sustained to the present, a diversification of Australian export markets was occurring toward the emerging economies of East Asia, which were recording growth rates above those of the mature industrial economies in Europe and North America. This diversification partially insulated Australia from what otherwise may have been a more dramatic slowdown in the 1970s.

Considered in isolation, the effect on domestic prosperity of the first oil-price shock was negative, with higher prices depressing real incomes. However, the indirect effects were partly beneficial, thus providing an offset. In some uses, natural gas and thermal coal are substitutes for oil, and since Australia had abundant supplies of both, and was export-competitive in these two products, the rise in the relative price of oil stimulated activity in the energy sector. Hence there are elements in the story about the end of the long boom that are specific to the domestic economy. In addition, as stressed previously in this book, the policy response to an external shock is domestically determined—however constrained the policy options may be. And to these I now return.

The Reemergence of a Booming Mining Sector

One critical determinant of economic conditions dating from the 1960s was the revival of activity in the Australian mining industry. As described in chapter 7, its contribution to the country's economic fortunes faded early in the twentieth century, and remained quite limited for several decades. Some major discoveries (especially of iron ore in the Pilbara region of Western Australia and bauxite on Cape York in far north Queensland), and the industrialization of natural-resource-poor Japan, resulted in the rapid expansion of mineral production and exports, to a degree reviving a nineteenth-century feature of growth in which minerals play a major role in underpinning the country's prosperity. This longer-run story will be taken up later in this chapter. Here our interest lies in the interaction between the spurt in mineral development in the 1960s and the deterioration in macroeconomic conditions in the 1970s.

Our discussion of the gold rushes in the middle of the nineteenth century in chapter 5 introduced the "booming sector" model as a framework for thinking about their economic impact. As noted there, this model was developed in the 1970s to account for the complex changes in a small, open economy experiencing a rapid expansion in activity in one key sector or industry.[6] In the case of the gold rush, the initial impetus was an increase in the known endowment of gold (a supply-side shock) rather than an increase in demand leading to a rise in its price (which at that time was fixed). In the minerals boom of the 1960s and beyond, the initial conditions differed in important respects relevant to its impact on the prosperity of Australians. In part, the boom was a lagged result of earlier discoveries. And in the case of energy-related resources such as natural gas and thermal coal, the sharp rise in world oil prices engineered by the OPEC producers' cartel in 1973 and again in 1979 was closer to a pure price-induced boom for the local energy-resources sector.

---

[6]Gregory (1976). This spawned a number of further Australian contributions. A survey of the wider literature at the time was offered by Corden (1984).

In the 1960s and 1970s, minerals production was highly capital intensive—requiring much more than a pan and shovel to enter the industry. So there was no rush phenomenon, no mass desertion of existing occupations, and no tidal wave of immigrants doubling the population within a decade, as had happened in the 1850s. Nonetheless the indirect and longer-term effects on the labor market were qualitatively similar. The high levels of profitability in mining resulted in wages in that industry becoming the pace-setters. The indirect demand for labor (infrastructure development, new towns to be constructed in remote mining locations, other inputs and supplies sourced from within Australia) ensured the spread to other sectors of higher wages and hence prices.

The booming sector model draws attention to the different effects likely to be observed in the nonbooming sectors of the economy. It predicts that export industries other than minerals, and industries whose products compete with imports in the domestic market, will both experience a *relative* contraction in activity. In contrast, the nontradeables sector will escape this adverse outcome.[7] In the circumstances facing Australia in the 1960s, this suggested that the mining boom would lead to a relative contraction in agriculture and manufacturing, but no necessary decline in the importance of the services sector. Another circumstance relevant to how the boom plays out is the exchange-rate regime in place. If the exchange rate is fixed, as it was in the 1960s, the boom in mining exports may lead to current account surpluses and the accumulation of foreign reserves, signaling that the currency may be undervalued, thus encouraging speculation of an imminent appreciation and inflow of capital. An upward adjustment of the domestic currency would, however, lower returns (in Australian dollars) to all exporters, but would improve the trading conditions facing import-competing firms. The distributional effects of a mining boom are complex even in theory.[8]

Perhaps the clearest implication of the models for Australia, and that popularly associated with the phrase "the Gregory effect," was the adverse impact of the mining boom on manufacturing. Manufacturers faced cost pressures emanating from the mining sector, and declining profitability because they were unable—because of import competition—to fully pass on these costs in higher

---

[7]The mechanism at work here is that the increased demand coming from the minerals sector will push up domestic costs—and not just wages. The trade-exposed parts of the economy have limited capacity to pass this on in higher prices, assuming that exporters are price takers in world markets, and that the (world) price of imports is unaffected by the mineral boom, both plausible assumptions in this case. The nontradeables sector (including many service industries) does not face import competition and hence is able to pass on the higher costs in higher prices without losing sales to imports.

[8]The analysis needs to take careful account of sequence. For example, currency speculators may predict a future mining boom soon after the discoveries are made but long before production or exporting begins. Also, there are general income effects of the boom that may reinforce or offset the sector-level relative price effects that have been described.

prices without losing market share. The relative size of manufacturing activity in the economy, whether measured by employment or output shares began to fall (figure 8.1). "Deindustrialization" was a term that acquired notoriety at the time; analytically it was a predictable corollary of the minerals boom. The revival in the importance of the minerals sector was forcing painful structural adjustments within the economy and society.

MACROECONOMIC MANAGEMENT IN THE 1970s

The mineral- and energy-resource discoveries represented major potential benefits to the community, but realizing this potential would require appropriate policy responses. The challenge, once again, was to escape any potential resource curse. Of interest here is whether the macropolicy decisions taken at the end of the 1960s and during the 1970s exacerbated rather than ameliorated the domestic impact of the deterioration under way in international economic conditions. Discussion of this issue in the 1970s occurred as part of a wider controversy surrounding the economic policies of the Whitlam government (1972–75). But there is agreement that at a critical time in the early 1970s, Australia persisted with an overvalued exchange rate after realigning it in 1971. This had the effect of reducing foreign demand for exports and switching domestic demand from goods produced locally to imported substitutes: "real exchange rate appreciation [1972 to 1974] was disastrous. Coming at a time when the rest of the world was about to move into a downturn induced by the first oil price shock, the policy quickly brought the long boom to an end."[9] There is general agreement, too, that real wage increases in the early 1970s were excessive, contributing to the rise in inflation as well as reducing the competitiveness of firms exposed to international competition. The government's policy was to use the federal public service as a pace-setter, starting with equal pay for women, which, however justified in principle, was unfortunately timed. The outcome was that the average weekly earnings of males rose in just one year (1975) by over 25 percent while those of women rose 31 percent. The deterioration in the labor market in the 1970s was in part due to inept policies.[10]

The subsequent commitment to give greatest priority to disinflationary policies, even at the expense of slower growth and higher unemployment, was a contentious one at the time, and it remains a matter of debate.[11] In this view (the so-called Treasury line), no return to golden-age-type performance of the

---

[9]Pagan (1987), p. 128.

[10]One recent Treasury assessment refers to a "legacy of inappropriately expansionary policies" from the 1970s: Gruen and Sayegh (2005). The earnings data relate to the year ending 31 December, and are from Vamplew (1987), Series LAB 153 and 154, p. 157.

[11]See Whitwell (1986), especially pp. 215–17.

economy would be possible without first securing a permanent lowering of inflationary expectations; and this would require some bitter monetary and/or fiscal medicine that, in the short run, would result in higher levels of unemployment and slower growth in living standards. The opponents of this policy approach (of "fighting inflation first") considered the short-run welfare costs in foregone output and employment too high. From hindsight, one alternative response can be seen in the institutional and political arrangements worked out under the Hawke government after 1983 known as the "Accord." Whereas the Whitlam administration pursued wage increases in the early 1970s despite their negative impact on employment and living standards, the Hawke administration devised institutional arrangements within which agreement was secured between business, labor unions, and the federal government on policies to curb wage demands and lower expectations regarding future price increases.[12]

An alternative perspective on macroeconomic performance in the 1970s and 1980s is provided by the experience in other countries. After all, stagflation appeared in all advanced economies at approximately the same time. What is striking, however, is that its defeat came at different times and by different means. And when viewed from a comparative perspective, the Australian record is not especially praiseworthy. At the time, there was a fascination with the incomes policies in such social democracies as Sweden and Austria. But given our focus here on longer-run growth and prosperity outcomes, comparison with the United States also seems warranted. Disinflation in the United States was achieved in the early 1980s by a severe monetary contraction. Engineered by the Federal Reserve chairman Paul Volcker, the American economy was pitched into a serious recession. The short-run social costs in terms of foregone output and increased unemployment were severe. The medium- and longer-run effect, however, was that expectations of persisting high inflation were ended. The 1980s in the United States are thus associated with better growth, inflation, and unemployment outcomes than attained by Australia.[13]

Differences in the two countries' institutional arrangements limit use of the United States as a benchmark for Australia in this instance. The Federal Reserve had much more policy independence than did the Reserve Bank at this time. The Reserve Bank could not have induced a recession in the early 1980s without government approval. Yet in the 1990s the need for a more independent central bank in Australia was accepted by both major political parties. And the low inflation of recent years has been attributed in part to the increased flex-

---

[12]The term "Accord" refers to the principles under which wages and related employment conditions were negotiated within Australia's centralized labor-market institutions from 1983 to the early 1990s. Thereafter a less regulated and decentralized system of wage bargaining and determination was introduced, as discussed below.

[13]Of course, other things complicate any glib comparisons of macroeconomic performance. In particular, under President Reagan there was considerable expansion of the federal debt as a result of a succession of budget deficits—a fiscal policy reversed in the 1990s under President Clinton.

ibility in monetary policy, especially the credibility of the low inflation target, made possible by this enhanced independence. Would Australia have seen an earlier return to a low inflation and higher growth environment had these institutional reforms been in place in the 1970s? The policy responses adopted—including the Accord—did not achieve immediate success. The return to sustained growth in a low-inflation environment, it has to be noted, followed a recession in 1990–91. The role of the Accord and associated policies in delivering Australia from the higher inflation and unemployment of the 1970s and 1980s is debated.[14] But in comparative perspective, it is evident that the policy options were constrained by institutional arrangements.

Behind the debates about macropolicy and performance of the economy during these years lies the role of economic theory. The Keynesian school of macroeconomics, which had been dominant since the war, faced a crisis with the emergence of stagflation in the 1970s, since orthodox or mainstream theory posited an inverse rather than a positive correlation between inflation and unemployment. Not only was there an empirical challenge to the theory, but also a challenge to its claims to policy relevance: these theoretical issues became more than matters of academic controversy. Some appreciation of this intellectual context is necessary before passing judgment on the conduct of macropolicy at this time, or assigning responsibility among governments for the deterioration in economic prosperity that occurred in the 1970s relative to the 1960s. We observed in chapter 7 in connection with the debates over the policy responses of government to the onset of the depression in the early 1930s that limitations in the economic theories prevailing at that time were exposed by an unexpected turn of economic events. While the slump persisted, the economic advisors struggled to agree on what policies to recommend. In light of this it has proved difficult to determine how much blame to assign to the political leaders of the day for not taking action that would have mitigated the collapse of economic activity during the depression. Similar considerations apply to any assessment of macropolicy in the stagflation of the 1970s.

ECONOMIC POLICY SHIFTS IN THE 1980s

The Australian economy in the 1980s recorded inflation and unemployment rates that were stubbornly high, and aggregate growth rates that were on average a little better than in the 1970s (3.5 percent per year compared to 3.0 percent) but highly variable. Indeed the decade was marked by a serious recession in 1982–83 and a severe stock-market downturn in 1987. Incomes rose a little more rapidly than in the 1970s at 1.9 percent per year compared to 1.3 percent, but there was no return to the prosperity associated with the 1960s

---

[14] For example, see Chapman (1990) and the comments thereon by Blandy (1990).

when the average increase had been 3.2 percent (figure 9.1).[15] The recession of 1982 probably reinforced the electorate's tolerance of more daring policy initiatives. The newly elected Hawke government (1983) thus embarked on a comprehensive program to improve prosperity, undertaking economic reforms of a range and significance eclipsing those in any decade since World War I. These reforms were designed to lift growth rates in the medium- to long run rather than produce an immediate and marked gain in living standards. Because this was, indeed, the outcome, an evaluation of their economic consequences is best deferred until the sources of the post-1990 boom are addressed. Here we briefly review the policy changes themselves before placing them in their historical context.

The principal policy shifts of relevance to long-run economic prosperity were intended either to increase economic efficiency by domestic market liberalization thus directly raising productivity, or to raise productivity indirectly by increasing the exposure of the domestic economy to international competitive forces. The first of these was loosely described at the time as "microeconomic reform." The second was summarized as the "opening" or "internationalizing" of the Australian economy. It was implied, and sometimes made explicit, that a failure to implement these policy changes would slow growth in incomes and lead Australia to a future wherein it would fall behind comparable countries in its level of economic prosperity. The federal treasurer in 1986 famously held out the prospect of "banana republic" status for the country should major changes in policy not be made. Reflecting the prevailing sense of pessimism, or the widespread impression that the economy was facing a critical decision about its future direction, a book written by two economic historians was published in 1984 with the ominous title *Australia and Argentina: On Parallel Paths*.[16]

The main policy shifts promoting greater integration of the domestic economy with the world economy included successive reductions in tariff protection to the manufacturing sector, the floating of the Australian dollar in 1983, and the easing of restrictions on the entry of foreign banks into the domestic retail banking sector. Principal elements in the microeconomic reform area included the "corporatization" or privatization of numerous public enterprises in utilities (telecommunications and postal services), banking, and the transport sector (the government-owned airlines). The major reforms continued in the years after 1990, with, most notably, the reform of the highly centralized labor market, the strengthening of the independence of the Reserve Bank, changes to the regulation of nonbank financial institutions, and the introduction of a goods and services tax to replace a plethora of indirect taxes.[17] But it is in the 1980s,

---

[15] Australian Bureau of Statistics, *National Accounts* (Cat. 5204.0), table 1. Decades are defined as 1961 to 1970, 1971 to 1980, and 1981 to 1990, respectively (years ending 30 June).

[16] Duncan and Fogarty (1984).

[17] Macfarlane (2006) offers an accessible and brisk overview of the evolution of policies and the reforms, albeit from the perspective of a central banker.

and especially with the Hawke government, that there occurred a sequence of major policy initiatives. From a historical perspective, how significant were these changes—and by what criteria is this significance to be determined?

At the time, there was debate as to whether there would be negative short-run effects of the liberalization of domestic markets and the associated structural shifts in the economy. For example, the relative decline in the manufacturing sector and increased dependence on imports following the reduction in protection for industry were seen by some as having contributed in the 1980s to recurring current account deficits and hence increases in the ratio of net overseas debt to GDP. The proponents of reform countered that these were temporary features of a transition to a more internationally competitive manufacturing sector, which would include export-oriented firms producing nontraditional products. And they felt the run-up in foreign debt would not carry the same risks as in the past because such risks would now be incurred primarily by the private rather than the government sector (known as the Pitchford thesis). Further, the newly adopted floating exchange-rate regime would prevent a return to the currency crises that had been a recurring feature of the country's history. The policy debates did not, in the main, run along party-political lines, as it was a left-of-center Labor government that initiated the burst of market liberalization, with the general support of its conservative political opponents. Rather, the criticism came from those who were not persuaded of either the necessity for or desirability of the adoption of more market-friendly policies on such a sweeping scale. Indeed, "economic rationalism" emerged as a pejorative label for the new policy direction.[18] Intellectual arguments for the policy reforms were advanced by several leading academic economists; while opposition predictably was voiced by interest groups—both employers and unions—representing those industries most dependent on protection, regulation, or public ownership. Less predictable from a political economy perspective was the remarkable role of the head of the government agency tasked with administering the tariff in the 1970s, G. A. Rattigan. Far from being "captured" by those benefiting from high protection, the Tariff Board under his direction became a major source of data and analysis documenting the level and incidence of the burden protection imposed on the wider community. Further, Rattigan became a prominent advocate of lower tariff levels, his work aptly described as an act of "bureaucratic heroism."[19]

On the so-called internationalization of the economy, it is important to recall the long-run trends. If measured by the trade to GDP ratio, a U-shaped pattern emerges, with the interwar period registering less openness than either the last

---

[18] The usage—or abusage—is revealing. One can compare the near contemporary use of "monetarism" in Thatcher's Britain and "Reaganomics" in the United States.

[19] This characterization is by Pincus (1995), p. 70. The Tariff Board subsequently acquired a much wider remit for its economic inquiries and analyses, evolving (after several changes of title) into the present-day Productivity Commission.

half of the nineteenth century or the final decades of the twentieth century (figure 5.2). A broadly similar story can be told if other measures of integration with the international economy are consulted. Immigration as a proportion of population increase, and the contribution of foreign savings to domestic investment, were both lower in the interwar decades than before or since. This suggests that what was under way in the decades after about 1960 was an outward *re*-orientation of the domestic economy—not something without precedent in the country's history. And the policy shifts in the direction of greater openness had begun prior to the 1980s: these included the treaty with Japan in 1957 and end of the ban on the export of certain minerals; the phasing out of the White Australia immigration policy (begun under the Gorton government, 1968–71); and the initial 25 percent tariff cut in 1973. Taken together, these nudged the economy in directions somewhat counter to those it had taken for much of the twentieth century. Thus the 1980s are best viewed as the period of most active and comprehensive policy change in this sense, but not of its origins.

Adopting a strictly national perspective could still lead one to the conclusion that in aggregate the 1980s policy reforms marked a historic shift in the strategy for sustaining growth and prosperity. Such an interpretation might, hypothetically, proceed as follows. For most of the nineteenth century the economy was outward-oriented and highly integrated into the international (mainly imperial) economy, and a development strategy was pursued in which its prosperity depended on the specialized production for export of a narrow range of natural-resource-intensive products. Following the crisis of the 1890s and federation, there was a shift in development strategy aimed at reducing the associated vulnerability to external shocks. Economic "security" was sought through a less narrowly based economic structure to be achieved by policies promoting import-substituting industrialization and the diversification of rural production. This second phase of the country's growth strategy runs from 1900 or 1914 to the 1960s or 1970s. It is marked by an inward orientation—the trade to GDP ratio declines—and the importance of the manufacturing sector grows from about 12 percent to a peak of about 28 percent of GDP. In parallel with this, the government sector accounts for a rising share of employment and final output, while private markets are subject to increasing degrees of regulation. Then, in the 1970s and 1980s, with a slower rate of improvement in living standards coinciding with higher unemployment and the decline in manufacturing, the social and political consensus underpinning the existing development strategy begins to fray—just as it had done seventy years earlier. A new strategy is sought to underpin a long-term revival of economic prosperity. Enter the third phase with its emphasis on raising productivity via increasing competitiveness in the economy through reverting to the outward orientation and less regulated policies of the first phase.

There are limitations to this simple view of growth strategies in Australian history as a three-act drama. It makes rough sense in relation to outward and inward orientation. In particular, it mirrors the three stages in globalization and is thus a reminder that what happened within Australia was in significant measure a response to what occurred elsewhere, and especially to the marked deterioration in the international economic environment that persisted from 1914 to 1945. But the three-phase perspective does not accord so well with the changing role of government in markets: the nature and extent of government's role in the economy had been constantly evolving since the foundation of the colony of New South Wales in 1788. Thus viewed, the policy shifts of the 1980s—and surrounding decades—represent a point of inflection in a longer historical trajectory rather than a major discontinuity.

There were other forces in play. After the Second World War the growth strategy options were again changing with the rise of Japanese (later East Asian) demand for Australia's widening array of natural resources. On the one hand, the economic costs of the inward-oriented policies of the preceding decades rose relative to a more outward-oriented alternative. This, I believe, is what fundamentally explains the gradual reorientation of the economy between the 1960s and 1990s. It was not due to a belated realization that a "wrong turn" in the development of the economy was taken earlier in the century. Indeed, the opposite case could be made. Given the less favorable international economic conditions Australia faced for much of the first half of the twentieth century, the pursuit of a policy of economic diversification emphasizing an expansion in manufacturing was a defensible choice. And there is, as yet, no clear evidence that living standards during that time were thereby significantly lowered relative to a counterfactual of, say, no protection for the manufacturing sector.[20]

On the other hand, the basic economic goals toward which the development strategy was directed, and which had not really varied since the early nineteenth century, underwent subtle change from about the 1960s. And this facilitated the policy shifts at the time. The goal of maximum population growth subject to real wage maintenance was, for the first time, called into question. Perhaps this was due to heightened concerns about world population pressures, and to rising awareness of the stresses placed on the natural environment by a growing population. Perhaps, too, the much more benign international political and military conditions following the Vietnam War played some role, as did the successful incorporation into Australian society of significant numbers of Asian immigrants. Thus it would be inaccurate to view the policies of the 1980s as simply a rejection of those adopted at the beginning of the century.[21]

---

[20]Recall the discussion in chapter 7 of the 1929 Brigden inquiry into the effects of the tariff, and subsequent assessments of the effects of interwar protection on the real wages or incomes of Australians.

[21]This seems to be the thesis of Kelly (1992), who describes as "the Australian settlement" the political consensus arrived at in the early twentieth century to pursue continued white immigration, guarantee high wages, and protect import-competing manufacturers.

REEVALUATIONS

The challenges to growth and prosperity that emerged at the end of the 1960s and in the 1970s resulted in especially vigorous policy advocacy by academic economists and by supporters of contending party political positions. To some extent, the winning side in the policy debates got to establish the dominant interpretation of the problem their preferred policies were designed to remedy. This in turn resulted in a degree of immunization against later reevaluation of those same problems, even if additional evidence or new theories emerged, or subsequent experience put a new perspective on events during the period. But this is common in historiography, and to be aware is to be forearmed. Two especially contentious policy areas illustrate this theme: the tariff, and the regulation of the labor market. We have previously discussed the history of these in relation to the period between federation and the Second World War; it is necessary to now consider the significance of the changes in these policies in the 1980s and 1990s.

Since the 1970s at least, the consensus view has been that by distorting prices and misallocating resources, the higher levels of postwar protection (tariff and nontariff) reduced productivity levels. The policy switch in 1973 ushered in a period of tariff reductions (figure 7.3). The improved macroeconomic performance of the economy since 1991 compared to that in the previous two decades has, in this view, been attributed in part to this policy shift. The different (and counterfactual) question posed here is whether higher growth rates in earlier decades of the twentieth century would have occurred had protection remained low at that time—say, no increases on that applying at federation. In the course of the policy debates in the 1970s and 1980s, it was sometimes implied that Australia had taken a welfare- and growth-reducing policy direction from the beginning of the century.[22] However, what is needed to support this assessment is an indication of the extent to which the *actual* policies adopted led to reduced growth, and whether that (putative) reduction varied over time—prior to 1914, during the 1920s, during the depression, and in the immediate aftermath of the Second World War. What evidence exists suggests that a more nuanced assessment of the impact of the tariff may be in order.

Recent cross-country historical analyses of tariffs and growth have raised the possibility that the robustly negative and significant relationship observed in studies of the final decades of the twentieth century may not be discernible in evidence for earlier periods.[23] These analyses, which often include Australia,

---

[22] For a discussion dating from this period, see Anderson and Garnaut (1987).

[23] This is a historical branch of a wider empirical debate about the relationship between openness and growth: key contributions include Frankel and Romer (1999) and Rodriguez and Rodrik (2001).

suggest that the inverse relationship is clearest only for the postwar decades (or even since about 1960); that there is no significant relationship during the turbulent interwar period; and that for the period prior to 1914 the relationship turns positive and significant.[24] One possible explanation is that the policies adopted by one's trading partners matter to the benefits obtained from decreased domestic protection—perhaps accounting for the inconclusive results for the interwar period. Another lies in closer analysis of the sectoral composition of pre-1914 trade, where the finding of a positive relationship between tariffs and growth may have been driven primarily by the evidence from commodity exporters (such as Australia). This suggests that period-specific factors were operating then but not after 1945 when manufactured products were more important in world trade.[25]

Was Australia an exception? There are few studies into this question, and the results to date are unclear.[26] Yet this line of historical inquiry is of considerable importance to how we assess the policy choices made. Also, we should note the conclusion in a recent study that the principal reason for relatively low volatility in the Australian economy despite repeated commodity terms-of-trade shocks since 1900 was the increase to about 1970 in the share of the manufacturing sector.[27] If lower volatility is favorable to long-run growth, this suggests another reason why protection for that sector may not always have been unambiguously growth-inhibiting. Finally, the role of the tariff in accounting for the increased share of manufacturing in output to 1939 may have been less than that of other sources, including changes in consumer demand patterns and technological change.[28] Insofar as the negative impact of the tariff on productivity and growth was thought to have arisen through an inefficient allocation of resources into the manufacturing sector, the importance of this transmission mechanism may have been overstated.[29]

Only an interim assessment of the implications of this recent work is possible. What is unaffected to date is the orthodox view that Australian growth would have been retarded by retention of the high tariffs and nontariff barriers in place during the postwar decades, and that the reduction in protection following the 1970s improved productivity and living standards. What is unclear is whether the counterfactual of significantly freer trade in either the interwar or

---

[24]See O'Rourke (2000), and Clemens and Williamson (2004).

[25]Lehmann and O'Rourke (2008).

[26]See the evaluations of Brigden's analysis by Siriwardana (1996) and Tyers and Coleman (2008).

[27]Bhattacharyya and Williamson (2009). A similar conclusion was earlier reported by Gillitzer and Kearns (2005).

[28]Merrett and Ville (2011).

[29]In a study of Canadian manufacturing productivity performance across the twentieth century, Keay (2000) has questioned the conventional view of a negative impact arising from that country's policies of tariff protection.

pre-1914 periods would have resulted in greater prosperity, and hence whether the increasingly protectionist policies pursued at those times were significantly growth-retarding or had relatively little impact on per capita incomes.

Similar importance attaches to the historical analysis of the effects of labor-market regulation on Australian growth. However, much less attention has been accorded the evidence about the impact of the choice of labor-market regime on growth in the long run than has been given its distributional consequences and especially the detailed history of its internal evolution. We have already noted the assessment that any economic impact of the postfederation changes to labor-market institutions was at best modest before the end of the First World War, but that changes made in the early 1920s most likely inhibited growth in that decade. Discussions of the impact of the labor market regime on the economy during the depression of the 1930s focus more on short-run distributional issues, including the unknown extent of informal noncompliance with legislated wages and conditions. With respect to the recent past, the debates are ongoing over the effects of the moves away from the centralized determination of wages and working conditions and toward the enterprise-based bargaining that occurred in the 1990s. More generally it seems unclear whether there exists any robust relationship between the labor-market regime and growth.[30] For assessments covering the longer sweep of Australian history, there appears to be some diffidence in claiming that a strong and empirically based relationship has been established between particular institutional arrangements in the labor market and productivity or growth performance.[31] Surprising, perhaps, but we lack empirical studies establishing the contribution of labor-market reforms to recent changes in productivity performance or growth relative to the contribution of other microeconomic reforms, computerization, globalization, and the resources boom.

To conclude this discussion of policy debates and reforms, it is worth reviewing the record of economic prosperity in the 1970s and 1980s. In the previous chapter I said that the assessment of the years between 1945 and 1973 as a "golden age" of economic prosperity was made at the time and has not required revision. In contrast, and given our focus on prosperity or living standards rather than macroeconomic conditions more broadly, there appears to be grounds for reassessing the interpretation by contemporaries of at least some aspects of the economy's performance during the period between 1973 and 1990. We have seen that this interpretation was almost uniformly negative, and

---

[30]For a survey stressing the "fragility" of the results in the cross-country studies, see Flanagan (1999)

[31]For example, see Hancock and Richardson (2004), especially pp. 185–86 and 194–97. Perhaps the task would be assisted by breaking it down into periods defined by regime changes more frequent than that implied by the conventional view of a single labor-market regime that persisted through all but the final decades of the twentieth century. Rosenbloom and Sundstrom (2009) illustrate the approach in their recent survey of U.S. experience.

based on the indisputable rise in inflation and unemployment, and the fall in growth rates—both aggregate and per capita. We have also suggested that this negative assessment resulted from an understandable adoption of a benchmark based on economic performance during the immediately preceding boom years, but an inappropriate (as described in the previous chapter) comparison with postwar growth rates elsewhere in the OECD.

So, just how bad was the record of prosperity in the period from 1973 to 1991? It is true that inflation in these years is without parallel in Australian history—at least since the gold rushes of the mid-nineteenth century and excluding the short spike that accompanied the Korean War wool boom. Of course its impact on real income or consumption is not observed in GDP-based time series because movements in the price level have already been taken into account. There may however be distributional consequences of a sustained period of abnormally high inflation. By contrast, the social impact of joblessness is immediate and potentially devastating for those affected. Although unemployment rates after 1973 were above the levels of the 1950s and 1960s, it must be remembered that the very low rates recorded in these two decades have never been regained (figure 7.4). By 1975 no one under the age of fifty would have experienced other than full employment throughout their adult lives. Hence it is no wonder that unemployment rates of 4 or 5 percent seemed so traumatic at the time, whereas such rates were the *best* obtained in the subsequent long boom, which began in 1991.

This disjunction between the picture painted by contemporary observers and the much less negative impression that emerges from an effort to put the period into a wider context, is evident in figure 9.1. For what it is worth, the very long-run growth rate of incomes for Australians since 1861 averages about 1.38 percent per year. As indicated earlier, the 1970s recorded a rate of 1.34 percent, and the 1980s 1.93 percent.[32] If this is our benchmark, even the 1970s turned in a near average performance. And recall that the average for the long boom prior to 1890 was also only 1.3 percent (table 2.1). The bottom line is that when the focus is on GDP per capita, the evidence suggests a rather different story than when the focus is on the performance of other macroeconomic indicators. Incomes across the 1970s were growing markedly more slowly only in comparison with the 1960s. This is consistent with the widespread impression at the time of diminished rates of improvement in living standards, and may also reflect disappointed expectations that the prosperity of the 1960s was not sustained. But surveying the entire era since the Second World War, and focusing on per capita GDP, it is the period just prior to 1973, not that immediately following, that looks unusual.

---

[32] These decade-long averages do not seem especially sensitive to the choice of end years: only for the shorter period 1975 to 1983, which includes three years of declines in incomes, does the average growth rate of GDP per capita fall below 1 per cent—to 0.9 percent.

Other changes were occurring during these decades that might qualify the use of GDP per capita as the primary indicator of living standards, though detailed analysis of these is beyond the scope of the present discussion. One is the evidence that the real earnings of average adult male wage earners stagnated across the two decades after 1975, while those workers earning the lowest wages experienced a decline. Only after the mid-1990s is there a sustained improvement in the level of real earnings of all male workers.[33] A second change is the increased participation of married females in the labor force. Two- (or multiple-) income households became more common. It is possible that this was, at least in part, a decision taken by the family or household unit in response to the slower growth in real wages. Of course any such endogenous response was occurring at the same time that social attitudes to the role of women in the workforce were shifting, and that women were closing the gap with men in respect to education and earnings. These complex shifts have implications also for the choice of an appropriate unit in the analysis of economic inequality. In figure 2.4 we reported the historical trends in the income shares of individuals; in recent years, complementary evidence relating to the distribution of income between households, following adjustment for their size and composition, would be appropriate in any more exhaustive inquiry into trends in postwar well-being.[34]

THE QUARRY ECONOMY: THE RETURN OF RESOURCES-BASED PROSPERITY

Following the recession of 1990–91, the Australian economy experienced another sustained period of growth and prosperity characterized by rising population and living standards, declining levels of unemployment and inflation, and only minor fluctuations in economic activity. Brief downturns occurred during the Asian economic crisis of 1997, the dot-com crash in 2001, and the global financial crisis beginning in 2008, but none resulted in a recession if this is defined as two successive quarters of negative change in aggregate GDP. In per capita terms, GDP rose in every year until 2009 when, despite there being no recession (aggregate GDP declined for just one quarter), annual growth in the economy was less than that in population, such that per capita GDP fell for the first time since 1991 (figure 9.1). At almost twenty years' duration at the time of writing, this period of sustained prosperity probably warrants the moniker of the "third golden age" in the country's economic history. It therefore invites comparison with the two long periods of prosperity that occurred prior

---

[33]Frijters and Gregory (2006) survey the evidence and canvas possible explanations.

[34]See, for example, Australian Bureau of Statistics: *Household Income and Income Distribution, Australia, 2007–08* (Catalogue 6523.0), August 2009.

to 1890 and between 1945 and 1973. Before embarking on such a comparative assessment, two features of the period require special attention because of their likely importance in accounting for the prosperity Australians enjoyed after 1990. One is the accelerated exploitation of a number of major natural resource deposits, some of which were only recently discovered. The second is the contribution of the economic reforms enacted after 1983 to subsequent improvements in productivity. As I have given prominence to both resource discoveries and major policy shifts in the analysis of what underpinned high per capita incomes in earlier periods, the explanation of the recent era of prosperity involves revisiting earlier themes.

The setting in which there occurred a return to resources-based prosperity was the continuing economic development of Asia. It was pointed out in the previous chapter that for the first time in Australia's history the postwar industrialization of Japan offered significant trade opportunities from within what might loosely be regarded as Australia's neighborhood. The industrialization of non-Japan Asia reinforced this highly beneficial development, spreading first to South Korea, Taiwan, Hong Kong, Singapore, and Malaysia, then to China during the 1980s. More recently India has increased its importance as a market for Australian merchandise exports—to rank fourth by 2009 behind Japan, China, and South Korea, and ahead of the United States. The United Kingdom ranked seventh, accounting for just 5 percent of merchandise exports—a far cry from its historic dominance of Australian trade. Taiwan, Singapore, and Thailand, together with New Zealand, round out the top ten export destinations. The key attribute of those Asian economies experiencing rapid growth was that their factor endowments were complementary to Australia's: as previously noted in relation to postwar Japan, most were labor abundant and resource poor such that, at this level of abstraction, they, too, looked much like Britain in the nineteenth century.

Turning from Asian demand to Australian supply, this period saw a dramatic expansion in the importance of minerals and energy production and exports, accompanying a diversification in their composition as described earlier. Of course this was possible only because of a succession of major resource discoveries that had occurred over several decades. One way to indicate the significance of these is to display Australia's estimated share of the world's known and "economic demonstrated reserves" of key minerals (figure 9.2). Australia has the largest such reserves of uranium, nickel, lead, zinc, and brown coal; the second largest of bauxite, copper, and silver; and the third or fourth largest of iron ore, industrial diamonds, and manganese ore.

An alternative measure of the expansion in the economic significance of the minerals sector is to observe the increasing contribution it makes to the country's exports. Changes in definitions inhibit the construction of a strictly consistent time series, but the trend is clear. In 1951 minerals and fuels represented just

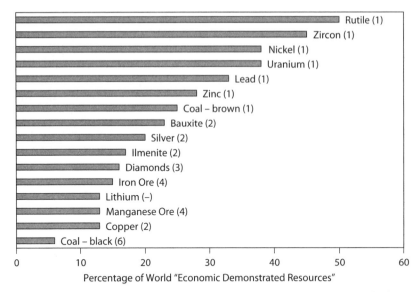

Figure 9.2. Australia's percentage of world "economic demonstrated resources" of major minerals, December 2008.

Note: Number in parenthesis is Australia's ranking in world holdings of "economic demonstrated resources."

Source: Australian Bureau of Statistics, *Year Book Australia, 2009–10* (Cat. 1301.0), Table 18.1.

over 1 percent of total exports. By 1974, with the first postwar mining boom well under way, this had increased to 18 percent, and by 1989 to 28 percent.[35] By 2009 mineral and fuels products accounted for 68 percent of the value of total *goods* exports. The leading items, in order of their importance, were iron ore and pellets, metallurgical (black) coal, refined gold, crude oil and related products, thermal (black) coal, copper, and liquefied natural gas. Considering the composition of *total* exports in the same year (that is, goods and services), minerals and fuels accounted for 55 percent, services for 19 percent, manufacturing for 11 percent, and rural products for a mere 10 percent.[36]

Manifestly, Australia had become increasingly dependent for its growth and prosperity on its nonrenewable resource base, a transition away from its historic export dependence on agriculture, rural land being a depletable but renewable resource. This justifies use of the shorthand description of Australia as a quarry economy. The increased importance of mining in the economy is not, however, reflected in a significantly enlarged share of the workforce being

---

[35] Pinkstone (1992), table 51, p.3 79, and table 59, p. 388.

[36] A further 5 percent comprised miscellaneous items. The source of these data is Australian Bureau of Statistics: *Australian Economic Indicators*, November 2010, tables 4 and 5.

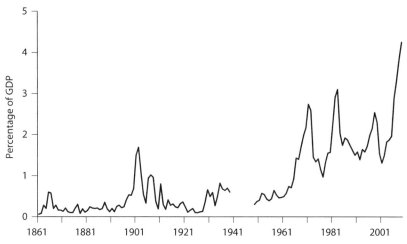

Figure 9.3. Mining investment as a percentage of GDP, 1861 to 2009.
Source: Battellino (2010), Graph 1.

directly employed in the sector: production techniques are way more capital intensive than the labor-intensive methods that were the hallmark of alluvial gold mining during the mid-nineteenth-century rushes (figure 5.1). This capital intensity of modern mining is dramatically illustrated by observing the rise in levels of investment in the sector. In figure 9.3 this is shown as a proportion not of total investment in the economy but of GDP. With capital the key input in the recent expansion of mining, this clearly traces the initial surge in the relative importance of the sector beginning in the late 1960s, with later surges around a rising trend culminating in a dramatic rise in the first decade of the twenty-first century.

One measure of the interaction between foreign demand for, and domestic supply of, the commodities that dominate Australia's exports is the price of those commodities. Just as at the time of the Korean War, there has been a marked rise in commodity prices, although in the recent episode the commodity price increase has been sustained over a longer period and despite very substantial increases in supply. A more informative indicator of the resultant boost to domestic prosperity is the terms of trade—the ratio of export prices to import prices. The striking increase of 77 percent in this index between 1999 and 2009 has been as dramatic as anything previously experienced (figure 8.3). And this improved "purchasing power" by Australians flows directly into some measures of living standards or economic prosperity. In figure 9.4, movements in the level of GDP per capita since 1960 are contrasted with those in real gross domestic income per capita, the latter incorporating the effect of changes in the terms of trade. Since there were neither major fluctuations nor marked secular trends in the terms of trade between 1960 and the 1990s, there is little difference

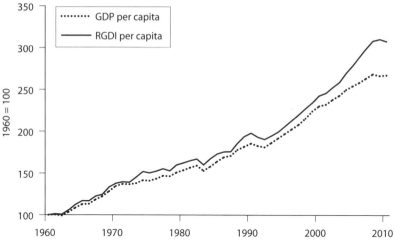

Figure 9.4. GDP per capita adjusted for the terms of trade, 1960 to 2010 (1960 = 100).
Notes: RGDI stands for Real Gross Domestic Income. Both GDP per capita and
RGDI per capita have been set equal to 100 at 1960.
Sources: Australian Bureau of Statistics, *National Accounts* (Cat. 5204.0), Table 1;
ABS, *Australian Historical Population Statistics, 2008* (Cat. 3105.0.65.001), Table 1.1.

between the series across these decades. The sharp upturn in the terms of trade
following the turn of the century results, however, in a clear divergence in these
two measures. The commodity price boom has added significantly to Australia's average incomes even though this is not fully reflected in the conventional
GDP measures.[37] To illustrate, in the eight years between 2002 and 2010, real
GDP per capita increased by 12 percent, while real gross domestic income per
capita increased by 22 percent.

The quarry-economy label conjures not only a reliance on nonrenewable
natural resources for growth and prosperity, but also the image of concentration on "raw" or unprocessed resource-based activity more widely in the
economy. And with some significant exceptions, this describes the situation
in Australia in recent decades. Put differently, for most resources, there is little
downstream processing or value-adding undertaken domestically. Most are
exported as commodities in a relatively untransformed state, hence the "commodity economy" label sometimes applied to Australia. To the historian, this
is reminiscent of the limited degree of processing that occurred with respect to
wool in the nineteenth century. It is true that some of the metal ores undergo
smelting and refining prior to export, as had occurred ever since the copper

---

[37]This arises since conversion to a "real" basis (specifically, deflating export receipts by an
export price index) is designed precisely to eliminate movements in prices.

boom in South Australia in the 1840s. Copper, bauxite/aluminum, lead, silver, zinc, and tin all fall into this category. And it is also true that the steel industry uses local iron ore and coking coal in the making of iron and steel products that in turn are used in the domestic production of such "elaborately transformed" manufactured products as motor vehicles, but the bulk of iron ore and coal production is exported.

In chapters 6 and 7 we highlighted the limited processing prior to export in earlier periods not just of wool but also of meat, fruit, and dairy products. And we there pondered why the linkages between the production of these rural commodities and their end use in domestic manufacturing were relatively weak, noting that the situation in Canada and especially in the United States appeared different. The terminology is a bit rough, but the possibility of a "staple trap" has been raised not just by Australian economic historians but also those looking at the experience of Argentina and New Zealand. We can revisit this perspective by questioning the limited onshore processing of Australia's mineral and energy industries in recent decades.

Most economists would not think this a useful question. The welfare and efficiency gains from trade necessarily involve specialization in domestic production and hence imply an increased dependence on imports. As a general proposition, this is unexceptionable. But the question needs sharpening. Either in theory or empirically, are the benefits of domestic production specialization through comparative advantage, relative to the risks, different for commodity exporters like Australia? If volatility in the terms of trade or in other trading conditions is greater for them than for exporters of manufactured goods or of services, or their domestic prosperity is more vulnerable to foreign trade barriers, does this shift the calculus regarding the net benefits from trade—and how significantly? There is also the possibility that specialization in natural-resource-intensive production, though justified by trade theory as income maximizing in the short run, offers less scope for future learning—a favorable externality—and therefore long-run productivity growth than does specialization in some other sector of the economy, but a sector that does not meet the comparative-advantage test in the short run.[38] This can be considered a refined version of the "staple trap" hypothesis. It is not clear that theory—trade or growth—can provide confident guidance to policy-makers on this vital question.[39]

The Canadian experience from the nineteenth century appears to suggest that its specialization in timber products and wheat resulted in a stronger stimulus to the development of domestic manufacturing than that observed in Australia, where there were weaker linkages running from wool and gold to

---

[38]The theoretical case is explored by Matsuyama (1992).

[39]See, for example, Hausmann, Hwang and Rodrik (2007).

manufacturing. As noted in chapter 7, the share of manufacturing in Canadian GDP was much higher much earlier than in Australia, though a thorough comparative analysis of the reasons remains to be undertaken.

The historical experience of the United States shows a different sequence, but one that throws light on Australia's circumstances. U.S. industrial development in the nineteenth century was heavily reliant on its abundant natural resources, and there is no suggestion that opportunities for the expansion of manufacturing based on adding value to domestically sourced raw materials were thereby foregone. Indeed, the location of much of this industry was determined by the proximity (around the Great Lakes, providing cheap water-based transportation) of major sources of coal and iron ore. So why did Australia not replicate this industrialization pattern in the latter half of the twentieth century? The size of the domestic market probably accounts for much of the difference. The U.S. domestic market was the largest in the world, and was well integrated following the construction of the railroad network. There were almost 100 million Americans by 1914. Scale economies in production and an efficient distribution network, spearheaded by the emerging institutional form of the corporation, could not be replicated in Australia. It should also be noted that there was tariff protection for U.S. manufacturing against import competition from Europe, though the effect of this on the growth of its infant industries remains a subject of debate.

To return to our central theme, getting a handle on the precise contribution of the expansion in the resources sector to the uninterrupted prosperity Australians have enjoyed since the early 1990s is not easy. Isolating the effects of activity in this disparate set of industries from all other contributing influences lies outside the scope of this discussion. But beyond the partial indicators already cited, there is an alternative perspective available, and one we have used in relation to earlier topics and periods. This is to imagine an Australia without minerals and energy, or at least those deposits discovered and developed in the last half century or so—what would the Australian economy today look like, and with what level of income for its (perhaps smaller) population?

If New Zealanders are asked why their standard of living has fallen behind that of Australians since the 1960s, the most likely response would include reference to the absence of major resource discoveries there. As we saw in chapter 2, per capita incomes in New Zealand were roughly comparable before 1960 to those enjoyed by Australians. The gap now may be more that 30 percent. From this simple correlation, can we treat the New Zealand experience as a natural experiment for an Australia without its post-1945 resources booms? This would be rash: too many other determinants of prosperity in the two countries are in play, one obvious example being the larger size of the Australian population (some five times that of New Zealand) and economy (now close to seven times New Zealand's). If scale economies matter to productivity and hence incomes, these would seem to work in Australia's favor, with or without mineral discoveries. Nonetheless, these size differences were also present during the period of parity in the incomes of the two countries prior to the minerals discoveries. Perhaps a better approach is to compare all the "regional" economies of Australasia. One such study compared the productivity levels in 2002 of the eight Australian states and territories with that of New Zealand, finding the latter's the lowest.[40] The explanation for New Zealand's poor showing did not lie in any significant differences in economic policies or in educational attainment. Rather it appears to have resided in geography (greater distance from other markets) and adverse patterns of labor utilization (participation rates and hours worked), and also the relative unimportance of mining in the New Zealand economy.

The importance of resources to Australian prosperity may also be observed in the variation in interstate prosperity. The nonrandom location of Australia's minerals and energy resources is reflected in the uneven spatial incidence of the direct economic effects of the mining boom. Recent resource developments are concentrated largely in Queensland, which accounts for much of the additional coal and bauxite production, and Western Australia, which is home to the iron-ore deposits of the Pilbara region and the natural gas fields of the North West Shelf. No surprise then that these two have recorded the fastest population growth. An analysis of the importance of the mining sector to variation in productivity performance at the state level found it to be marked, such that "[o]nce mining is removed, productivity growth rates across the states look very similar."[41] Thus the location of mineral and energy resources significantly determined the *regional* pattern of prosperity within the country, again illustrating the crucial role played by such endowments in the *national* economy.

THE CONTRIBUTION OF ECONOMIC REFORMS TO PRODUCTIVITY

For countries that are not resource rich the most important mechanism for increasing prosperity is raising productivity—the efficiency with which the existing stock of all productive resources is utilized. Even for the resource rich, this remains the best guarantee of sustained increases in living standards in the long run. Thus we explored (in chapters 5 and 6) the contribution of productivity to Australia's stellar performance in the late nineteenth century and its waning at the beginning of the twentieth, and speculated as to the most important sources of the levels of productivity recorded for that period. Here I resume consideration of the economy's productivity performance, complementing the emphasis just accorded the recent resources boom.

---

[40] Davis and Ewing (2005).

[41] Ibid., pp. 26–27.

Comprehensive and reliable estimates of Australia's productivity trends are not available until the 1960s. A crude measure of labor productivity can be obtained by dividing GDP by the number of workers, and this can be refined by adjusting employment for the average number of hours worked per year. Higher rates of productivity growth so defined are evident in the years to 1984 (reflecting in part that the rising levels of unemployment in those years disproportionately affected less productive workers) before a marked slowdown occurred for the remainder of the 1980s. During the 1990s there was an increase in the rate of improvement in this measure of productivity, consistent with the view that the economic reforms following 1983 had, with a lag, begun to yield the hoped-for results. However, since 1999 the pace of improvement has once again fallen back.[42] Of course, too much weight should not be put on any one indicator of efficiency. And further adjustments might be made to this particular measure of productivity, such as incorporating the average skill or educational levels in the workforce, which would identify the human capital contribution to output. But workers can also become more productive as a result of an increase in the amount of capital equipment they each have—increases in capital intensity. And this can occur on farms (e.g., agricultural mechanization) or in the service sector (e.g., computers) as well as in factories. To incorporate an allowance for capital deepening into an analysis of multifactor productivity (MFP), reliable capital stock estimates are needed, but these are not available historically for every sector in the economy.

The one attempt to measure economy-wide MFP in Australia prior to the 1960s indicated that this had been a relatively minor contributor to increased output between 1901 and 1979—some 34 percent.[43] That is, during this period as a whole two-thirds of the growth of Australia's economy arose from the accumulation of additional workers and capital rather than from efficiency improvements in their utilization. From the perspective of modern growth economics, this is surprising since technological change is believed to be the principal source of growth in advanced economies. However, taking a longer perspective, and considering especially Australia's status as a settler economy, the result may be less surprising. In the history of the United States, also a settler economy, and one for which better data on productivity are available from the nineteenth century, MFP made only a limited contribution to growth until the beginning of the twentieth century. Around that time the sources of growth shifted, and factor accumulation declined in importance relative to technological change broadly defined.[44]

---

[42] The average annual rates of change in GDP per hour worked are 2.5 percent from 1975 to 1984; 0.5 percent from 1984 to 1990; 2.3 percent from 1990 to 1999; and 1.3 percent from 1999 to 2009. The underlying data are reported in Australian Bureau of Statistics, *National Accounts* (Cat. 5204), table 1.

[43] Kaspura and Weldon (1980).

[44] Abramovitz and David (2000).

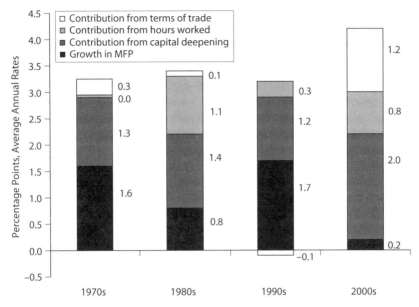

Figure 9.5. Estimated contributions to growth in real aggregate gross domestic income, 1970 to 2009.
Note: Gross domestic income is GDP adjusted for changes in the terms of trade.
Source: Productivity Commission, *Annual Report 2009–10* (October 2010), Appendix A, Figure A.1, p. 57.

It is not clear that Australia has yet made this same transition in the proximate sources of its growth, at least on a sustained basis. The greatly improved productivity data available from 1970 indicate that MFP has made a significant contribution to the growth of output in the economy only in the 1970s and 1990s but not in the 1980s or 2000s. This temporal pattern is consistent with the evidence cited earlier of GDP per hour worked. However, it is preferable to employ an output measure that allows us to observe also the impact of the recent improvement in Australia's terms of trade. Hence in figure 9.5, real aggregate gross domestic income is the basis on which the estimates of contributions to (or sources of) growth have been made. The first feature of interest is the favorable impact after 2000 of the sharp upturn in the prices of Australia's resource exports, as noted in figure 9.4, and of the relative importance of the contribution of this source of recent prosperity. This is a further window onto the impact of this latest natural-resource-based boom in the economy.

The second interesting feature, already noted in the data of GDP per hour worked, is that the rise in the contribution of multifactor productivity growth to increases in real aggregate gross domestic income in the 1990s was short-lived. In this area of economic statistics, it is especially important to be cautious about overinterpreting short-run movements: productivity measures are highly volatile, hence sensitive to the choice of end points for any analysis of trends. With this caveat, the decline in rates of improvement in MFP in the early 2000s appears not to be just some temporary blip but to mark the end of the favorable performance during the previous decade. This interpretation of trends is critical, as these data are central to the debate concerning the productivity impact of the economic reforms of the 1980s and 1990s, a debate to which we now turn.

It is one thing to note the positive correlation between economic reforms beginning in the 1980s and enhanced productivity performance in the 1990s. It is another to establish a clear causal relationship, or to assess the importance of the reforms relative to other factors contributing to the lift in productivity. What we would like to know is the path the economy would have taken, including its productivity performance, *in the absence of* the reforms dating from 1983. Then the payoff to the community in increased efficiency and living standards from the reforms would be evident. It may surprise those who lived through the period and witnessed the importance attached by governments of both persuasions to the implementation of these reforms, that a decade or more later we do not have such conclusive evidence, as the effects of the reforms were pervasive, often indirect, spread over many years, and confounded with other major influences also in play.

It may also be surprising that the recorded lift in productivity in the 1990s had seemingly run its course by the end of that decade. In the period since 1998, productivity growth has returned to around its historic (post-1965) rate. This suggests on a superficial reading that the efficiency dividend from the earlier reforms was short-lived in the sense of producing a one-off lift in the underlying *level* of efficiency but not a sustained increase in the *rate* of efficiency improvement. But care must be taken with the implicit counterfactual: in the absence of the reforms, Australian productivity performance since 1998 may have been even poorer, that is, below its historic average. All this explains the cautious assessments of the impact of the reforms on productivity even by those government agencies most closely associated with advocating the reform agenda—the Australian Treasury and the Productivity Commission.[45]

One way to get a little closer to the role of the reforms in accounting for the productivity improvement in the 1990s is to look at industry-level evidence. When seeking an explanation for the shifts in Australia's levels of income relative to those of the United States at the end of the nineteenth century, we noted (in chapter 6) that a disaggregation of the economy-wide estimates of growth and productivity can be especially revealing. With respect to the last few decades, it might have been anticipated that the sectors and industries showing the most improvement in efficiency would be those previously most protected

---

[45]Parham (2004), Dolman, Parham and Zheng (2007), and Australian Treasury (2009).

or regulated, and for whom the reforms were intended to result in a more bracing trading environment. In fact the industry-level evidence on productivity does not closely match such expectations. In particular there has been no significant improvement in productivity in the manufacturing sector.[46] Of course many industry-specific influences are at work: for example, drought will lower measured productivity in agriculture; and a mining investment boom will at least temporarily depress measured efficiency in the minerals sector.

A second approach to assessing the productivity trends is to look at experience elsewhere. Since the sweep of the reforms undertaken by Australia after 1983 were not matched anywhere else among the advanced economies apart from in New Zealand, some comparative analysis might provide leverage on their impact on productivity. There is evidence that a surge in productivity growth also occurred in Canada and the United States in the 1990s; and that in Canada, as in Australia, this was short-lived.[47] This raises the possibility of common factors at work, with candidates including globalization and the adoption of new information technology. However, some European countries did not experience comparable productivity gains in that decade. The most detailed comparative analysis for Australia has been with the United States. This choice was made for the same reason the United States was the selected comparator in chapters 5 and 6, namely, that it most closely approximates the productivity or technological "frontier." In the 1970s and 1980s Australia's *level* of productivity was a little over 80 percent that of the United States. Toward the end of the 1990s, this briefly rose to a peak of over 85 percent, following which it has fallen back almost to 80 percent.[48] Of course, this comparison reflects what is happening to productivity *growth* in both countries, and in particular a slowdown in Australia since 1998 not matched in the United States.

The "failure" of Australia to reach parity in productivity levels with the United States, especially in the 1990s following the extensive reforms designed to increase relative economic performance, may be read as evidence of the modest achievement of the reforms themselves, or as evidence supporting the need to undertake even more radical changes within the domestic economy. Perhaps it should be read as neither. Possibly there are other factors, beyond policy influence, constraining Australian firms and industries from achieving American levels of productivity. Some of these have been raised before in this book, including the small size of the national market together with its geographically fragmented nature, and the relatively isolated location of Australia from the world's major economies. I have previously noted the possible importance of these barriers to Australians achieving incomes per capita that were the equal of those in the United States. And in chapter 6 I argued that where

---

[46] Parham (2004), pp. 246, 248.

[47] Inklaar, Timmer, and van Ark (2007).

[48] Australian Treasury (2009), p. 54, and Young et al. (2008), p. 46.

that parity had been reached—and exceeded—unusual and transitory factors played a critical role.

There is evidence to support the view that in recent times Australia's productivity and hence incomes are indeed constrained by geographical factors. One is isolation from other major centers of economic activity. This location disadvantage is greater than for any other OECD economy—New Zealand having the advantage of being relatively closer to the much larger Australian economy.[49] Gravity models of trade indicate that this has a bearing on the openness of an economy as measured by the trade-to-GDP ratio. Australia scores relatively low among advanced economies in its openness, and it has been estimated that trade levels would rise by about 50 percent were Australia relocated off the coast of Europe to occupy the position of Britain.[50] However, another dimension of geography, the natural-resource endowment, works in Australia's favor. This resource abundance raised Australia's GDP per capita by almost 2 percent relative to the OECD average, a benefit comparable to that for Canada, and exceeded only in the case of Norway.[51]

It is not just through the effects of a less open *national* economy that the location disadvantage negatively impacts Australia's level of productivity. Analysis of *state*-level productivity across Australia and the United States indicates that proximity to other regions of economic activity has an independent effect on efficiency. Indeed, according to one study, some 45 percent of the gap between the Australian and U.S. average levels of productivity is attributable to this proximity effect.[52] Geography is not destiny, of course, as policies also matter. And there is still a sizable productivity gap to explain. Among other identified determinants of the variation in state-level productivity is human capital, with the Australian states (excepting the Australian Capital Territory) coming in close to the lowest in the proportion of college graduates in (measured) labor input across all states in the two countries.

It is possible that there will never be settled agreement among economists regarding the precise contribution of the reforms after 1983 to the productivity surge in the 1990s, or on the extent to which their longer-lasting impact was obscured by other factors, such as the rises in resource-related investment, output and exports in the following decade. Perhaps the last word on this discussion of the reforms and their effects on productivity can be left to two Treasury economists: "Australia's performance should continue to be considered in the context of a geographically remote economy with a unique history and set of natural resource endowments. By recognizing the role of these factors, the

---

[49] Wilkie and McDonald (2008).
[50] Battersby and Ewing (2005). See the related findings in Guttman and Richards (2006).
[51] Cited in Wilkie and McDonald (2008), p. 8.
[52] Battersby (2006).

successes and shortcomings of economic policy can be fairly identified and appropriately responded to."[53]

Before leaving this review of productivity trends, and recalling our discussion in chapter 2, it should not be overlooked that measured gains in efficiency do not always indicate that an increase in well-being has thereby resulted. Changes wrought by productivity-enhancing reforms, as with those resulting from globalization or computerization, may have also occasioned reduced leisure or resulted in other adjustments to the operation of an average Australian household that were not willingly embraced. Efficiency may have risen but "utility" fallen. For example, John Quiggin thinks increased work intensity and unrecorded increases in hours worked may have contributed significantly to the rise in productivity in the 1990s.[54] The lack of good evidence on trends in work intensity should not lead to the conclusion that it may safely be ignored: economists are prone to tailor their explanations to what is readily measurable, or to the availability of data.

If there has indeed been some increased work intensity resulting from the economic reforms following 1983, was this a new phenomenon for Australian workers, or did it represent a return to earlier conditions of employment? If the latter, then the immediate postwar era is cast as unusual in recording increases in both income and well-being more broadly defined. But this would, in turn, lead to the question not just of whether the "golden age" was sustainable, as canvased earlier, but whether any adverse effects of the policy changes of the 1980s and 1990s should be attributed, ultimately, to longer-run and deeper forces. Globalization generally, and Asian industrialization in particular, arguably imposed new constraints on the ability of many Australian households to simultaneously improve both material living standards and leisure time. The economic reforms were, in this view, society's collective decision to in part wind back some of the working conditions previously achieved in order to preserve as much material prosperity as possible in the new international economic environment that was less favorable to some workers.

Sustaining Prosperity through Boom and Bubble— A Historical Perspective

The period of growth and prosperity following 1991 had many features that would be familiar to a time traveler from the decades before 1890, or one from the years immediately following 1945. Most obviously, growth after 1991 seemed driven by the interaction of rising foreign demand for Australian natural

---

[53] Battersby and Ewing (2005), p. 18.
[54] Quiggin (2000).

resources and an expanding domestic resource base, with this occurring in an open and stable international economic environment. The commodity mix of exports was not wholly new, as wool, copper, and gold had been prominent before 1890, and wool, wheat, and meat/beef had been leading exports in the postwar era. But some would be unfamiliar to our time travelers, including diamonds, aluminum, natural gas, iron ore, coal, oil, and uranium. The Asian destinations of exports would also surprise a visitor from the late nineteenth century, when most trade was with the United Kingdom. But perhaps the most startling feature of the composition of exports to our time travelers would be the expansion of service exports. Inbound tourism, educational services (foreign fee-paying students), and a range of financial and related services contributed significantly to total current account receipts, whereas they were of minuscule importance until late in the twentieth century.

This "compare and contrast" exercise across the three booms could be extended. All three periods saw high levels of immigration and foreign investment and relative stability in domestic macroeconomic conditions, and all recorded low rates of both inflation and unemployment. It is possible that economic inequality may have increased in the pre-1890 period, though our evidence is fragmentary, while it declined in the post-1945 period, with inequality trends since 1990 again showing some increase. All three periods were free of serious political or social tension.

It was pointed out in chapter 5 that despite gold production declining only very gradually over the three decades following its peak in the 1850s, there was a transition in the sources of prosperity. Gold had kick-started that long boom, but the traditional resource-based industry, farming, had replaced it as the principal engine of growth within twenty years, such that together they underpinned the rapidly growing urban economy. Reflecting on this, it is natural to ask what may happen to the structure of the early twenty-first-century economy and to the levels of prosperity it has supported if the current boom conditions in the minerals and energy sector fade. We have seen that the tariff and labor-market policies introduced after the turn of the twentieth century were in part a response to the perceived vulnerabilities inherent in the resource-based economy of the nineteenth century. Diversification of the economic structure was at that time thought to reduce the risk of a repeat of such a major negative shock. In the modern "quarry economy," the minerals and energy industries offer limited direct opportunities for employment growth, recalling the concern a century ago with the future employment potential of the agricultural industries. Then it was manufacturing that was seen as the future provider of jobs for a growing population; now it is the service sector.

Other macroeconomic consequences of a sustained resources boom may also be viewed historically. Before 1890 prosperity was sustained not just by an expansion of the resource base in gold and copper discoveries and in the land devoted to farming, but by the inflow of large amounts of foreign capital that greatly assisted the expansion of urban-based economic activity. That is, a chronic deficit on current account underwrote both a larger population (in part through immigration) and high living standards. Foreign savings augmented domestic savings, permitting a higher level of domestic investment to be maintained without reducing consumption levels. Similarly, the recent boom has been accompanied by persisting deficits on current account, with foreign investment making a significant contribution to sustaining domestic growth and prosperity. The view that these deficits were a reflection of the investment stage of resources developments, and hence temporary, has been discredited as resource-driven growth has been sustained, and so have the deficits. Indeed, they have increased (as a percentage of GDP) from an average of 2.6 percent between 1960 and 1983 to 4.5 percent between 1984 and 2006.[55]

Despite obvious points of similarity with recent trends, there are important differences. We have noted (in chapter 6) that in the nineteenth century the exchange rate was fixed under the gold standard, leaving no scope for its adjustment in response to shocks. And the borrowers of foreign capital were primarily colonial governments. The exchange rate is now floating, allowing shocks to be absorbed partly by changes in relative prices rather than falls in domestic output and employment—as illustrated during the Asian crisis of 1997. But the floating exchange rate has brought other problems not so evident in the nineteenth century: short-term speculative capital flows such as the carry-trade phenomenon, and the sensitivity of the exchange rate to expected developments in the resources sector rather than to conditions in the remainder of the tradeables sector—which accounts for a far higher proportion of domestic employment.

A corollary of the boom has been a long run-up in foreign debt, as in the late nineteenth century and again in the 1920s. Net foreign debt grew from 32 percent of GDP in 1990 to 41 percent in 2000 and to 52 percent in 2010.[56] Of course, the foreign debt is now mainly private rather than government, though in a financial crisis, as recent events have highlighted, the distinction may matter less than had earlier been argued. Prior to the global financial crisis of 2008, the Pitchford thesis had become conventional wisdom with respect to the Australian current account deficit; though larger since the floating of the exchange rate than before, it therefore was regarded as at a sustainable level; and it was thought that the ensuing increase in the ratio of foreign debt to GDP would eventually stabilize.[57] Further, external negative shocks were viewed as less likely than in the past to inflict serious damage on the Australian economy.

---

[55] Belkar, Cockerell, and Kent (2007), p. 3.

[56] Australian Bureau of Statistics, *Balance of Payments and International Investment Position, Australia, June 2010* (Cat. 5302.0), table 52; and A.B.S., *National Accounts, 2009–10* (Cat. 5204.0), table 2.

[57] Belkar, Cockerell, and Kent (2007), and Edey and Gower (2000).

Among the reasons advanced for this break from historical patterns were not just the floating of the exchange rate but also the ability to borrow abroad in bonds denominated in Australian dollars, the greater flexibility in the domestic economy resulting from pervasive microeconomic reforms, hedging, robust financial market institutions, and a good track record of monetary and fiscal policy outcomes. In light of the recent global financial crisis, such optimism may have been premature.

If there is any "lesson" to be drawn from past balance of payments or debt crises it is that the next crisis may well arrive from an unexpected quarter and/ or in unfamiliar guise. So it was in 2008. Australian banks had borrowed in international capital markets in order to lend for house mortgages in Australia. As was the case during the residential construction boom up to 1890, these investments were not into directly productive assets, nor did they contribute directly to net export earnings and hence foreign debt servicing. The rise in the ratio of house prices to household incomes raised concerns about a possible speculative component. The federal government intervention with bank guarantees in late 2008 brought this Faustian bargain into the open.[58] And there are further echoes of the housing boom prior to 1890. Both periods saw rapid population growth underpinned by high levels of immigration, the consequent diversion of investment activity into capital widening rather than capital deepening, a concentration of population growth in the large cities, and a financial and banking sector operating in a less regulated environment than, say, that during the decades immediately after the Second World War. Unfortunately, economic theory offers little guidance as to whether a run-up in the prices of a particular asset class constitutes a speculative bubble, assigning the determination of this to hindsight!

The attention of our time travelers would also be drawn to some sectoral aspects of the economic landscape. Since manufacturing now accounts for less than half its previous share of employment, and the employment shares of the rural and mining sectors remain small, the productivity of firms and industries in the service sector increasingly determine productivity in the economy as a whole. Should there be another period of depressed demand for Australian commodities, there is no reason to anticipate a revival of manufacturing based on value-adding or downstream processing of mineral and energy products. Illustrating the point, the domestic motor-vehicle industry seems unable to achieve international competitiveness, as it continues to receive subsidies even as tariff protection has been reduced. High wage costs and an unfavorable exchange rate, both resulting in part from the resources boom, are part of the story. Within the service sector, tourism, education, and finance have developed sizable export markets, diversifying the composition of exports in new directions. However, the potential for further growth in these is unclear. The

---

[58]The recent increase is not in public debt: see Di Marco, Pirie and Au-Yeung (2009).

export of higher education services is ultimately quality determined, and the recent expansion in foreign student numbers may have already compromised the standards of domestic suppliers. The scope for Australia to host a major financial center in the western Pacific seems limited for reasons of location, and may fade further with the continued growth and increased sophistication of economies more centrally located in the region. Tourism, the largest of the export service industries, may have greater growth potential over the long run, but is characterized by generally modest skill levels and limited scope for productivity enhancement.

Finally, our time travelers would note a major shift in community values with respect to economic growth. Beginning in the 1960s or 1970s, the priority historically accorded to extensive growth as a paramount national goal was questioned. One symptom of this shift was the debate about environmental quality, including a muddled conflation of growth in the size of the economy with environmental degradation. A second was a questioning of the link between measured increases in incomes and improvements in some wider concept of welfare or well-being. Yet another symptom was the reduction in the importance given the goal of very rapid population expansion, reflected in part in the decline in the birth rate following the postwar baby boom. However, in the first decade of the twenty-first century, financial incentives to raise the fertility rate have been introduced, inspired in part by concerns about the rising burden of publicly provided welfare on future generations of taxpayers as the population ages. At the same time, there has been a rise in the level of immigration since the mid-1990s, in this case spurred in part by perceived shortages of particular skills among native-born entrants to the labor market that can be more quickly and cheaply filled from abroad than by increasing domestic supply. It remains to be seen whether any of this constitutes a permanent rather than a transitory reversion to historical priorities.

CHAPTER 10

The Shifting Bases of Prosperity

The fox knows many things, but the hedgehog knows one big thing.
   —Archilochus[1]

There are such things as historical and theoretical temperaments. That is to say, there are types of mind that take delight in all the colors of historical processes and of individual cultural patterns. There are other types that prefer a neat theorem to everything else. We have use for both. But they are not made to appreciate each other.
   —Schumpeter[2]

WHEN EMBARKING ON THIS JOURNEY tracing Australia's economic prosperity, we looked (in figure 2.1) at the level of its per capita GDP since the early nineteenth century relative to that of the United States and the other settler economies—Argentina, Canada, and New Zealand—and also that of the United Kingdom. And in chapter 2 we examined alternative measures of living standards or economic well-being such as the human development index (HDI) to assess the extent to which per capita GDP might serve as a reliable proxy measure for these. In chapter 6 we speculated on the reasons for Australia briefly leading the world in incomes during the late nineteenth century, and why it subsequently fell behind. And in chapter 9, using productivity data, we assessed Australia's performance relative to the United States. Perhaps it is appropriate, therefore, that I bookend this topic by noting the most recent comparative evidence on Australia's standing, both with respect to GDP and the HDI. Figure 10.1 shows, for 2010, the International Monetary Fund's estimates of GDP per capita, purchasing-power parity adjusted, and the United Nations Development Program's estimates of the HDI. Australia ranks second behind Norway out of the 169 countries included in the HDI rankings. New Zealand ranks third, the United States fourth, Canada eighth, the United Kingdom twenty-sixth, and Argentina forty-sixth. In the GDP per capita rankings Australia comes in tenth—though this is behind some city-states or microstates: Qatar, Luxembourg, Singapore, Brunei, and Hong Kong. Taking these out of the comparison

---

[1]Greek poet of the seventh century BC, quoted in Berlin (1967), p. 1
[2]Schumpeter (1954), p. 815

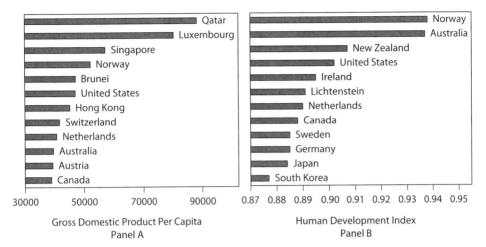

Figure 10.1. Comparative GDP per capita and comparative HDI rankings, 2010.
Notes: Top 12 and top 10 countries shown (in Panels A and B respectively). GDP per capita in current international dollars.
Sources: Panel A: Comparative GDP Per Capita, 2010. International Monetary Fund, *World Economic Outlook Database—October 2010.* Panel B: Comparative HDI Rankings, 2010. United Nations Development Programme, *Human Development Reports,* Human Development Index (HDI)—2010 Rankings.

again leaves Norway in the top spot followed by the United States, Switzerland, the Netherlands, and then Australia. Canada ranks just two behind Australia, the United Kingdom twenty-first, New Zealand thirty-third, and Argentina fifty-second.[3]

• • •

It would be tidy to conclude this story of the historical sources of Australia's economic prosperity with the assertion that a single dominant influence tells us most of what we need to know. Prosperity was primarily due to luck rather than human effort or wise decisions. It was primarily the result of the extensive natural resource endowment relative to the small population. It was primarily a tale of overcoming an initial handicap of distance. Or it was primarily the consequence of an inheritance of institutions and culture from Britain rather than another European colonial power such as Portugal, the Netherlands, or France. But we have seen that monocausal explanations of something as complex as

---

[3]As discussed in chapter 8, crude country rankings can be misleading because of close bunching between them. With respect to the HDI, Australia is only 0.1 percent below Norway, and just 3.9 percent above the United States; in terms of GDP per capita, it is 25 percent below Norway, and 16 percent below the United States.

Australia's sustained prosperity fail to survive close inspection. Thus to be persuasive the story has balanced the understandable desire for parsimony against the messy complexity of the historical record. Of course, this is precisely the challenge faced by economists in their "elusive quest" to unravel the "mystery" of economic growth more generally.[4]

Rather than adopting any single or dominant theme around which to center the narrative, my reading of the evidence has emphasized two features. First, explaining long-run growth in Australia requires that attention be paid to the *interaction* between the potential contributing sources suggested either by growth theory or in the writings of historians. This represents an advance over a laundry list of ostensibly independent influences. It also complements the approach of those writers who elevate a single theme to special status—such as luck, distance, investment, risk, imperialism, or the market.[5] I have argued that any persuasive interpretation of the Australian story must assign prominence to the interactions between, say, resource abundance and institutional quality, or between international economic conditions and the policy responses to them. As noted in chapter 2, such an approach also reflects current trends in growth economics, illustrated by the recent debate over the relationship between institutions and geography in cross-country growth regressions. Both theory and empirical research now also distinguish another dimension to such interactions between the many determinants of growth. Some influences on, or sources of, growth have a direct or proximate impact on a country's level of prosperity; with others the impact is indirect or deeper, but nonetheless essential. For example, attention was given to constitutional and political developments in the early colonial period in chapters 4 and 5 because of their importance in accounting for the efficient operation of the markets for labor and land at that time.

Second, I have stressed, throughout, the *shifting* bases of prosperity. Some of this has been obvious, such as the rise and fall of the importance of particular commodities within total exports. Also obvious have been the occasions on which domestic prosperity was impacted, favorably or unfavorably, by shifts in the international economic environment. Favorable examples stretch from the rising demand for fine wools in the London market in the early nineteenth century to the growth in demand for energy by the industrializing countries of Asia in the early twenty-first century. Some of the shifts are less dramatic, such as those arising from secular swings in the terms of trade, from the gradually increasing levels of human capital required in the labor force, from the realignment of key economic policies, or from the evolution of institutional arrangements.

---

[4] The reference is to the titles of two recent books on growth by Easterly (2002) and Helpman (2004) cited in chapter 2.

[5] I am thinking here of, respectively, Horne (1964), Blainey (2001 [1966]), Butlin (1964), White (1992), Fitzpatrick (1971 [1939]) and (1969 [1941]), and Shann (1948 [1930]).

For such reasons, the story offered here has been told chronologically, where the loosely defined periods reflected a set of determinants of growth and prosperity whose relative importance differed to some degree from those prevailing in previous and subsequent periods. We have seen that the international economic conditions facing Australia varied dramatically over time. Natural-resource discoveries and their exploitation figure prominently in many periods after 1820, though fade for much of the interwar era. Institutional change is especially important in the early and mid-nineteenth century, and again around the time of federation. Geography may have mattered both negatively, during periods in which distance from markets restricted the range of potential exports to nonperishable products with unusually high value-to-weight ratios, and positively, when Asian industrialization, together with the invention of bulk-carrier shipping, stimulated the production for export of a new range of commodities.

The initial sources of prosperity among non-indigenous Australians included the sizable subsidies from British taxpayers, and the "efficiency" of the convict economy. In the first few decades of European settlement, the high masculinity and low dependency ratios in the population led to an unusually high workforce participation rate. Even had the labor force been less productive per worker than, say, their British counterparts, income per capita would still have been high. In this sense, the convict basis for the labor force was well suited to the needs of the pioneer community. Then, by the 1820s, the development of the wool export trade provided an additional source of prosperity. Economic fortunes were now heavily dependent on conditions in the international economy—or more accurately the British economy. The production technology adopted in the pastoral industry ensured that wages would be high in this land-abundant but labor- and capital-scarce economy. Prosperity was thus sustained even as the British subsidies were gradually phased out, and as the labor market evolved from coercive to free. Indeed, it was the high wages and related economic opportunities that attracted increasing numbers of free settlers. Australia had successfully made the transition from an inherently temporary basis for its prosperity to one that was to be more durable. All this occurred within the institutional and political context of colonial status, and in a society drawn (not quite randomly) from British society. For, as we saw, the intersection with Aboriginal society and its economy was limited: the high-wage settler economy was built from scratch.

Many of the key elements in later phases of Australian growth are thus present almost from the outset. These include the unusually favorable demographic and workforce participation characteristics; the exploitation of a comparative advantage in the export of products intensive in the abundant natural resource; an institutional framework that did not impede the emergence and flourishing of risk-taking and profit-seeking enterprise—and that was capable of peaceful adaptation when it threatened to choke off prosperity; and a cultural context, or set of social norms, necessary to the maintenance of good governance. It is the interrelatedness of these elements that was crucial. For instance, consider a no-convict initial settlement comprising families, with its higher dependency and lower workforce participation rates. The early experience of some seventeenth-century settlements in the British North American colonies indicates the time possibly required to achieve even modest levels of prosperity.

As preceding chapters have outlined, sustaining and augmenting the initially high level of prosperity has not easily or always been achieved, and has faced repeated obstacles. International economic conditions deteriorated in the early 1840s, sometimes called Australia's first depression, but the wool industry and colonial economy recovered later in the decade. Negative external economic shocks were to recur in the 1890s, 1930s, and 1970s, but there was no general economic breakdown. Political institutions and social cohesion were tested but did not collapse, and living standards were eventually restored and improved upon. The two world wars similarly constituted major shocks to the economy—the first overwhelmingly negative, the second more mixed in its economic impact. There have also been developments potentially favorable to prosperity but which, if mismanaged, could have led to a reduction in living standards. The discovery of good grazing land in the 1820s, and gold in the 1850s, seemed an unalloyed boon to contemporaries. But a natural-resource boom can also lead to economic stagnation, distributional conflict, and even social breakdown. Australia has experienced only minor or transitory symptoms of this disease. I have detailed the near miss with respect to the squatter era before the granting of responsible government; the wide distribution of access to the alluvial gold "lottery"; and the partial redistribution of agricultural land to selectors from the 1860s. And the resource rents from the successive mineral booms since the 1960s have been spread among the entire community by means of messy redistributive systems of taxation and expenditure within the federal political system.

A related observation is that, as a small open economy, Australia has generally been successful in capturing the opportunities arising from favorable conditions in the international economy. The one exception occurred in the late 1890s and early 1900s. As we have seen, the combination of deep financial readjustment following the crisis of the early 1890s in the household, banking and government sectors, and a severe drought, overwhelmed the positive effects of rural diversification and rising world commodity prices. The high levels of international lending and migration at this time flowed to the other settler economies.

Geography has also played a role in this story. One aspect has been made famous by Blainey's description of distance as resulting in a "tyranny" that "shaped" Australian history. Yet what is remarkable about the years down to the Second World War is how Australia's trade, investment, and migration links were closest with a country as far away as it was possible to be. With respect to distances within Australia, what also seems remarkable is that so small a population, scattered around an area the size of the continental United States, maintained income levels at or close to American levels. So why was distance not a tyrant—at least in its economic effects? As noted previously, one reason is that Australia was able to specialize in export products that overcame high transport costs. The list runs from wool and gold initially, to wheat, frozen meat, dairy products from the late nineteenth century, and a wide portfolio of minerals and energy products in the last half century together with tourism and educational services most recently. Laying out this list indicates the second reason. Technological change in intercontinental transport lowered its cost. The innovations of most importance to Australian prosperity were the replacement of sailing with steamships; the invention of bulk carriers making possible the shipment of low-value and bulky mineral and energy products; and the decline in the cost of long-distance air travel following the arrival of jet aircraft.

Another dimension of geography that has been a major challenge to sustaining prosperity arises from Australia's physical attributes. Poor-quality soils, low rainfall, and highly variable climatic conditions characterize much of the continent. Yet, from the first squatters' attempts to graze the natural grasslands of New South Wales, learning, adaptation, and innovation have been the drivers of changes in rural production methods and products that have kept Australian farmers world competitive with relatively low levels of subsidy and protection. These physical attributes have meant, however, that dreams of Australia becoming a second United States, possessing a large and fertile inland drained by navigable river systems, soon faded. But these attributes impacted the limits of extensive growth, and limited the total population: they did not seriously threaten the maintenance of a high-wage economy, albeit of a smaller size.

The absence of navigable inland waterways—even the Murray-Darling river system was unreliable for year-round shipping—and infrequency of natural harbors have contributed to a pattern of concentrated urban development in a few widely separated locations around the coast. With the exception of Queensland, the colonial-era railway networks reinforced this pattern. Yet the nature of early rural and mineral production did not require that there be cities nearby. On the one hand, the significant distances between the major cities may have reduced potential scale economies in some branches of manufacturing and the service sector compared to a counterfactual in which the relatively small domestic economy and its population were contained within a much reduced area—say that of Victoria. On the other hand, this potential disadvantage was more likely to have applied in the later twentieth century than in the nineteenth. And by then the size of at least two of the urban economies, those based around Sydney and Melbourne, offered offsetting advantages in agglomeration economies.

Of course, inappropriate policies and institutions can prevent the achievement of sustained prosperity even if other conditions are highly favorable to growth. And there have been occasions on which the direction of policy or institutional changes threatened to retard the improvement of Australian living standards. I have noted examples from the ending of convict transportation and the restrictions placed on squatters' property rights in the early nineteenth century to the so-called microeconomic reforms in the last two decades of the twentieth century. Other examples continue to attract the attention of scholars. One is the extent to which the depression of the 1890s was caused or exacerbated by a lack of appropriate regulatory constraints on markets, and by policies of rural and urban expansion based on unsustainable levels of foreign borrowing. A second is whether labor market institutions and policies inhibited productivity growth by limiting the best allocation of labor—particularly in the 1920s and again in the 1970s. A further example is the putative negative impact of protection for the manufacturing sector, especially in the decades following the Second World War. But these remain academic debates precisely because policy shifts and institutional reforms were made and long-run stagnation or sustained decline avoided. This contrasts with the historical record of Argentina.

The willingness to adopt new institutional arrangements and adapt existing ones in order to sustain or restore prosperity has been a recurring theme in this story. I have also speculated at several points as to what accounts for this tendency, and why the results were generally growth promoting. With respect to the period leading up to responsible government, I have emphasized the influence of British attitudes and policies toward the colonies. These in turn were shaped by the loss of the American colonies and, more immediately, by political instability in Upper and Lower Canada. Timing is important also in accounting for the domestic pressures for changes to political and economic institutions following the granting of responsible government. The attitudes and aspirations of the flood of immigrants arriving after the discovery of gold reflected those in mid-Victorian Britain where reform of the corrupt and class-based political system and concern at social and economic inequalities were much in evidence. The resulting democratic and egalitarian temperament of nineteenth-century Australians was surely a major source of their preparedness to challenge existing institutions and policies, including when it appeared they were not conducive to the maintenance or improvement of their living standards. Their response to the severe and prolonged depression of the 1890s demonstrates this preparedness. It not only saw the emergence of trade unions and labor-affiliated political parties, but accelerated the most dramatic institutional change of all— the federation of the six colonies.

These same social and cultural traits persisted through the twentieth century. The homogeneity of the predominantly Anglo-Celtic population until after 1945 is worth noting as a factor perhaps contributing to the resilience of a society that endured two wars and a depression without serious social or political strains. The greater diversity of ethnic backgrounds in the population arising as a result of large-scale immigration from Continental Europe from the late 1940s and from Asia from the 1970s does not appear to have altered social norms or attitudes toward institutional and policy changes aimed at promoting growth. Perhaps this is unsurprising in a society in which immigrants or the descendants of recent immigrants comprise a significant proportion of the population, and where the principal motivation for the decision to migrate has been economic betterment. As described in chapter 9, the reshaping of some key economic institutions and the shifts in economic-policy settings that negatively affected some groups in society were accepted by voters in the last decades of the twentieth century as necessary to the maintenance of their prosperity.

It is no great challenge to observe from hindsight that certain institutional changes or redirections in policy were followed by an improved productivity performance or raised incomes. Ascertaining the causal connections between these events, and the relative importance of other influences, is more difficult, as we saw in the previous chapter in relation to the impact of the reforms of the 1980s and 1990s. It is an even more challenging task to account for how it is that institutional and policy changes took the form they did rather than an alternative form with possibly different implications for prosperity. I have offered some speculations on this theme mainly in relation to institutional and policy changes in the nineteenth century, because they appear to have received less attention in the literature than that accorded later changes. Perhaps better understood is the rent-seeking behavior during the twentieth century of key interest groups, and the political-economy context within which major policy decisions affecting growth were made. For example, the impact of the labor movement—both unions and their affiliated political party—on policies such as labor-market regulation, minimum wages, social welfare, and tariff protection for manufacturing has been extensively documented by historians. Thus in chapter 7 I noted its role in the establishment of new labor-market institutions following federation, and in chapter 9 its participation in the novel Accord arrangements to combat stagflation in the 1980s. A second example, referred to in chapter 8, relates to the circumstances surrounding the switch from a protectionist to a liberalizing stance with respect to tariff policies in the 1970s.

• • •

For all small open economies, a tension exists between exploiting comparative advantage and increased vulnerability to external shocks. Arguably this tension is greater for those resource-abundant countries specializing in a narrow range of exports and thereby exposed to the terms of trade volatility arising from commodity price fluctuations. Taking a very long view, an almost dialectic process appears to operate in Australian history between the confident pursuit of rapid growth and openness when international economic conditions are favorable, and, after a deterioration in these conditions reveals the downside risk inherent in the earlier growth strategy, there is a reaction. The search for economic security or stability is then assigned greater weight even though this may require trading off a higher rate of economic progress—growth through openness. This process is evident at the political level in reversals in policy directions, as well as at the intellectual level in changes in the relative influence on policy formation of contending economic theories. These transitions are especially clear in the 1900s and interwar years, but seem to recur over a longer span of Australia's history. A mid-nineteenth-century example is the rise in protectionism partly in response to the end of the initial boom phase of the Victorian gold rushes. A more recent one is the policies of the Hawke government after 1983, which were adopted in part in reaction to the shocks and slowdown of the 1970s. As current debates on the merits of free trade, globalization, foreign investment, and population growth all attest, nothing gets settled—at least beyond the next major shock.

It is against this background that, in the previous chapter, I discussed the conventional assessment, dating from the 1970s, of the inward-oriented phase of development circa1900–60, as constituting a "wrong turn" in policy direction. This seems a somewhat ahistorical interpretation of the feasible growth strategies available to Australia under the adverse international economic conditions prevailing at the time, and in the absence of a major new resource discovery. I have suggested that the goal of diversifying the economic base by encouraging industrialization may, for a period, have been an appropriate means of securing the social objectives of high population growth through immigration and the maintenance of real wages. In hindsight it is clear that encouraging manufacturing through tariff protection resulted in Australia being much better placed to secure economic benefits during the war against Japan, and, following the war, manufacturing made a significant contribution to exports, thereby easing the recurring balance of payments constraint on growth at that time. No doubt some efficiency gains from a freer trade regime were forgone: but how significant these were in terms of average incomes remains unclear; and how important these were as an offset to the other benefits noted is a matter of speculation. From the 1960s the combination of postwar resource discoveries and Asian industrialization offered Australia the opportunity, once again, to shift the basis of its growth and prosperity. That this occurred, and has proven successful, does not constitute evidence that the earlier strategy was inappropriate prior to these two major changes in the country's economic environment.

A related theme in this book has been that the implications of resource abundance appear in many guises—not just pervasive corruption and blatant, large-scale misallocation of resources. Partly for this reason I have highlighted the story of the squatters' access to and property rights in rural land as potentially constituting a brake on nineteenth-century prosperity—in two phases as described in chapters 4 and 5. Federation in 1901 may in part be ascribed to institutional weaknesses exposed by the pre-1890 boom and ensuing crisis. And the institutional changes associated with the major economic policy reforms of the 1980s and 1990s illustrate the adjustments believed necessary to enhance living standards in the face not just of changed external economic conditions but also the re-emergence of a booming minerals and energy sector.

A further implication of Australia's resource abundance is the tension that arises during resource-based booms between the goals of rapid population increase and the growth in income per capita—extensive versus intensive growth. The trade-off is illustrated by the additional investment in infrastructure required during periods of high immigration, as in the 1850s to 1880s, 1950s and 1960s, and again in recent years. Savings and investment are diverted from the capital deepening required to raise productivity to the capital widening required to prevent a decline in the living standards of the more rapidly growing population. I earlier noted that social objectives appeared to have undergone a historic shift from the 1960s with less emphasis placed on a larger population as an end in itself, one to be achieved through high rates of immigration. But the recent commodities-based boom has revived the historic tensions. There has been a dramatic increase in the immigration of workers required—directly or indirectly—to rapidly exploit a series of major mineral and energy discoveries. This echoes the response to labor scarcity resulting from the discovery of pastoral and agricultural land in the early nineteenth century. Similarly, during the last decade or so, there reappeared worrisome symptoms familiar to any student of previous booms: a decline in household savings rates and rise in household indebtedness; a dramatic rise in the ratio of house prices to incomes; increased reliance on foreign savings leading to a rise in the current account deficit as a proportion of GDP; an increase in overseas net indebtedness as a proportion of GDP; and a heightened vulnerability of the banking system—and hence domestic prosperity generally—to any interruption to its ability to raise capital overseas, a vulnerability exposed in 2008 during the global financial crisis.[6]

Another corollary of a resource boom is that expectations regarding the benefits arising from actual or anticipated resource rents may lead economic agents to behave in ways that undermines growth in the long run. The pre-1890s boom ended in a deep and prolonged bust in some degree because it increasingly acquired speculative elements. And we discussed in chapter 6 the likelihood that the high incomes achieved at that time were in part derived from the depletion of the economy's stock of natural resources: current consumption levels were inherently unsustainable. Arguably this may be regarded as a variant of the "curse" of resource abundance.

---

[6] At the time of writing, some of these trends have been halted or reversed—at least temporarily. Although Australia avoided a recession and bank collapses in 2008, the financial turmoil and economic downturns elsewhere appear to have had an impact on the behavior of consumers. Household savings rates have risen from zero or even slightly negative in the years just prior to 2007, to around 10 percent of disposable income, levels not seen for two decades. The rapid rise in house prices has slowed. Both these outcomes result also from a tightening of monetary policy designed to restrain the inflationary pressures arising from the continuing resources boom.

In recent years per capita incomes have been raised on the back of historically very high terms of trade (figure 9.4) and the exploitation of large quantities of mineral and energy resources. But this has masked a slowdown in the rate of productivity improvement (figure 9.5). The reforming impulse among political leaders that most likely contributed to the productivity gains recorded during the 1990s has subsequently waned. And to date, the windfall gains arising from this latest resources boom have largely been dissipated through higher current consumption spending by both the private and public sectors. The rise of so-called middle-class welfare might illustrate a form of resource-rent dissipation through the political process that encourages entitlement expectations that can only be met under boom conditions. Meanwhile serious bottlenecks have emerged in road and rail transport and port facilities, and urban water supplies have become less secure, reflecting underinvestment in infrastructure. There has been no serious attempt to raise the quality of education and skills to enhance the stock of human capital. And there has been no major or sustained effort to divert resource rents from the booming minerals sector into a Norway-style sovereign wealth fund designed to support living standards when the boom passes. As a consequence, maintaining prosperity relative to that achieved elsewhere in the event of a steep decline in commodity prices, or following the depletion of a major natural resource, or in the face of raised trade barriers, may prove extremely challenging. Australia has experienced both brief and prolonged periods of resource-based prosperity in the past; adjusting to their demise has invariably been wrenching.

At the same time, appreciation of the potential threat to longer-run prosperity posed by the current resource boom, and of the continuing ability to creatively engage in the institutional innovation required to sustainably manage it, is illustrated by the creation by the Howard government in 2006 of the Future Fund.[7] Furthermore, levels of awareness in the community of the nonrenewable nature of the resources underpinning living standards, and also of the uncertainty surrounding future foreign demand for them, are probably higher than was the case during the natural-resource-based boom of the late nineteenth century. Perhaps these are examples of Australians learning from their past.

---

[7] The Future Fund is designed to offset the unfunded pension liabilities of the federal government, receiving capital injections directly from the federal budget, but it operates much like a sovereign wealth fund. At the end of 2010 it had $72 billion in assets (see http.futurefund.gov.au).

Appendix

Note on Statistics and Sources

Currency Units

The pound was the principal Australian currency unit until 1966 when the Australian dollar was introduced at the conversion rate of two dollars to each pound. Where the original source expresses values in pounds, this has been retained, especially for the nineteenth century. Otherwise most pre-1966 values have been converted to dollars.

Real and Nominal Values

The historical time series most frequently referred to in this book (aggregate GDP, per capita GDP, etc.) are expressed in "real" or "deflated" values unless otherwise indicated.

Calendar and Financial Years

During the colonial period (1788 to 1900), most annual statistics relating to the economy were reported in relation to the year ending 31 December. Thereafter the reporting year shifted to years ending 30 June. The six colonies were not always consistent in this; and following federation in 1901, there was a period in which these inconsistencies survived in the state-level components of some statistics relating to the Australian economy as a whole.

The convention in Australia is to express financial-year data in hyphenated form, for instance, 2003–04 for the year ended 30 June 2004, or with a forward slash—2003/04. To simplify, and avoid possible confusion that two years are being referred to, the practice here is to label this as 2004. Thus, all economic series such as GDP relate to the calendar year to 1900 and the year ended 30 June from 1901. Any exceptions will be noted in the text.

Statistical Sources and Abbreviations

The principal statistical agency of the Australian government is the Australian Bureau of Statistics (previously, the Commonwealth Bureau of Census and Statistics), whose standard abbreviation is ABS. Most of its publications either in print or on the Web (at http.abs.gov.au) are defined by a catalogue number (abbreviation, Cat.). For example, the annual summary of economic and related statistics is *1301.0—Year Book Australia*. A second major official source of economic statistics is the Reserve Bank of Australia, whose abbreviation is RBA (and Web address is http.rba.gov.au). In particular frequent reference is made to *Australian Economic Statistics 1949–50 to 1996–97*, Occasional Paper No. 8, accessible at www.rba.gov.au/statistics/frequency/occ-paper-8.html. The principal collection of historical statistics, also frequently utilized in this book, is *Australians: Historical Statistics*, a collaborative venture edited by Wray Vamplew and published in 1987: it is referred to here not by the author of the individual chapters but as "Vamplew (1987)."

Unpublished Papers

Some references are to sources other than books and journals, and are available on the Web. The most frequently cited are the following:

   Australian Treasury working papers (www.treasury.gov.au, then "Working Paper Series")

   Australian Treasury *Economic Roundup* (www.treasury.gov.au, then "Publications" then "Economic Roundup")

   National Bureau of Economic Research working papers (www.nber.org/papers.html)

   Reserve Bank of Australia research discussion papers (www.rba.gov.au/publications/rdp)

References

Abramovitz, Moses, and Paul A. David. 2000. "American Macroeconomic Growth in the Era of Knowledge-Based Progress: The Long-Run Perspective." In Stanley L. Engerman and Robert E. Gallman (editors), *The Cambridge Economic History of the United States, Volume III: The Twentieth Century.* New York: Cambridge University Press, pp. 1–92.

Acemoglu, Daron. 2009. *Introduction to Modern Economic Growth.* Princeton, NJ: Princeton University Press.

Acemoglu, Daron, Simon Johnson, and James A. Robinson. 2001. "The Colonial Origins of Comparative Development: An Empirical Investigation." *American Economic Review,* Vol. 91, No. 5 (December), pp. 1369–1401.

———. 2002. "Reversal of Fortune: Geography and Institutions in the Making of the Modern World Income Distribution." *Quarterly Journal of Economics,* Vol. 117, No. 4 (November), pp. 1231–94.

———. 2005. "Institutions as a Fundamental Cause of Long-Run Economic Growth." In *Handbook of Economic Growth Vol. 1A,* Philippe Aghion and Steven N. Durlauf (editors). Amsterdam: Elsevier, pp. 385–472.

Acemoglu, Daron, and James A. Robinson. 2006a. *The Economic Origins of Dictatorship and Democracy.* Cambridge: Cambridge University Press.

———. 2006b. "Persistence of Power, Elites and Institutions." Working Paper 12108, National Bureau of Economic Research, Cambridge, Mass. (March).

Adelman, Jeremy. 1994. *Frontier Development: Land, Labour, and Capital on the Wheatlands of Argentina and Canada 1890–1914.* Oxford: Clarendon Press of Oxford University Press.

Aghion, Philippe, and Steven N. Durlauf (editors). 2005. *Handbook of Economic Growth, Vols. 1A and 1B.* Amsterdam: Elsevier.

Albouy, David Y. 2008. "The Colonial Origins of Comparative Development: An Investigation of the Settler Mortality Data." Working Paper 14130, National Bureau of Economic Research, Cambridge, Mass. (June).

Allen, Robert C. 1994. "Real Incomes in the English-Speaking World, 1879–1913." In *Labour Market Evolution: The Economic History of Market Integration, Wage Flexibility and the Employment Relation,* George Grantham and Mary MacKinnon (editors). London: Routledge, pp. 107–38.

———. 2009. *The British Industrial Revolution in Global Perspective.* Cambridge: Cambridge University Press.

Anderson, Kym, and Ross Garnaut. 1987. *Australian Protectionism: Extent, Causes and Effects.* Sydney: Allen & Unwin.

Aristotle. 2009. *The Nicomachean Ethics,* trans. David Ross. Oxford: Oxford University Press.

Atkinson, Anthony B,. and Andrew Leigh. 2007. "The Distribution of Top Incomes in Australia." *Economic Record,* Vol. 83, No. 262 (September), pp. 247–61.

Attard, Bernard. 1989. "Politics, Finance and Anglo-Australian Relations: Australian Borrowing in London, 1914–1920." *Australian Journal of Politics and History*, Vol. 35, No. 2, pp. 142–63.

Australian Treasury. 2009. "Raising the Level of Productivity Growth in the Australian Economy." *Economic Roundup*, Issue 3 (September), pp. 47–66.

Auty, Richard M. 2001. "The Political Economy of Resource-Driven Growth." *European Economic Review*, Vol. 45, Nos. 4–6 (May), pp. 839–46.

Barnard, Alan. 1958. *The Australian Wool Market 1840–1900*. Carlton, Vic.: Melbourne University Press.

Barr, Neil, and John Cary. 1992. *Greening a Brown Land: The Australian Search for Sustainable Land Use*. Melbourne: Macmillan.

Barro, Robert J., and Xavier Sala-i-Martin. 1995. *Economic Growth*. New York: McGraw-Hill.

Battellino, Ric. 2010. "Mining Booms and the Australian Economy." Address to the Sydney Institute, 23 February 2010. Available at www.rba.gov.au/speeches/2010.

Battersby, Bryn. 2006. "Does Distance Matter? The Effect of Geographic Isolation on Productivity Levels." Treasury Working Paper 2006–03 (April), Australian Treasury, Canberra.

Battersby, Bryn, and Robert Ewing. 2005. "International Trade Performance: The Gravity of Australia's Remoteness." Treasury Working Paper 2005–03 (June), Australian Treasury, Canberra.

Belkar, Rochelle, Lynne Cockerell, and Christopher Kent. 2007. "The Current Account Deficits: The Australian Debate." Research Discussion Paper 2007–02 (March), Reserve Bank of Australia, Sydney.

Bentick, B. L. 1969. "Foreign Borrowing, Wealth, and Consumption: Victoria 1873–1893." *Economic Record*, Vol. 45 (September), pp. 415–31.

Berlin, Isaiah. 1967. *The Hedgehog and the Fox: An Essay on Tolstoy's View of History*. London: Weidenfeld and Nicolson 1967.

Bhattacharyya, Sambit, and Jeffrey G. Williamson. 2009. "Commodity Price Shocks and the Australian Economy Since Federation." Working Paper 14694, National Bureau of Economic Research (January).

Blainey, Geoffrey. 1964. "Technology in Australian History." *Business Archives and History*, Vol. 4, No. 2 (August), pp. 117–37.

———. 1970. "A Theory of Mineral Discovery: Australia in the Nineteenth Century." *Economic History Review*, Vol. 23, No. 2 (August), pp. 298–313.

———. 1982. *A Land Half Won*. Melbourne: Macmillan (revised edition).

———. 1983. *Triumph of the Nomads: A History of Ancient Australia*. Melbourne: Sun Books (revised edition).

———. 2001. *The Tyranny of Distance: How Distance Shaped Australia's History*. Sydney: Macmillan (revised edition; first published in 1966).

———. 2003a. *The Rush That Never Ended: A History of Australian Mining*. Carlton, Vic: Melbourne University Press (fifth edition; first published in 1963).

———. 2003b. *Black Kettle and Full Moon: Daily Life in a Vanished Australia*. Camberwell, Victoria: Viking.

Blanchflower, David G., and Andrew J. Oswald. 2005. "Happiness and the Human Development Index: The Paradox of Australia." *Australian Economic Review*, Vol. 38, No. 3 (September), pp. 307–18.

———. 2006. "On Leigh-Wolfers and Well-Being in Australia." *Australian Economic Review*, Vol. 39, No. 2 (June), pp. 185–86.

Blandy, Richard. 1990. "Discussion." In *The Australian Macro-Economy in the 1980s*, Stephen Grenville (editor). Sydney: Reserve Bank of Australia, pp. 66–72.

Blattman, Christopher, Jason Hwang, and Jeffrey G. Williamson. 2007. "Winners and Losers in the Commodity Lottery: The Impact of Terms of Trade Growth and Volatility in the Periphery 1870–1939." *Journal of Development Economics*, Vol. 82, No. 1 (January), pp. 156–79.

Boehm, E. A. 1971. *Prosperity and Depression in Australia 1887–1897*. Oxford: Clarendon Press.

Bolton, Geoffrey. 1992. *Spoils and Spoilers: A History of Australians Shaping Their Environment*. Sydney: Allen & Unwin (second edition).

Boyer, George R. 2007. "The Convergence of Living Standards in the Atlantic Economy, 1870–1930." In *The New Comparative Economic History: Essays in Honor of Jeffrey G. Williamson*, Timothy J. Hatton, Kevin H. O'Rourke, and Alan M. Taylor (editors). Cambridge, Mass.: The MIT Press, pp. 317–42.

Brash, Donald T. 1966. *American Investment in Australian Industry*. Canberra: Australian National University Press.

Brigden, J. B. 1929. *The Australian Tariff: An Economic Enquiry*. Melbourne: Melbourne University Press.

Broadberry, Stephen, and Douglas A. Irwin. 2006. "Labor Productivity in the United States and the United Kingdom during the Nineteenth Century." *Explorations in Economic History*, Vol. 43, No. 2 (April), pp. 257–79.

———. 2007. "Lost Exceptionalism? Comparative Income and Productivity in Australia and the UK, 1861–1948." *Economic Record*, Vol. 83, No. 262 (September), pp. 262–74.

———. 2008. "Real Product and Productivity of Industries since the Nineteenth Century: A Reply to Bryan Haig." *Economic Record*, Vol. 84, No. 267 (December), pp. 515–16.

Broome, Richard. 1994. "Aboriginal Workers on South-Eastern Frontiers." *Australian Historical Studies*, Vol. 26, No. 103 (October), pp. 202–20.

Brunnschweiler, Christa N., and Erwin H. Bulte. 2008. "The Resource Curse Revisited and Revised: A Tale of Paradoxes and Red Herrings." *Journal of Environmental Economics and Management*, Vol. 55, No. 3 (May), pp. 248–64.

Buckley, Ken, and Ted Wheelwright. 1988. *No Paradise for Workers: Capitalism and the Common People in Australia 1788–1914*. Melbourne: Oxford University Press.

Burroughs, Peter. 1967. *Britain and Australia 1831–1855: A Study in Imperial Relations and Crown Lands Administration*. Oxford: Clarendon Press.

Butlin, M. W. 1977. "A Preliminary Annual Database 1900/01 to 1973/74." Research Discussion Paper 7701 (May), Reserve Bank of Australia, Sydney.

Butlin, N. G. 1962. *Australian Domestic Product, Investment and Foreign Borrowing 1861–1938/39*. Cambridge: Cambridge University Press.

———. 1964. *Investment in Australian Economic Development 1861–1900*. Cambridge: Cambridge University Press.

———. 1970. "Some Perspectives of Australian Economic Development, 1890–1965." In *Australian Economic Development in the Twentieth Century*, Colin Forster (editor). London: Allen & Unwin, pp. 266–327.

———. 1983. *Our Original Aggression: Aboriginal Populations of Southeastern Australia 1788–1850.* Sydney: Allen & Unwin.

———. 1986. "Contours of the Australian Economy 1788–1860." *Australian Economic History Review*, Vol. 26, No. 2 (September), pp. 96–125.

———. 1994. *Forming a Colonial Economy, Australia 1810–1850.* Cambridge: Cambridge University Press.

Butlin, N. G., and J. A. Dowie. 1969. "Estimates of Australian Work Force and Employment, 1861–1961." *Australian Economic History Review*, Vol. 9, No. 2 (September), pp. 138–55.

Butlin, N. G., and W. A. Sinclair. 1986. "Australian Gross Domestic Product 1788–1860: Estimates, Sources and Methods." *Australian Economic History Review*, Vol. 26, No. 2 (September), pp. 126–47.

Butlin, S. J. 1953. *Foundations of the Australian Monetary System 1788–1851.* Melbourne: Melbourne University Press.

———. 1955. *War Economy 1939-1942.* Canberra: Australian War Memorial.

Butlin, S. J., and C. B. Schedvin. 1977. *War Economy 1942–1945.* Canberra: Australian War Memorial.

Campbell, Judy. 2002. *Invisible Invaders: Smallpox and Other Diseases in Aboriginal Australia 1780–1880.* Carlton South, Vic.: Melbourne University Press.

Carter, Michael, and Rodney Maddock. 1984. "Working Hours in Australia: Some Issues." In *Understanding Labour Markets in Australia*, Richard Blandy and Owen Covick (editors). Sydney: Allen & Unwin, pp. 222–45.

———. 1987. "Leisure and Australian Wellbeing." *Australian Economic History Review*, Vol. 27, No. 1 (March), pp. 30–43.

Cashin, Paul. 1995. "Economic Growth and Convergence across the Seven Colonies of Australasia: 1861–1991." *Economic Record*, Vol. 71, No. 213 (June), pp. 132–44.

Caves, Richard E., and Lawrence B. Krause. 1984. "Introduction." In *The Australian Economy: A View from the North*, Caves and Krause (editors). Washington, D.C.: The Brookings Institution, pp. 1–23.

Chapman, Bruce. 1990. "The Labour Market." In *The Australian Macro-Economy in the 1980s*, Stephen Grenville (editor). Sydney: Reserve Bank of Australia, pp. 7–65.

Clark, David. 1975. "Australia: Victim or Partner of British Imperialism?" In *Essays in the Political Economy of Australian Capitalism, Vol. 1*, E. L. Wheelwright and Ken Buckley (editors). Sydney: Australia and New Zealand Book Co., pp. 47–71.

Clark, Gregory. 2007. *A Farewell to Alms: A Brief Economic History of the World.* Princeton, NJ: Princeton University Press.

Clark, Manning. 1987. *A Short History of Australia.* New York: Mentor (third edition).

Clay, Karen, and Randall Jones. 2008. "Migrating to Riches? Evidence from the California Gold Rush." *Journal of Economic History*, Vol. 68, No. 4 (December), pp. 997–1027.

Clay, Karen, and Gavin Wright. 2005. "Order without Law? Property Rights during the California Gold Rush." *Explorations in Economic History*, Vol. 42, No. 2 (April), pp. 155–83.

Clemens, Michael A., and Jeffrey G. Williamson. 2001. "A Tariff-Growth Paradox? Protection's Impact the World Around 1875–1997." Working Paper 8459, National Bureau of Economic Research, Cambridge, MA (September).

———. 2004. "Why Did the Tariff-Growth Correlation Change after 1950?" *Journal of Economic Growth*, Vol. 9, No. 1 (March), pp. 5–46.

Cochrane, Peter. 2006. *Colonial Ambition: Foundations of Australian Democracy*. Carlton, Vic.: Melbourne University Press.

Copland, D. B. 1988. "Australia in the World War: (III) Economic." In *Australia: Cambridge History of the British Empire, Vol. 7, Part. 1*, Ernest Scott (editor). Cambridge: Cambridge University Press, pp. 585–604 (first published in 1933).

Corden, W. M. 1984. "Booming Sector and Dutch Disease Economics: A Survey." *Oxford Economic Papers*, Vol. 36, No. 3 (November), pp. 359–80.

Cornish, Selwyn. 1993. "The Keynesian Revolution in Australia: Fact or Fiction?" *Australian Economic History Review*, Vol. 33, No. 2 (September), pp. 42–68.

Cortes Conde, Roberto. 1985. "Some Notes on the Industrial Development of Argentina and Canada in the 1920s." In *Argentina, Australia and Canada: Studies in Comparative Development 1870-1965,*. D.C.M. Platt and Guido di Tella (editors). New York: St Martin's Press, pp. 149–60.

Crafts, N.F.R. 1995. "Exogenous or Endogenous Growth? The Industrial Revolution Reconsidered." *Journal of Economic History*, Vol. 55, No. 4 (December), pp. 745–72.

Crafts, Nicholas. 2002. "The Human Development Index, 1870–1999: Some Revised Estimates." *European Review of Economic History*, Vol. 6, No. 3 (December), pp. 395–405.

Crawford, R. M. 1979. *Australia*. London: Hutchison (fourth edition).

David, Paul A., and Gavin Wright. 1997. "Increasing Returns and the Genesis of American Resource Abundance." *Industrial and Corporate Change*, Vol. 6, No. 2. Pp. 203–45.

Davidson, Bruce R. 1981. *European Farming in Australia: An Economic History of Australian Farming*. Amsterdam: Elsevier.

———. 1982. "A Benefit Cost Analysis of the New South Wales Railway System." *Australian Economic History Review*, Vol. 22, No. 2 (September), pp. 127–50.

Davis, Graeme, and Robert Ewing. 2005. "Why Has Australia Done Better Than New Zealand? Good Luck or Good Management?" Treasury Working Paper 2005–01 (January), Australian Treasury, Canberra.

Diamond, Jared. 1998. *Guns, Germs and Steel: A Short History of Everybody for the Last 13,000 Years*. London: Vintage.

Diaz Alejandro, Carlos. 1985. "Argentina, Australia and Brazil before 1929." In D.C.M. Platt and Guido di Tella (editors), *Argentina, Australia and Canada: Studies in Comparative Development 1870-1965*. New York: St Martin's Press, pp. 95–109.

Dick, Trevor J. O. 1982. "Canadian Newsprint, 1913–1930: National Policies and the North American Economy." *Journal of Economic History*, Vol. 42, No. 3 (September), pp. 659–87.

Di Marco, Katrina, Mitchell Pirie, and Wilson Au-Yeung. 2009. "A History of Public Debt in Australia." *Economic Roundup* (Australian Treasury), Issue 1 (March), pp. 1–15.

Dingle, Tony. 1988. *Aboriginal Economy: Patterns of Experience*. Melbourne: McPhee Gribble/Penguin Books.

Dolman, Ben, Dean Parham, and Simon Zheng. 2007. "Can Australia Match US Productivity Performance?" Staff Working Paper, Australian Government Productivity Commission (March).

Doran, D. R. 1984. "An Historical Perspective on Mining and Economic Change." In *The Minerals Sector and the Australian Economy* (L. H. Cook and M. G. Porter, editors). Sydney: Allen & Unwin, pp. 37–84.

Dowrick, Steve, and Tom Nguyen. 1989. "Measurement and International Comparison." In *Australian Economic Growth: Essays in Honour of Fred H. Gruen*, Bruce Chapman (editor). South Melbourne: Macmillan, pp. 34–59.

Duncan, Tim. 1985. "Australia and Argentina: A Tale of Two Political Cultures." In A. E. Dingle and D. T. Merrett (editors), *Argentina and Australia: Essays in Comparative Economic Development*. Clayton, Vic.: Economic History Society of Australia and New Zealand, pp. 37–56.

Duncan, Tim, and John Fogarty. 1984. *Australia and Argentina: On Parallel Paths*. Carlton, Vic.: Melbourne University Press.

Dunsdorfs, Edgars. 1956. *The Australian Wheat-Growing Industry 1788–1948*. Melbourne: Melbourne University Press.

Easterlin, Richard A. 1974. "Does Economic Growth Improve the Human Lot? Some Empirical Evidence." In *Nations and Households in Economic Growth: Essays in Honor of Moses Abramovitz*, Paul A. David and Melvin W. Reder (editors). New York: Academic Press, pp. 89–125.

Easterly, William. 2002. *The Elusive Quest for Growth: Economists' Adventures and Misadventures in the Tropics*. Cambridge, MA: The MIT Press.

Easterly, William, and Ross Levine. 2003. "Tropics, Germs, and Crops: How Endowments Influence Economic Development." *Journal of Monetary Economics*, Vol. 50, No. 1 (January), pp. 3–39.

Edelstein, Michael. 1982. *Overseas Investment in the Age of High Imperialism: The United Kingdom, 1850–1914*. New York: Columbia University Press.

———. 1988. "Professional Engineers in Australia: Institutional Response in a Developing Economy." *Australian Economic History Review*, Vol. 28, No. 2 (September), pp. 8–32.

———. 1994. "Imperialism: Cost and Benefit." In *The Economic History of Britain since 1700, Volume 2: 1860–1939*, Roderick Floud and Donald McCloskey (editors). Cambridge: Cambridge University Press, pp. 197–216.

Edey, Malcolm, and Luke Gower. 2000. "National Savings: Trends and Policy." In David Gruen and Sona Shrestha (editors), *The Australian Economy in the 1990s: Proceedings of a Conference*. Sydney: Reserve Bank of Australia, pp. 277–311.

Eichengreen, Barry. 1988. "The Australian Recovery of the 1930s in International Comparative Perspective." In *Recovery from the Depression: Australia and the World Economy in the 1930s*, R. G. Gregory and N. G. Butlin (editors). Cambridge: Cambridge University Press, pp. 33–60.

———. 1992. *Golden Fetters: The Gold Standard and the Great Depression 1919–1939*. New York: Oxford University Press.

———. 1994. "Institutional Prerequisites for Economic Growth: Europe after World War II." *European Economic Review*, Vol. 38, Nos. 3/4 (April), pp. 883–90.

———. 1996. "Institutions and Economic Growth: Europe after World War II." In *Economic Growth in Europe since 1945*, Nicholas Crafts and Gianni Toniolo (editors). Cambridge: Cambridge University Press, pp. 38–72.

Eichengreen, Barry, and Ian W. McLean. 1994. "The Supply of Gold under the Pre-1914 Gold Standard." *Economic History Review*, Vol. 47, No. 2 (May), pp. 288–309.

Eichengreen, Barry, and Jeffrey Sachs. 1985. "Exchange Rates and Economic Recovery in the 1930s." *Journal of Economic History*, Vol. 45, No. 4 (December), pp. 925–46.

Elliott, J. H. 2006. *Empires of the Atlantic World: Britain and Spain in America, 1492–1830*. New Haven: Yale University Press.

Engerman, Stanley L., and Kenneth L. Sokoloff. 1997. "Factor Endowments, Institutions, and Differential Paths of Growth among New World Economies." In *How Latin*

America Fell Behind, Stephen Haber (editor). Stanford: Stanford University Press, pp. 260–304.

———. 2002. "Factor Endowments, Inequality, and Paths of Development among New World Economies." Working Paper 9259, National Bureau of Economic Research. Cambridge, Mass. (October).

———. 2003. "Institutional and Non-Institutional Explanations of Economic Differences." Working Paper 9989, National Bureau of Economic Research. Cambridge, Mass. (September).

———. 2005a. "Colonialism, Inequality, and Long-Run Paths of Development." Working Paper 11057, National Bureau of Economic Research. Cambridge, Mass. (January).

———. 2005b. "The Evolution of Suffrage Institutions in the New World." *Journal of Economic History*, Vol. 65, No 4 (December), pp. 891–921.

Ferguson, Niall, and Moritz Schularick. 2006. "The Empire Effect: The Determinants of Country Risk in the First Age of Globalization, 1880–1913." *Journal of Economic History*, Vol. 66, No. 2 (June), pp. 283–312.

Findlay, Ronald, and Kevin O'Rourke. 2007. *Power and Plenty: Trade, War, and the World Economy in the Second Millennium*. Princeton, NJ: Princeton University Press.

Fisher, Allan G. B. 1935. *The Clash of Progress and Security*. London: Macmillan.

Fitzpatrick, Brian. 1971. *British Imperialism and Australia 1783–1833: An Economic History of Australasia*. Sydney: Sydney University Press (first published 1939).

———. 1969. *The British Empire in Australia: An Economic History 1834–1939*. South Melbourne: Macmillan (first published 1941).

Flanagan, Robert J. 1999. "Macroeconomic Performance and Collective Bargaining: An International Perspective." *Journal of Economic Literature*, Vol. 37, No. 3 (September), pp. 1150–75.

Flannery, Timothy Fridtjof. 1994. *The Future Eaters: An Ecological History of the Australasian Lands and Peoples*. Frenchs Forest, NSW: Reed New Holland.

Fleurbaey, Marc. 2009. "Beyond GDP: The Quest for a Measure of Social Welfare," *Journal of Economic Literature*, Vol. 47, No. 4 (December), pp. 1029–75.

Flood, Josephine. 2006. *The Original Australians: Story of the Aboriginal People*. Crows Nest, NSW: Allen & Unwin.

Forster, Colin. 1953. "Australian Manufacturing and the War of 1914–18." *Economic Record*, Vol. 29 (November), pp. 211–30.

———. 1977. "Federation and the Tariff." *Australian Economic History Review*, Vol. 17, No. 2 (September), pp. 95–116.

———. 1985. "An Economic Consequence of Mr Justice Higgins." *Australian Economic History Review*, Vol. 25, No. 2 (September), pp. 95–111.

———. 1989. "The Economy, Wages, and the Establishment of Arbitration." In *Foundation of Arbitration: The Origins and Effects of State Compulsory Arbitration 1890–1914*, Stuart Macintyre and Richard Mitchell (editors). Melbourne: Oxford University Press, pp. 203–24.

Frankel, Jeffrey A. 2010. "The Natural Resource Curse: A Survey." Working Paper 15836 (March), National Bureau of Economic Research. Cambridge, Mass.

Frankel, Jeffrey A., and David Romer. 1999. "Does Trade Cause Growth?" *American Economic Review*, Vol. 89, No. 3 (June), pp. 379–99.

Frijters, Paul, and Robert Gregory. 2006. "From Golden Age to Golden Age: Australia's 'Great Leap Forward'?" *Economic Record*, Vol. 82, No. 257 (June). Pp.207–24.

Frost, Lionel. 2000. "Government and the Colonial Economies: An Alternative View." *Australian Economic History Review*, Vol. 40, No. 1 (March), pp.71–85.

Frost, Warwick. 1995. "Soil Exhaustion in Late Nineteenth Century Victoria: A Reinterpretation." Paper presented at the Australian and New Zealand Economic History Society Conference, University of Melbourne, 31 March–2 April.

Gammage, Bill. 1990. "Who Gained, and Who Was Meant to Gain, from Land Selection in New South Wales?" *Australian Historical Studies*, Vol. 24, No. 94 (April), pp. 104–22.

Gerschenkron, Alexander. 1962. *Economic Backwardness in Historical Perspective: A Book of Essays*. Cambridge, Mass: Belknap Press of Harvard University Press.

Gillitzer, Christian, and Jonathan Kearns. 2005. "Long-Term Patterns in Australia's Terms of Trade." Research Discussion Paper 2005-01, Reserve Bank of Australia (April).

Giuliano, Paola, and Antonio Spilimbergo. 2009. "Growing Up in a Recession: Beliefs and the Macroeconomy." Working Paper 15321, National Bureau of Economic Research, Cambridge Mass. (September).

Glick, Reuven, and Alan M. Taylor. 2010. "Collateral Damage: Trade Disruption and the Economic Impact of War." *Review of Economics and Statistics*, Vol. 92, No. 1 (February), pp. 102–27.

Goldin, Claudia. 1998. "America's Graduation from High School: The Evolution and Spread of Secondary Schooling in the Twentieth Century." *Journal of Economic History*, Vol. 58, No. 2 (June), pp. 345–74.

Gould, J. D. 1977. Review of W. A. Sinclair, "The Process of Economic Development in Australia." *Australian Economic History Review*, Vol. 17, No. 2 (September), pp. 170–71.

Greasley, David, and Les Oxley. 2009. "The Pastoral Boom, the Rural Land Market, and Long Swings in New Zealand Economic Growth, 1873–1939." *Economic History Review*, Vol. 62, No. 2 (May), pp. 324–49.

Green, Alan M. 2000. "Twentieth-Century Canadian Economic History." In *The Cambridge Economic History of the United States, Vol.3*, Stanley L. Engerman and Robert. E Gallman (editors). Cambridge: Cambridge University Press, pp. 191–247.

Gregory, R. G. 1976. "Some Implications of the Growth of the Mining Sector." *Australian Journal of Agricultural Economics*, Vol. 20, No. 2 (August), pp. 71–91.

Gregory, R. G., and N. G. Butlin (editors). 1988. *Recovery from the Depression: Australia and the World Economy in the 1930s*. Cambridge: Cambridge University Press.

Grey, Jeffrey. 2008. *A Military History of Australia*. New York: Cambridge University Press (third edition).

Gruen, David, and Amanda Sayegh. 2005. "The Evolution of Fiscal Policy in Australia." Treasury Working Paper 2005-04, Australian Treasury, Canberra (November).

Gruen, F. H. 1986. "How Bad Is Australia's Economic Performance and Why?" *Economic Record*, Vol. 62, No. 177 (June), pp. 180–93.

Guttmann, Simon, and Anthony Richards. 2006. "Trade Openness: An Australian Perspective." *Australian Economic Papers*, Vol. 45, No. 3 (September), pp. 188–203.

Gylfason, Thorvaldur. 2001. "Natural Resources, Education, and Economic Development." *European Economic Review*, Vol. 45, Nos. 4–6 (May), pp. 847–59.

Haig, Bryan. 1989. "International Comparisons of Australian GDP in the 19th Century." *Review of Income and Wealth*, Vol. 35, No. 2 (June), pp. 151–62.

———. 2001. "New Estimates of Australian GDP: 1861–1948/49." *Australian Economic History Review*, Vol. 41, No. 1 (March), pp. 1–34.

———. 2008. "Real Product and Productivity of Industries since the Nineteenth Century: A Comment on 'Lost Exceptionalism' by Broadberry and Irwin." *Economic Record*, Vol. 84, No. 267 (December), pp. 511–14.

Haig, Bryan, and Jennifer Anderssen. 2007. "Australian Consumption Expenditure and Real Income: 1900 to 2003–2004." *Economic Record*, Vol. 83, No. 263 (December), pp. 416–31.

Haig, Bryan D., and Neville G. Cain. 1983. "Industrialization and Productivity: Australian Manufacturing in the 1920s and 1950s." *Explorations in Economic History*, Vol. 20, No. 2 (April), pp. 183–98.

Haig-Muir, Marnie. 1995. "The Economy at War." In *Australia's War 1914–18*, Joan Beaumont (editor). St Leonards, NSW: Allen & Unwin, pp. 93–124.

Hall, A. R. 1963a. "Some Long Period Effects of the Kinked Age Distribution of the Population of Australia 1861–1961." *Economic Record*, Vol. 39 (March), pp. 43–52.

———. 1963b. *The London Capital Market and Australia 1870–1914*. Social Science Monograph No. 21. Canberra: The Australian National University.

———. 1968. *The Stock Exchange of Melbourne and the Victorian Economy 1852–1900*. Canberra: Australian National University Press.

Hall, Robert E., and Charles I. Jones. 1999. "Why Do Some Countries Produce So Much More Output per Worker than Other Countries?" *Quarterly Journal of Economics*, Vol. 114, No. 1 (February), pp. 83–116.

Hancock, Keith, and Sue Richardson. 2004. "Economic and Social Effects." In Joe Issac and Stuart Macintyre (editors), *The New Province for Law and Order: 100 Years of Australian Industrial Conciliation and Arbitration*. Cambridge: Cambridge University Press, pp. 139–206.

Hatton, Timothy J., Kevin H. O'Rourke, and Alan M. Taylor (editors). 2007. *The New Comparative Economic History: Essays in Honor of Jeffrey G. Williamson*. Cambridge, MA: The MIT Press.

Hatton, Timothy J., and Jeffrey G. Williamson. 1998. *The Age of Mass Migration: Causes and Economic Impact*. New York: Oxford University Press.

Hausmann, Ricardo, Jason Hwang, and Dani Rodrik. 2007. "What You Export Matters." *Journal of Economic Growth*, Vol. 12, No. 1 (March). Pp. 1–25.

Helpman, Elhanan. 2004. *The Mystery of Economic Growth*. Cambridge, MA: Harvard University Press.

Hirst, J. B. 1983. *Convict Society and Its Enemies: A History of Early New South Wales*. Sydney: Allen & Unwin.

———. 1988. *The Strange Birth of Colonial Democracy: New South Wales 1848–1884*. Sydney: Allen & Unwin.

Horne, Donald. 1964. *The Lucky Country: Australia in the Sixties*. Ringwood, Vic: Penguin.

Huberman, Michael. 2004. "Working Hours of the World Unite? New International Evidence of Worktime, 1870–1913." *Journal of Economic History*, Vol. 64, No. 4 (December), pp. 964–1001.

Hughes, Helen. 1961. "The Eight-Hour Day and the Development of the Labour Movement in Victoria in the Eighteen-Fifties." *Historical Studies of Australia and New Zealand*, Vol. 9, No. 36 (May), pp. 396–412.

Hughes, Robert. 1987. *The Fatal Shore: The Epic of Australia's Founding*. New York: Random House.

Inklaar, Robert, Marcel P. Timmer, and Bart van Ark. 2007. "Mind the Gap! International Comparisons of Productivity in Services and Goods Production." *German Economic Review*, Vol. 8, No. 2 (May), pp. 281–307.

Irwin, Douglas A. 2006. "The Impact of Federation on Australia's Trade Flows." *Economic Record*, Vol. 82, No. 258 (September), pp. 315–24.

———. 2007. "Australian Exceptionalism Revisited." *Australian Economic History Review*, Vol. 47, No. 3 (November), pp. 217–37.

Issac, Joe. 2008. "The Economic Consequences of Harvester." *Australian Economic History Review*, Vol. 48, No. 3 (November), pp. 280–300.

Jackson, R. V. 1992. "Trends in Australian Living Standards since 1890." *Australian Economic History Review*, Vol. 32, No. 1 (March), pp. 24–46.

Jones, Charles I. 1995. "Time Series Tests of Endogenous Growth Models." *Quarterly Journal of Economics*, Vol. 110, No. 2 (May), pp. 495–525.

Jones, E. L. 1987. *The European Miracle: Environments, Economies and Geopolitics in the History of Europe and Asia*. Cambridge: Cambridge University Press (second edition).

———. 1988. *Growth Recurring: Economic Change in World History*. Oxford: Oxford University Press.

Kalix, Z., L. M. Fraser, and R. I. Rawson. 1966. *Australian Mineral Industry: Production and Trade, 1842–1964*. Canberra: Commonwealth of Australia, Department of National Development, Bureau of Mineral Resources, Geology and Geophysics, Bulletin No. 81.

Kaspura, Andre, and Geoff Weldon. 1980. "Productivity Trends in the Australian Economy 1900–01 to 1978–79." Working Paper No. 9, Research Branch, Department of Productivity, Canberra (August).

Keating, M. 1973. *The Australian Workforce 1910–11 to 1960–61*. Canberra: Department of Economic History, Research School of Social Sciences, Australian National University.

Keay, Ian. 2000. "Canadian Manufacturers' Relative Productivity Performance, 1907–1990." *Canadian Journal of Economics*, Vol. 33, No. 4 (November), pp. 1049–68.

Kelley, Allen C. 1965. "International Migration and Economic Growth: Australia, 1865–1935." *Journal of Economic History*, Vol. 25, No. 3 (September), pp. 333–54.

———. 1968. "Demographic Change and Economic Growth: Australia, 1861–1911." *Explorations in Entrepreneurial History*, Vol. 5, No. 3 (Spring/ Summer), pp. 207–77.

Kelly, Paul. 1992. *The End of Certainty: The Story of the 1980s*. St Leonards, NSW: Allen & Unwin.

Kenwood, A. G., and A. L. Lougheed. 1999. *The Growth of the International Economy 1820–2000*. London: Routledge (fourth edition).

Kindleberger, Charles P. 1986. *The World in Depression, 1929–1939*. Berkeley: University of California Press (revised edition).

Kinsella, John (editor). 2009. *The Penguin Anthology of Australian Poetry*. Camberwell, Vic.: Penguin.

La Croix, Sumner J. 1992. "Property Rights and Institutional Change during Australia's Gold Rush." *Explorations in Economic History*, Vol. 29, No. 2 (April), pp. 204–27.

Lamb, P. N. 1964. "Early Overseas Borrowing by the New South Wales Government." *Business Archives and History*, Vol. 4, No. 1 (February), pp. 46–62.

Landes, David S. 1998. *The Wealth and Poverty of Nations: Why Some Are So Rich and Some So Poor*. New York, NY: Norton.

Lehmann, Sibyelle, and Kevin H. O'Rourke. 2008. "The Structure of Protection and Growth in the Late 19th Century." Discussion Paper No. 269, Institute for International Integration Studies (November).

Leigh, Andrew, and Justin Wolfers. 2006. "Happiness and the Human Development Index: Australia Is Not a Paradox." *Australian Economic Review*, Vol. 39, No. 2 (June), pp. 176–84.

Levine, Ross. 2005. "Law, Endowments and Property Rights." *Journal of Economic Perspectives*, Vol. 19. No. 3 (Summer), pp. 61–88.

Lindert, Peter H. 2004. *Growing Public: Social Spending and Economic Growth Since the Eighteenth Century. Vol. 1, The Story*. Cambridge: Cambridge University Press.

Lloyd, Peter. 2008. "100 Years of Tariff Protection in Australia." *Australian Economic History Review*, Vol. 48, No. 2 (July), pp. 99–145.

Lougheed, A. L. 1968. "International Trade Theory and Economic Growth." *Australian Economic History Review*, Vol. 8, No. 2 (September), pp. 99–109.

Macfarlane, Ian. 2006. *The Search for Stability: Boyer Lectures 2006*. Sydney: ABC Books.

MacKinnon, Mary. 1989a. "Years of Schooling: The Australian Experience in Comparative Perspective." *Australian Economic History Review*, Vol. 29, No. 2 (September), pp. 58–78.

———. 1989b. "Schooling: Examining Some Myths." In *Australia's Greatest Asset: Human Resources in the Nineteenth and Twentieth Centuries*, David Pope and Lee Alston (editors). Annandale NSW: The Federation Press, pp. 102–29.

Maddison, Angus. 2003. *The World Economy: Historical Statistics*. Paris: Development Centre of the Organisation for Economic Co-operation and Development.

———. 2010. *Historical Statistics of the World Economy: 1–2008 AD*. Groningen Growth and Development Centre, www.ggdc.net/maddison.

Maddock, Rodney, and Ian W. McLean. 1984. "Supply-Side Shocks: The Case of Australian Gold." *Journal of Economic History*, Vol. 44, No. 4 (December), pp. 1047–67.

———(editors). 1987a. *The Australian Economy in the Long Run*. New York: Cambridge University Press.

———. 1987b. "The Australian Economy in the Very Long Run." In *The Australian Economy in the Long Run*, Rodney Maddock and Ian W. McLean (editors). New York: Cambridge University Press, pp. 5–29.

Matsuyama, Kiminori. 1992. "Agricultural Productivity, Comparative Advantage, and Economic Growth." *Journal of Economic Theory*, Vol. 58, No. 2 (December), pp. 317–34.

May, Dawn. 1994. *Aboriginal Labour and the Cattle Industry: Queensland from White Settlement to the Present*. Melbourne: Cambridge University Press.

McCarty, J. W. 1964. "The Staple Approach in Australian Economic History." *Business Archives and History*, Vol. 4, No. 1 (February), pp. 1–22.

McInnis, R. M. 1986. "Output and Productivity in Canadian Agriculture, 1870–71 to 1926–27." In *Long-Term Factors in American Economic Growth*, eds. Stanley L. Engerman and Robert E. Gallman. Chicago: University of Chicago Press, pp. 737–78.

McLean, I. W. 1968. "The Australian Balance of Payments on Current Account 1901 to 1964–65." *Australian Economic Papers*, Vol. 7 (June), pp. 77–90.

———. 1973a. "The Adoption of Harvest Machinery in Victoria in the Late Nineteenth Century." *Australian Economic History Review*, Vol. 13, No. 1 (March), pp. 41–56.

———. 1973b. "Growth and Technological Change in Agriculture: Victoria 1870–1910." *Economic Record*, Vol. 49 (December), pp. 560–74.

———. 1976. "Anglo-American Engineering Competition, 1870–1914: Some Third-Market Evidence." *Economic History Review*, Vol. 29, No. 3 (August), pp. 452–64.

———. 1982. "The Demand for Agricultural Research in Australia 1870–1914." *Australian Economic Papers*, Vol. 21, No. 39 (December), pp. 294–308.

———. 1987. "Economic Wellbeing." In *The Australian Economy in the Long Run*, Rodney Maddock and Ian W. McLean (editors). Cambridge: Cambridge University Press, pp. 319–43.

———. 1989a. "South Australian Manufacturing Since 1907: A Comparative Analysis of Structure and Productivity." In *South Australian Manufacturing in Transition*, T. J. Mules (editor). Adelaide: Wakefield Press, pp. 4–41.

———. 1989b. "Growth in a Small Open Economy: An Historical View." In *Australian Economic Growth*, Bruce Chapman (editor). Melbourne: Macmillan, pp. 7–33.

———. 1994. "Saving in Settler Economies: Australian and North American Comparisons." *Explorations in Economic History*, Vol. 31, No. 4 (October), pp. 432–52.

———. 2004. "Australian Economic Growth in Historical Perspective." *Economic Record*, Vol. 80, No. 250 (September), pp. 330–45.

———. 2006. "Recovery from Depression: Australia in an Argentine Mirror 1895–1913." *Australian Economic History Review*, Vol. 46, No. 3 (November), pp. 215–41.

———. 2007. "Why Was Australia So Rich?" *Explorations in Economic History*, Vol. 44, No. 4 (October), pp. 635–56.

McLean, Ian W., and Jonathan J. Pincus. 1982. "Living Standards in Australia 1890–1940: Evidence and Conjectures." Working Paper in Economic History No. 6 (August), Australian National University.

———. 1983. "Did Australian Living Standards Stagnate between 1890 and 1940?" *Journal of Economic History*, Vol. 43, No. 1 (March), pp. 193–202.

McLean, Ian W., and Alan M. Taylor. 2003. "Australian Growth: A California Perspective." In *In Search of Prosperity: Analytic Narratives on Economic Growth*, Dani Rodrik (editor). Princeton, NJ: Princeton University Press, pp. 23–52.

McMichael, Philip. 1984. *Settlers and the Agrarian Question: Foundations of Capitalism in Colonial Australia*. Cambridge: Cambridge University Press.

McMinn, W. G. 1979. *A Constitutional History of Australia*. Melbourne: Oxford University Press.

Mehlum, Halvor, Karl Moene, and Ragnar Torvik. 2006. "Institutions and the Resource Curse." *Economic Journal*, Vol. 116 (January), pp. 1–20.

Meinig, D. W. 1962. *On the Margins of the Good Earth: The South Australian Wheat Frontier 1869–1884*. Chicago: Rand McNally.

Melbourne, A.C.V. 1988a. "New South Wales and Its Daughter Colonies, 1821–1850." In *Australia: The Cambridge History of the British Empire, Volume VII, Part I*, Ernest Scott (editor). Cambridge: Cambridge University Press (first published 1933), pp. 146–83.

———. 1988b. "The Establishment of Responsible Government." In *Australia: The Cambridge History of the British Empire, Volume VII, Part I*, Ernest Scott (editor). Cambridge: Cambridge University Press (first published 1933), pp. 272–95.

Mellor, D. P. 1958. *The Role of Science and Industry: Australia in the War of 1939–1945, Series Four, Civil, Volume V*. Canberra: Australian War Memorial.

Meredith, David, and Barrie Dyster. 1999. *Australia in the Global Economy: Continuity and Change*. Cambridge: Cambridge University Press.

Meredith, David, and Deborah Oxley. 2005. "Contracting Convicts: The Convict Labour Market in Van Diemen's Land 1840–1857." *Australian Economic History Review*, Vol. 45, No. 1 (March), pp. 45–72.

Merrett, D. T. 1989. "Australian Banking Practice and the Crisis of 1893." *Australian Economic History Review*, Vol. 29, No. 1 (March), pp. 60–85.

———. 1997. "Capital Markets and Capital Formation in Australia, 1890–1945." *Australian Economic History Review*, Vol. 37, No. 3 (November), pp. 181–201.

Merrett, David, and Simon Ville. 2011. "Tariffs, Subsidies and Profits: A Re-Assessment of Structural Change in Australia 1901–39." *Australian Economic History Review*, Vol. 51, No. 1 (March), pp. 46–70.

Mitchener, Kris James, and Ian W. McLean. 1999. "U.S. Regional Growth and Convergence, 1880–1980." *Journal of Economic History*, Vol. 59, No. 4 (December), pp. 1016–42.

Mitchener, Kris James, and Marc Weidenmier. 2008. "Trade and Empire." *Economic Journal*, Vol. 118, No. 533 (November), pp. 1805–34.

Mokyr, Joel. 2009. *The Enlightened Economy: An Economic History of Britain 1700–1850*. New Haven: Yale University Press.

Nelson, Richard R., and Gavin Wright. 1992. "The Rise and Fall of American Technological Leadership: The Postwar Era in Historical Perspective." *Journal of Economic Literature*, Vol. 30, No. 4 (December), pp. 1931–64.

Nicholas, Stephen (editor). 1988. *Convict Workers: Reinterpreting Australia's Past*. Cambridge: Cambridge University Press.

Nicholas, Stephen. 1990. "Reinterpreting the Convict Labour Market." *Australian Economic History Review*, Vol. 30, No. 2 (September), pp. 50–66.

———. 1991. "Understanding Convict Workers." *Australian Economic History Review*, Vol. 31, No. 2 (September), pp. 95–105.

Nunn, Nathan. 2009. "The Importance of History for Economic Development." Working Paper 14899, National Bureau of Economic Research, Cambridge, Mass. (April).

Obstfeld, Maurice, and Alan M. Taylor. 2003. "Sovereign Risk, Credibility and the Gold Standard: 1870–1913 versus 1925–31." *Economic Journal*, Vol. 113, No. 487 (April), pp. 241–75.

Offer, Avner. 1993. "The British Empire, 1870–1914: A Waste of Money?" *Economic History Review*, Vol. 46, No. 2 (May), pp. 215–38.

———. 1999. "Costs and Benefits, Prosperity, and Security." In *The Oxford History of the British Empire, Vol. 3: The Nineteenth Century*, Andrew Porter (editor). Oxford: Oxford University Press, pp. 690–711.

Olmstead, Alan L., and Paul W. Rhode. 2008. *Creating Abundance: Biological Innovation and American Agricultural Development*. Cambridge: Cambridge University Press.

O'Rourke, Kevin H. 2000. "Tariffs and Growth in the Late 19th Century." *Economic Journal*, Vol. 110 (April), pp. 456–83.

O'Rourke, Kevin H., and Jeffrey G. Williamson. 1999. *Globalization and History: The Evolution of a Nineteenth-Century Atlantic Economy*. Cambridge, MA: The MIT Press.

Pagan, Adrian. 1987. "The End of the Long Boom." In *The Australian Economy in the Long Run*, Rodney Maddock and Ian W. McLean (editors). New York: Cambridge University Press, pp. 106–30.

Parham, Dean. 2004. "Sources of Australia's Productivity Revival." *Economic Record*, Vol. 80 (June), pp. 239–57.

Persson, Torsten, and Guido Tabellini. 2003. *The Economic Effects of Constitutions.* Cambridge, MA: The MIT Press.

Pincus, Jonathan. 1995. "Evolution and Political Economy of Australian Trade Policies." In *Australia's Trade Policies*, Richard Pomfret (editor). Melbourne: Oxford University Press, pp. 53–73.

Pinkstone, Brian. 1992. *Global Connections: A History of Exports and the Australian Economy.* Canberra: Australian Government Publishing Service.

Pomeranz, Kenneth. 2000. *The Great Divergence: China, Europe, and the Making of the Modern World Economy.* Princeton, NJ: Princeton University Press.

Pomfret, Richard. 1981. "The Staple Theory as an Approach to Canadian and Australian Economic Development." *Australian Economic History Review*, Vol. 21, No. 2 (September), pp. 133–46.

Pope, Alan. 1988. "Aboriginal Adaptation to Early Colonial Labour Markets: The South Australian Experience." *Labour History*, Vol. 54 (May), pp. 1–15.

Pope, David. 1982. "Wage Regulation and Unemployment in Australia: 1900–30." *Australian Economic History Review*, Vol. 22, No. 2 (September), pp. 103–26.

———. 1986. "Protection and Australian Manufacturers' International Competitiveness: 1901–1930." *Australian Economic History Review*, Vol. 26, No. 1 (March), pp. 21–39.

Prados del la Escosura, Leandro. 2000. "International Comparisons of Real Product, 1820–1990: An Alternative Data Set." *Explorations in Economic History*, Vol. 37, No. 1 (January), pp. 1–41.

Quiggin, John. 2000. "Discussion." In David Gruen and Sona Shrestha (editors), *The Australian Economy in the 1990s: Proceedings of a Conference.* Sydney: Reserve Bank of Australia, pp. 268–71.

Raby, Geoff. 1996. *Making Rural Australia: An Economic History of Technical and Institutional Creativity, 1788–1860.* Melbourne: Oxford University Press.

Reynolds, Henry. 1995. *The Other Side of the Frontier: Aboriginal Resistance to the European Invasion of Australia.* Ringwood, Vic.: Penguin Books (second edition).

Roberts, Stephen H. 1924. *History of Australian Land Settlement 1788–1920.* Melbourne: Macmillan.

———. 1964. *The Squatting Age in Australia 1835–1847.* Parkville, Vic.: Melbourne University Press (first published 1935).

———. 1988. "The Wool Trade and the Squatters." In *Australia: The Cambridge History of the British Empire, Volume VII, Part I*, Ernest Scott (editor). Cambridge: Cambridge University Press (first published 1933), pp. 184–206.

Rodriguez, Francisco, and Dani Rodrik. 2001. "Trade Policy and Economic Growth: A Skeptic's Guide to the Cross-National Evidence." In *NBER Macroeconomics Annual 2000*, Ben S. Bernanke and Kenneth Rogoff (editors). Cambridge, MA: The MIT Press, pp. 261–325.

Rodrik, Dani. 1999. "Where Did All the Growth Go? External Shocks, Social Conflict, and Growth Collapses." *Journal of Economic Growth*, Vol. 4, No. 4 (December), pp. 385–412.

Rodrik, Dani, Arvind Subramanian, and Francesco Trebbi. 2004. "Institutions Rule: The Primacy of Institutions over Geography and Integration in Economic Development." *Journal of Economic Growth*, Vol. 9, No. 2 (June), pp. 131–65.

Roe, Michael. 1974. "1830–1850." In *A New History of Australia*, F. K. Crowley (editor). Melbourne: Heinemann, pp. 82–123.

Rogoff, Kenneth, and Carmen M. Reinhart. 2009. *This Time Is Different: Eight Centuries of Financial Folly*. Princeton, NJ: Princeton University Press.

Rosenbloom, Joshua L., and William A. Sundstrom. 2009. "Labor-Market Regimes in U.S. Economic History." Working Paper 15055, National Bureau of Economic Research (June).

Rubinstein, W. D. 1979. "The Distribution of Personal Wealth in Victoria 1860–1974." *Australian Economic History Review*, Vol. 19, No. 1 (March), pp. 26–41.

Ruzicka, Lado T. 1989. "Long Term Changes in Australian Life Expectancies." In David Pope and Lee J. Alston (editors), *Australia's Greatest Asset: Human Resources in the Nineteenth and Twentieth Centuries*. Annandale, NSW: The Federation Press, pp. 38–52.

Sachs, Jeffrey D., and Andrew M. Warner. 1995. "Natural Resource Abundance and Economic Growth." Working Paper 5398, National Bureau of Economic Research, Cambridge, MA (December).

———. 2001. "The Curse of Natural Resources." *European Economic Review*, Vol. 45, Nos. 4–6 (May), pp. 827–38.

Salisbury, Neal. 1996. "The History of Native Americans from Before the Arrival of the Europeans and Africans until the American Civil War." In *The Cambridge Economic History of the United States, Volume 1: The Colonial Era*, Stanley L. Engerman and Robert E. Gallman (editors). Cambridge: Cambridge University Press, pp. 1–52.

Schedvin, C. B. 1970. *Australia and the Great Depression: A Study of Economic Development and Policy in the 1920s and 1930s*. Sydney: Sydney University Press.

———. 1979. "Midas and the Merino: A Perspective on Australian Economic Historiography." *Economic History Review*, Vol. 32, No. 4 (November), pp. 542–56.

———. 1990. "Staples and Regions of Pax Britannica." *Economic History Review*, Vol. 43, No. 4 (November), pp. 533–59.

Schumpeter, Joseph A. 1954. *History of Economic Analysis*. New York: Oxford University Press.

Scott, Ernest. 1989. *Australia during the War: The Official History of Australia in the War of 1914–1918, Volume XI*. St Lucia: University of Queensland Press in association with The Australian War Memorial (first published 1936).

Serle, Geoffrey. 1963. *The Golden Age: A History of the Colony of Victoria 1851–1861*. Melbourne: Melbourne University Press.

Shann, Edward. 1948. *An Economic History of Australia*. Cambridge: Cambridge University Press (first published 1930).

Shann, E.O.G. 1988. "Economic and Political Development 1860–1885. In *Australia: The Cambridge History of the British Empire, Volume VII, Part I*, Ernest Scott (editor). Cambridge: Cambridge University Press (first published 1933), pp. 296–323.

Shiller, Robert J. 2000. *Irrational Exuberance*. Princeton, NJ: Princeton University Press.

Shlomowitz, Ralph. 1982. "Melanesian Labor and the Development of the Queensland Sugar Industry, 1863–1906." In *Research in Economic History*, Paul Uselding (editor). Greenwich Conn.: JAI Press, Vol. 7. pp. 327–61.

———. 1990. "Convict Workers: A Review Article." *Australian Economic History Review*, Vol. 30, No. 2 (September), pp. 67–88.

Sinclair, Keith. 1980. *A History of New Zealand*. Harmondsworth: Penguin Books (revised edition).

Sinclair, W. A. 1970. "Capital Formation." In *Australian Economic Development in the Twentieth Century* (Colin Forster, editor). London: Allen & Unwin, pp. 11–65.

———. 1976. *The Process of Economic Development in Australia*. Melbourne: Longman Cheshire.

———. 1996. "Victoria's Economy in the Long Run." *Australian Economic History Review*, Vol. 36, No. 2 (September), pp. 3–29.

Siriwardana, Mahinda. 1995. "The Causes of the Depression in Australia in the 1930s: A General Equilibrium Analysis." *Explorations in Economic History*, Vol. 32, No. 1 (January), pp. 51–81.

———. 1996. "The Economic Impact of Tariffs in the 1930s in Australia: The Brigden Report Re-examined." *Australian Economic Papers*, Vol. 35, No. 67 (December), pp. 320–89.

Smith, Adam. 1979. *The Theory of Moral Sentiments*. Oxford: Clarendon Press (first published 1759).

Sokoloff, Kenneth L., and Stanley L. Engerman. 2000. "Institutions, Factor Endowments, and Paths of Development in the New World." *Journal of Economic Perspectives*, Vol. 14, No. 3 (Summer), pp. 217–32.

Solberg, Carl E. 1987. *The Prairies and the Pampas: Agrarian Policy in Canada and Argentina, 1880–1930*. Stanford, CA: Stanford University Press.

Stevenson, Betsey, and Justin Wolfers. 2008. "Economic Growth and Subjective Well-Being: Reassessing the Easterlin Paradox." Working Paper 14282. National Bureau of Economic Research, Cambridge, Mass. (August).

Stutchbury, Michael. 1984. "The Playford Legend and the Industrialization of South Australia." *Australian Economic History Review*, Vol. 24, No. 1 (March), pp. 1–19.

Thomas, Mark. 1995. "'A Substantial Superiority'? Anglo-Australian Comparisons of Consumption and Income in the Late Nineteenth Century." *Australian Economic History Review*, Vol. 35, No. 2 (September), pp. 10–38.

Trollope, Anthony. 1987. *Australia*. New York: Hippocrene Books, 2 vols. (first published 1873).

Twain, Mark. 1989. *Following the Equator: A Journey Around the World*. New York: Dover (first published 1897).

Tyers, Rod, and William Coleman. 2008. "Beyond Brigden: Australia's Inter-War Manufacturing Tariffs, Real Wages and Economic Size." *Economic Record*, Vol. 84 (March), pp. 50–67.

Urquhart, M. C. 1986. "New Estimates of Gross National Product, Canada, 1870–1926: Some Implications for Canadian Development." In *Long-Term Factors in American Economic Growth*, Stanley L. Engerman and Robert E. Gallman (editors). Chicago: University of Chicago Press, pp. 9–88.

Valentine, T. J. 1987. "The Causes of the Depression in Australia." *Explorations in Economic History*, Vol. 24, No. 1 (January), pp.43-62.

———. 1988. "The Battle of the Plans: A Macroeconometric Model of the Interwar Economy." In *Recovery from the Depression: Australia and the World Economy in the 1930s*, R. G. Gregory and N. G. Butlin (editors). Cambridge: Cambridge University Press, pp. 151–71.

Vamplew, Wray (editor). 1987. *Australians: Historical Statistics*. Broadway, NSW: Fairfax, Syme & Weldon.

van der Ploeg, Frederick, and Anthony J. Venables. 2011. "Harnessing Windfall Revenues: Optimal Policies for Resource-Rich Developing Economies." *Economic Journal*, Vol. 121 (March), pp. 1–30.

Ville, Simon. 2000. *The Rural Entrepreneurs: A History of the Stock and Station Agent Industry in Australia and New Zealand*. Cambridge: Cambridge University Press.

Vonyo, Tamas. 2008. "Post-War Reconstruction and the Golden Age of Economic Growth." *European Review of Economic History*, Vol. 12, No. 2 (August), pp. 221–41.

Walker, E. Ronald. 1947. *The Australian Economy in War and Reconstruction*. New York: Oxford University Press.

Ward, Russel. 1992. *Concise History of Australia*. St. Lucia.: University of Queensland Press.

Waterman, A.M.C. 1972. *Economic Fluctuations in Australia, 1948 to 1964*. Canberra: Australian National University Press.

Weisdorf, Jacob. 2009. "Why Did the First Farmers Toil? Human Metabolism and the Origins of Agriculture." *European Review of Economic History*, Vol. 13, No. 2 (August), pp. 157–72.

White, Colin. 1992. *Mastering Risk: Environment, Markets and Politics in Australian Economic History*. South Melbourne: Oxford University Press.

Whitwell, Greg. 1986. *The Treasury Line*. Sydney: Allen & Unwin.

Whitwell, Greg, Christine de Souza, and Stephen Nicholas. 1997. "Height, Health, and Economic Growth in Australia, 1860–1940." In *Health and Welfare during Industrialization*, Richard H. Steckel and Roderick Floud (editors). Chicago: University of Chicago Press, pp. 379–422.

Whitwell, Greg, and Stephen Nicholas. 2001. "Weight and Welfare of Australians, 1890–1940." *Australian Economic History Review*, Vol. 41, No. 2 (July), pp. 159–75.

Wilkie, Joann, and Tony McDonald. 2008. "Economic Geography and Economic Performance in Australia." *Economic Roundup* (Australian Treasury), Issue 3 (October), pp. 1–15.

Withers, Glenn. 1987. "Labour." In Rodney Maddock and Ian W. McLean (editors), *The Australian Economy in the Long Run*. New York: Cambridge University Press, pp. 248–88.

———. 1989. "The Immigration Contribution to Human Capital Formation." In *Australia's Greatest Asset: Human Resources in the Nineteenth and Twentieth Centuries*, David Pope and Lee Alston (editors). Annandale, NSW: The Federation Press, pp. 53–71.

Wright, Gavin. 1990. "The Origins of American Industrial Success, 1879–1940." *American Economic Review*, Vol. 80, No. 4 (September), pp. 651–68.

Wright, Gavin, and Jesse Czelusta. 2007. "Resource-Based Growth, Past and Present." In *Natural Resources: Neither Curse Nor Destiny*, Daniel Lederman and William F. Maloney (editors). Washington, DC: World Bank, and Palo Alto, CA: Stanford University Press, pp. 183–211.

Young, Adam, Joann Wilkie, Robert Ewing, and Jyoti Rahman. 2008. "International Comparisons of Industry Productivity." *Economic Roundup* (Australian Treasury), Issue 3 (October), pp. 45–61.

Index

THE PRINCETON ECONOMIC HISTORY OF THE WESTERN WORLD

Joel Mokyr, Series Editor

Growth in a Traditional Society: The French Countryside, 1450–1815, by Philip T. Hoffman

The Vanishing Irish: Households, Migration, and the Rural Economy in Ireland, 1850–1914, by Timothy W. Guinnane

Black 47 and Beyond: The Great Irish Famine in History, Economy, and Memory, by Cormac Ó Gráda

The Great Divergence: China, Europe, and the Making of the Modern World Economy, by Kenneth Pomeranz

The Big Problem of Small Change, by Thomas J. Sargent and François R. Velde

Farm to Factory: A Reinterpretation of the Soviet Industrial Revolution, by Robert C. Allen

Quarter Notes and Bank Notes: The Economics of Music Composition in the Eighteenth and Nineteenth Centuries, by F. M. Scherer

The Strictures of Inheritance: The Dutch Economy in the Nineteenth Century, by Jan Luiten van Zanden and Arthur van Riel

Understanding the Process of Economic Change, by Douglass C. North

Feeding the World: An Economic History of Agriculture, 1800–2000, by Giovanni Federico

Cultures Merging: A Historical and Economic Critique of Culture, by Eric L. Jones

The European Economy since 1945: Coordinated Capitalism and Beyond, by Barry Eichengreen

War, Wine, and Taxes: The Political Economy of Anglo-French Trade, 1689–1900, by John V. C. Nye

A Farewell to Alms: A Brief Economic History of the World, by Gregory Clark

Power and Plenty: Trade, War, and the World Economy in the Second Millennium, by Ronald Findlay and Kevin O'Rourke

Power over Peoples: Technology, Environments, and Western Imperialism, 1400 to the Present, by Daniel R. Headrick

Unsettled Account: The Evolution of Banking in the Industrialized World since 1800, by Richard S. Grossman

States of Credit: Size, Power, and the Development of European Polities, by David Stasavage

Creating Wine: The Emergence of a World Industry, 1840–1914, by James Simpson

The Evolution of a Nation: How Geography and Law Shaped the American States, by Daniel Berkowitz and Karen B. Clay

Distant Tyranny: Markets, Power, and Backwardness in Spain, 1650–1800, by Regina Grafe

The Chosen Few: How Education Shaped Jewish History, 70–1492, by Maristella Botticini and Zvi Eckstein

Why Australia Prospered: The Shifting Sources of Economic Growth, by Ian W. McLean